International Fraud Handbook

International Fraud Handbook

Dr. Joseph T. Wells

WILEY

Cover design: Wiley
Cover image: © Tetra Images/Getty Images

Published by John Wiley & Sons, Inc., Hoboken, New Jersey.

Published simultaneously in Canada.

For general information on our other products and services or for technical support, please contact our
Customer Care Department within the United States at (800) 762–2974, outside the United States at (317)
572–3993, or fax (317) 572–4002.

Wiley publishes in a variety of print and electronic formats and by print-on-demand. Some material
included with standard print versions of this book may not be included in e-books or in print-on-demand.
If this book refers to media such as a CD or DVD that is not included in the version you purchased, you
may download this material at http://booksupport.wiley.com. For more information about Wiley products,
visit www.wiley.com.

Library of Congress Cataloging-in-Publication Data:
Names: Wells, Joseph T., author.
Title: International fraud handbook / Dr. Joseph T. Wells.
Description: Hoboken, New Jersey : John Wiley & Sons, Inc., [2018] | Includes
  index. |
Identifiers: LCCN 2018017403 (print) | LCCN 2018017692 (ebook) | ISBN
  9781118728550 (Adobe PDF) | ISBN 9781118728536 (ePub) | ISBN 9781118728505
  (hardcover)
Subjects: LCSH: Fraud. | Fraud–Prevention. | Fraud investigation. |
  Fraud–Law and legislation.
Classification: LCC HV6691 (ebook) | LCC HV6691 .W454 2018 (print) | DDC
  364.16/3–dc23
LC record available at https://lccn.loc.gov/2018017403

Printed in the United States of America.

V079139_051818

For Andi McNeal

This book would not have been possible without her superb efforts.

Contents

Preface

My 40-year career has been devoted to the investigation and prevention of white-collar crimes. And while I have witnessed much change, I have also seen so much stay the same.

Through the ebbing and flowing trends and the technological advances, I have learned several enduring lessons about fraud and human nature. First, fraud is timeless; as long as people are put in positions of trust, fraud will occur. Second, the variations on fraud are not limitless. As explored in my previous publication, *Corporate Fraud Handbook*, frauds tend to fall into time-tested and universal categories. Finally, ignoring the problem will never solve the problem. In fact, quite the opposite is true: all organizations are inherently vulnerable to fraud, but the ones that are reluctant to admit it are the ones most at risk.

Along with these truths, I have also seen the evolution of our profession. Technology has helped both the fraudsters and the fraud fighters accomplish their tasks more effectively and efficiently. Governments in numerous countries have enacted new regulations and bolstered their enforcement efforts against fraud, resulting in an increased focus on compliance in many organizations. Business operations – and frauds – now routinely span geographical borders, requiring new knowledge and skill sets for those attempting to prevent, detect, and investigate white-collar crimes. As the fraud examination profession has grown globally and the fight against fraud has grown more complex, the need for information and professional connection has never been greater.

It is out of this need, demonstrated by the numerous and increasing requests that the ACFE receives every year for resources to assist in this international effort, that the inspiration for this book arose. It focuses solely on combatting those frauds perpetrated against organizations; frauds against individuals are pervasive and devastating, and consequently merit separate, in-depth discussion.

The foundation for effectively addressing fraud against organizations – the tools of the trade used to prevent, detect, and respond to these crimes – look about the same throughout most of the world. However, important geographical nuances and considerations exist. Thus, to help fraud examiners everywhere, the material in this book is provided in two parts:

- Part I delves deeply into ways organizations can understand and mitigate their fraud risks, as well as how they can, and should, respond when the unthinkable happens.
- Part II explores regional and country-specific information about fighting fraud around the world.

Much like the fight against fraud, this book was truly a global effort. Each section discussing specific countries in Part II lists the specific ACFE members who contributed that material. My deepest gratitude to these volunteers – listed individually in the Acknowledgments section – who helped us with this significant undertaking.

My appreciation also goes to the members of the ACFE team who helped research, compile, and review various parts of this publication. In particular, I'd like to thank John Gill, JD, CFE; Andi McNeal, CFE, CPA; Ron Cresswell, JD, CFE; Jordan Underhill, JD, CFE; Mason Wilder, CFE; Bobbie Dani; and Mark Blangger.

And finally, my thanks and admiration go to the fraud fighters everywhere who have dedicated their professional lives to the prevention and detection of fraud. As the first US president, George Washington, said, *"Truth will ultimately prevail where pains is taken to bring it to light."* By sharing information and joining forces as part of the worldwide anti-fraud community, we can continue to bring truth to light and be successful in the global fight against fraud.

Dr. Joseph T. Wells
Austin, TX
February 2018

Acknowledgments

Thanks to the following individuals for their time and effort in assisting with this publication. The information they provided in Part II of this book is invaluable in highlighting the anti-fraud environment and resources in their respective countries.

Syed Zubair Ahmed, MBA, CFE, MCom
ACFE Islamabad Chapter Secretary
Islamabad, Pakistan

Gertrudis Alarcon, CFE
ACFE Spain Chapter President
Senior Managing Director, Grupo GAT
Madrid, Spain

Abdallah Alomari, CFE
ACFE Jordan Chapter Treasurer
Managing Director, KYC Jordan
Amman, Jordan

Mukesh Arya, CFE
ACFE India Chapter Treasurer
Managing Director, Red Flag
Gurgaon, India

Tomasita Pazos Aurich, CFE, CRISC
ACFE Lima Chapter President
Fraud Prevention Manager, Banco de Crédito del Perú (BCP)
Lima, Peru

Adel Ayyoub
ACFE Jordan Chapter Secretary
Amman, Jordan

S.K. Bansal, CFE
ACFE India Chapter President
Managing Partner, Bansal & Co., LLP, Chartered Accountants
New Delhi, India

Alison Benbow, CFE, CMIIA
ACFE Oman Chapter Secretary
Muscat, Oman

Vibeke Bisschop-Mørland, CFE
Senior Manager, BDO Norway
Oslo, Norway

Dom Blackshaw, CFE
ACFE Perth Chapter President
Manager, Corporate Governance, Risk and Compliance, Finders Resources Limited
Perth, Australia

Thomas Bøgballe, CFE
ACFE Denmark Chapter Treasurer and Board Member
Head of Fraud and Forensics, Novozymes A/S
Bagsværd, Denmark

Stefano Bordoli
Consultant, Deloitte Forensic
Santiago, Chile

Dr. Jose A. Brandin, MBA, CFE, CIA, CISA
ACFE Spain Chapter Board Member
Head of Audit Spain, International Airlines Group
Barcelona, Spain

Muna D. Buchahin, PhD, CFE, CFI, CGAP, CRMA
ACFE Mexico Chapter Vice President
Director General, Forensic Audit, SAO Mexico
Mexico City, Mexico

Bandish Bundhoo, CFE
ACFE Mauritius Chapter Secretary
Riviere du Rempart, Mauritius

Nereyda López Canales
Lima, Peru

Piotr Chmiel, CFE, CISA, CIA
ACFE Poland Chapter President
Compliance Manager, T-Mobile
Warsaw, Poland

Sun Hee Cho
Bae, Kim & Lee, LLC
Seoul, South Korea

Shamsa Dagane, CFE
Nairobi, Kenya

Dr. Anna Damaskou, CFE, PhD, LLM
Chair of the Board of Transparency International — Greece
Black Sea Trade & Development Bank — Compliance & Operational Risk Management Office
Thessaloniki, Greece

Sandra Damijan, PhD, CFE
Partner, Western Balkans Forensic Leader, Grant Thornton
Ljubljana, Slovenia

Fadi Daoud, MBA, CACM, CIPT
ACFE Jordan Chapter Board Member
Education and Youth Advisor, Talal Abu Ghazaleh Organization
Amman, Jordan

Roger Darvall-Stevens, MBA, MA, CFE
Former ACFE Melbourne Chapter President; ACFE Regent Emeritus
Partner and National Head of Fraud and Forensic Services, RSM Australia
Melbourne, Australia

Mario B. Demarillas, CFE, CPISI, CRISC, CISM, CISA, CIA
ACFE Philippines Chapter Board Member
ISACA Manila Chapter President and Board Member
Partner, Advisory Services, Reyes Tacandong & Co. (RSM Philippines)
Makati City, Philippines

Evangelia Dimitroulia, CFE, CIA
ACFE Greece Chapter President
Partner, Fraud Education Center
Athens, Greece

John Ederer, CFE, FCA
ACFE Switzerland Chapter Vice President
Chartered Accountant, JADEN Consulting LLC
Gattikon-Zurich, Switzerland

Hossam El Shaffei, CFE
ACFE Jordan Chapter Vice President
Amman, Jordan

Mahmoud Elbagoury, GRCA, CPFA, CICA, CACM
ACFE Egypt Board Member
Head of Audit and Compliance, Union Group
Cairo, Egypt

Hossam Elshafie, CFE, CRMA, CCSA, CFCI
ACFE Egypt Chapter President
Partner, RSM Egypt
Cairo, Egypt

Hazem Abd Eltawab
ACFE Egypt Chapter Vice President
Board Member, Egyptian Society of Accountants and Auditors (ESAA)
Cairo, Egypt

Acknowledgments

Edward J. Epstein, LLB, LLM
Solicitor, Hong Kong, England &
Wales, Australia, and the Republic
of Ireland
Shanghai, China

Marco Antonio E. Fernandes
Director, Berkeley Research Group
São Paulo, Brazil

Dante T. Fuentes, CFE, CPA, CAMS
ACFE Philippines Chapter President
Chief Compliance Officer, Security
Bank Corporation
Association of Bank Compliance
Offices, Inc., President
Good Governance Advocates &
Practitioners of the Philippines, Inc.,
Senior Adviser
Makati City, Philippines

Atty. Laureano L. Galon Jr., CFE, CPA
ACFE Philippines Chapter Secretary
Partner, Rodriguez Casila Galon &
Associates Law Firm
Manila, Philippines

Gertjan Groen
ACFE Netherlands Chapter President
Business Line Manager Forensics &
Incident Response, Fox-IT
Rotterdam, Netherlands

Makito Hamada, CFE, CPA
ACFE Japan Chapter President
Visiting Professor, Rikkyo University
Tokyo, Japan

Tim Harvey, CFE, JP
ACFE Global Head of Chapter
Development
ACFE UK Chapter President
London, UK

Sandra Hauwert, CFE
ACFE Netherlands Chapter
Communication Chair
Netherlands

Adv. Jan Henning, SQ
Bloemfontein, South Africa

Pavla Hladká, CFE
ACFE Czech Republic Chapter
President
Associate Partner of Forensic Services,
EY
Czech Republic

Francis Hounnongandji, CFE, CFA
ACFE France Chapter President
President, Institut Français de Prévention
de la Fraude (IFPF)
Paris, France

Shun Hsiung Hsu, CFE, CPA
ACFE Taiwan Chapter President
Managing Partner, YMH Company CPAs
Taipei, Taiwan

Katie Huchler, CFE
Manager, BDO Norway
Oslo, Norway

Siti Zeenath Shaik Ibrahim
Head, Group Corporate Crime
Prevention, Kenanga Investment
Bank Berhad
Kuala Lumpur, Malaysia

Vladimir Ikonomov, CFE
ACFE Bulgaria Chapter President
Project Manager, First Investment Bank
Sofia, Bulgaria

Jaco de Jager, CFE
ACFE South Africa CEO
Pretoria, South Africa

Wong Siew Jiuan, CFE
Head, Group Legal, Kenanga Investment
Bank Berhad
Kuala Lumpur, Malaysia

Peter Juestel, CFE, CAMS
ACFE Switzerland Chapter Secretary
Attorney, Lustenberger Rechtsanwaelte
Zurich, Switzerland

Deoraj Juggoo
ACFE Mauritius Chapter Board Member
Mauritius

Agata Kamińska, Master in International
Relations
Gdańsk, Poland

Hyeon Kang, CFE
ACFE South Korea Chapter Board
Member
Bae, Kim & Lee, LLC
Seoul, South Korea

Maheswari Kanniah, CFE
Group Chief Regulatory & Compliance
Officer, Kenanga Investment Bank
Berhad
Kuala Lumpur, Malaysia

Andrew H. Kautz, CFE
ACFE Faculty
Manager, Special Investigations Unit,
Great-West Life Assurance Company
London, Ontario, Canada

Umaer Khalil
Bae, Kim & Lee, LLC
Seoul, South Korea

Robert Kilian, CFE
ACFE Germany Chapter President
Managing Director, DRB Deutsche
Risikoberatung GmbH
Frankfurt, Germany

Kwang Jun Kim
Bae, Kim & Lee, LLC
Seoul, South Korea

Mojca Koder, CFE
ACFE Slovenia Chapter President
Senior Manager in Forensics, PwC
Slovenia
Ljubljana, Slovenia

Aniket Kolge
Senior Manager, EY LLP
Mumbai, India

Sara Koski
Senior Associate, Compliance, DLA
Piper
Paris, France

Mihael Kranjc
ACFE Slovenia Chapter Board
Member
CEO, Sasa Accounting Services and Tax
Consulting, Ltd
Ljubljana, Slovenia

Sharad Kumar, CFE
ACFE India Chapter Secretary
Officer on Special Duty, Ministry of
External Affairs
New Delhi, India

Eric Lasry
Partner, Baker & McKenzie AARPI
Paris, France

Jun Ho Lee
Bae, Kim & Lee, LLC
Seoul, South Korea

Dr. Sheree S. Ma, CPA
ACFE Taiwan Chapter Vice President
Professor of Accounting, National
Chengchi University
Taipei, Taiwan

Sumit Makhija, CFE
ACFE India Chapter Vice President
Partner, Deloitte Touche Tohmatsu
India, LLP
Gurgaon, India

Jose Damian Garcia Medina, CFE
ACFE Spain Chapter Vice President
Corporate Security Director, Vodafone
Spain
Madrid, Spain

Nicoleta Mehlsen, MBA, CFE
ACFE Denmark Chapter Board
Member
Head of Internal Audit, Danfoss
Nordborg, Denmark

Acknowledgments

Ahmed Mokhtar, CFE, CRMA
ACFE Egypt Chapter Board Member
Internal Audit Manager, Al-Mansour
Automotive
Cairo, Egypt

Iyad Mourtada, CFE, CIA, CCSA,
CRMA, CSX
ACFE Authorized Trainer in the United
Arab Emirates
Open Thinking Academy
Dubai, United Arab Emirates

Bernard M. K. Muchere, CFE
ACFE Kenya Chapter President
Nairobi, Kenya

Lukelesia Namarome, CFE
Nairobi, Kenya

Ralf Neese, CIA
Associate Director, DRB Deutsche
Risikoberatung GmbH
Frankfurt, Germany

New Zealand ACFE Chapter members and
committee members

Qosai Obidat
ACFE Jordan Chapter Board Member
Amman, Jordan

Carsten Allerslev Olsen, CFE
ACFE Denmark Chapter Board Member
Assistant Professor, Copenhagen
Business School
Frederiksberg, Denmark

Miguel Angel Osma, CFE
ACFE Spain Chapter Board Member
Investigations & LI Manager, Vodafone
Spain
Madrid, Spain

Zulhisham Osman
Vice President, Group Chief Regulatory &
Compliance Officer's Office, Kenanga
Investment Bank Berhad
Kuala Lumpur, Malaysia

Luis Navarro Pizarro
Lima, Peru

Chris Porteous
Senior Forensic Advisory Specialist,
Electricity Networks Corporation
Perth, Australia

Tony Prior, MBA, CFE, CAMS
ACFE Sydney Chapter President
Director, Compliance, AUSTRAC
Sydney, Australia

Sagar Rajkumar, MBA, CFE, PJSC
Risk Management, Finance House P.J.S.C.
Abu Dhabi, United Arab Emirates

Andrea Rondot, CFE
Manager, Deloitte Forensic
Santiago, Chile

George Rostantis, CFE
ACFE Cyprus Chapter Secretary
Manager Network Audits &
Investigations, Internal Audit
Division, Bank of Cyprus
Nicosia, Cyprus

Pooja Roy, CA
Senior Manager, EY LLP
Mumbai, India

Raymond A. San Pedro, CPA, CICA
ACFE Philippines Chapter Operations
Manager
Makati City, Philippines

Dong Woo Seo, CFE
ACFE South Korea Chapter Board
Member
Bae, Kim & Lee, LLC
Seoul, South Korea

Hazem Adel Shahin, CFE
ACFE Jordan Chapter President
Amman, Jordan

Sameh Abu Shamaleh, CFE
ACFE Jordan Chapter Board Member
Finance Director, Adidas Group
Amman, Jordan

Mukul Shrivastava, CFE, CA
ACFE Mumbai Chapter Vice President
Partner, EY LLP
Mumbai, India

Rajkumar Shriwastav, CFE, Lawyer
ACFE Mumbai Chapter Manager
Director, EY LLP
Mumbai, India

Arpinder Singh, CFE, CA, Lawyer
ACFE Mumbai Chapter President
Partner and Head — India and Emerging
Markets, EY LLP
Mumbai, India

Tae Kyung Sung, PhD, CFE
ACFE South Korea Chapter President
Kyonggi University
Seoul, South Korea

Agis Taramides, CFE, FCA
ACFE Cyprus Chapter Treasurer
Managing Director, Navigant
Consultants Limited
Nicosia, Cyprus

Sabrina Tatli-Van der Valk
ACFE Netherlands Chapter Treasurer
Netherlands

Pedro Trevisan, CFE
ACFE Chile Chapter President and
Board Member
Senior Manager, Deloitte Forensic
Santiago, Chile

Sachie Tsuji, CFE, CPA
ACFE Japan Chapter Board Member
President & CEO, SPLUS Co., Ltd.
Tokyo, Japan

Ayumi Uzawa, CFE, CPA
ACFE Japan Chapter Board Member
Representative, Uzawa Accounting Firm
Tokyo, Japan

Adv. Chris van Vuuren, CFE
Pretoria, South Africa

Josephat K. Wainaina, CFE
Nairobi, Kenya

Loes Wenink, CFE
ACFE Netherlands Chapter Events
Chair
Amsterdam, Netherlands

Caoyu Xu
Due Diligence Analyst
Menlo Park, California, United States

Toshiaki Yamaguchi, CFE
ACFE Japan Chapter Board Member
Lawyer, Yamaguchi Law Office
Osaka, Japan

Rodrigo Yáñez
ACFE Chile Chapter Secretary and
Board Member
Senior Manager, Deloitte Forensic
Santiago, Chile

Sherlyn Yeo
ACFE Singapore Chapter Marketing
and Event Coordinator
Singapore

George Yiallouros, CFE
ACFE Cyprus Chapter Board Member
Internal Auditor — Investigations,
Internal Audit Division, Bank of
Cyprus
Nicosia, Cyprus

Nagy Mohammed Ibrahim Yousef
CEO, Bit Al-khabera Financial
Dubai, United Arab Emirates

Daisuke Yuki, CFE
ACFE Japan Chapter Board Member
Partner Attorney, Nozomi Sogo
Attorneys at Law
Tokyo, Japan

Hervé Zany, CFE
Managing Director, Financial
Intelligence & Processing (FIP)
Paris, France

About the ACFE

The Association of Certified Fraud Examiners (ACFE) is the world's largest anti-fraud organization and premier provider of anti-fraud training and education. Together with nearly 85,000 members, the ACFE is reducing business fraud worldwide and inspiring public confidence in the integrity and objectivity within the profession.

Established in 1988, with headquarters in Austin, Texas, the ACFE supports the anti-fraud profession by providing expert instruction, practical tools, and innovative resources in the fight against fraud. The ACFE hosts conferences and seminars year-round while offering informative books and self-study courses written by leading practitioners to help members learn how and why fraud occurs and to build the skills needed to fight it effectively. Members of the ACFE also have the ability to expand their anti-fraud knowledge and assert themselves as experts in the anti-fraud community by obtaining the Certified Fraud Examiner (CFE) credential. This globally preferred certification indicates expertise in fraud prevention, deterrence, detection, and investigation.

The ACFE oversees the CFE credential by setting standards for admission, administering the CFE examination, and maintaining and enforcing the ACFE Code of Professional Ethics.

The ACFE is also committed to providing educational resources to the academic community and has established the Anti-Fraud Education Partnership to address the unprecedented need for fraud examination education at the university level. In pursuit of this objective, the ACFE has provided free training and educational materials to institutions of higher learning throughout the world.

Criminologist and former FBI agent Dr. Joseph T. Wells, CFE, CPA, is chairman and founder of the ACFE. Dr. Wells has lectured to tens of thousands of business professionals, and is the author of 22 books, and scores of articles and research projects. His writing has won numerous awards, including the top articles of the year for both the *Internal Auditor* and the *Journal of Accountancy* magazines, and he is a winner of the Innovation in Accounting Education Award presented by the American Accounting Association. He was named nine times to *Accounting Today* magazine's annual list of the "Top 100 Most Influential People" in accounting. In 2010, for his contributions to the anti-fraud field, he was honored as a Doctor of Commercial Science by York College of the City University of New York.

Labeled "the premier financial sleuthing organization" by *The Wall Street Journal*, the ACFE has also been cited for its efforts against fraud by media outlets such as the BBC, *U.S. News & World Report*, *The New York Times*, CNN, CNBC, *Fortune*, ABC-TV's *Nightline* and *20/20*, and CBS News' *60 Minutes*.

Further information about the ACFE is available at www.acfe.com, or 800-245-3321.

PART I

PART I

CHAPTER 1

Introduction

In the world of commerce, organizations incur costs to produce and sell their products or services. These costs run the gamut: labor, taxes, advertising, occupancy, raw materials, research and development, and, yes, fraud and abuse. The latter cost, however, is fundamentally different from the former: the true expense of fraud and abuse is hidden, even if it is reflected in the profit-and-loss figures.

For example, suppose a company's advertising expense is $1.2 million. But unknown to the company's executives, the marketing manager is colluding with an outside ad agency and has accepted $300,000 in kickbacks to steer business to that firm. That means the true advertising expense is overstated by at least the amount of the kickbacks – if not more. The result, of course, is that $300,000 comes directly off the bottom line, out of the pockets of the investors and the workforce. Similarly, if a warehouse foreman is stealing inventory or an accounting clerk is skimming customer payments, the company suffers a loss – one it likely does not know about, but one that must be absorbed somewhere.

The truth is, fraud can occur in virtually any organization. If an organization employs individuals, at some point one or more of those individuals will attempt to lie, cheat, or steal from the company for personal gain. So this hidden cost – one that offers no benefit to the company and, in fact, causes numerous kinds of damage to the company even beyond the direct financial consequence – is one that all organizations, in all countries, in all industries, and of all sizes, will encounter. However, the risk of fraud is most significant – that is, it has the potential to cause the most damage – for organizations that are unaware of, ignore, or underestimate whether and how fraud can occur within their operations.

The risk is also evolving due to changes in technology, globalization, regulatory environments, and other factors. These changes can present challenges to those charged with preventing, detecting, investigating, and responding to fraud. Nonetheless, the concepts behind fraud remain timeless – the perpetrators seek to trick victims out of financial or other resources for personal gain. As a result, the foundational concepts in fighting fraud are still effective.

WHAT IS FRAUD?

The term *fraud* is commonly used to encompass a broad range of schemes: employee embezzlement, identity theft, corrupt government officials, cybercrimes, fraud against the elderly, health care schemes, loan fraud, bid rigging, credit card skimming, counterfeit goods, and dozens of others. While the range of schemes that fall under the

---

Portions of this chapter are adapted from the following Association of Certified Fraud Examiners (ACFE) publications: *Ten Common External Threats to Your Organization*, the materials for the *Auditing for Internal Fraud* and *Controlling the Risk of Asset Misappropriation* seminars, and the "Financial Transactions" and "Fraud Schemes" sections of the *Fraud Examiners Manual*.

umbrella of fraud is extensive, a general definition and an understanding of the common elements of these schemes are useful in preventing and detecting these acts.

Fraud can be generally defined as any crime for gain that uses deception as its principal modus operandi. Consequently, fraud includes any intentional or deliberate act to deprive another of property or money by guile, deception, or other unfair means. As such, all types of fraud have the following common elements:

- A material false statement (i.e., a misrepresentation)
- Knowledge that the statement was false when it was uttered (i.e., intent)
- The victim's reliance on the false statement
- Damages resulting from the victim's reliance on the false statement

Components of Fraud

An act of fraud normally involves three components, or steps:

1. The act
2. The concealment
3. The conversion

To successfully perpetrate a fraud, offenders generally must complete all three steps: they must commit the act, conceal the act, and convert the proceeds for their personal benefit or the benefit of another party.

The Act

The fraud act is normally the theft or deception – the action that leads to the gain the perpetrator is seeking.

The Concealment

Once the perpetrator accomplishes the act, the individual typically makes efforts to conceal it. Concealment is a cornerstone of fraud. As opposed to traditional criminals, who make no effort to conceal their crimes, fraud perpetrators typically take steps to keep their victims ignorant. For example, in the case of the theft of cash, falsifying the balance in the cash account would constitute concealment. Although some individuals commit fraud without attempting to conceal it (e.g., taking cash from a register drawer with no attempt to cover the theft), fraud investigations generally uncover such schemes quickly, reducing the perpetrator's chances of repeating the offense and increasing the likelihood of being caught.

The Conversion

After completing and concealing the fraudulent act, the perpetrator must convert the ill-gotten gains for the individual's own benefit or the benefit of another party. In the case of the theft of petty cash, conversion generally occurs when the perpetrator deposits the funds into the individual's own account or makes a purchase with the stolen funds.

4

Exhibit 1.1   The Fraud Triangle

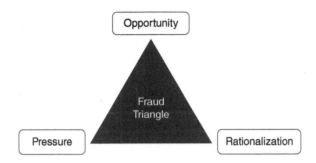

WHAT FACTORS LEAD TO FRAUD?

Individuals and groups perpetrate frauds to obtain money, property, or services; to avoid payment or loss of services; or to secure personal or business advantage. However, most people who commit fraud against their employers are not career criminals. In fact, the vast majority are trusted employees who have no criminal history and who do not consider themselves to be lawbreakers. So the question is: What factors cause these otherwise normal, law-abiding individuals to commit fraud?

The Fraud Triangle

The best and most widely accepted model for explaining why people commit fraud is the Fraud Triangle. (See Exhibit 1.1.) Dr. Donald Cressey, a criminologist whose research focused on embezzlers (whom he called *trust violators*), developed this model.

According to Cressey, three factors must be present at the same time for an ordinary person to commit fraud:

1. Pressure
2. Perceived opportunity
3. Rationalization

Pressure

The first leg of the Fraud Triangle represents *pressure*. This is what motivates the crime in the first place. The individuals might have a financial problem they are unable to solve through legitimate means, so they begin to consider committing an illegal act, such as stealing cash or falsifying a financial statement. The pressure can be personal (e.g., too deep in personal debt) or professional (e.g., job or business in jeopardy).

Examples of pressures that commonly lead to fraud include:

- Inability to pay one's bills
- Drug or gambling addiction
- Need to meet earnings forecast to sustain investor confidence
- Need to meet productivity targets at work
- Desire for status symbols, such as a bigger house or nicer car

Opportunity

The second leg of the Fraud Triangle is *opportunity*, sometimes referred to as *perceived opportunity*, which defines the method by which an individual can commit the crime. The person must see some way to use (abuse) a position of trust to solve a financial problem with a low perceived risk of getting caught.

It is critical that fraud perpetrators believe they can solve their problem in secret. Many people commit white-collar crimes to maintain their social status. For instance, they might steal to conceal a drug problem, pay off debts, or acquire expensive cars or houses. If perpetrators are caught embezzling or falsifying financial information, it hurts their status at least as much as the underlying problem they were trying to conceal. So the fraudster has to not only be able to steal funds, but also be able to do it in such a way that the person is unlikely to be caught and the crime itself will go undetected.

Rationalization

The third leg of the Fraud Triangle is *rationalization*. The majority of fraudsters are first-time offenders with no criminal past. They do not view themselves as criminals. They see themselves as ordinary, honest people caught in a bad set of circumstances. Consequently, fraudsters must justify their crime to themselves in a way that makes it an acceptable or justifiable act; that is, they must be able to rationalize their scheme. Common rationalizations include the following:

- "I was only borrowing the money."
- "I was entitled to the money."
- "I had to steal to provide for my family."
- "I was underpaid; my employer cheated me."
- "My employer is dishonest to others and deserved to be defrauded."

Limitations of the Fraud Triangle

The Fraud Triangle applies to most embezzlers and occupational fraudsters, but it does not apply to the *predatory employees* – those who take a job with the premeditated intent of stealing from their employer.

Also, while a rationalization is necessary for most people to begin a fraud, perpetrators often abandon rationalization after committing the initial act. Most frauds are not one-time events. They usually start as small thefts or misstatements and gradually increase in size and frequency. As the perpetrator repeats the act, it becomes easier to justify, until eventually there is no longer a need for justification.

Why Sanctions Alone Don't Deter Fraud

The Fraud Triangle also implies that simply punishing people who are caught committing fraud is not an effective deterrent. There are several reasons why:

- Fraud perpetrators commit their crimes when there is a perceived opportunity to solve their problems in secret. In other words, they do not anticipate getting caught.

The threat of sanctions does not carry significant weight because they never expect to face them.

- Fraud perpetrators rationalize their conduct so that it seems legal or justified. Thus, they do not see their actions as something that warrants sanctioning.
- Because status is frequently the motivation for individuals to commit fraud, the greatest threat they face is the detection of their crime, which would result in loss of status. Any formal sanctions that follow are a secondary consideration.

Control Weaknesses

On the organizational side, control weaknesses create the opportunity for fraud to occur. While this is only one factor in the Fraud Triangle, it is the element of fraud that organizational leaders typically have the greatest ability to control, and thus tend to focus most of their efforts and resources on. However, deficiencies in such controls are a notable factor in many frauds that occur. According to the 2018 *Report to the Nations on Occupational Fraud and Abuse*, published by the Association of Certified Fraud Examiners (ACFE), nearly half of all occupational fraud cases occur primarily due to a lack of internal controls or an override of existing controls. (Specific control activities to prevent and detect fraud are discussed in detail in Chapters 3 and 4.)

THE IMPACT OF FRAUD

All Organizations Are Susceptible to Fraud

Fraud is an uncomfortable risk to address. Most directors, executives, and managers would much rather believe that their organization's employees would never steal from the company. However, companies with management that is least attentive to the potential for fraud are at the greatest risk.

The truth is that fraud occurs in all organizations, regardless of size, industry, or location. No entity is immune. The fundamental reason for this is that fraud is a human problem, not an accounting problem. As long as organizations are employing individuals to perform the business functions, the risk for fraud exists. Only by recognizing and proactively and continually addressing this risk can organizations mitigate the potentially devastating impact.

The High Cost of Occupational Fraud

In its 2018 *Report to the Nations on Occupational Fraud and Abuse*, the ACFE analyzed data from 2,690 cases of occupational fraud that were investigated worldwide between January 2016 and October 2017. To compile this information, the ACFE surveyed the Certified Fraud Examiners (CFEs) who investigated those cases about the costs, methods, victims, and perpetrators involved in the frauds. The fraud cases in the study came from 125 nations – with more than half of the cases occurring in countries outside the US – providing a truly global view into the plague of occupational fraud.

Survey participants estimated that the typical organization loses 5% of its annual revenue to fraud. Applied to the estimated 2016 gross world product,[1] this figure translates to a potential total fraud loss of nearly US $4 trillion worldwide. Further, the median loss caused by the occupational fraud cases in the study was US $130,000, with 22% of the frauds resulting in losses of at least US $1 million.

The Indirect Costs

The impact of a fraud extends well beyond the actual dollar amount stolen by the perpetrator or the amount of the financial statement manipulation. In the wake of a fraud, employees might lose confidence in the security of their jobs, leading to loss of productivity. Moreover, the company's image is tarnished, decreasing its reputation in the eyes of existing and potential customers and vendors. In some instances, competitors have even used reports of fraud as a recruiting advantage in attracting top talent away from the victim company.

TYPES OF FRAUD AFFECTING ORGANIZATIONS

Occupational Fraud

Occupational fraud, also called *internal fraud*, is defined as "the use of one's occupation for personal enrichment through the deliberate misuse or misapplication of the organization's resources or assets." Simply stated, occupational fraud occurs when an employee, manager, or executive commits fraud against the employer. *Occupational fraud* is commonly synonymous with terms like *employee fraud* or *embezzlement*, although the term *occupational fraud* is broader and better reflects the full range of employee misconduct through which organizations lose money.

Although perpetrators are increasingly embracing technology and new approaches in committing and concealing these types of schemes, the methodologies used in such frauds generally fall into clear, time-tested categories. To identify and delineate the schemes, the ACFE developed the *Occupational Fraud and Abuse Classification System*, also known as the *Fraud Tree*. (See Exhibit 1.2.) This organization of schemes is especially helpful in designing, implementing, and assessing internal controls and other activities undertaken to manage the risk of fraud.

As illustrated in the Fraud Tree, there are three primary types of occupational fraud: asset misappropriation, corruption, and financial statement fraud; each of these types also has several distinct categories of subschemes.

The ACFE's 2018 *Report to the Nations* shows that, of the three primary categories of occupational fraud, asset misappropriation schemes are by far the most common and the least costly. In contrast, financial statement fraud schemes cause the greatest damage, but occur in just 10% of occupational fraud schemes. Corruption schemes fall in the middle in terms of both frequency and financial impact. (See Exhibits 1.3 and 1.4.)

Asset Misappropriation

Asset misappropriation schemes are frauds in which an employee misappropriates the organization's resources (e.g., cash, inventory, or proprietary information) for personal

Exhibit 1.2   The Fraud Tree

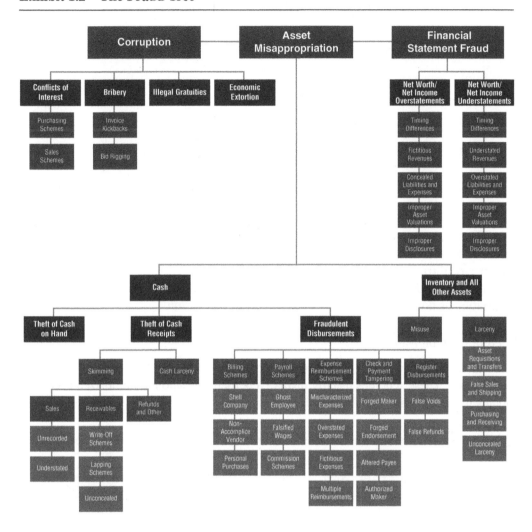

Exhibit 1.3   Occupational Frauds by Category – Frequency

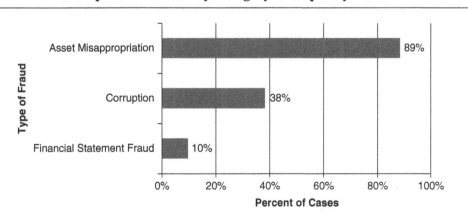

Exhibit 1.4   Occupational Frauds by Category – Median Loss

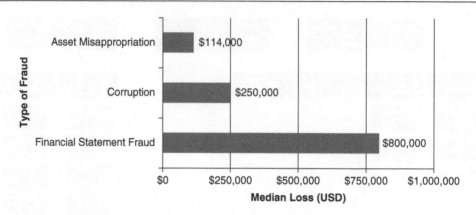

gain. These schemes include both the *theft* of company assets (such as stealing inventory from the warehouse) and the *misuse* of company assets (such as using a company car for a personal trip).

Exhibit 1.5 shows the frequency and median loss of the various forms of asset misappropriation as noted in the ACFE's 2018 *Report to the Nations*.

Theft of Cash on Hand

Theft of cash on hand refers to cash that resides in a secure, central location, such as a vault or safe. These schemes usually involve a perpetrator who has authorized access to monies in the safe or vault.

Exhibit 1.5   Frequency and Median Loss of Asset Misappropriation Subschemes

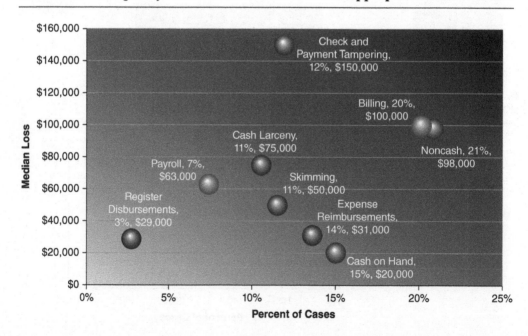

Theft of Cash Receipts

Perpetrators often target incoming cash payments, whether from sales, payments on customer accounts, or some other source. These schemes can take the form of skimming or cash larceny, depending on when the cash is stolen.

Skimming

Skimming is the theft of incoming cash before an employee records it in the accounting system; thus, it is an *off-book scheme*, meaning these schemes leave no direct audit trail. Because the stolen funds are never recorded, the victim organization might not be aware that the cash was ever received.

Skimming can occur at any point where money enters a business, so almost anyone who deals with the process of receiving incoming payments might be in a position to skim money. However, the most common places for skimming schemes to occur are in sales and accounts receivable.

Sales Skimming

Most skimming schemes involve the theft of incoming payments received from sales. This is probably because money skimmed from sales can remain completely unrecorded, whereas skimmed receivables might leave warning signs in the form of aged account balances.

> **Example**
>
> Johannes is a sales associate at a men's clothing store. One afternoon, a customer approaches the cash register with three shirts that he would like to purchase. Johannes charges the customer for all three shirts, but rings up the sale for only two of the shirts. When the customer hands over cash as payment for the purchase, Johannes puts the money for the two shirts he rang up in the register drawer and puts the money for the other shirt in his pocket.

Receivables Skimming

It is generally more difficult to hide the skimming of receivables than the skimming of sales because receivables payments are expected. When receivables are skimmed, the missing payment is shown on the books as a delinquent account. To conceal a skimmed receivable, the perpetrator must somehow account for the payment that was due to the company but never received. Consequently, schemes in which the fraudster skims receivables usually involve one of the following concealment methods:

- Lapping, in which one customer's payment is used to cover the theft of another customer's payment
- Account write-offs
- Falsified discounts, allowances, or other account adjustments

Example

Marjorie worked in the accounts receivable department of XYZ Corp. When Marjorie's personal debts grew larger than her income, she began embezzling incoming payments from XYZ's customers to finance the shortfall. After stealing Customer A's payment, Marjorie hid the documentation for that payment until the following day, when she took money from Customer B's payment to cover it. Then she used a payment from Customer C to cover the shortage in Customer B's payment. The cycle continued, with Marjorie repeatedly taking some of the incoming payments for herself, until a customer noticed a discrepancy between the payments and the account statement and called the accounting manager to complain.

Cash Larceny

Cash larceny involves the theft of money *after* an employee records it in the accounting system; thus, it is an *on-book scheme*. Accordingly, these schemes leave an audit trail on the company's books and are thus much harder to get away with than skimming schemes. Like skimming schemes, cash larceny can take place anywhere an employee has access to cash, but the most common schemes are:

- Theft of cash from the register
- Theft of cash from the deposit

Theft of Cash from the Register

The register is a popular place for cash larceny schemes for one reason – that's where the money is. In a scheme involving theft of cash from the register, an employee opens the register and simply removes the cash. The fraudster might do so while a sale is rung up or by opening the cash drawer with a "no sale" transaction. Unlike skimming schemes, cash larceny results in an imbalance in the register because the remaining cash in the drawer is less than the amount indicated on the register transaction log.

Example

A manager at a retail store signed onto a coworker's register when that person was on break, rang a "no sale" transaction, and took cash from the drawer. Over a period of two months, the manager took approximately $6,000 through this simple method. The resulting cash shortage therefore appeared in an honest employee's register, deflecting attention from the true thief.

Theft of Cash from the Deposit

When a company receives cash, someone must deposit it into a financial institution. In this scheme, an employee steals currency or checks before depositing them into the company's account but after recording the payment as received. This causes an out-of-balance condition, unless the thief alters the deposit slip after it has been validated.

Example

Soon after being given the responsibility of taking his company's deposit to the bank (and knowing that his employer's record keeping was less than effective), Gregory began a scheme involving theft of cash from the deposit. He simply took money from the deposit and altered the deposit slip to reflect the amount he actually deposited. His scheme worked well until the company hired a new employee in the accounting department who immediately began reconciling the bank account with the recorded cash receipts.

Fraudulent Disbursements

In a fraudulent disbursement scheme, an employee uses falsified documentation or other misstatements to induce the organization to disburse company funds for a dishonest purpose. Examples of fraudulent disbursements include submitting false invoices, altering time cards, and falsifying expense reports. On their face, the fraudulent disbursements do not appear any different from valid cash disbursements. Someone might notice the fraud based on the amount, recipient, or destination of the payment, but the method of payment is legitimate.

Common forms of fraudulent disbursements include:

- Check and payment tampering schemes
- Billing schemes
- Cash register disbursement schemes
- Expense reimbursement fraud
- Payroll fraud

Check and Payment Tampering Schemes

Check and payment tampering is a form of fraudulent disbursement scheme in which an employee either prepares a fraudulent payment (whether by check or by electronic funds transfer) for personal benefit or intercepts a payment intended for a third party. While the use of checks for business payments has declined dramatically over recent decades – and is almost nil in some countries – these schemes still proliferate. According to the 2018 *Report to the Nations*, check and payment tampering schemes, including those involving checks, were involved in 12% of occupational frauds and caused a median loss of US $150,000.

Check and payment tampering schemes include:

- Forged maker schemes
- Forged endorsements
- Altered checks
- Authorized maker schemes
- Electronic payment schemes

Forged Maker Schemes   In a forged maker scheme, the perpetrator steals blank company checks, fills them out, and negotiates them at a bank, check-cashing store, or other establishment. Commonly, the perpetrator finds unsecured checks and takes several from the bottom of the stack. The theft of the checks might not be discovered until much later (i.e., when the checks would have been issued), when someone notices that the check numbers do not match up with the check register. A variation of this scheme involves stealing checks from an inactive bank account, filling them out, and then cashing them.

Forged maker schemes can be easily concealed if the person who steals the checks also reconciles the bank account upon which the checks are drawn. In this case, the fraud will probably not be caught as long as there is money in the account.

Example

An accountant for a small organization was highly trusted and had responsibility over all accounting functions. She also had unrestricted access to blank checks, and she began writing checks to herself from the company account. To conceal the scheme, she would let large sales go unrecorded in the company's books, then write fraudulent checks in the amount of the unrecorded sales. Since the perpetrator was also the sole recipient of the company's bank statement, she could destroy the fraudulent checks and adjust the reconciliation to show the account as being in balance.

Forged Endorsements   Forged endorsements occur when an employee fraudulently negotiates a check written to someone else. The perpetrator might forge the recipient's signature or double-endorse the check.

Example

A manager stole and converted approximately $130,000 worth of company checks that had been returned to the company due to noncurrent addresses for the recipients. The nature of his company's business was such that the recipients of the rerouted checks were often not aware that the victim company owed them money, so they did not complain when their checks failed to arrive. In addition, the perpetrator had complete control over the bank reconciliation, so he could issue new checks to those payees who did complain, then "force" the reconciliation, making it appear that the bank balance and the book balance matched when, in fact, they did not.

Altered Checks   Rather than forging a signature, the fraudster might change the payee on a previously written check by manually altering the payee or by using a computer to change the payee. One way to alter a check is by adding letters or words at the end of the payee. For example, a check made payable to "ABC" could be changed to "ABCollins" and probably wouldn't be detected when negotiated. Alternatively, if the fraudster has responsibility for check creation, the individual might write the check in pencil to allow for easy alteration later.

> **Example**
>
> An administrative employee misappropriated funds from her organization by preparing checks for fraudulent expenses. The employee would draw a manual check for a miscellaneous expense, have the check approved and signed by an authorized employee, and then alter the check by inserting her own name as the payee. The employee was in charge of the bank statement and would destroy the altered checks when they were returned to the company after payment. Bank staff detected the fraud during a review of manual checks on the account. One check appeared to be irregular, so a bank employee contacted the victim organization, and the perpetrator was interviewed. She admitted to having "borrowed" funds on one occasion. In fact, she had written more than 10 fraudulent checks totaling approximately $50,000.

Authorized Maker Schemes   In an authorized maker scheme, an employee with signature authority on a company account writes fraudulent checks for his own benefit and signs his name as the maker. Because the perpetrator is authorized to sign checks, there is no need to forge signatures or intercept signed checks. The perpetrator simply writes and signs the instruments in the same manner as with any legitimate check.

The perpetrator of an authorized maker scheme can conceal a fraud the same way a forged maker does. Additionally, since perpetrators of authorized maker schemes are usually high-level employees, they can use their influence to discourage employees from asking questions when they override controls. Intimidation can play a large part in the concealment of any type of occupational fraud where powerful individuals are involved.

> **Example**
>
> The manager of a sales office stole approximately $150,000 from his employer over a two-year period. The manager had primary check-signing authority and abused this power by writing company checks to pay his personal expenses. Certain members of his staff knew about the fraud, but he had control over their careers. Fear of losing their jobs, plus the lack of a proper whistle-blowing structure, prevented these employees from reporting his fraud.

Electronic Payment Tampering   As businesses moved to using electronic payments – such as automated clearinghouse (ACH) payments, online bill payments, and wire transfers – in addition to or instead of traditional checks, fraudsters have adapted their methods to manipulate these payments as well. Some of these fraudsters abuse their legitimate access to their employer's electronic payment system; these schemes are similar to traditional check tampering frauds carried out by authorized makers. Others gain access through social engineering or password theft, or by exploiting weaknesses in their employer's internal control or electronic payment system. Regardless of how they log in to the system, dishonest employees use this access to fraudulently initiate or divert electronic payments to themselves or their accomplices.

As with other schemes, after making a fraudulent payment, employees must cover their tracks. However, the lack of physical evidence and forged signatures can make concealment of fraudulent electronic payments less challenging than other forms of check and payment tampering schemes. Some fraudsters attempt to conceal their schemes by altering the bank statement, miscoding transactions in the accounting records, or sending fraudulent payments to a shell company with a name similar to that of an existing vendor. Others rely on the company's failure to monitor or reconcile its accounts.

Billing Schemes

Billing schemes are those in which the fraudster manipulates the organization's purchasing and accounts payable functions to generate a fraudulent payment. The purchases used by the fraudster to generate the payment might be real or fictitious.

The following are common categories of billing schemes:

- False invoicing through shell companies
- Overbilling schemes involving existing vendors
- Making personal purchases with company funds

False Invoicing through Shell Companies   False invoicing occurs when a fraudulent invoice is set up for payment through the normal processing channels. The perpetrator creates fictitious backup documentation for the transaction (e.g., a purchase order or requisition) and attaches an invoice to generate the fraudulent payment. The perpetrator might either be the purchasing agent or be from a user area.

These schemes often involve the use of *shell companies*, which are business entities that typically have no physical presence (other than a mailing address) and no employees, and generate little, if any, independent economic value. Such companies might be nothing more than a fabricated name and a post office box that the fraudster uses to collect disbursements from the false billings. However, because the payments generated are made out in the name of the shell company, the perpetrator normally sets up a corresponding bank account in the shell company's name to deposit and cash the fraudulent checks.

To successfully commit a shell company scheme, the fraudster needs to be able to do all of the following:

- Form the shell company.
- Obtain the victim organization's approval of the shell company as a vendor.
- Submit an invoice from the shell company.
- Collect and convert the payment.

Example

A purchasing manager set up a dummy company using his residence as the mailing address. Over a two-year period, he submitted more than $250,000 worth of false invoices. Eventually, the scheme was detected by an accounts payable clerk when she was processing an invoice and noticed that the address of the vendor was the same as the purchasing manager's address. Had the perpetrator used a post office box instead of his home address on the invoices, his scheme might have continued indefinitely.

Overbilling through Existing Vendors   Billing schemes sometimes involve the use of legitimate vendors. In these cases, the perpetrator uses an existing vendor to bill the victim organization for goods or services that are nonexistent or overpriced.

The perpetrator might manufacture a fake invoice for a vendor that regularly deals with the victim organization, or might resubmit an invoice that has already been paid and then intercept the new payment. Because the bill is fictitious, the existing vendor is not out any money. The victim is the organization, which pays for goods or services that it does not receive.

A variation of these schemes, called a *pay-and-return scheme*, involves an employee intentionally mishandling legitimate payments that are owed to existing vendors. A perpetrator might do this by purposely double-paying an invoice, then requesting and intercepting the refund for overpayment. Alternatively, the fraudster might intentionally pay the wrong vendor. The perpetrator tells the vendor to return the check to the perpetrator's attention, intercepts the returned check, and then runs the vouchers through the accounts payable system a second time so the correct vendor eventually gets paid.

Example

A co-owner of a privately held company generated several hundred thousand dollars' worth of fraudulent income through false invoicing. The perpetrator submitted falsified invoices from one of the victim company's regular suppliers. The invoices were prepared with the help of an employee of the supplier. The fraudulent bills were paid on the perpetrator's authority, and the payments were intercepted by the employee of the supplier, who split the proceeds with the company co-owner.

Personal Purchases with Company Funds   Some frauds involve employees purchasing goods or services for personal use and billing the purchase to their employer. Fraudsters might use company funds to buy items for themselves, their businesses, their families, or their friends. Instead of generating cash, the perpetrator reaps the benefit of the purchases. From the victim organization's perspective, the loss is the same. In either case, the victim ends up expending funds on something that it does not receive.

In some of these schemes, the fraudster purchases the personal items but has the invoice sent to the organization's accounts payable department for payment. Another variation involves the purchase of personal items using a corporate credit card.

Example

A purchasing supervisor started a company for his son and had his employer purchase all the materials and supplies necessary for the son's business. In addition, the supervisor purchased materials through his employer that were used to add a room to his own house. The perpetrator used company money to buy nearly $50,000 worth of supplies and materials for himself.

Cash Register Disbursement Schemes

Register disbursement schemes involve removing cash from the register during a transaction, but they differ from skimming schemes because there is a record of the transaction on the register transaction log. And unlike cash larceny schemes, these frauds do not result in an imbalanced register. The most common methods are false refunds and false voids.

False Refunds   When a customer returns merchandise, an employee generates a refund and gives the customer the funds. Two types of false refunds are included in this category. The first involves refunds made for the entire amount of purchase without a customer actually returning the merchandise. The second involves overstated refunds in which part of the refund is legitimate, but the sales associate rings up a larger refund than the customer is owed and keeps the difference in cash. Another variation of this scheme is a refund through a credit card – the sales associate rings up a refund on the associate's own credit card.

Although false refund schemes are most common in the retail industry, they also occur in the service industry. Often in such frauds, the customer is in collusion with the fraudster. In a typical scheme, a customer receives the services requested, an employee at the service provider bills the customer, the customer submits a payment and it is processed, but then the employee issues a refund based on "unperformed" or "unsatisfactory" services. The two conspirators then split the fraudulent refund.

False Voids   False voids are similar to false refunds, except the sales clerk withholds the customer's receipt in anticipation of the fraud. Knowing that most establishments require a receipt to void a purchase, the perpetrator rings up the legitimate sale, keeps the customer's receipt, and then voids the transaction and pockets the sale amount. The sales clerk later submits the customer's receipt to the supervisor to justify the void.

Expense Reimbursement Schemes

Another common form of fictitious disbursements involves employees submitting falsified claims for expense reimbursement. There are four basic types of fraudulent expense reports:

1. Fictitious expenses
2. Altered or overstated expenses
3. Mischaracterized expenses
4. Duplicate reimbursements

Fictitious Expenses   Fictitious expenses are expenses that never occurred. The following are examples of common ways that employees fabricate expense report items:

- Claiming mileage that was never incurred
- Claiming lodging charges that were never incurred
- Submitting air travel receipts for trips that were never taken
- Requesting reimbursement for taxi fare when the hotel provided free service from the airport or the employee was picked up by a friend or relative without charge

- Submitting small items, such as tips and parking, that were never incurred
- Claiming meals that were paid for by other parties
- Claiming business trips that were never taken

Example

On his expense report, an employee claimed hotel expenses that his client had actually paid. He attached photocopies of legitimate hotel bills to the expense report as though he had paid for his own room.

Altered or Overstated Expenses   Employees might also alter documentation for legitimate expenses to fraudulently increase the amount of reimbursement received. Common altered expense schemes include:

- Altering the amount or date of the expense incurred
- Sharing a taxi with someone but submitting the full fare
- Submitting reimbursement for expensive meals by indicating that more than one person dined
- Altering the identities of individuals entertained so that the expense is reimbursable
- Submitting air travel for first class but flying coach

Mischaracterized Expenses   Mischaracterized expenses are expenses incurred by the employee but that are not eligible for reimbursement. Examples include:

- Disguising alcohol as meals
- Paying for personal meals and expenses, such as a family outing, and disguising them as business-related entertainment
- Claiming mileage for personal errands
- Claiming nonallowed entertainment expenses as meals
- Claiming gifts as meals
- Paying for personal vacations and claiming them as business trips

---

Example

Two midlevel managers ran up $1 million in inappropriate expenses over a two-year period. Their executive supervisors did not properly oversee their travel or expense requests, allowing them to spend large amounts of company money on international travel, lavish entertainment of friends, and the purchase of expensive gifts. They claimed they incurred these expenses entertaining corporate clients.

Duplicate or Multiple Reimbursements   Duplicate reimbursements occur when a legitimate expense is paid more than once. For example, an airline trip might be reimbursed from the passenger receipt as well as from the credit card receipt. The same might be true for meals; both the actual receipt and the credit card receipt are submitted for reimbursement.

Example

In one case of duplicate expense reimbursements, the perpetrator was an executive in a company that another organization purchased. The acquired company continued to operate in a fairly independent manner, and the books of the two companies were maintained separately. The perpetrator held a credit card in the name of the smaller, acquired company, which he used for business expenses. He would retain receipts for expenses charged to this credit card and submit them for reimbursement to the accounting office of the acquiring company. Thus, the perpetrator was able to receive a double reimbursement for his expenses.

Payroll Schemes

Payroll schemes occur when employees fraudulently generate more compensation than they are owed. These schemes are similar to billing schemes in that the perpetrator typically produces a false document or makes a false claim for distribution of funds by the employer. In billing schemes, the false claim typically comes in the form of a fraudulent invoice. In payroll schemes, the false claim generally occurs when the fraudster falsifies payroll records, timekeeping records, or other types of documents related to payroll or personnel functions. The most common forms of payroll fraud schemes are:

- Ghost employees
- Overpayment of wages
- Commission schemes

Ghost Employees   A perpetrator might use a fictitious employee placed on the payroll – called a *ghost employee* – to generate fraudulent paychecks. The ghost employee might be an ex-employee kept on the payroll after termination; a newly hired employee put on the payroll before employment begins; an accomplice, such as a friend or relative who does not work for the organization; or a fictitious person.

For a ghost employee scheme to work, the following things must happen:

- The ghost must be added to the payroll.
- Timekeeping information must be collected (if the ghost is set up as an hourly employee).
- A paycheck must be issued to the ghost.
- The check must be delivered to the perpetrator or an accomplice and converted for personal use.

Example

A high-ranking school employee added several fictitious employees to the school district's payroll. The scheme succeeded principally because of a lack of segregation of duties. The perpetrator had the authority to hire new employees and approve payroll expenditures. The bookkeepers for the school district relied on the perpetrator's authority in processing and recording payroll transactions. Payroll checks were distributed through the perpetrator's office, under his supervision. The perpetrator always took direct responsibility for distributing the paychecks to the fictitious employees.

Overpayment of Wages   The most common method of misappropriating funds from the payroll involves overpayment of wages. These schemes involve the fraudsters inducing the victim organization into paying them more than they are owed for a pay period.

For employees who are paid on an hourly basis to fraudulently increase the amounts of their paychecks, they must either falsify the number of hours worked or change their wage rates. Because salaried employees do not receive compensation based on hours worked, they usually generate fraudulent wages by increasing their rates of pay. Thus, schemes involving the overpayment of wages include:

- Falsified hours reported (hourly)
- Overtime abuses (hourly)
- Falsified pay rate (hourly and salaried)
- False reporting of paid time off (hourly and salaried)
- Retroactive pay increases (hourly and salaried)

Example

An individual who worked for a government agency committed fraud by falsely claiming overtime. The perpetrator was employed at a remote location and was the only individual who worked in this office, so no one was overseeing her activities. The employee would fill out false time cards, crediting herself with an average of 10 hours of overtime per week. Because there was no supervisor in the office, the perpetrator simply signed the time cards and forwarded them to headquarters.

Commission Schemes   Employees who are paid on commission might falsify the amount of sales made – and thus inflate their pay – by creating fictitious sales, altering the pricing list on sales documents or claiming the sales of other employees. Alternatively, they might fraudulently increase their own commission rates. However, to do so, they (or an accomplice) must obtain access to the payroll records, enter the change in the system, and save it.

Noncash Asset Schemes

In addition to stealing cash from an employer, an employee might steal or misuse other assets. These schemes range from taking a box of pencils home to stealing millions of dollars' worth of company equipment or misappropriating proprietary information from the company.

Misappropriation of Physical Assets

Employees can misappropriate a physical noncash asset through two basic methods: misuse and outright theft.

Misuse of Physical Assets   Asset misuse is the less egregious of the two categories of noncash misappropriation of physical assets. Misuse typically occurs with fixed assets such as company vehicles, computers, and other office equipment. In such schemes, these assets are not stolen; they are simply used by employees for nonbusiness purposes.

   Employees might also use office supplies, computers, and other office equipment to perform personal work on company time. For instance, they might use their computers at work to write letters, print invoices, or complete other work connected with a business they run on the side. In many cases, these side businesses are of the same nature as the employer's business, so the employee is essentially using the employer's equipment to compete with the employer.

Example

An employee used his employer's machinery to run his own snow removal and excavation business. He generally performed this work on weekends and after hours, falsifying the logs that recorded mileage and usage on the equipment. The employee had formerly owned all the equipment but had sold it to his current employer to avoid bankruptcy. As a term of the sale, he agreed to operate the equipment for his current employer, but he also never stopped running his old business.

Theft of Inventory, Supplies, and Fixed Assets   While the misuse of company property might be a problem, the theft of company property is of greater concern because it deprives the organization of the ability to use and profit from the assets completely. The most common methods of stealing noncash assets are:

- Unconcealed larceny
- Fraudulent requisitions and transfers
- Falsified receiving reports
- Fraudulent shipments of merchandise
- Theft of scrap inventory

Unconcealed Larceny   The most basic method for stealing noncash assets is unconcealed larceny, where an employee takes inventory, supplies, or other assets from the victim organization's premises without attempting to conceal the theft in the victim's books and records.

Example

A warehouse manager stole merchandise from his employer and resold it for his own profit. The perpetrator was taking inventory on weekends when the company was closed for business. He would enter the warehouse, load a company truck with various types of merchandise, and drive to a commercial storage facility where he kept the stolen items. From there, the fraudster ran his illicit business, selling the merchandise at discounted rates.

Fraudulent Requisitions and Transfers   Some employees falsify internal documents pertaining to the requisition or internal movement of noncash assets in order to steal those assets. They use these documents to justify the transfer or reallocation of inventory, supplies, or fixed assets by enabling access to items that they otherwise might not be able to reach. Examples of this type of scheme include overstating the amount of materials required for a project, requesting merchandise for an improper purpose, and fraudulently transferring inventory from one site to another within the victim organization.

Example

An employee of a telecommunications company used false project documents to request approximately $100,000 worth of computer chips, allegedly to upgrade company computers. Knowing that this type of requisition required verbal authorization from another source, the employee set up an elaborate phone scheme to get the project approved. The fraudster used her knowledge of the company's phone system to forward calls from four different lines to her own desk. When the confirmation call was made, it was the perpetrator who answered the phone and authorized the project.

Falsified Receiving Reports   Another relatively common method for misappropriating noncash assets is to falsify receiving reports or skim goods from incoming deliveries. For example, a warehouse supervisor or clerk might falsify a receiving report to show that a shipment was short or that some of the goods in the shipment were defective. The perpetrator then steals the "missing" or "substandard" merchandise.

The problem with this kind of scheme is that the receiving report does not reconcile to the vendor's invoice. If the vendor bills for 1,000 units of merchandise, but the receiving report only shows receipt of 900 units, someone has to explain the missing 100 units. This kind of scheme can be avoided by matching up support documents before paying invoices.

> **Example**
>
> Two employees conspired to misappropriate incoming merchandise by marking shipments as short. The fraudsters concealed the theft by falsifying only one copy of the receiving report. The copy that was sent to accounts payable indicated receipt of a full shipment so that the vendor would be paid without any questions. The copy used for inventory records indicated a short shipment so that the assets on hand would equal the assets in the perpetual inventory.

Fraudulent Shipments of Merchandise   Some employees misappropriate inventory by creating false sales orders or other shipping documents. These false documents might indicate sales made to fictitious persons or companies, real customers who are unaware of the scheme, or accomplices of the perpetrator. The victim organization's shipping department sends the inventory as if it had been sold; however, there is no sale, and the merchandise is delivered to the perpetrator or an accomplice.

> **Example**
>
> A warehouse employee misappropriated inventory from his employer's distribution center by creating fraudulent shipments. This individual had access to the organization's inventory control and shipping/receiving programs. He created shipments of inventory to an accomplice who worked for a competitor of the victim company. He also had merchandise delivered to a commercial storage facility he had leased. The victim organization had recently relaxed its controls over the shipping and inventory control processes to meet deadlines and improve efficiency. Consequently, the fraudster was able to enter shipping information into the victim's computer system, wait until the shipment was sent, and then cancel the orders and delete all the files associated with the transaction.

Theft of Scrap Inventory   Assets are sometimes written off *before* they are stolen, making them susceptible to theft. If a fraudster can have the target assets designated as scrap, it can be easier to conceal their misappropriation. Fraudsters might be able to take the supposedly useless assets for themselves, sell them to an accomplice at a greatly reduced price, or simply give them away.

> **Example**
>
> A warehouse foreman abused his authority to declare inventory obsolete. The foreman wrote off perfectly good inventory as scrap, and then transferred it to a shell corporation that he secretly owned. Using this scheme, the fraudster took more than $200,000 worth of merchandise from his employer.

Concealing Shrinkage   When a fraudster steals inventory, supplies, or fixed assets, the key concealment issue is usually shrinkage. *Shrinkage* is the unaccounted-for reduction in an organization's inventory that results from theft. Shrinkage is one of the red flags of noncash asset misappropriation. The goal of the fraudster is to avoid detection and prevent anyone from looking for missing assets. This means concealing the shrinkage that occurs from inventory theft. Common ways fraudsters attempt to conceal inventory shrinkage include:

- Altering inventory records
- Padding the physical inventory
- Recording fictitious sales and accounts receivable
- Writing off the missing assets

Misappropriation of Intangible Assets

Any valuable information that an organization collects, creates, develops, or stores is susceptible to theft or misappropriation.

Types of Intangible Assets That Are Misappropriated   The two intangible assets most susceptible to misappropriation are intellectual property and personally identifiable information.

INTELLECTUAL PROPERTY The World Intellectual Property Organization defines *intellectual property* as "creations of the mind, such as inventions; literary and artistic works; designs; and symbols, names, and images used in commerce."[2] The term encompasses many different forms of subject matter, which in some cases might overlap through copyrights, patents, trademarks, industrial design rights, and trade secrets.

Of these, trade secrets are particularly susceptible to theft because they are the most likely to confer a competitive advantage when misappropriated. The potential for theft and abuse increases as management invests time, money, and energy into developing information, processes, techniques, and other forms of trade secrets that provide an edge over competitors. The precise definition of a *trade secret* tends to vary by jurisdiction, but three elements are common to most:

1. The information is not generally known to the relevant portion of the public.
2. It confers an economic benefit on its holder (derived specifically from its not being generally known, not just from the value of the information itself).
3. It is the subject of reasonable efforts to maintain its secrecy.

Consequently, trade secrets can include a variety of confidential information used by an organization to gain a competitive advantage in its market, including:

- Business processes (e.g., those used in manufacturing, sales, or marketing)
- Sales information, such as customer data, historical sales, and cost and pricing information
- Research findings
- Methodologies

- Business plans and strategic plans
- Unreleased marketing information
- Source code and algorithms
- Documents and forms

PERSONALLY IDENTIFIABLE INFORMATION *Personally identifiable information* (PII) is information that can be used on its own or with other information to identify, contact, or locate a person, or to identify an individual in context. PII includes but is not limited to:

- Full name, maiden name, mother's maiden name, or alias
- Street address or email address
- Government identification number, passport number, driver's license number, taxpayer identification number or financial account, or credit card numbers
- Information about an individual that is linked or linkable to one of the previously listed items (e.g., date of birth, place of birth, race, religion, weight, activities, geographical indicators, employment information, medical information, education information, and financial information)

Organizations often have databases of PII for employees and customers. Such information can be extremely valuable to fraudsters because it can be used to commit identity theft, obtain fraudulent credit cards, or hack into individuals' bank accounts.

How Do Employees and Other Insiders Misappropriate Information?
Gaining access to sensitive information can be a complex feat for an outsider, but an employee might already have access to the targeted information. Even employees who do not have access are likely to know who does and how get to the information. Departing employees are often the greatest source of concern regarding information theft because they might see an opportunity to use company information to help get ahead at a new job or to get revenge on an organization they believe has wronged them.

As technology evolves, so do the methods used to misappropriate information. Ranging from crude to sophisticated, the methods used by insiders have a commonality: They serve a different – and usually legitimate – purpose within the business's normal operations. The following are some mechanisms that fraudsters might use to transfer the valuable information they are misappropriating:

- Email
- Removable media (e.g., USB drives, CDs, hard disks, and external drives)
- Smart phones and other mobile devices
- Printed documents and files
- Images and screen captures
- Instant messaging
- Social media
- File transfer protocols (e.g., FTP and SFTP)
- Peer-to-peer file-sharing programs
- Cloud storage

Corruption

Corruption involves employees' use of their influence in business transactions in a way that violates their duty to the employer and for the purpose of obtaining a benefit for themselves or someone else. These schemes create an unhealthy situation for businesses.

Corruption is a significant problem for organizations, particularly due to the drive for growth in international markets. As a result, many countries have enacted laws specifically designed to combat this risk. (Information about these country-specific laws is contained in Part II of this handbook.) Despite the multitude of anti-corruption legislation and increased enforcement efforts around the world, corruption is still prevalent.

Corruption can be broken down into the following four scheme types:

1. Bribery and kickbacks
2. Illegal gratuities
3. Economic extortion
4. Conflicts of interest

Bribery and Kickbacks

Bribery can be defined as "the offering, giving, receiving, or soliciting of corrupt payments (i.e., items of value paid to procure a benefit contrary to the rights of others) to influence an official act or business decision." At its heart, a bribe is a business transaction, albeit an illegal or unethical one. A person "buys" influence over the recipient of the bribe to procure a benefit that is contrary to the duty or the rights of others. Thus, bribery involves collusion between at least two parties – typically one inside and one outside the organization.

Bribery often takes the form of kickbacks, a form of negotiated bribery in which a commission is paid to the bribe taker in exchange for the services rendered. Thus, *kickbacks* are improper, undisclosed payments made to obtain favorable treatment. In the government setting, kickbacks refer to the giving or receiving of anything of value to obtain or reward favorable treatment in relation to a government contract. In the commercial sense, kickbacks refer to the giving or receiving of anything of value to influence a business decision without the employer's knowledge and consent.

Usually, kickback schemes are similar to the billing schemes described previously. They involve the submission of invoices for goods and services that are either overpriced or fictitious. However, kickbacks are classified as corruption schemes rather than asset misappropriations because they involve collusion between employees and third parties.

In a common type of kickback scheme, a vendor submits a fraudulent or inflated invoice to the victim organization, and an employee of that organization helps make sure that a payment is made on the false invoice. For this assistance, the employee receives a kickback payment from the vendor.

Most kickback schemes attack the purchasing function of the victim organization; therefore, these frauds are often undertaken by employees with purchasing responsibilities. Purchasing employees usually have direct contact with vendors and therefore have an opportunity to establish a collusive relationship.

Example

A purchasing agent redirected a number of orders to a company owned by a supplier with whom the agent was conspiring. In return for the additional business, the supplier paid the purchasing agent more than half the profits from the additional orders.

Illegal Gratuities

Illegal gratuities are something of value given to reward a decision *after* it has been made, rather than to influence it before the decision is made. Illegal gratuities are similar to bribery schemes except that, unlike bribery schemes, illegal gratuity schemes do not necessarily involve an intent to influence a particular decision before the fact; it is enough to show that the employee accepted an award based on the employee's performance. For example, instead of paying an employee to make a decision (i.e., award a contract), the vendor pays the employee because a favorable decision was made.

In the typical illegal gratuities scenario, a decision is made that happens to benefit a certain person or company. The party who benefited from the decision then gives a gift to the person who made the decision. The gift is merely offered as a thank-you for something that has been done.

Example

A city commissioner negotiated a land development deal with a group of private investors. After the deal was approved, the private investors rewarded the commissioner and his wife with a free, all-expenses-paid, international vacation.

At first glance, it might seem that illegal gratuity schemes are harmless as long as the business decisions in question are not influenced by the promise of payment. But most organizations' ethics policies forbid employees from accepting unreported gifts from vendors. One reason for such blanket prohibitions is that illegal gratuity schemes can (and frequently do) evolve into bribery schemes. Once an employee has been rewarded for an act such as directing business to a particular supplier, the employee might reach an understanding with the gift giver that future decisions will also be made to benefit the gift giver. Additionally, even though no outright promise of payment has been made in an illegal gratuity, employees might direct business to certain companies in the hope that they will be again rewarded with money or gifts.

Economic Extortion

An extortion scheme is often the other side of a bribery scheme. Economic extortion is present when an employee or official, through the wrongful use of actual or threatened force or fear, demands money or some other consideration to make a business decision. A demand for a bribe or kickback, coupled with a threat of adverse action if the payment is not made, might constitute extortion. For example, a government official might refuse to pay a legitimate invoice from a contractor unless the contractor pays the official a percentage.

Example

A plant manager for a utility company started a business on the side. The manager forced vendors who wanted to do work for the utility company to divert some of their business to the manager's side business. Those that did not agree to the manager's terms lost their business with the utility company.

Conflicts of Interest

Conflicts of interest occur when an employee or agent of the organization (or a spouse or close family member) has an undisclosed financial interest in a matter that could influence the person's professional role. As with other corruption frauds, conflict of interest schemes involve the exertion of an employee's influence to the principal's detriment. In contrast to bribery schemes, in which fraudsters are paid to exercise their influence on behalf of a third party, conflict of interest cases involve self-dealing by employees or agents.

Conflicts of interest frequently arise in the procurement process. These conflicts usually involve employees who make decisions that would allow them to give preference or favor to a vendor or contractor in exchange for anything of personal benefit to themselves or their friends and families.

Conflicts of interest can occur in various ways. For example, they often arise when an employee:

- Buys goods or services through a broker or intermediary that the employee controls
- Is involved in other business ventures with a vendor or contractor or its employees
- Has an interest in a business that competes with the employer
- Accepts inappropriate gifts, favors, travel, entertainment, or "fees" (kickbacks) from a vendor or contractor
- Engages in unapproved employment negotiations or accepts employment with current or prospective vendors or contractors

Most conflicts of interest occur because the fraudster has an undisclosed economic interest in a transaction, but a conflict can exist when the fraudster's hidden interest is not economic. In some scenarios, employees act in a manner detrimental to their employer to provide a benefit for a friend or relative, even though the fraudster receives no direct financial benefit.

Conflicts of interest do not necessarily constitute legal violations, as long as they are properly disclosed. Thus, to be classified as a conflict of interest scheme, the employee's interest in the transaction must be undisclosed. The crux of a conflict case is that the fraudster takes advantage of the employer; the victim organization is unaware that its employee has divided loyalties. If an employer knows of the employee's interest in a business deal or negotiation, there can be no conflict of interest, no matter how favorable the arrangement is for the employee.

Financial Statement Fraud

Financial statement fraud is the deliberate misrepresentation of the financial condition of an enterprise accomplished through the intentional misstatement or omission of amounts or disclosures in the financial statements to deceive financial statement users. Like all types of fraud, financial statement fraud involves an intentional act. As stated in the International Standard on Auditing (ISA) 240, *The Auditor's Responsibility Relating to Fraud in an Audit of Financial Statements*, "misstatements in the financial statements can arise from error or fraud. The distinguishing factor between error and fraud is whether the underlying action that results in the misstatement of the financial statements is intentional or unintentional."[3]

The financial statements are the responsibility of the organization's management. Accordingly, financial statement fraud is unique in that it almost always involves upper management. Also, in contrast to other frauds, the motivation for financial statement fraud is not only personal gain. Most commonly, financial statement fraud is used to make a company's reported earnings look better than they actually are. Specifically, some of the more common reasons people commit financial statement fraud are:

- To demonstrate increased earnings per share or partnership profits interest, thus allowing increased dividend/distribution payouts
- To cover inability to generate cash flow
- To avoid negative market perceptions
- To obtain financing, or to obtain more favorable terms on existing financing
- To encourage investment through the sale of stock
- To receive higher purchase prices for acquisitions
- To demonstrate compliance with financing covenants
- To meet company goals and objectives
- To receive performance-related bonuses

Most financial statement schemes involve one or more of the following:

- Overstatement of assets or revenues
- Understatement of liabilities or expenses
- Improper disclosures[4]

Overstated Assets or Revenues

One of the most direct ways to improve the organization's financial appearance is to artificially inflate the reported revenues, assets, or both. However, recording revenue or assets in a way that is not in accordance with generally accepted accounting principles can result in fraudulent financial statements.

Common schemes used to overstate asset or revenue include:

- Fictitious revenues
- Timing differences
- Improper asset valuation

Fictitious Revenues

Fictitious revenue schemes involve recording sales that never occurred. The purpose of fictitious sales is to overstate or inflate reported revenue to make the organization appear more profitable than it is. Fictitious revenues can be recorded for fake sales of both goods and services.

Fictitious revenue schemes most often involve fake or phantom customers, but can also involve legitimate customers. For example, an invoice is prepared for a legitimate customer and then the goods are not shipped or the services are not rendered. At the beginning of the next accounting period, the sale is reversed. Another method involves altering (e.g., artificially inflating) invoices to legitimate customers so that they reflect higher amounts or quantities than were actually sold.

Timing Differences

Financial statement fraud can involve timing differences (i.e., recognizing revenue or expenses in improper periods). In general, revenue should be recognized in the accounting records when the sale is complete; for the sale of goods, this generally is when title is passed from the seller to the buyer. In the case of services, revenue is typically recognized when the services have been rendered.

Examples of schemes that involve fraudulent timing differences include:

- Improper matching of revenues and expenses
- Early revenue recognition

Improper Matching of Revenues and Expenses   In general, under the accounting concept of the *matching principle*, revenues and their corresponding expenses should be recorded in the same period. An example of improper matching of revenues and expenses occurs when a company accurately records sales for an accounting period, but then fails to simultaneously record the expenses corresponding to those sales. This mismatch of income and expenditures has the effect of overstating net income in the period the sales occurred, and subsequently understating net income when the expenses are recorded.

Early Revenue Recognition   Generally, revenue should be booked when the sale is complete – when the title has passed from the buyer to the seller or when services have been rendered. However, intentionally booking revenue before it is earned results in overstated income. For example, a company receives fees from a customer for management services that it has not yet rendered. If the company reports the fees as revenue in the period received, the financial statements for the period will be misstated. The same is true for the sale of merchandise that is booked but not shipped. In addition, the income for the reporting period in which the sales are finally complete will be lower than it should be due to the cost of goods sold recorded in that period without matching revenue to offset it.

Improper Asset Valuation

The cost principle in generally accepted accounting principles requires that assets be recorded at their original cost. Some assets are reported at the lower of cost or market value, but asset values are generally not increased to reflect current market value. Even so, it is still sometimes necessary to use estimates in valuing and accounting for assets. For example, estimates are used in determining the salvage value and useful life of a depreciable asset. Whenever estimates are used, there is an opportunity for fraud. For this reason, some assets are especially susceptible to manipulation.

While any asset can be manipulated for financial reporting purposes, the most common assets subject to improper valuation are:

- Inventory
- Accounts receivable
- Fixed assets

Inventory Inventory can be overstated by manipulating the physical inventory count, failing to relieve inventory for costs of goods sold, and many other methods. One of the most popular methods of overstating inventory is by reporting fictitious (phantom) inventory. Fictitious inventory schemes usually involve the creation of fake documents, such as inventory count sheets and receiving reports. In some instances, a co-conspirator claims to be holding inventory for the company in question. Alternatively, some fraudsters insert fake count sheets or change the quantities recorded on the count sheets during the inventory observation.

Accounts Receivable Accounts receivable are subject to manipulation in the same manner as sales and inventory, and in many cases the schemes are conducted together. The two most common schemes involving accounts receivable are:

- Fictitious receivables (which usually accompany fictitious revenues)
- Failure to write down accounts receivable as bad debts or the failure to establish adequate reserves for future collectability problems

Fixed Assets Fixed asset values can be falsified through several different schemes. Some of the more common schemes are:

- Fictitious fixed assets
- Misrepresenting valuations of fixed assets

Understated Liabilities and Expenses

Understating liabilities and expenses is another way financial statements can be manipulated to make a company appear more profitable than it is. Liability understatement has a positive effect on the balance sheet in that the company appears to owe less to creditors than it actually does. Furthermore, the reported amount of either assets or equity increases by the amount of understated liabilities to keep the books in balance. Understating expenses, conversely, has the effect of artificially inflating net income. Both actions make the financial statements more attractive to the user.

Concealed liabilities and expenses can be difficult to detect because frequently there is no audit trail to follow. If there is nothing in the books, it makes the manipulation difficult to uncover using normal audit and review techniques.

Common methods of concealing liabilities and expenses involve:

- Liability or expense omissions
- Improper capitalizing of costs

Liability or Expense Omissions

The easiest method of concealing liabilities and expenses is to simply fail to record them. Liability omissions are probably one of the hardest schemes to detect. A thorough review of all transactions after the financial statement date, such as increases and decreases in accounts payable, might help uncover any liabilities that management omitted from the financial statements. Also, a review and analysis of the company's contractual obligations might reveal contingent liabilities that were intentionally omitted.

Improper Capitalizing of Costs

All organizations incur costs. However, it is not always clear how an organization should record those costs. Suppose ABC Company has a piece of property in need of some repairs. If the work performed simply fixes any problems and brings the property back to its original state, then the costs associated with the repair would appear as an expense on the income statement in the year they were incurred. Net income would be reduced by this amount, and the balance sheet would remain unaffected.

However, suppose work is done that not only repairs but increases the value of the property. Any expenditures made that increase the book value of the property would need to be capitalized – that is, added to the company's assets reported on the balance sheet. In other words, these costs would be added to the asset value on ABC's balance sheet and then depreciated as an expense over time.

Either way, the costs associated with repairs or improvements are on ABC's income statement as an expense. The difference is in the timing. Capitalizing an expenditure and depreciating it over a number of years makes a significant difference in the bottom line of the financial statements in the year the work was done. Conversely, expensing the same amount of costs in the same year results in a much lower net income that year.

Improperly capitalizing expenses is another way to increase income and assets and make the entity's financial position appear stronger. If expenditures are capitalized as assets and not expensed during the current period, both income and assets will be overstated. As the assets are depreciated, income in following periods will be understated.

Improper Disclosures

Generally accepted accounting principles require that financial statements and notes include all the information necessary to prevent a reasonably discerning user of the financial statements from being misled. The most common fraud schemes resulting from improper disclosures involve:

- Related-party transactions
- Liability omissions
- Subsequent events
- Management fraud
- Accounting changes

Related-Party Transactions

Related-party transactions occur when a company does business with another entity whose management or operating policies can be controlled or significantly influenced by the company or by some other party in common. The financial interest that a company official has might not be readily apparent. For example, common directors of two companies that do business with each other, any corporate general partner and the partnerships with which it does business, and any controlling shareholder of the corporation with which it does business could be related parties. Family relationships can also be considered related parties, such as all direct descendants and ancestors, without regard to financial interests.

Related-party transactions are sometimes referred to as *self-dealing*. While these transactions are sometimes conducted at arm's length, often they are not. There is nothing inherently wrong with related-party transactions, as long as they are fully disclosed. If the transactions are not fully disclosed, the company might injure shareholders by engaging in economically harmful dealings without their knowledge.

Liability Omissions

Improper disclosures related to liability omissions include the failure to disclose loan covenants or contingent liabilities. Loan covenants are agreements, in addition to or as part of a financing arrangement, that a borrower has promised to keep as long as the financing is in place. The agreements can contain various types of covenants, including certain financial ratio limits and restrictions on other major financing arrangements. Contingent liabilities are potential obligations that will materialize only if certain events occur in the future. A corporate guarantee of personal loans taken out by an officer or a private company controlled by an officer is an example of a contingent liability.

Subsequent Events

Events occurring or becoming known after the close of the period that could have a significant effect on the entity's financial position must be disclosed. Fraudsters typically avoid disclosing court judgments and regulatory decisions that undermine the reported values of assets, that indicate unrecorded liabilities, or that adversely reflect upon management's integrity. A review of subsequent financial statements, if available, might reveal whether management improperly failed to record a subsequent event that it had knowledge of in the previous financial statements.

Management Fraud

Management has an obligation to disclose to the shareholders information about significant fraud committed by officers, executives, and others in a position of trust. When management is aware that fraud has occurred and the subjects are under criminal proceedings, disclosure is required.

Accounting Changes

In general, three types of accounting changes must be disclosed to avoid misleading the user of financial statements: changes in accounting principles, estimates, and reporting entities. Although the required treatment for these accounting changes varies for each type and across jurisdictions, they are all susceptible to manipulation. For example, fraudsters might fail to retroactively restate financial statements for a change in accounting principles if the change causes the company's financial statements to appear weaker. Likewise, they might fail to disclose significant changes in estimates such as the useful lives and estimated salvage values of depreciable assets, or the estimates underlying the determination of warranty or other liabilities. They might even secretly change the reporting entity by adding entities owned privately by management or by excluding certain company-owned units to improve reported results.

External Fraud

External fraud against a company covers a broad range of schemes committed by a broad range of parties. While management often places considerable attention on the potential for employee fraud, it must ensure that the organization's leaders are aware of the ways the organization can be defrauded by outside parties and that anti-fraud measures address the risks posed by these threats as well.

Many external fraud schemes are dependent upon the relationship the perpetrator has with the organization, and thus the opportunities presented to commit the fraud.

Fraud Committed by Vendors and Contractors

Dishonest vendors and contractors might engage in schemes to defraud the organization of cash or other resources. Common examples of fraud committed by vendors include:

- Billing the company for goods or services not provided
- Submitting inflated or duplicate billings for payment
- Bribing company employees to gain or keep the company's business
- Delivering goods or services that do not meet the specified requirements, but not disclosing the substitution

Colluding with Other Vendors or Contractors

Some contractors might seek to circumvent the competitive bidding process – and thus to defraud the company – by colluding with their competitors. In these schemes, competitors in the same market collude to defeat competition or to inflate the prices of goods and services artificially. When competitors commit such schemes, the procuring entity is cheated out of its right to the benefits of free and open competition.

The most common forms of collusion between competitors involve the following types of schemes:

- *Complementary bidding* (also known as *protective*, *shadow*, or *cover bidding*) occurs when competitors submit token bids that are not serious attempts to win the contract (e.g., are too high or deliberately fail to meet other requirements). These bids give the appearance of genuine bidding but are actually intended only to influence the contract price and who is awarded the contract.
- *Bid rotation* (also known as *bid pooling*) occurs when two or more contractors conspire to alternate the business between/among themselves on a rotating basis. Instead of engaging in competitive contracting, the bidders exchange information on contract solicitations to guarantee that each contractor will win a share of the purchasing entity's business.
- *Bid suppression* occurs when two or more contractors enter into an illegal agreement whereby at least one of the conspirators refrains from bidding or withdraws a previously submitted bid. The goal of this type of scheme is to ensure that a particular competitor's bid is accepted.
- *Market division* occurs when competitors agree to divide and allocate markets and to refrain from competing in each other's designated portion of the market. The result of these schemes is that competing firms will not bid against each other, or they will submit only complementary bids when a solicitation for bids is made by a customer or in an area not assigned to them. The customer thereby loses the benefit of true competition and ends up paying a higher price than would be dictated by fair bidding under normal economic forces.

Colluding with Company Employees

In addition to bribing company employees to gain or keep the company's business, some dishonest vendors collude with company insiders to rig the procurement or contract bidding process. The manner in which these schemes are perpetrated generally depends on the corrupt employee's level of influence. The more power a person has over the process being manipulated, the more likely it is that the person can influence which entity is awarded the contract.

Fraud schemes involving collusion between the contractor and the purchasing entity's employees generally include the following:

- *Need recognition schemes*, in which a company employee receives a bribe or kickback for convincing the employer to recognize a need for a particular product or service
- *Bid tailoring* (also known as *specifications schemes*), in which an employee with procurement responsibilities, often in collusion with a contractor, drafts bid specifications in a way that gives an unfair advantage to a certain contractor
- *Bid manipulation schemes*, in which a procuring employee attempts to influence the selection of a contractor by restricting the pool of competitors from which

bids are sought, thereby improving the collusive vendor's chances of winning the contract

- *Leaking bid data*, in which an employee of a procuring entity leaks confidential information from competing bidders to a favored bidder, giving that bidder an unfair advantage in the bidding process
- *Bid splitting*, in which a dishonest employee breaks up a large project into several small projects that fall below the mandatory bidding level and awards some or all of the component jobs to a contractor with whom the employee is conspiring

Fraud Committed by Customers

Likewise, dishonest customers might take advantage of company sales and return policies for personal gain or might attempt to obtain company goods or services for free. Examples of frauds committed by customers include:

- Placing orders on other customers' accounts (account takeover fraud)
- Submitting bad checks or falsified account information for payment
- Paying for purchases with stolen or counterfeit credit cards
- Attempting to return stolen, broken, or counterfeit products for a refund
- Claiming goods were never received (even though they were) and requesting a refund or replacement order
- Overpaying for a product or service using a fraudulent payment method (e.g., counterfeit check or stolen credit card) and then requesting the organization to wire the difference between the overpayment and the true cost to the fraudster or a third party
- Manipulating customer loyalty and reward programs to obtain benefits the fraudster isn't entitled to
- Making multiple warranty claims or claims for issues not covered by the warranty

Fraud Committed by Agents, Brokers, and Fiduciaries

Other parties, such as financial and legal advisers, might also have the opportunity to defraud organizations. For example, an investment adviser might steal an organization's funds or undertake transactions on the organization's behalf simply to generate excess fees and commissions. Such schemes are similar to schemes perpetrated against consumers, but organizations can fall victim to dishonest agents, brokers, and fiduciaries as well.

Fraud Committed by Unrelated Third Parties

In addition to watching for schemes perpetrated by parties known to the organization, management must also be aware of threats from unknown outside parties.

Business ID Theft

While individuals are the usual targets of identity theft, identity thieves sometimes target businesses. *Business identity theft* occurs when a fraudster impersonates a business to commit financial fraud. For identity thieves, there are a number of reasons to target businesses instead of individuals:

- The potential rewards are greater, as businesses tend to have larger bank account balances, easier access to credit, and higher credit limits than individuals.
- Employees are less likely to notice new or unusual financial transactions, because businesses tend to engage in more transactions than individuals.
- The information necessary to commit business identity theft (e.g., business or tax identification numbers) is often publicly available online or in government records.

Methods of Business ID Theft

To operate legally in most jurisdictions, company owners must file certain documents with the appropriate government agency. Such documents might include business registration forms, organizational documents (e.g., articles of incorporation), governance agreements (e.g., shareholder agreements), and tax forms. Fraudsters often commit business identity theft by changing the information in these government filings. In addition to impersonating an existing business, identity thieves can use these government filings to reinstate or revive a closed or dissolved business. Identity thieves tend to target companies that recently closed, because there is usually a legal time limit for reinstatement (e.g., two years from closure). Once they find a suitable company, the identity thieves can reinstate the company by filing the required reinstatement documents and paying a filing fee. The owners of the closed or dissolved company generally do not discover the fraud until creditors of the reinstated company contact them.

Fraudsters also commit business identity theft by creating a new business with a name similar to an existing business. For example, identity thieves could impersonate a company named Windsor Homes, Inc., by creating a new company named "Windsor Homes, LLC" or "Windsor Home, Inc." In such cases, the fraudsters attempt to trick careless third parties (e.g., creditors, vendors, customers) into doing business with the similarly named company.

In one of the more audacious and risky schemes, fraudsters sometimes commit business identity theft by renting office space in the same building as the targeted company.

Example

Barney, Cooper, & Smith (BCS) is a large law firm that occupies the ninth and tenth floors of an office building. After researching BCS for months, a fraudster rents a suite on the eighth floor of the same building, calls several of BCS's vendors, and orders $50,000 worth of computers and office equipment. The fraudster pretends to represent BCS and gives the address of his suite. Because his address is the same as that of BCS (except for the suite number), the vendors deliver the goods to the fraudster's suite. The fraudster then vacates the building. BCS discovers the fraud a month later when it receives invoices from the vendors.

Data Breaches

External fraudsters are increasingly attacking organizations' networks and systems to steal sensitive information. In these data breach schemes, the fraudster exploits weaknesses stemming from default configurations and passwords, design flaws, coding issues, and software vulnerabilities. Wide-ranging and often sophisticated techniques, such as SQL injection, malware, automated attack tools, exploit kits, and other hacking tools can be used by ambitious fraudsters. Conversely, many data breaches are accomplished using simple social engineering techniques, such as phishing schemes, tech support impersonation schemes, or schemes targeting the customer contact center.

Upon gaining access to systems, the attackers search to identify the valuable information before misappropriating it from the organization's controls. These attacks can be either obvious or unnoticeable to the victim organization, depending on the attackers' skill levels.

While many data breaches are committed by unrelated third parties, the possible perpetrators – and the specific motivations for the attacks – vary. Such schemes might be perpetrated or assisted by:

- Contractors or vendors, which often have access to the same information as employees but without the same controls
- Competitors, which are seeking to misappropriate trade secrets, ideas, processes, blueprints, or source code, or to acquire commercial information such as client lists, pricing, or bid information to gain an undue advantage
- Nation-state actors, who have become extremely active in industrial and commercial ventures so their industries can perform at a higher level than those of competing nations
- Organized crime groups, who seek personally identifiable information in support of criminal endeavors

Ransomware

Ransomware is a type of malicious software (malware) that locks a computer's operating system and restricts access to data until the victim pays a ransom to the perpetrator. Fraudsters use ransomware to extort money from businesses. A typical ransomware attack on a business involves the following three steps:

1. *A company computer or network is infected with ransomware.* The infection usually occurs when an employee clicks on a malicious link in an email, opens or downloads an infected file, or visits a compromised website. Ransomware can also infect mobile devices through links in text messages. Some ransomware spreads automatically through the Internet, infecting computers without the need for any action by computer users. However, this method of infection is uncommon; most ransomware infections occur because a user unwittingly downloads it. After infecting one computer, the ransomware often spreads throughout the company's computer network, endangering all data residing on the network.

2. *The ransomware encrypts or blocks access to data on the infected computer or the entire network.* Some ransomware programs also encrypt the targeted data so that the victim cannot access the data without a decryption key provided by the fraudster. Other ransomware programs simply delete the data and then falsely claim that it has been encrypted, thus tricking the victim into paying a ransom for data that no longer exists.

3. *A ransom demand is displayed on the computer screen.* Generally, the ransomware disables the infected computer and displays a message on the computer screen stating that the victim's data will be deleted unless a ransom is paid by a specified date. To intimidate victims, the message might contain threatening accusations that the victim has viewed illegal videos, downloaded pirated media, or otherwise accessed forbidden content. The message might also include police insignia or an official-looking government logo. Other ransomware messages are more direct and make no effort to conceal their obvious attempts at extortion. Increasingly, such messages demand payment in bitcoin, the most popular type of cryptocurrency. Historically, fraudsters have kept the ransom amount relatively low to encourage more victims to pay, especially in ransomware campaigns that are widespread and indiscriminate. However, the ransom amount tends to be higher when a specific company is targeted. In addition, many companies do not recover their data after paying the ransom. Some fraudsters destroy the ransomed data regardless of management's response, and others raise the ransom amount after receiving an initial payment.

Business Email Compromise

In a traditional *business email compromise* scheme, a fraudster uses a fake email from a company executive (e.g., CEO, CFO, president) to trick an employee into sending money or other information to the fraudster. Business email compromise schemes are also commonly known as *BEC scams* or *CEO fraud*.

How BEC Scams Work

Social engineering refers to the psychological manipulation of people to trick them into revealing information or taking some action. After researching a victim, social engineers often impersonate someone the victim trusts, such as an authority figure or a business associate.

One common social engineering method is *phishing*, which involves the use of emails to impersonate trusted persons or entities. In traditional phishing schemes, fraudsters send out thousands of emails indiscriminately. Only a small percentage of recipients fall for the scheme, but the fraudsters rely on the sheer volume of their emails to achieve results. By contrast, *spear phishing* schemes target specific individuals or businesses. BEC scams are a type of spear phishing scheme. They generally require more preparation than a traditional phishing scheme, but the rewards can be great.

Prior to initiating the BEC scam, fraudsters generally perform extensive research on the company, the executive they will impersonate, and the employee who will receive the fake email. Fraudsters can gather much of this information from public sources, such as the company's website and social media accounts. In addition, fraudsters might use phishing or other social engineering methods, malware, and hacking to learn about the company's employees, organizational structure, and payment procedures. Some victims have reported being the target of a ransomware attack prior to a BEC scam.

The fake emails used in BEC scams are often well written, and they sometimes mimic language used by the executive in prior emails. Fraudsters can compromise the executive's email account through social engineering or computer intrusion techniques (e.g., malware). Additionally, fraudsters sometimes spoof emails by adding, removing, or changing characters in the email address. For example, if a CEO's email address is John.Smith@ABCINC.com, the fake email might come from John.Smit@ABCINC.com (the "h" in "Smith" is missing) or John.Smith@ACBINC.com (the letters "B" and "C" in "ABCINC" are transposed). This makes it difficult to spot the fake email address.

Types of BEC Schemes

Although BEC scams can take numerous forms, the FBI has identified five common scenarios by which BEC scams are perpetrated.[5]

1. Fraudsters posing as a company's longstanding supplier (often a foreign supplier) send an email to an employee of the company and request that funds be transferred to an alternate account controlled by the fraudsters. The scenario is sometimes known as the bogus invoice scheme, supplier swindle, or invoice modification scheme.
2. The compromised email account of a high-level executive is used to ask an employee to transfer funds to the fraudsters' account. This scenario is sometimes known as CEO fraud, business executive scam, masquerading, or financial industry wire fraud.
3. Fraudsters use an employee's hacked personal email account to identify the company's vendors or business contacts and ask them to transfer funds to the fraudsters' account.
4. Fraudsters posing as the company's attorney contact an employee and request a transfer of funds to the fraudsters' account. The fraudsters often insist that the employee act quickly and secretly.
5. The compromised email account of a high-level executive is used to contact the company's human resources department and request employees' payroll data, tax information, or other personally identifiable information. Unlike traditional BEC schemes, this scheme seeks to obtain information about employees instead of money. Fraudsters then use the employee information to commit identity theft or one of the other BEC schemes described earlier.

NOTES

1. Estimated 2016 gross world product of US $79.58 trillion (www.cia.gov/library/publications/the-world-factbook/geos/xx.html), retrieved January 22, 2018.
2. www.wipo.int/about-ip/en/index.html
3. www.ifac.org/system/files/downloads/a012-2010-iaasb-handbook-isa-240.pdf

4. Because financial reporting standards can vary by jurisdiction, the details of those standards – and intentional violations thereof – are beyond the scope of this discussion. Consequently, the schemes discussed in this section reflect high-level accounting principles and the general approaches used to manipulate the financial statements; experts in applicable financial reporting standards should be consulted if financial statement fraud is suspected.
5. www.ic3.gov/media/2017/170504.aspx

CHAPTER 2

Legal Issues Pertaining to Fraud

A variety of legal issues may arise during the course of a fraud investigation. This chapter covers some of the basic principles relating to evidence, legal privileges, privacy, and employee rights. However, it is important to keep in mind that the legal systems in different countries or jurisdictions can vary dramatically. As a result, fraud examiners should consult with counsel regarding relevant local laws and regulations. More information about the laws and practices of specific countries is contained in Part Two of this handbook.

TYPES OF LEGAL SYSTEMS

At a very basic level, legal systems can be divided into several categories.

Religious and Secular Systems

Religious systems derive their laws from interpretations of religious texts and treat them as divine mandates. However, today few countries rely exclusively on religious law. Instead, it is often used in conjunction with secular law. For example, some countries that use religious law restrict its application to issues such as divorce, inheritance, and child custody, while using secular law to govern criminal and commercial law.

The majority of legal systems are secular systems. This means that the laws are not based on any particular religion. Instead, they are designed and implemented by the relevant governmental authorities.

Common Law and Civil Law Systems

Most legal systems also fall under the umbrella of one of two legal "families" – common law systems and civil law systems. The term *common law* refers to judge-made law. Countries that incorporate common law into their legal system generally recognize the extensive application of judicial precedent. In the legal context, precedent refers to an earlier court ruling that applies to a particular dispute. For example, if the highest court in a particular jurisdiction issues a ruling regarding government searches, lower courts within that jurisdiction are obligated to follow that ruling whenever the relevant issue arises.

In contrast, judges play less crucial roles in civil law systems. In these systems, judge-made law is either a minor aspect or completely absent. Instead, civil law countries formally codify their laws. Civil law countries often do not recognize judicial precedence,

---

Portions of the material in this chapter are adapted from the following Association of Certified Fraud Examiners (ACFE) publications: *Legal Issues in Fraud Examinations* (International Edition), *Conducting Internal Investigations: Gathering Evidence and Protecting Your Company*, the course material for the *Legal Elements of Fraud Examinations* seminar, and the "Law" section of the *Fraud Examiners Manual* (International Edition).

or they utilize it in a more limited manner than common law jurisdictions. This means that civil law courts do not shape the law to the same extent as their counterparts in common law countries. Civil law has its roots in ancient Roman law and is by far the most common basis for legal systems worldwide.

Adversarial and Inquisitorial Proceedings

A further distinction between common law and civil law systems is the process used to settle legal disputes. Most common law countries use *adversarial proceedings*, where the presiding judge essentially acts as a referee between the two parties to the dispute. Each party presents its case and has the opportunity to challenge or rebut arguments advanced by the opposing side. Then, a judge, group of judges, or jury issues a decision based on the facts presented.

In contrast, civil law countries frequently use *inquisitorial proceedings* (sometimes referred to as *nonadversarial proceedings*) to settle legal disputes. Judges play much more active roles in inquisitorial systems, where they are generally tasked with actively investigating the case. For example, in adversarial systems, the parties involved in the dispute are generally tasked with collecting evidence and questioning witnesses at trial. In countries that use an inquisitorial system, the presiding judge may question witnesses and supervise the gathering of evidence. After the completion of an investigation, the judge, a group of judges, or a jury will decide the outcome of the case.

Hybrid Systems

It is important to note that there is significant crossover between common law and civil law systems and that many countries use hybrid systems that incorporate aspects of both. For example, most countries that use common law do not rely exclusively on judicial decisions as the source of law. Generally, these countries have legislatures that draft and enact laws. However, the judiciary generally has the power to shape those laws (or to strike them down as unconstitutional) if they arise during a legal dispute. Additionally, countries that predominantly use adversarial systems might task judges with more active responsibilities in certain kinds of cases (e.g., minor traffic violations, administrative decisions).

DEFINITION OF EVIDENCE

In the most general sense, evidence is anything that tends to prove or disprove some claim or assertion. In the legal sense, *evidence* refers to the testimony, documents, exhibits, and other tangible objects offered to prove or disprove the existence of an alleged fact during court proceedings.

Most legal systems have intricate sets of principles that govern the admission of evidence. The purpose of these principles is to ensure that only relevant and probative evidence is admitted in court proceedings, and that irrelevant, unreliable, and prejudicial evidence is excluded so that cases can be decided fairly and expeditiously.

Rules of evidence affect every aspect of a legal case – from filing the complaint to the presentation of witnesses and exhibits. These rules often govern not just what counts as evidence, but also how that evidence is gathered, handled, and presented.

Of course, the rules of evidence vary significantly among countries and legal systems. Some countries maintain extensive rules that regulate the admission of evidence. For example, in Canada, the Canada Evidence Act regulates the rules of evidence in federal cases. Similarly, the Federal Rules of Evidence (FRE) govern evidence in US federal courts.

In contrast, many countries (particularly those with civil law legal systems) do not have explicit evidentiary rules or have less detailed rules. As a result, judges in these countries are often afforded greater discretion regarding the admission of evidence.

The rules of evidence in a particular jurisdiction are often complex, and can involve not only explicit rules, but judicial interpretations of those rules. As a result, fraud examiners should consult legal counsel if an important question of evidence arises during a fraud investigation. Additionally, rules of evidence vary by jurisdiction, even within the same country. For example, in the US, state courts maintain their own evidentiary rules that might differ from the Federal Rules of Evidence. Likewise, each province of Canada maintains its own evidence act for provincial proceedings.

Three Basic Forms of Evidence

There are three basic forms that evidence can take: testimonial, real, and demonstrative.

Testimonial Evidence

Testimonial evidence refers to the oral or written statements made by witnesses under oath. In general, there are two types of testimonial witnesses: lay witnesses and expert witnesses. A *lay witness* (or *fact witness*) is a nonexpert witness who must testify from personal knowledge about a matter at issue. An *expert witness* is a person who, by reason of education, training, skill, or experience, has the requisite qualifications to render an opinion or otherwise testify in areas relevant to resolution of a legal dispute.

Real Evidence

Real evidence refers to physical objects that played a part in the issue(s) being litigated. The term includes both documentary evidence such as bank statements, invoices, ledgers, and letters, as well as other types of physical evidence (e.g., fingerprints, fibers, tire tracks). Therefore, a printer in a case involving questioned documents is clearly real evidence, as is an audio recording since members of the court can experience the sounds firsthand.

Demonstrative Evidence

Demonstrative evidence is a tangible item that illustrates some material proposition (e.g., a map, a chart, or a summary). Demonstrative evidence differs from real evidence because it was not part of the underlying event; it was created specifically for the legal proceeding. For example, a computer-generated video might be used to show how a car accident likely occurred. The purpose of demonstrative evidence is to provide a visual aid for the fact finder. As long as it meets the relevant evidentiary standards, demonstrative evidence can be introduced to assist the fact finder in reaching a verdict.

Direct versus Circumstantial Evidence

There are also two basic types, as distinguished from forms, of admissible evidence: direct evidence and circumstantial evidence. *Direct evidence* is evidence that tends to prove or disprove a fact in issue directly, such as eyewitness testimony or a confession. *Circumstantial evidence* is evidence that tends to prove or disprove facts in issue indirectly, by inference. Many fraud cases are proved entirely by circumstantial evidence, or by a combination of circumstantial and direct evidence, but seldom by direct evidence alone. The most difficult element to prove in many fraud cases – fraudulent intent – is usually proved circumstantially, and necessarily so, because direct proof of the defendant's state of mind, absent a confession or the testimony of a co-conspirator, is often impossible.

ADMISSIBILITY OF EVIDENCE

The rules of evidence in a particular jurisdiction govern whether a piece of evidence is admissible. However, because civil law systems do not rely on juries to the extent that common law systems do, there is a relative lack of restrictions on the admissibility of evidence. In contrast, challenges to the admissibility of certain pieces of evidence are a frequent occurrence in common law systems, where the evidentiary rules tend to be stricter or more detailed.

In common law systems using *adversarial processes* – those in which the litigating parties drive the discovery process – questions involving the admissibility of evidence occur when one party objects to another party's offer of evidence. If a judge sustains an objection, the evidence is not admitted. If, however, the judge overrules the objection, the evidence is admitted and can be considered by the fact finder.

Relevant

The admissibility of evidence largely depends on the discretion of the presiding judge, but a basic requirement of admissibility in both common and civil law systems is that evidence must be relevant.

For example, Section 55 of Australia's Evidence Act 1995 states, "The evidence that is relevant in a proceeding is evidence that, if it were accepted, could rationally affect (directly or indirectly) the assessment of the probability of the existence of a fact in issue in the proceeding." Further, Section 56 states that all relevant evidence is admissible (and evidence that is not relevant is not admissible) unless it is falls under a specific exclusion.

However, in common law systems using juries, the fact that an item of evidence is relevant does not automatically mean that it will be admitted. Relevant evidence might be excluded if it is unduly prejudicial, threatens to confuse or mislead the jury, threatens to cause unnecessary delay or waste of time, or is merely cumulative. Thus, evidence of drug addiction might technically be relevant to prove motive for embezzlement or fraud, but it might be excluded if the judge determines that its evidentiary value is outweighed by the danger of prejudice to the defendant. Relevant evidence might also be excluded if it is subject to certain legal privileges noted later in this chapter.

Additionally, whether a particular piece of evidence is relevant depends on what the evidence is offered to prove. For example, in the US, evidence of other crimes, wrongs, or acts committed by the defendant are not admissible if offered to prove that the defendant is generally a bad person and thus is likely guilty of the crime charged. The evidence is not relevant in this case because the mere fact that a defendant has a criminal past says little about whether the individual is guilty of the current charge. However, evidence of past crimes committed by the defendant might be relevant and admissible if offered to prove modus operandi – that is, that the crime bears the notably distinctive features of previous crimes committed by the defendant. In this situation the evidence of past crimes is relevant because it speaks directly to the crime in question.

Relevant evidence can be either inculpatory or exculpatory. *Inculpatory evidence* is evidence that tends to show that an individual is guilty or at fault. *Exculpatory evidence* is evidence that tends to clear an individual from fault or guilt. Evidence that is neither exculpatory nor inculpatory is likely irrelevant.

Authentic

Authentic evidence is evidence that has been proven to be genuine. That is, the evidence is not a forgery and accurately represents the fact or situation it is offered to prove or disprove. The authenticity of evidence is an important concept in both civil law and common law systems, though some differences exist between the systems.

Authenticity in Civil Law Systems

Civil law systems usually do not impose a requirement of authenticity for the admission of evidence. However, authentication is relevant in civil law systems because it affects the evidential value or weight the fact finder gives the evidence. That is, in civil law systems, authenticity is a factor to be considered by the fact finder in deciding, in light of all the evidence presented at trial, just how much weight to give the evidence. For example, if a relevant item of evidence is not authenticated, it will be less reliable and less helpful to the fact finder in ascertaining the truth. Consequently, the fact finder will give it less weight than authenticated evidence.

Authenticity in Common Law Systems

In common law systems using adversarial processes, evidence will not be admissible unless it is established as authentic. There are a variety of ways to authenticate a piece of evidence. For example, if a party wants to introduce a handwritten document as evidence, the party might offer the testimony of a witness familiar with the purported author's handwriting to establish that the document is not a forgery. Additionally, depending on the jurisdiction, some evidence is considered "self-authenticating" and does not need to be formally authenticated (e.g., newspapers and other periodicals, official government publications, certified copies of public records).

Admissibility of Testimonial Evidence

The rules around the admissibility of testimonial evidence in civil law jurisdictions are more lenient than in common law jurisdictions. Generally, in civil law jurisdictions, testimonial evidence is admitted if the presiding judge decides it is relevant.

In contrast, to be admissible in common law countries, testimony generally must be relevant and based on:

- Fact, not speculation or opinion (unless the witness is testifying as an expert)
- Direct knowledge, not hearsay

Very generally, a witness has direct knowledge if the witness:

- Performed the act or participated in it
- Saw the act being performed
- Heard about the act from the defendant (or in some circumstances, from a co-conspirator)

EXAMPLES OF COMMON EVIDENTIARY RULES IN ADVERSARIAL PROCEEDINGS

Legal systems that use adversarial processes often have a variety of rules that restrict the admission of evidence. These rules might not be present in civil law systems that use inquisitorial proceedings because such systems often give wider discretion to the presiding judge to determine the reliability or relevance of specific items of evidence.

These rules are often intended to exclude evidence that lacks reliability. A few common examples of these rules are:

- The rule against character evidence
- The rule against opinion testimony
- The rule against hearsay

The Rule against Character Evidence

In civil and criminal trials in common law systems, there is often a strong policy against character evidence. *Character evidence* (sometimes called *propensity evidence*) refers to testimony or exhibits that purport to establish a trait of character or a propensity to behave in a particular way, such as cautiously, violently, or in a cowardly manner.

There are several reasons why common law rules exclude character evidence. If used improperly, character evidence has the potential to be unreliable and unfair. Also, if character evidence is admitted, the jury might draw conclusions about the general propensity of the individual who is the subject of the evidence. Similarly, juries might be inclined to punish a defendant for perceived bad character, rather than for actual guilt. Additionally, character evidence is subject to interpretation – one person's "antisocial" is another's "introspective" or "pensive." Moreover, the introduction of character evidence might involve time-consuming ventures into issues that ultimately have little bearing on the merits of the case.

Finally, testimony about character has the potential to be mistaken, misleading, or invented. It is always possible to misjudge someone, especially if that person is known in a limited capacity (e.g., from work or a university class). Moreover, it is easy to fabricate incidents about character or to present testimony intended to cast an individual in a misleading or false light.

While many jurisdictions restrict the admission of character evidence – as with many rules of evidence – there are often exceptions that allow the introduction of character evidence in criminal and civil trials. Some of the common exceptions for the use of character evidence are:

- In criminal trials, the defendant may offer evidence of good character, in which case the prosecution may introduce evidence of the defendant's bad character.
- Character evidence may be admissible to reflect on the credibility of a witness.

Additionally, character evidence may be admissible if it is offered for a purpose other than showing character. In some jurisdictions, character evidence may be used to:

- Show the accused's knowledge, intent, or motive for the crime.
- Prove the existence of a larger plan of which the charged crime is a part.
- Show the accused's preparation to commit the charged crime.
- Show the accused's ability and means of committing the crime (possession of a weapon, tool, or skill used in the commission of the act).
- Show the accused's opportunity to commit the crime.
- Show threats or expressions of ill will by the accused.
- Link the accused to physical evidence at the scene.
- Show the accused's conduct and comments during arrest.
- Show the accused's attempt to conceal the accused's identity.
- Show the accused's attempt to destroy evidence.
- Present valid confessions.

Conversely, because civil law jurisdictions do not rely as heavily on juries as many common law jurisdictions, the laws of evidence in these jurisdictions are less concerned with rules intended to protect jurors from inappropriate or prejudicial evidence. Therefore, most civil law systems have less rigorous restrictions on the use of character evidence.

The Rule against Opinion Testimony

During trial in adversarial proceedings, most evidence is introduced through the testimony of witnesses. Evidence on which the jury can make factual determinations must be introduced in the form of admissible testimony or documentary evidence by lay or fact (i.e., nonexpert) witnesses.

However, evidentiary rules often limit the testimony of lay witnesses – nonexpert witnesses who testify from personal knowledge about a matter at issue. Generally, lay witnesses are allowed to testify only about their factual, firsthand observations. Thus, lay witnesses report on what they witnessed and generally must keep their opinions and speculation to themselves.

However, many jurisdictions have exceptions that allow lay witnesses to offer opinion testimony in certain circumstances. For example, exceptions might allow lay witnesses to give opinions if the statement is "rationally based" on their own perceptions and if the opinion helps provide a clearer understanding of their testimony.

In contrast to lay witnesses, expert witnesses are allowed to give opinion testimony because they are hired to render a professional opinion about a matter that requires specialized knowledge. Experts possess education, training, skill, or experience in drawing conclusions from certain types of data or information that lay witnesses do not possess. For example, a forensic fire investigator might testify that, in the investigator's professional opinion, the burn patterns at the site of an alleged arson were consistent with the use of accelerants.

The Rule against Hearsay

Many countries with common law systems restrict the admission of hearsay statements at trial. *Hearsay* is "a statement, other than one made . . . at the trial or hearing, offered in evidence to prove the truth of the matter asserted."[1] Basically, hearsay involves the following elements:

- *A statement:* A statement is anything intended to be an assertion; statements can be oral, written, or nonverbal conduct, such as nodding a head.
- *That is made outside the court's supervision:* Statements made at trial or during deposition are not hearsay because they are made during court proceedings, but a statement made at work or at a crime scene is outside the court's supervision and could be hearsay if the other elements are also present.
- *That is offered to prove the truth of the matter asserted:* For example, Julia testifies that she spoke to John from her home phone and John told her, "I wasn't home yesterday." If legal counsel offers this testimony as proof that John wasn't home on the referenced date, then it is hearsay. However, if it is offered to prove something that is auxiliary to the actual statement – for example, that the power was working at Julia's house at the time that she spoke to John – then it is not hearsay.

Hearsay rules are intended to allow only the most reliable evidence into a trial. For example, if Oliver testifies that "Lucia told me that she saw the defendant at noon," that testimony is likely to be perceived as less reliable than Lucia directly testifying about seeing the defendant at noon. Rules against hearsay are to ensure the reliability of testimony and to preserve each side's right to cross-examine witnesses.

However, like other evidentiary rules, there are often exceptions to hearsay rules. For example, in the US Federal Rules of Evidence there are three separate rules (803, 804, and 807) dedicated to the various exceptions to the rule against hearsay. Likewise, Canadian courts recognize several categories of exceptions to the hearsay rule. These exceptions are generally premised on the idea that certain kinds of hearsay evidence are sufficiently reliable and necessary to the disposition of a case.

Hearsay in Civil Law Systems

Because judges play a more active role as fact finders in civil law countries that use inquisitorial processes, these countries often do not have explicit rules regarding hearsay. For example, in German courts, hearsay is generally admissible, and it is up to the court to determine whether the hearsay evidence is convincing. Rules against hearsay are generally based on the concern that juries might give inappropriate weight to unreliable hearsay evidence, but because juries are uncommon in civil law systems, these concerns are less relevant.

CHAIN OF CUSTODY

If evidence is subject to change over time, or is susceptible to alteration, the offering party might need to establish that the evidence has not been altered or changed from the time it was collected through its production in court. This is done by establishing a chain of custody, which can be an important factor in authenticating evidence.

The *chain of custody* memorializes (1) who has had possession of an object and (2) what they have done with it. It is a way to track evidence and establish that there has not been a material change or alteration to a piece of evidence. Thus, establishing the chain of custody for an item of evidence demonstrates its authenticity.

In general, establishing the chain of custody consists of documenting:

- Each person who had control or custody of the evidence
- How and when it was received
- How it was maintained or stored while in each person's possession
- What changes, if any, it underwent in that person's custody
- How it left that person's custody

The end result is a chain of testimony that accounts for the movement and location of evidence from the time it is obtained to the time it is proffered at trial. The goal is to show that access to the evidence was limited to those who testified in the chain of custody and thereby demonstrate that the evidence has not been materially altered.

Gaps in the chain of custody (e.g., when it is not clear what occurred with a set of records) or outright mishandling (e.g., documents that were not properly sealed) can often derail or weaken a case. Evidence that has been mishandled may be excluded from trial. However, in some cases courts have found that even though there were mistakes in the chain of custody, the mistakes affect the weight, though not the admissibility, of evidence. That is, the evidence will still be allowed into the record, but it is accompanied by a forthright description of any improprieties that occurred in the chain of custody. The fact finders are supposed to consider the improprieties relating to the evidence when they deliberate, which could affect the eventual verdict.

In fraud cases, the chain of custody for the array of physical evidence – all the paper documents and audio and video recordings – should be closely monitored. Additionally, fraud examiners should ensure the careful handling of computers, phones, servers, and other places where electronic evidence might be stored.

The following are some general guidelines that will help fraud examiners document the chain of custody for all physical documents obtained during an investigation:

- If records are received via mail or courier-receipted delivery, keep copies of the postmarked envelope or the delivery receipts.
- If a cover letter is included, make sure to keep it.
- If the cover letter or transmittal letter includes a list of the documents, check the package immediately to ensure all documents are there. If something is missing, make a note in the file and notify the sender immediately.
- If documents are received in person, create a memo stating the date and time the documents were received, who delivered the documents, where that individual obtained the documents, and a complete list of the documents received.
- If the documents were directly obtained from the original source (desk, file cabinet, etc.), create a memo describing the date, time, and exact location of where the documents were found, and make a complete list of the documents obtained.
- Keep the originals of these memos or delivery receipts in the case file, and keep a copy with the documents (it will be much easier to identify where the documents came from if that information is included with the documents).

Additionally, because electronic evidence can be easily altered or destroyed, a chain of custody must be maintained for all such evidence gathered and analyzed in an investigation. At a minimum, the following chain of custody procedures should be followed:

- Identify each item that contains relevant information.
- Document each item, including:
  - From whom it was received
  - Who authorized its removal
  - The location of the item
  - The date and time the item was received
- Maintain a continuous record of the item's custody as it changes hands.

PRIVILEGES AND PROTECTIONS

In addition to the various rules governing the admission of evidence, many jurisdictions recognize certain evidentiary privileges and protections that affect what types of evidence are discoverable or produced during trial. Generally, if a privilege applies to information, the court and the parties seeking the information may not access it, and judges and juries must disregard any evidence initially introduced if it is deemed privileged afterward.

The privileges and protections available and the scope of each vary substantially by jurisdiction. Generally, countries with common law systems offer broader evidentiary protections than countries with civil law systems. However, civil law jurisdictions often have doctrines that serve the same function as privileges and protections in common law jurisdictions, even if such doctrines are not classified as privileges. For example, many civil law systems have general professional privileges that prohibit the admission of communications made through the exercise of certain professional duties.

Some of the more common privileges and protections are discussed below.

Legal Professional Privileges

Legal professional privileges preclude disclosure of confidential communications between professional legal advisers (e.g., solicitor, barrister, attorney) and their clients. These privileges are intended to encourage open and honest communications between legal professionals and their clients. This type of privilege is referred to with different names depending on the jurisdiction. For example, in the US, it is known as the *attorney-client privilege*; in the UK, it is known as the *legal advice privilege*; in Canada, it is known as the *solicitor-client privilege*; and in most European countries and many others (e.g., South Africa, Australia), it is known as the *legal professional privilege*.

The requirements for the application of these privileges vary among jurisdictions, but generally, the following elements must be present for communications to be protected:

- A communication was made between a legal professional and a client.
- The communication was made to seek or give legal advice.
- The parties intended the communications to be confidential (i.e., the communications must not be disclosed to third parties such as vendors, customers, auditors, or governmental officials).

To be protected under a legal professional privilege, it is not necessary that the communication take place after the commencement of a legal action.

Waiver of the Privilege

Legal professional privileges, however, are not absolute. Because these privileges protect only confidential communications, the protection will be waived for communications disclosed to third parties who have little or nothing to do with the client's legal representation, because such disclosures demonstrate a lack of confidentiality.

Generally, waiver occurs when the client, who holds the privilege, voluntarily discloses (or consents to or encourages someone else's disclosure) any significant part of the privileged communications. Although the client holds the privilege, in some circumstances the privilege can be waived by the client's legal professional or by a third party.

The legal professional privilege can be waived in various ways, including:

- The client testifies about confidential communications.
- The legal professional testifies about confidential communications at the client's command or request.
- The client puts confidential communications in question.
- The client, the legal professional, or a third party carelessly or inadvertently discloses confidential communications to an outside party (which sometimes results in waiver).

Although legal professional privileges apply only to confidential communications between legal professionals and their clients, in most jurisdictions the protection afforded by these privileges extends to communications with third-party consultants hired to help provide legal advice to the client (e.g., fraud examiners, accountants, bankers, or other experts). Thus, waiver does not occur when a legal professional shares privileged information with an outside consultant hired in a role that concerns the client's pursuit of legal representation, and when the communication was made for the purpose of effectuating legal representation for the client.

Legal Work Privileges

Many countries recognize privileges that protect materials prepared in anticipation of litigation. These privileges are often referred to as *litigation privileges*. Additionally, some jurisdictions recognize this privilege as part of the general legal professional privilege, rather than as a distinct doctrine.

The protection offered by these privileges can extend beyond information and documents prepared by attorneys to those prepared by third-party consultants and examiners hired by those attorneys. For instance, communications between an attorney and an expert (e.g., fraud examiner, accountant) and any work or analysis done by that expert for the attorney might be protected. However, that protection would likely be waived if the expert testifies at trial.

Typically, privileges relating to legal work product generally arise once litigation is reasonably anticipated. Thus, documents and tangible things prepared in the course of an in-house or other prelitigation investigation, even if at the direction of an attorney, might not be covered by these privileges.

While litigation privileges protect documents and things prepared in anticipation of litigation from compelled disclosure, they do not render the facts themselves confidential, privileged, or nondiscoverable. Thus, while reports, interview notes, and transcripts might be protected, the underlying facts are not. Similarly, litigation privileges do not prevent discovery of the identity of witnesses and the existence of interview notes, tapes, or transcripts.

Additionally, like the legal professional privilege, litigation privileges can be waived.

Self-Evaluation Privilege

The *self-evaluation privilege* (also referred to as the *self-critical privilege*) can provide some protection for the work product of an internal investigation. The basis of this privilege is the need to encourage companies to undertake voluntary internal reviews and develop compliance programs. If it applies, it will protect the work product of an organization's investigation from discovery during legal proceedings if the organization can demonstrate that (1) it is attempting to police itself in an area of public interest, and (2) disclosure of its work product would prejudice its efforts to police itself.

Normally, for this privilege to apply, the information must be prepared by the organization with the expectation that it would be kept confidential, and the information must have remained confidential.

The self-evaluation privilege may apply even in the absence of anticipated litigation, and it does not require the participation of a legal adviser.

This privilege is a relatively new concept and is not recognized in all jurisdictions. Even in those jurisdictions that do recognize it, it is generally regarded as much weaker than the legal professional and litigation privileges.

Marital Privilege

In many jurisdictions, the *marital privilege* (also called the *spousal privilege*) protects communications between spouses. It is intended to encourage harmony within a marriage. As with other legal privileges, the scope of the marital privilege differs among countries.

Some countries recognize two forms of the marital privilege: (1) the confidential communications privilege, and (2) the adverse testimony privilege. The *confidential communications privilege* protects the contents of confidential communications between spouses during their marriage, and it enables either spouse to prevent the other from testifying about a confidential communication made during marriage. The *adverse testimony privilege* protects spouses from being compelled to testify against each other while they are married. Usually, the confidential communications privilege continues after the termination of the marriage; the adverse testimony privilege does not.

However, the spousal privilege is often subject to exceptions under which an individual's spouse might be compelled to testify.

Parent-Child Privilege

Many European jurisdictions recognize a privilege that allows parents and children to refrain from testifying against each other. Similarly, some jurisdictions recognize a more general familial privilege that might apply to other close relatives.

Law Enforcement Privilege to Withhold the Identity of an Informant

In some jurisdictions, law enforcement agencies may legitimately withhold the identity of an informant unless disclosure is necessary to ensure that the defendant receives a fair trial. In such circumstances, the prosecution has to decide whether to forgo prosecution or disclose the identity of the informant. In the private sector, there generally is no equivalent privilege. Fraud examiners or others who are investigating on behalf of a private client may be compelled by court order to disclose the identity of an informant or any other witness. This possibility should be disclosed to potential witnesses who may request confidentiality.

Accountant-Client Privilege

Some jurisdictions recognize an *accountant-client privilege* that protects the communications between an accountant and a client, but it is generally rare or very limited in scope. In fact, some jurisdictions actually require accountants to report suspected misconduct by their clients to the proper authorities. Additionally, in some jurisdictions, communications between an accountant and a client might be protected by the relevant legal professional privilege if the accountant was working on behalf of a legal professional involved in the investigation.

Other Privileges

There are a number of other privileges that are less likely to arise in fraud actions, including the *priest-penitent* and *physician-patient* privileges. Fraud examiners should consult with legal counsel in the relevant jurisdictions to determine which privileges might be available and how to comply with the respective requirements.

Judicial Treatment of Privileges from Foreign Jurisdictions

The rise of global markets and multijurisdictional transactions has resulted in an increase in disputes that span multiple jurisdictions, and, as the previous discussion on privileges demonstrates, legal privileges vary substantially by jurisdiction. There are no standardized rules and, in some cases, privileges might conflict. For example, the litigants in a cross-border dispute might be required in one jurisdiction to disclose information that is privileged in another jurisdiction.

Generally, individuals involved in cross-border litigation should not expect the legal privileges of their own jurisdiction to apply when engaged in litigation abroad. There are several reasons for this. First, courts are more inclined to apply their own laws because they are more familiar with local law than the laws of foreign jurisdictions. Second, characterizations and conceptualizations of privileges vary among different countries. For instance, common law jurisdictions typically view privileges as the right of the client. In contrast, communications in many civil law countries are protected by secrecy or privacy laws that require confidentiality.

INDIVIDUAL RIGHTS DURING EXAMINATIONS

Because fraud examinations might lead to legal action, fraud examiners should be familiar with the basic rights and freedoms of those involved in investigations, especially of those suspected of fraud. Being knowledgeable about an individual's legal rights is particularly important for fraud examiners conducting investigations that could result in criminal action. The gathering of evidence, for instance, in violation of the law could result in the exclusion of that evidence later at a criminal trial. Additionally, inappropriate behavior on the part of an investigator could result in a lawsuit by the subject against the investigator or the investigator's employer.

This section presents some general concepts regarding individual rights that are common in many countries, particularly those operating under the common law and civil law systems, but it first examines employees' duties and rights during investigations.

EMPLOYEES' DUTIES AND RIGHTS

Employees involved in investigations of suspected fraud generally have certain duties and rights, whether they are merely bystanders who have relevant information or they are suspected of wrongdoing.

Employee duties and rights vary among jurisdictions and from case to case, but generally such duties and rights apply to employees who work in both government and private-sector workplaces. Thus, both private and government employers might violate their employees' legal rights if they act imprudently.

Employees' Duty to Cooperate

In most jurisdictions, a duty to cooperate exists in every employer-employee relationship, but such duties vary between jurisdictions. Some jurisdictions have statutes defining the scope of this duty; in others, the duty is found to be implied from the basic nature of the employment relationship. Additionally, many employers include provisions in their employee handbooks outlining a duty to cooperate in internal investigations.

Generally, the duty to cooperate extends to workplace investigations; therefore, employees have a duty to cooperate during an internal investigation as long as what is requested from them is reasonable. What is considered reasonable is determined by the relevant facts of the particular case and by the scope of an employee's work duties. For example, if inventory items are missing, it would be reasonable to request that a warehouse supervisor review inventory records because this falls within the scope of the supervisor's work duties. But under such facts, it might not be reasonable to ask the same supervisor to review detailed transaction records from the company's cash registers, and it almost certainly would not be reasonable to ask the warehouse supervisor to let company investigators search his personal vehicle.

The issue of whether an employee has a duty to cooperate often comes up when investigators seek to interview employees about suspected workplace misconduct. In general, interviews are reasonable if they address matters within the scope of the employees' actions or duties.

Duty to Preserve Information Relevant to Litigation

Employees might also have a duty to preserve relevant information during the course of a legal action. Common law jurisdictions, in which litigants are usually obligated to disclose relevant information to the opposing side, impose a duty on litigants to take affirmative steps to preserve relevant evidence. This duty might arise prior to the official commencement of litigation. It typically arises when litigation is reasonably anticipated or contemplated.

When an organization is involved in litigation, this duty to preserve evidence applies to the organization's management, and it extends to all employees likely to have relevant information. A violation of this duty occurs when information that could be relevant to anticipated or existing litigation is lost, destroyed, or otherwise made unavailable.

In civil law systems, in which the primary responsibility for discovering evidence is placed on the presiding judge, there are often no specific rules requiring litigants to preserve information for discovery, because there is no common-law-style discovery in civil law systems. Consequently, civil law systems tend to have a narrower view of what evidence is requisite for litigation, and the issue of when to take affirmative steps to preserve evidence is established by the court. Nonetheless, the destruction of evidence is rarely permitted and often constitutes a violation of judicial procedures.

Violating the duty to preserve relevant information (whether accidentally or intentionally) can result in sanctions for the offending party. The adverse consequences can include, but are not limited to, monetary penalties (e.g., paying the opposing party's legal fees), the drawing of adverse inferences of fact, and criminal penalties. The theory behind such consequences is that the individual who makes evidence unavailable following the probable initiation of a lawsuit is aware of its detrimental effect and might be deliberately attempting to obstruct the case.

Examples of situations that could give rise to sanctions for failing to preserve evidence include intentionally or accidentally:

- Erasing computer files (e.g., documents, images, databases, etc.)
- Losing or destroying physical evidence
- Losing, destroying, or altering documents or records
- Failing to suspend the routine destruction of electronic data (e.g., emails, chat logs, etc.)

Employees' Contractual Rights

Employees might have contractual rights that are enforceable against their employers. That is, employers and employees might enter into contracts that govern the employment relationship, and if the employer violates the contract, the employee can sue for breach of contract. Contractual rights might limit the ability of the employer to compel full cooperation from an employee in a fraud examination.

Often, employee contractual rights at issue during investigations arise from a union contract, a collective bargaining agreement, or an employment contract. For example, a union employee might be subject to a union contract or collective bargaining agreement that contains restrictions on the employer's investigatory procedures.

Additionally, employees might have a written employment agreement containing provisions concerning the employees' rights during an investigation. Generally, such contracts can be express or implied. Just because the employer does not have a written, signed, and formalized contract with an employee does not mean that there is no agreement in place. Many courts have held that company policies, employee manuals, and past practices can create "implied" contractual relationships between the employer and the employee.

Whistle-Blower Protections

Many jurisdictions have whistle-blower laws designed to protect individuals who report suspected misconduct within their organizations. The purpose of these laws is to shield employees from retaliation by their employers. Whistle-blower laws do not, however, prevent individuals from being terminated for engaging in unrelated fraudulent behavior.

Many governments recognize the importance of whistle-blower protection to uncover wrongdoing. For example, in 1999, the Council of Europe ratified the Civil Law Convention on Corruption. This convention is binding on many European countries and includes a section requiring the protection of whistle-blowers from retaliation. However, while many countries adopted partial or comprehensive measures to protect whistle-blowers, their effectiveness varies across jurisdictions.

Employees' Privacy Rights in the Workplace

Employees have certain privacy rights that can affect numerous aspects of the employer-employee relationship, such as conducting investigations, surveillance and monitoring, and workplace searches. An employee's privacy rights can arise from, and be protected by, various sources of law, including constitutional law, statutory law, common law, human rights law, labor law, data protection law, and contract law.

Some countries have privacy laws that prohibit unreasonable workplace searches and surveillance in areas where employees have a reasonable expectation of privacy. Depending on the circumstances, an employee might have a reasonable expectation of privacy in a desk drawer, a file cabinet, a locker, or even an entire office. Reasonable expectations of privacy can also attach to communications, such as data stored on hard drives and other electronic communications like phone calls, emails, and text messages.

Often, the key issue to consider when assessing the existence of a reasonable expectation of privacy is whether a reasonable person would expect the area or item to be free from intrusion. Employees tend to regard purses, briefcases, and other personal effects as personal items that they reasonably expect to be private. An employee does not need to have an ownership interest in, or legal custody over, the area or item to have a reasonable expectation of privacy in it. Thus, even if an employer owns the office where employees work, the employees can still have a reasonable expectation of privacy in parts of their workspace.

Another important factor is the amount of control an individual exercises over the area. If an employee has exclusive control over an area, this tends to show that the employee has a reasonable expectation of privacy in that area. Therefore, if an employee is exclusively assigned to a specific office, desk, wastebasket, locker, or other area, the employee might have a reasonable expectation of privacy regarding such areas. Conversely, an employee probably cannot claim a privacy expectation in a work area that is open to the public and shared with other employees (e.g., a shared kitchen, a conference room).

In terms of workplace surveillance, employees are likely to have reasonable privacy expectations in restrooms, changing rooms, and other personal areas within the workplace.

Generally, the best method employers can use to lower the expectation of privacy is to adopt a written privacy policy and require employees to sign it. Such policies should provide that, to maintain the security of operations, the company may monitor and search all work areas (subject to any applicable laws). Also, the policy should notify employees that computer systems (including the Internet, email communications, hardware, and files) are solely for business use, and that the company reserves the right to monitor, review, audit, and disclose all matters sent over the system or placed in storage.

Employee Privacy Rights in the EU

In most European countries, privacy is a fundamental human right. For that reason, European countries tend to have robust privacy rights, even in the workplace, and workplace searches and employee monitoring are subject to greater legal restrictions. Those restrictions take the form of constitutional laws, data privacy laws, labor laws, EU regulations, and collective bargaining agreements.

Most European countries are members of the EU, a coalition of member states linked by a series of treaties. The EU has the power to issue regulations, directives, recommendations, opinions, and decisions that may be binding or nonbinding on member states. Some of these sources address issues of workplace privacy and employee monitoring, either expressly or implicitly.

While the details of the various EU directives, decisions, recommendations, opinions, and regulations that address privacy, employment, or both are beyond the scope of this chapter, a number of common themes run through them. Based on those themes, employers in EU member countries should adhere to the following principles before conducting a workplace search or crafting an employee monitoring policy:

- *Necessity:* The search or monitoring must be absolutely necessary to achieve a legitimate business purpose, such as protecting the business from significant threats.
- *Finality:* The data must be collected for a specific, explicit, and legitimate purpose and not used for any other purpose.
- *Transparency:* The employer must give employees clear and comprehensive notice of its search or monitoring policy.
- *Proportionality:* The intrusion upon employees' privacy should be no greater than is necessary to address the particular risk.
- *Legality:* The search or monitoring must comply with all applicable laws.
- *Accuracy and retention of data:* Any collected employee data must be updated as required to keep it accurate, and the data should be retained for no longer than necessary (generally no longer than three months).
- *Security:* The employer must implement appropriate technical and organizational measures to ensure that collected employee data is safe.[2]

The aforementioned principles are minimum requirements; most European countries have additional legal requirements for workplace searches and employee monitoring. For example, in some countries where employees are commonly represented by works councils, employers must consult or notify the relevant works council before implementing an employee monitoring program. In addition, under data protection laws in most European countries, employees have the right to access and correct personal data collected by their employers. In some European countries, the right to search employees' computers depends on whether the employees have permission to use their computers for personal tasks.

In some countries, such as Germany and Italy, employees must give voluntary written consent to any form of employee monitoring, and the consent may be challenged in court on the ground that it was not truly voluntary. In France, employers generally cannot access employee emails that are identified as "private" or "personal." Finland also restricts the ability of employers to access any type of employee emails.

Employee Privacy Rights in Other Countries

Outside of Europe, privacy laws vary significantly. Some countries, such as India and Singapore, have few laws that explicitly regulate workplace monitoring. Other countries, such as Japan and Australia, require notice of employee monitoring in most cases but not explicit consent. Others, like the United Arab Emirates, require employers to obtain consent from all affected employees.

Most countries prohibit *covert* employee monitoring, unless a specific criminal activity has been identified. Therefore, nearly every employer is required to notify its employees before implementing an employee monitoring program. The notice should be clear and comprehensive, and it should be in writing.

The laws governing workplace privacy are complex and vary by jurisdiction. Therefore, legal counsel should always be consulted before conducting a workplace search or implementing an employee monitoring program.

Individuals' Rights and Obligations under Criminal Law

Generally, individuals arrested or questioned by the police for suspected involvement in criminal activity have certain rights, such as the right to remain silent and the right to counsel. This section examines some of the more common rights available under criminal law.

Right to Remain Silent

A tenet of many legal systems is that a criminal suspect or person accused of a crime has the right to remain silent both at the investigative stage and at the trial stage of criminal cases. The right to remain silent applies to individuals being questioned by government authorities, but not someone who is being questioned by a private party acting on its own behalf. Accordingly, the right to remain silent generally does not apply in private internal investigations, and private employers might be able to terminate employees for refusing to answer questions (i.e., refusing to cooperate).

The right to remain silent is often recognized in both common law and civil law systems. This right generally guarantees that individuals have the right to refuse to answer questions or to provide certain personal information during a criminal investigation. Note, however, that the right does not protect the defendant from being ordered to provide other types of evidence, such as the weapon used in an alleged assault or a sample fingerprint.

If the subject has a right to remain silent, government authorities might also be required to inform the subject of this right (as well as other applicable legal rights) before questioning begins. For example, the EU published a directive on the right to information in criminal proceedings. Under the directive, suspects detained in the EU receive a letter listing their basic rights during criminal proceedings.

Even when the right to remain silent applies, it is not necessarily absolute. Some common law jurisdictions have explicit exceptions to this right. For instance, in England and Wales, certain government institutions can compel individuals to provide information or face potential criminal sanctions for noncompliance. Some jurisdictions also allow prosecutors, juries, or judges to draw adverse inferences based on a defendant's refusal to answer questions (although this is normally limited to very specific instances, such as when a defendant chooses to be selectively silent, rather than completely silent).

Right to Counsel

The right to counsel is the right of criminal defendants to have a legal professional assist in their defense, even if they cannot afford to pay for one. Thus, if an individual is the subject of a criminal investigation by government authorities, the subject may have the right to consult with legal counsel or have a legal professional appointed to represent him.

This right is generally found in both civil and common law jurisdictions, though the point at which this right attaches varies across jurisdictions. For example, in Japan, the right to counsel normally attaches after a defendant has been formally indicted. In other countries, the right to counsel might arise at other specific points in the judicial process, such as when an individual is taken into police custody or when judicial proceedings are first initiated.

As with many legal rights, the right to counsel does not normally apply if there is no government action. Thus, in most cases, a private employer can interview an employee without the presence of the employee's legal representative.

Generally, subjects can waive their right to counsel, but, to be valid, any waiver must be voluntary and premised on a true appreciation of the consequences of giving up that right. For example, if the detainee waives the right to counsel while intoxicated, the waiver is not likely to stand because, under such circumstances, the subject cannot make a meaningful determination of whether to waive this right.

Many jurisdictions create exceptions to the right to counsel in criminal trials, the most typical being when the crime charged is a very minor violation.

Right to a Trial by Jury

Some jurisdictions afford defendants the right to a trial by jury in criminal prosecutions. Juries are most common in jurisdictions with common law, adversarial systems, but many countries with civil law systems also use juries.

In a trial by jury, the judge and jury both serve important roles. In most common law jurisdictions, the jury is responsible for reaching a verdict based on the evidence presented, while the judge provides instructions to the jury regarding relevant aspects of the law and rules on the admissibility of evidence, and generally moderates the proceeding to ensure a fair trial.

Typically, the availability of a trial by jury depends on the nature of the crime charged. For example, jury trials might be available only for very serious charges (e.g., treason, murder) or for offenses that are punishable by incarceration of a specified length of time (e.g., crimes punishable by incarceration of more than six months).

The composition of juries and requirements to be a juror also vary across jurisdictions. Some jurisdictions use juries that include both lay citizens and judges. For example, in France, serious crimes are heard by criminal trial courts that use a panel of three judges and six or nine lay jurors.

Some jurisdictions that recognize the right to a trial by jury allow the defendant to waive that right. However, this waiver might be subject to certain limitations. Some jurisdictions allow the prosecution or the presiding judge to refuse to accept a defendant's waiver. Normally, if a defendant successfully waives this right, the judge will then decide the case in what is called a *bench trial*.

Some countries – such as Chile, the Czech Republic, Hungary, India, Israel, Mexico, the Netherlands, and South Africa – do not use juries at all.

Limits on Using Confessions in Criminal Cases

Depending on the jurisdiction, there might be laws limiting the use of a suspect's confession (i.e., admission of misdeeds) in a criminal case. In criminal cases, statements made by the accused to persons in authority are valuable as evidence and are often incriminating.

In some jurisdictions, confessions made out of court by the accused may be admitted into evidence only if the prosecution shows that the statement was made freely and voluntarily. In general, a confession is considered voluntary if it is not coerced by physical or psychological means, though such a determination is dependent on the specific facts of a case. In many jurisdictions, courts may admit a voluntary confession even if it is obtained through deception.

In jurisdictions limiting the admissibility of confessions, the law might require the government to establish the accuracy of the statement if it intends to use it against the accused. Courts might give more credence to written statements (in the defendant's own handwriting) or audio recordings of confessions than to nonrecorded oral statements.

THE LAW RELATING TO GOVERNMENT SEARCH AND SEIZURE

Laws relating to search and seizure tend to be extremely complex. In many countries, the state derives its power of search and seizure from the complicated interplay of both common law and statutory law. The treatment of search and seizure can even vary within a country based on the laws and regulations of particular territories or provinces.

Additionally, most countries have laws that recognize the right to be free from unreasonable search and seizure by government authorities. For example, Article 5 of the

European Convention on Human Rights recognizes that everyone has the right to liberty and security of person, and that individuals can be deprived of this right only under particular circumstances (e.g., lawful arrest or detention). Similarly, in Canada, Section 8 of the Canadian Charter of Rights and Freedoms recognizes the right to be secure from unreasonable search and seizure.

Search Warrants

Countries with laws that provide the public with the right to be free from unreasonable search and seizure might require the government to obtain authorization (e.g., a search warrant) from a judicial officer or other authorized person before it conducts a search of a person, location, or vehicle for evidence of a crime.

A *search warrant* is a court order that grants government authorities the right to search a premises or property for information pertinent to a case, regardless of whether the owner consents to the search. If a court finds that a search was executed improperly or that the underlying search warrant is invalid, any evidence obtained during the search could be inadmissible and the individual harmed by the improper search might have cause for legal action against the party that conducted the search.

Reasonableness

In general, searches must be reasonable in scope and conducted in a reasonable manner. For example, if a police officer obtains a warrant to search an individual's apartment for a stolen laptop, it would not be reasonable for the officer to rifle through the individual's wallet or purse because they are too small to conceal a laptop. The reasonableness of a search is normally determined by the totality of the circumstances.

Exceptions to the Warrant Requirement

Even if a warrant is technically required, most jurisdictions recognize certain exceptions. Two common exceptions are consent searches and evidence in plain view.

Consent Searches

Voluntary consent is a common exception to the requirement that government agents must obtain a warrant before they search a person, location, or vehicle for evidence of a crime. However, if agents obtain consent by force, duress, or bribery, then it may be held to be involuntary and invalid – potentially causing the exclusion from trial of any evidence gained during the search. Jurisdictions are mixed, however, as to whether consent obtained by deceit constitutes a valid waiver. Also, there is generally no requirement that government agents warn suspects that they have a right to refuse consent. Additionally, in the context of workplace searches, individuals' consent might not be voluntary if it requires a choice between exercising their legal rights and remaining employed.

Consent might be implied in circumstances where the individual can choose between entering an area and submitting to a search or not entering, such as when an individual enters a secured courthouse, boards an airplane, or crosses an international border.

In some cases, third parties may consent to searches of property that they coinhabit with the suspect. Thus, a roommate who shares an apartment with the suspect may be able to consent to a search of the apartment's common areas. However, the roommate likely would not have the power to consent to a search of the suspect's bedroom. Of course, judicial treatment of third-party consent varies across jurisdictions.

Evidence in Plain View

Some countries recognize the plain view doctrine as an exception to the general rule that the government must obtain a search warrant before seizing an item. Under this doctrine, an officer who observes an item from an area where the officer is lawfully present may seize that item if:

- The officer can lawfully access the item.
- The officer has reason to believe the item is evidence of a crime or is contraband.

For example, in countries that recognize this doctrine, a government official who inadvertently discovers contraband or evidence of another crime during a search or arrest may seize that evidence, even if it is outside the scope of the arrest or search.

INVESTIGATIONS IN PRIVATE ACTIONS

The right for businesses and organizations to investigate, examine, or audit for fraud is implicit in most countries. Of course, investigations in private actions are subject to certain legal limitations, some of which – such as the laws prohibiting unauthorized electronic surveillance – are enforced with criminal as well as civil penalties. Over-zealous or imprudent acts by private parties (even if technically legal) can result in civil suits, complaints, and other issues that can delay, disrupt, or even completely derail an otherwise meritorious case. Thus, fraud examiners must keep in mind the rights of those involved in any private investigation.

The following is a brief discussion of some legal issues that might arise as a result of an investigation, particularly one conducted in an irresponsible manner, carried out without predication, or conducted in a way that blatantly violates the rights of those involved. These issues are avoidable if fraud examiners employ common sense and professional standards to accomplish legitimate objectives. Fraud examiners should always pursue the facts, not people; should ask rather than accuse; and should seek to prove rather than allege.

Defamation

Many countries have defamation laws that provide redress against harm to reputation. Generally speaking, *defamation* refers to the unprivileged publication of false statements about a person that harm that person's reputation.

Defamation can be a crime or a civil violation, depending on the particular jurisdiction where the alleged offense occurred. Additionally, some jurisdictions treat certain kinds of defamation as civil violations and other types as crimes punishable by incarceration.

In most common law jurisdictions, the law of defamation comes in two forms: libel and slander. *Libel* refers to defamatory statements in writing, and *slander* refers to spoken statements, although the distinction often is unclear in cases involving electronic media. Thus, the key difference between libel and slander is the form in which an individual made the defamatory statement. However, not all jurisdictions make a distinction between libel and slander.

The threat of a defamation lawsuit is always present when there are allegations of wrongdoing made against employees. For example, a claim of defamation might arise in the context of an interview if the interviewer makes unfounded accusations or statements in the presence of a third party.

If a plaintiff (i.e., the party who initiates a legal action) is successful in a claim for defamation, that party may recover economic damages (e.g., lost business, lost earning potential), noneconomic damages (e.g., pain and suffering, emotional distress), and punitive damages, which can be substantial. The types of damages available vary across jurisdictions and depend on the nature of the case.

Elements of Defamation

While the treatment of defamation (whether it is libel or slander) varies by jurisdiction, the following are the most common elements necessary to support a claim:

- The defendant made an untrue statement of fact.
- The statement was communicated (published) to third parties.
- The statement was made on an unprivileged occasion.
- The statement caused injury to the subject.

Untrue Statement of Fact

To be defamatory, a statement must be a statement of fact (not opinion) and be untrue. Thus, truth is an absolute defense to defamation.

Communicated to Third Parties

To be defamatory, a statement must be conveyed, either orally or in writing, to one or more third parties. Defamation does not occur when one accuses another directly and in the presence of no other parties; to be defamatory, a statement must be heard or read by a third party.

Unprivileged Occasion

For a statement to qualify as defamatory, the occasion in which the statement is made must be an unprivileged one. Many jurisdictions recognize that there are some circumstances in which the need to share information is so important that people should be free to make mistakes without having to worry about being sued for defamation. Statements made in these circumstances are said to be privileged.

Assuming that an employee can establish that an individual made and communicated defamatory statements about the employee to a third party, some of the most common recognized privileges include:

- Statements made during a judicial proceeding
- Statements made in preparation of judicial proceedings
- Statements made between a legal professional (e.g., solicitor or attorney) and client
- Good faith statements made to protect a legitimate interest of the speaker or recipient, such as a communication between an employee and employer regarding an important business matter or the results of an examination into suspected fraud

Accordingly, in many jurisdictions, a number of privileges protect prudent fraud examiners from defamation claims.

Injury

Additionally, to be considered defamatory, a statement must cause some kind of injury. This often takes the form of reputational damage. For example, a plaintiff might argue that he lost business opportunities and income because the statement damaged his professional reputation.

Privacy Laws

Privacy laws protect the rights of individuals to be left alone. However, jurisdictions vary substantially in how they treat privacy rights. Some countries explicitly recognize privacy rights in their constitutions. In other countries, privacy rights might be derived from case law or specific statutes.

For example, Article 8 of the European Convention on Human Rights, which is the authoritative human rights instrument in Europe, provides that individuals have the right to respect for private and family life. The Treaty Establishing the European Union, in recognizing Article 8, requires member states to respect the fundamental rights guaranteed therein. Consequently, many European legal systems tend to impose greater legal restrictions on employee monitoring or workplace surveillance than other jurisdictions. Also, the Charter of Fundamental Rights of the European Union, which sets forth a binding list of rights for the EU and its member states, affirms that everyone has the right to respect for one's private and family life, home, and communications.

In contrast, the Constitution of the Republic of Singapore does not explicitly recognize any rights to privacy. However, Singapore has laws that regulate the handling and collection of personal data, such as the Personal Data Protection Act and the Computer Misuse and Cybersecurity Act.

Civil Invasion of Privacy

Invasion of privacy laws protect people's right to keep their lives private and free from intrusion. In many countries, invasion of privacy is a civil wrong that can be redressed through the judicial system. The two most common forms of invasion of privacy applicable to fraud examinations are intrusion into an individual's private matters and publicity of private facts.

Intrusion into an Individual's Private Matters

The civil wrong regarding intrusion into an individual's private matters (sometimes referred to as *intrusion upon seclusion*) occurs when an individual intentionally intrudes into another individual's private matters in a way that would be highly offensive or objectionable to a reasonable person. The common elements of this civil wrong include:

- The intrusion was intentional.
- The intrusion was into an area where an individual has a reasonable expectation of privacy.
- The intrusion would be highly offensive or objectionable to a reasonable person.

There is no intrusion if the information at issue is open to public view or has been disclosed to others.

An intrusion claim can be based on physical intrusions, wiretapping, eavesdropping, and other forms of surveillance. Thus, liability for this civil wrong can arise from conducting an unwarranted search of another's personal property, performing intensive physical surveillance, or obtaining private bank account information, absent legal authority. Also, questioning employees about activities not related to their job performance might constitute an intrusion upon seclusion.

Public Disclosure of Private Facts

Public disclosure of private facts occurs when one party makes public statements about another party's private life that are not of public concern. For instance, disclosing information obtained in an interview conducted as part of a fraud investigation to individuals not involved in the investigation might constitute public disclosure of private facts.

To establish liability for public disclosure of private facts, many jurisdictions require the plaintiff to prove the following elements:

- The defendant made public statements about another party's private life.
- The statements were not about a matter of public concern.
- The statements would be highly offensive to a reasonable person.

Also, unlike the requirements to establish a claim for defamation, liability for this cause of action can arise even if the statements at issue are true. Because publicizing true, but private, information about an employee can provide grounds for a claim for public disclosure of private facts, the need to communicate information about the employee must be balanced against the intrusion into the employee's privacy. Thus, fraud examiners must exercise caution when disclosing investigatory materials or conclusions.

The gist of this civil wrong is the unwarranted publicity of private facts, not the discovery of private facts. For example, an internal investigator who reports an individual's credit information to an insurance company would not necessarily be susceptible to a claim for the publicity of private facts. However, if the investigator shared this information in a companywide email, the result could be different.

Other Legal Actions That Could Arise during Private Investigations

A variety of other legal actions could arise during the course of internal investigations. This section examines a few of the most common ones.

False Imprisonment

Many countries have laws that protect individuals from unlawful confinement. *False imprisonment* is the unlawful restraint of an individual by someone without consent or legal justification. Many jurisdictions treat false imprisonment both as a tort (i.e., a civil wrong) and as a crime. Some countries do not have statutes that explicitly cover false imprisonment, but might have similar laws relating to kidnapping, abduction, or the deprivation of liberty.

To recover for a civil claim of false imprisonment, many jurisdictions require the plaintiff to prove the following elements:

- The defendant used words or actions intended to restrain the plaintiff.
- The defendant's words or actions resulted in the restraint of the plaintiff without the plaintiff's consent (i.e., against the plaintiff's will) and without legal justification.
- The plaintiff was aware of the confinement.

A claim of false imprisonment might arise if an employee is detained in any way during a search or an interview. Generally, an employer may question an employee at work about a violation of company policy as long as the employee submits to the questioning voluntarily – that is, not as a result of threats or force.

Courts generally consider a variety of factors to determine whether a defendant is liable for false imprisonment, including:

- Whether the interview was conducted in a room that was small and confined in nature (e.g., windowless, not easily accessible)
- The use of physical force to direct the employee or to keep the individual in a room (e.g., holding the employee's arm to escort the individual or pushing the employee into a chair)
- The use of violent behavior of any kind during the interview, including yelling, pounding on a desk, or kicking furniture or walls
- The use of a physical barrier to restrain the employee (e.g., locking the door or standing in front of the exit)
- Whether the defendant used threats of immediate physical force to restrain the employee

Intentional Infliction of Emotional Distress

Intentional infliction of emotional distress is a civil cause of action available mainly in common law countries. It refers to any unprivileged conduct that is so outrageous and egregious that it exceeds all bounds usually tolerated by civilized society and is intended to cause injury to another (or was committed with reckless disregard of the likely harmful consequences of the action).

Generally, to recover for intentional infliction of emotional distress, the plaintiff must prove the following elements:

- The defendant acted intentionally or recklessly.
- The defendant's conduct was extreme and outrageous.
- The plaintiff suffered severe emotional or mental distress as a result of the defendant's conduct.

For liability to attach, the offending conduct must "outrage the sensibilities of a reasonable person." Mere angry words or insults, or allegations or implications of wrongdoing (if based on reasonable grounds), are generally not enough. Also, it is not enough that the individual is merely upset by the conduct. Emotional distress tends to describe extreme mental suffering or anguish and can encompass feelings of paranoia, anxiety, depression, fright, or extreme stress.

Wrongful Discharge

Wrongful discharge occurs when an employer discharges an employee for an improper reason (e.g., unlawful discrimination) in violation of an actual or implied employment contract or company policies. The scope for wrongful discharge, however, varies by jurisdiction.

Data Privacy

Most countries have data privacy laws (also known as *information privacy laws* or *data protection laws*) that protect individuals' personal information from disclosure, unauthorized access, and misuse. As innovations in technology make it easier to track, compile, and process personal information about individuals, fraud examiners who deal with personal information must take steps to comply with local and international data privacy laws. These laws can significantly affect data collection, data use, and cross-border transfer.

Typically, these laws address:

- How personal information is collected
- How personal information is handled
- How personal information is used
- Who has access to personal information
- Notification requirements when personal information is amended, changed, and deleted

It is important to note that while data privacy laws focus on personal information, they often define *personal information* in different ways. Nevertheless, on a general basis, personal information refers to any information about an identifiable individual, such as:

- An individual's personal characteristics (e.g., name, gender, age, government identification number, household income, home address or phone number, race and ethnicity, physical characteristics, family status, marital status, and employment status)
- An individual's health information (e.g., medical appointment history, health conditions, received health services)
- An individual's activities and views (e.g., religious affiliations, political views, personal opinions)

Data privacy laws are often based on the concept of Fair Information Practices, which refers to the standards and practices that countries and organizations should adhere to when collecting and handling personal data. The Organisation for Economic Co-operation and Development (OECD) was influential in developing Fair Information Practices with its *Guidelines on the Protection of Privacy and Transborder Flows of Personal Data* (OECD Privacy Guidelines). These guidelines harmonize national privacy legislation and prevent interruptions in international flows of data.

The OECD Privacy Guidelines set out eight principles for the processing of data by private and public sectors that are the foundation for many national laws and international agreements regarding privacy. Even though countries have their own requirements for the protection of data privacy, most countries impose requirements that converge around the OECD principles:

- Personal data should be obtained fairly and lawfully.
- Collected data should be relevant to its stated purpose, accurate, and kept up to date.
- The purpose of the data collection should be specifically stated no later than the time it is collected.
- Data should be used only for its original, specified purpose.
- Data should be protected by reasonable security safeguards.
- There should be a general policy of openness concerning developments, practices, and policies with respect to personal data.
- Individuals should have the right to obtain confirmation that a data controller has personal data relating to them, and should be able to challenge that data.
- A data controller should be held accountable for failing to abide by data collection and maintenance rules.[3]

European Union

The EU Data Protection Directive (also known as EU Directive 95/46/EC) is the principal data protection instrument in the EU and is influential across many jurisdictions. The EU Data Protection Directive regulates the processing, using, and transferring of personal data within the EU, and it places limits on transmitting personal data to non-EU countries.

The EU Data Protection Directive establishes the blueprint for data privacy laws across Europe, and it mandates that all EU member states enact laws and regulations that satisfy certain minimum standards, which include, among other things, requirements that data controllers:

- Give their identity and purpose when collecting data directly from the subject.
- Notify the subject of their identity, the type of information they are collecting, and their purpose when collecting data from a third party.
- Collect data for only specific, legitimate purposes.
- Avoid processing data unless certain conditions are met.
- Avoid processing data unless necessary to achieve a specific, legitimate purpose.
- Keep data confidential and secure.
- Give data subjects the right to information about the processing of their personal data.
- Give data subjects the right to access and correct any inaccurate data.

In 2016, the European Parliament adopted the General Data Protection Regulation (GDPR), which replaced EU Directive 95/46/EC on May 25, 2018. The GDPR generally increases data privacy, but it contains broad exemptions for law enforcement. The GDPR's new requirements include:

- Data protection generally extends to all companies that process data about EU residents, even if those companies do not have a presence in the EU.
- Except where otherwise stated in the GDPR, individuals must be notified and consent to processing of their personal information.
- Individuals will have the ability to request that their personal data be transferred to other data providers, and they can demand that their data history be erased under certain circumstances.
- Organizations must notify the state's data protection authority about data breaches without undue delay, and adversely affected individuals also must be notified.
- Law enforcement authorities are largely exempt from privacy restrictions during investigations.

International Data Transfers

Many countries have adopted legal restrictions on international data transfers. Thus, an important issue that arises in transnational investigations concerns the transmission of personal data between two or more countries. Data transfers cover any sharing, transferring, disclosing, or giving access to information to third parties (e.g., corporate entities and government authorities).

Additionally, countries that regulate cross-border data transfers differ regarding what types of data are protected, how the regulations are enforced, and what entities are subject to them. For example, member states of the EU impose specific restrictions on cross-border transfers. In particular, member states of the EU have laws that prohibit the transfer of personal information to jurisdictions outside the EU unless the country of final destination offers an adequate level of protection for data. The European Commission, which is the executive of the EU, has the authority to make an "adequacy" finding as to whether a country offers an adequate level of protection for data.

Similarly, Malaysia's Personal Data Protection Act 2010 imposes restrictions on cross-border data transfers. In general, data can be transferred only to countries that are included on a white list maintained by Malaysia's Personal Data Protection Commissioner. However, there are exceptions that enable organizations to transfer data to non-white-listed countries (e.g., when the data subject consents to the transfer).

In contrast to the restrictions on cross-border transfers in the EU, Canada applies an organization-to-organization approach under the Personal Information Protection and Electronic Documents Act (PIPEDA), which governs how private-sector organizations collect, use, and disclose personal information in the course of commercial business. PIPEDA provides that organizations that collect data are responsible for protecting personal information transferred to other jurisdictions. Additionally, organizations that collect data must take all reasonable steps to protect personal information from unauthorized disclosures while it is in the custody of third parties. That is, under PIPEDA, organizations must be satisfied that a recipient of personal information has appropriate policies and procedures in place to ensure the protection of personal information in its custody.

In general, there are three basic ways by which management can legitimize cross-border transfers of personal information:

1. Obtain the consent of the data subject.
2. Establish a contract between the entities exchanging the information (i.e., between the transmitting entity and the receiving entity).
3. If transmitting from the EU to non-EU countries, rely on adequacy decisions by the European Commission. That is, limit the transfer of data to countries that offer an adequate level of protection to safeguard that data.

However, given the wide range of legislation and practices regarding cross-border transfer laws and restrictions, fraud examiners working in other countries must become familiar with laws governing privacy and must adapt their procedures to comply with local rules.

NOTES

1. Black's Law Dictionary, 7th ed.
2. Article 29 Data Protection Working Party, "Working Document on the Surveillance of Electronic Communications in the Workplace," WP 55 (adopted May 29, 2002); Miriam H. Wugmeister and Christine E. Lyon, *Global Employee Privacy and Data Security Law*, 2nd ed., ch. 10 (BNA Books, 2011).
3. The full OECD Privacy Guidelines are accessible here: www.oecd.org/sti/ieconomy/ oecdguidelinesontheprotectionofprivacyandtransborderflowsofpersonaldata.htm.

CHAPTER 3

Fraud Risk Assessment

For an organization to effectively prevent and detect fraud, it must first understand where and how it is most vulnerable to being victimized by the various fraud schemes; that is, it must identify and assess the entity's fraud risks.

WHAT IS FRAUD RISK?

As discussed earlier, the Fraud Triangle indicates that there are three interrelated elements that enable someone to commit fraud: the *motive* or *pressure* that drives a person to want to commit the fraud, the *opportunity* that enables the individual to commit the fraud, and the *ability to rationalize* the fraudulent behavior. The vulnerability that an organization has to those capable of overcoming all three of these elements is *fraud risk*. Fraud risk can come from sources both internal and external to the organization and is one of many risks that organizational leaders must manage.

Factors That Influence Fraud Risk

The following are among the many factors that influence an organization's fraud risks.

The Nature of the Business

The types of risks an organization faces are directly connected to the nature of the business in which it is engaged. For example, the fraud risks faced by hospitals and medical practices are vastly different from those faced by banks and financial institutions, construction companies, educational institutions, or retail organizations.

Economic Conditions

Overall economic conditions can have an effect on fraud risks. In particular, poor economic conditions can increase the financial pressure on the organization and its employees, thereby increasing the likelihood that someone will attempt to perpetrate a fraud. Similarly, internal resource constraints during periods of economic hardship might result in staffing reductions or process restructuring, which can lead to additional opportunities for fraud.

The Operating Environment

The environment in which the organization operates has a direct impact on its vulnerability to fraud. Brick-and-mortar businesses have a very different risk profile from

---

Portions of the material in this chapter also appear in the course material for the Association of Certified Fraud Examiners (ACFE) *Fraud Risk Management* seminar.

Internet businesses. Likewise, local businesses have different risk profiles from those that operate in the international arena.

The Company's Ethical Culture and the Ethics of Employees

It stands to reason that a strong ethical culture would help counteract the likelihood of fraud occurrence within an entity. However, it is extremely difficult, if not impossible, to have a company made up of individuals whose ethics and values are fully aligned with those of the organization. Any gap in alignment can significantly increase an organization's fraud risk.

Technology

As organizational leaders deploy new technology or modify how they use existing technology, fraud risks often change. Specifically, technological developments might result in the creation of a completely new fraud risk, the elimination of an existing fraud risk, or an increase or decrease in the likelihood or potential impact of a fraud risk.

The Legal Environment

A highly regulated industry, with numerous and complex laws and regulations, might create an environment in which people look for ways to cut corners or circumvent the rules in order to work more efficiently or succeed in business. Such intentional noncompliance can cross over into fraud when these acts personally benefit the individual (e.g., a salesperson increases his bonus compensation by violating a bribery law).

Effectiveness of Internal Controls

No system of internal controls can fully eliminate the risk of fraud, but well-designed and effective internal controls can deter the average fraudster by reducing the opportunity to commit the fraud and increasing the perception of detection.

Types of Fraud Risks

When considering the fraud risks faced by an organization, management should analyze how significant a risk is before and after its response to that risk. Risks that are present before management action are described as *inherent risks*. Risks that remain after management action are *residual risks*.

For example, there is an inherent risk that the employee in charge of receiving customer payments at a small company might embezzle incoming cash. Controls, such as segregation of duties and oversight from the company owner, can be implemented to help mitigate this risk; however, even with such controls in place, there will likely remain some residual risk that the bookkeeper could still manage to embezzle funds. The objective of the controls is to make the residual risk significantly smaller than the inherent risk.

WHAT IS A FRAUD RISK ASSESSMENT?

A *fraud risk assessment* is a process aimed at proactively identifying and addressing an organization's vulnerabilities to both internal and external fraud. If performed and used correctly, a fraud risk assessment can be a powerful tool in the fight against fraud for any business.

Because every organization is different, the fraud risk assessment process is often more an art than a science. Thus, the assessment should be planned with consideration for the nuances of the specific organization; what is evaluated and how it is assessed should be tailored to the organization – there is no one-size-fits-all approach.

Additionally, organizational fraud risks continually change. A change in any of the factors discussed earlier (business, economic, operating, ethical, technological, legal, or internal controls) can affect the organization's fraud risks. Therefore, the fraud risk assessment should be an ongoing, continuous process rather than a one-time or periodic activity. And management should strive to keep the process alive and relevant through ongoing dialogue, active oversight of action plans, and development of procedures to ensure that the assessment is appropriately revisited and maintained.

Through a fraud risk assessment, management can identify where fraud is most likely to occur, and design and implement proactive measures to address the risks to reduce the chance of fraud. The strategic reasoning used in an assessment requires a skeptical mindset and involves asking questions such as:

- How might a perpetrator exploit weaknesses in the system of controls?
- How might a perpetrator override or circumvent controls?
- How might a perpetrator conceal the fraud?

Benefits of a Fraud Risk Assessment

Every organization should conduct a fraud risk assessment and build procedures to keep the assessment process current and relevant. Not only is this practice good corporate governance, but it also makes good business sense. Specifically, engaging in a fraud risk assessment provides a number of benefits to an organization.

Improve Communication and Awareness about Fraud

A fraud risk assessment provides an opportunity to open a dialogue and raise awareness about fraud with employees and other stakeholders. When employees engage in open discussions about fraud, the conversations themselves can play a role in reducing fraud vulnerability. Such discussions help remind employees that the organization's leaders care about preventing fraud, and they feel empowered to come forward if they suspect fraud is occurring. Open communication and awareness about fraud can also deter potential fraudsters by reducing their ability to rationalize bad behavior and increasing their perception that someone might notice and report their actions.

Detect Vulnerabilities

Management must know where the company is most vulnerable to fraud to prevent it from happening. For most companies, the normal course of business generally involves many different activities; however, not all the activities that the company engages in are equal in terms of exposure to fraud. The fraud risk assessment helps management focus on the activities that put the company at greatest risk.

Identify Risk Contributors

Certain individuals put the organization at greater risk for fraud, whether due to the nature of their position or their behavior. The increased risk can be direct (e.g., an individual has a greater propensity to commit fraud) or indirect (e.g., an individual does not adhere to company policies and controls, which creates an opportunity for other employees to commit and conceal fraud). The fraud risk assessment can help identify those people and activities that might increase the company's overall fraud risk.

Develop Plans to Mitigate Fraud Risk

If management knows where the greatest fraud risks are, it can develop and implement plans to reduce or mitigate those risks. The results of the fraud risk assessment can be used to create alignment among various stakeholders and to drive preventive action.

Develop Investigative Techniques

Assessing an area as having a high fraud risk does not conclusively mean that fraud is occurring there. Nevertheless, the fraud risk assessment is useful in identifying areas that should be proactively investigated for evidence of fraud. In addition, putting high-risk areas under increased scrutiny can deter potential fraudsters by increasing their perception of the likelihood of detection.

Assess Internal Controls

Many organizations rely heavily on their internal control systems to prevent and detect fraud. Although internal controls play a critical role in fraud prevention and detection, they are dynamic systems that require constant reevaluation to detect any weaknesses. Performing a fraud risk assessment provides management with the opportunity to review the company's internal control system for effectiveness, with the following considerations:

- Controls that might have been eliminated due to restructuring efforts (e.g., elimination of separation of duties due to downsizing)
- Controls that might have eroded over time due to reengineering of business processes
- New opportunities for collusion
- Lack of internal controls in a vulnerable area

- Nonperformance of control procedures (e.g., control procedures compromised for the sake of expediency)
- Inherent limitations of internal controls, including opportunities for those responsible for a control to commit and conceal fraud (e.g., through management and system overrides)

Compliance with Regulations and Professional Standards

Fraud risk assessments can assist management and auditors (both internal and external) in satisfying regulatory requirements and complying with professional standards pertaining to their responsibility for fraud risk management.

WHO IS RESPONSIBLE FOR THE FRAUD RISK ASSESSMENT?

When possible, management and auditors should share ownership of the fraud risk assessment process and accountability for its success. While both parties have a responsibility to prevent and detect fraud within the organization, each brings a unique perspective to the process and the risks faced by the organization.

Management has an intricate familiarity with day-to-day business operations, responsibility for assessing business risks and implementing organizational controls, authority to adjust operations, influence over the organization's culture and ethical atmosphere, and control over the organization's resources (e.g., people and systems).

Auditors, conversely, are trained in risk identification and assessment and have an expertise in evaluating internal controls, which is critical to the fraud risk assessment process. Consequently, the assessment is most effective when management and auditors share ownership of the process and accountability for its success.

Designating the Best Sponsor

Having the right sponsor for a fraud risk assessment is extremely important in ensuring its success and effectiveness. The sponsor must be senior enough in the organization to command the respect of the employees and elicit full cooperation in the process.

The sponsor also must be someone with strong determination and fortitude to learn the truth about where the company's fraud vulnerabilities are – the sponsor must be a truth seeker, not someone prone to rationalization or denial. Ideally, the sponsor is an independent board director or audit committee member; however, a chief executive officer or other internal senior leader can be equally effective.

Organizational culture plays a key role in influencing the organization's vulnerability to fraud. If the company's culture is shaped by a strong and domineering leader, obtaining candid participation from the people in the business might be difficult if that leader were to sponsor the fraud risk assessment.

The right sponsor is willing to hear the good, the bad, and the ugly. For example, a fraud risk assessment may reveal that one of the greatest fraud risks facing the organization is bribery, based on the close relationship between one of the key business leaders and the company's business partners. For the fraud risk assessment to be effective, the sponsor must be independent and open in this evaluation of the situation and, most important, appropriate in his response to the identified risks.

Who Should Conduct the Fraud Risk Assessment?

A fraud risk assessment can be a complex process. Consequently, management and the designated sponsor should assemble a team to conduct the fraud risk assessment team that consists of individuals with diverse knowledge, skills, and perspectives. The size of the team will depend on the size of the organization and the methods used to conduct the assessment. The team should include individuals who are credible and have experience in gathering and eliciting information.

Team members can include internal and external resources such as:

- Accounting and finance personnel who are familiar with the financial reporting processes and internal controls
- Nonfinancial business unit and operations personnel who have knowledge of day-to-day operations, customer and vendor interactions, and issues within the industry
- Risk management personnel who can ensure that the fraud risk assessment process integrates with the organization's enterprise risk management program
- General counsel or other members of the legal department
- Members of any ethics or compliance functions within the organization
- Internal auditors
- Internal security or investigative personnel who are familiar with investigations of past fraud incidents
- External consultants with fraud and risk expertise
- Any business leader with direct accountability for the effectiveness of the organization's fraud risk management efforts

When forming the fraud risk assessment team, the following factors must be considered.

Thorough Understanding of the Business

The individuals leading and conducting the fraud risk assessment must have a thorough understanding of the business's operations, working environment, and strategic goals and plans. Every organization is unique; even companies that appear similar have characteristics that differentiate them – and their fraud risks – from their competitors. Some of those differences can be obvious, whereas others are subtle.

To have a sufficient understanding of the business, the team members must know, beyond a superficial level, what the business does and how it operates. They must also understand what makes the organization both similar to and different from other companies in related lines of business.

In forming this requisite knowledge base, information about broad industry fraud risks from external sources can be helpful. Such sources include industry news; criminal, civil, and regulatory complaints and settlements; and resources provided by relevant professional organizations.

Independence and Objectivity

Independence and objectivity are key factors in deciding who should be on the team. While a fraud risk assessment can be effectively conducted by people either inside or outside the organization, it is critical that those leading and conducting the fraud risk assessment remain independent and objective throughout the assessment process. Additionally, they must be perceived as independent and objective by others.

The people leading and conducting the work should be mindful of any personal biases they might harbor regarding the organization and the staff and take steps to reduce or eliminate such biases. For example, if an employee on the fraud risk assessment team had a bad experience with someone in the accounts payable department, she might allow that experience to affect her evaluation of the fraud risks in that area of the business. To preclude this possibility, someone else should perform the fraud risk assessment work related to the accounts payable department's activities.

Access to People at All Levels of the Organization

It is often said that perception is reality. In other words, how individuals perceive a situation is their reality of that situation. In an organization, it is important that the perceptions of people at all levels are included in the fraud risk assessment process.

Leaders of a business or function often have perspectives very different from their subordinates on how something is perceived or executed; however, this does not mean that one perspective is right and the other is wrong. What it does mean is that expectations and perceptions within the organization are not aligned, which could increase fraud risk.

Risk assessments created or performed by management and auditors without the input of the staff who perform the operational tasks will be ineffective. It is crucial to include members of all levels of the organization in the risk assessment process to ensure that all relevant risks are addressed and reviewed from many different perspectives. Additionally, asking employees at lower levels of the organization specific questions about the company culture or their ideas to strengthen internal controls can provide valuable information that might not be obtainable from any other source.

Engendered Trust

If management and employees do not trust the people leading and conducting the fraud risk assessment, they will not be open and honest about the realities of the business, its culture, and its vulnerability to fraud. Trust is not something that can be granted by authority; it must be earned through words and actions. As the people leading and conducting the fraud risk assessment engage with employees throughout the business, they should deliberately and carefully plan the initial contact with an effort to develop rapport and gain trust.

Ability to Think the Unthinkable

Most honest people are not naturally inclined to think like a criminal. In fact, many large-scale frauds that have occurred would have been deemed unthinkable by people closest to the events. However, a necessary part of conducting an effective fraud risk assessment involves thinking like a fraudster. Consequently, the people leading and conducting the assessment must be expansive in their consideration and evaluation of fraud risk. Thoughts of "it couldn't happen here" should not be allowed to moderate the evaluation of fraud risk.

PREPARING FOR THE FRAUD RISK ASSESSMENT

Properly preparing the company for the fraud risk assessment is critical to its success. The culture of the organization should influence the approach used in preparation for the assessment.

Identify the Information to Be Gathered

The fraud risk assessment team should begin by identifying the information the team needs to gather to fully understand the organization's fraud risk landscape. This information typically includes:

- Information regarding the organization's inherent fraud risks
- Past known fraud incidents and how they were handled
- Information regarding the likelihood and impact of identified risks
- Perceptions regarding the overall control environment
- Perceptions regarding the operating effectiveness of specific anti-fraud controls

Determine the Best Techniques to Use in Conducting the Fraud Risk Assessment

The assessment team should also consider the best ways to gather candid information from people throughout all levels of the organization, starting by understanding what techniques are commonly and effectively used throughout the organization in general, as well as whether any specific areas need to be handled differently. For example, in a single organization, interviews might be effective for a small, centralized accounting team, while surveys are more appropriate for a larger sales team that is geographically disbursed.

The following are some examples of methods that can be used to conduct the fraud risk assessment.

Interviews

Interviews can be an effective way to gather information by having candid, one-on-one conversations with specific individuals. However, the outcome depends on how willing people in the organization are to be open and honest in a direct dialogue with the interviewer. The assessment team should consider whether interviews are typically and successfully used to gather information from employees in the organization. They should also speak with individuals who have conducted past interviews to glean lessons learned. With each potential interviewee, the team should gauge the person's willingness to provide candid information; some people might be good interview candidates, whereas others might need to be engaged differently.

Interviews used in the fraud risk assessment process can be structured or semistructured. In a *structured interview*, the interviewee is presented with questions or scenarios that have been prepared ahead of time by the interviewer. Structured interviews result in a focused use of interviewees' time and consistency among interviews. The interviewer does not deviate from the planned list of questions. In contrast, a *semistructured interview* allows for follow-up questions and flexibility in the direction of the interview. Semistructured interviews are more conversational in nature.

Focus Groups

Focus groups (sometimes referred to as *workshops*) allow the assessment team to observe employee interactions as they discuss a particular question or issue. Some topics lend themselves to being discussed in an open forum if people feel comfortable with their colleagues. Additionally, when discussing sensitive issues in a group, an anonymous, real-time voting tool can be an effective way of promoting a dialogue. Focus groups can be especially useful with employees at lower levels of the organization.

The success of a focus group is highly dependent on the facilitator's skill. If focus groups are used as part of the fraud risk assessment, they should be led by an experienced facilitator the group can relate to and trust. Getting a group to open up and talk honestly can be very difficult. An experienced facilitator can read the group and use techniques, such as group icebreakers, to make the session a success.

Like interviews, focus groups can involve structured or semistructured discussions. In a structured environment, the facilitator presents the group with prepared questions or scenarios and does not deviate from the list. In a semistructured approach, the facilitator deviates from their prepared questions to delve further into issues that arise during the discussion. Given that one of the primary benefits of the focus group approach is the interaction of the people involved, a semistructured approach is generally preferable. However, the facilitator must be skilled enough to keep the group discussion on track and productive.

Another possible approach to the focus group is an *unstructured* format. Similar to a brainstorming session, the group is presented only with very broad issues or questions, such as "How might fraud occur in this area?" An unstructured approach encourages creativity because the group is not limited in the scope of its discussion. However, the group can also lose focus quickly if allowed to wander too far into various discussion points. Thus, the facilitator must be particularly adept at handling these types of discussions if an unstructured approach is used.

A final consideration with focus groups is whether participants should come from a single department or multiple functions. At the early stages of the fraud risk assessment (e.g., when identifying inherent fraud risks), a single-function group is usually gathered to help ensure each functional area's fraud risks are thoroughly identified. Later, when the process of assessing identified risks begins, cross-functional groups are preferred, as they help incorporate multiple perspectives into the conversation.

Surveys

Surveys can be a convenient tool to gather information from large or geographically disbursed groups of individuals. They also provide a more flexible option for scheduling purposes; employees can answer on their own time and can start and stop the survey as needed. Surveys can also be easily customized to different groups based on the specific information sought. However, because surveys are remotely administered and based on predefined questions, they do not provide the same opportunities for open discussion or clarification that interviews or focus groups do.

Additionally, surveys can be anonymous or directly attributable to individuals. Some people might be more willing to share openly when they do not have to engage in a face-to-face conversation – especially if they are able to provide responses anonymously. Thus, in an organizational culture that discourages open and free discussions, an anonymous survey can be an effective way to get feedback. However, employees might be skeptical about the true anonymity of a survey; for example, employees would have reason to doubt the anonymous nature of the survey if the organization solicits feedback anonymously but sends follow-up emails to individual delinquent respondents. Consequently, if the fraud risk assessment team determines that an anonymous survey is an appropriate technique to use to gather information, they should clearly and explicitly explain to employees how anonymity will be maintained.

Other Anonymous Feedback Mechanisms

In some organizations, anonymous suggestion boxes or similar mechanisms are used to encourage employee feedback. In these companies, information pertaining to the fraud risk assessment can be requested in the same way. Additionally, anonymous feedback mechanisms can be effective in an environment where people are less likely to be open and honest through other methods and techniques.

One approach to effectively using the anonymous feedback technique involves establishing a question of the day that is prominently displayed above a collection box. A sample question is: "If you thought fraud were occurring in the company, would you come forward? Why or why not?"

Another approach involves using a table lineup of five to 10 opaque boxes, each with a statement posted above it. Employees are provided with poker chips in two different colors and told that one color indicates "I agree" and the other indicates "I disagree." Employees are then encouraged to respond to each statement by putting a corresponding chip in each box to indicate their response.

Obtain the Sponsor's Agreement on the Work to Be Performed

Before the fraud risk assessment procedures begin, the sponsor and the assessment team need to agree on:

- The scope of work to be performed
- The individuals who should participate

- The methods to use for collecting information
- The content of the chosen methods
- The form of output for the assessment

Educate Employees and Openly Promote the Process

The fraud risk assessment process should be visible and communicated throughout the business. Employees are more inclined to participate in a process when they understand the purpose and expected outcomes.

The sponsor should also be involved in openly promoting the process. The more personalized the communication from the sponsor, the more effective it will be in encouraging employees to participate. Whether through a video, town hall meeting, or companywide email, the communication should be aimed at eliminating any reluctance employees have about participating in the fraud risk assessment process.

CONDUCTING THE FRAUD RISK ASSESSMENT

Fraud risk assessments can be executed in many ways. To ensure the assessment's success, the approach should be structured, rational, and tailored to the organization.

When conducting a fraud risk assessment, it is helpful to use a framework for performing, evaluating, and reporting the results of the work. Fraud risk can be analyzed and reported both qualitatively and quantitatively using a consistent framework. In adopting a framework, however, the assessment team must ensure that the specific needs and culture of the organization are addressed. Without tailoring the approach to the specific organization, the team might miss important factors or obtain unreliable or meaningless results.

The following sample framework illustrates how the elements of fraud risk assessment are applied under different approaches. This framework is based on the fraud risk assessment process provided in the *Fraud Risk Management Guide*, a resource jointly published by the Committee of Sponsoring Organizations of the Treadway Commission (COSO) and the Association of Certified Fraud Examiners (ACFE).[1] Additionally, a downloadable Excel template to assist with the application of this framework is available at www.acfe.com/fraudrisktools/tools.aspx.

Using this framework, the fraud risk assessment team incorporates the following steps into their strategy:

- Identify potential inherent fraud risks and schemes.
- Assess the likelihood of occurrence of the identified, inherent fraud risks.
- Assess the impact of each inherent fraud risk to the organization.
- Evaluate which parties are most likely to commit fraud.
- Identify and map existing internal controls to the relevant inherent fraud risks.
- Evaluate whether the identified controls are operating effectively and efficiently, resulting in a controls assessment.
- Identify, evaluate, and respond to residual fraud risks that need to be mitigated.

The following table provides a visual representation of the steps involved in this framework, and can be filled in as the fraud risk assessment is performed.

Identified Fraud Risks and Schemes	Likelihood	Impact	Personnel/ Departments Involved	Existing Fraud Control Activities	Effectiveness of Existing Control Activities	Residual Fraud Risks	Fraud Risk Responses
Financial Statement Fraud:							
Asset Misappropriation:							
Corruption:							
External Fraud Risks:							

Identify Potential Inherent Fraud Risks and Schemes

One of the first steps in a fraud risk assessment involves identifying potential fraud risks inherent to the organization. Identification begins with gathering knowledge from throughout the entity using the techniques determined to be most appropriate. Knowledge of actual frauds and fraud investigations that have taken place in the company should also be introduced early in this phase of the fraud risk assessment.

In addition to these internal sources, management might turn to external sources to help identify inherent fraud risks. One such method is *benchmarking*, in which similar organizations share information regarding real and perceived threats.

Next, with this information, the fraud risk assessment team should brainstorm to identify the inherent fraud risks that could apply to the organization in order to refine and potentially expand the list of identified risks already gathered. Brainstorming should include discussions regarding:

- Incentives, pressures, and opportunities to commit fraud
- Risk of management's override of controls
- The population of fraud risks from both internal sources and external sources
- The risk of regulatory and legal misconduct
- Reputation risk

Incentives, Pressures, and Opportunities to Commit Fraud

When assessing incentives, pressures, and opportunities to commit fraud, the team should evaluate:

- Incentive programs and how they might affect employees' behavior when conducting business or applying professional judgment
- Pressures on individuals to achieve performance or other targets and how such pressures might influence employees' behavior
- Opportunities to commit and conceal fraud that arise from:
  - A person's position (i.e., given the person's responsibilities and authority)
  - Weak internal controls, such as a lack of separation of duties
  - Collusion
- Highly complex business transactions and how they might be used to conceal fraudulent acts

Risk of Management's Override of Controls

When considering the potential for management's override of controls, the fraud risk assessment team should keep in mind that:

- Management personnel within the organization generally know the controls and standard operating procedures that are in place to prevent fraud.
- Individuals who are intent on committing fraud might use their knowledge of the organization's controls to do it in a manner that will conceal their actions.

Population of Fraud Risks

The fraud risk identification process requires an understanding of the universe of fraud risks and the subset of risks that apply to a particular organization. It includes gathering information about the business itself, including its business processes, industry, and operating environment, as well as all associated fraud risks. Such information can be obtained from external sources (e.g., industry news outlets; criminal, civil, and regulatory complaints and settlements; and professional organizations and associations) and from internal sources by interviewing and brainstorming with personnel, reviewing whistle-blower hotline complaints, and performing analytical procedures.

As discussed in Chapter 1, fraud risks from internal sources can be classified into three major areas: financial statement fraud, asset misappropriation, and corruption. Fraud risks from external sources (e.g., vendors, customers, competitors, unrelated third parties) should also be considered.

Risk of Regulatory and Legal Misconduct

Regulatory and legal misconduct includes a wide range of risks, such as conflicts of interest, insider trading, theft of competitor trade secrets, anti-competitive practices, environmental violations, and trade and customs violations. These are acts for which a company could have liability if noncompliance is detected (normally by a government agency). Intentional circumvention by employees or agents to facilitate other aspects of operations might constitute a fraud risk, in addition to being a compliance risk. Depending on the organization and the nature of its business, some or all of these risks might be applicable and should be considered in the fraud risk assessment process.

Reputation Risk

Reputation risk must be considered as part of the organization's risk assessment process, because fraudulent acts can damage the organization's reputation with customers, suppliers, investors, lenders, and others. For example, fraud leading to a financial restatement can damage an organization's reputation in capital markets, which can increase the organization's cost of borrowing and depress its market capitalization. Additionally, the assessment team should consider the organization's reputational capital – that is, how much stakeholder value is derived from the organization's reputation in the marketplace.

Assess the Likelihood of Occurrence of the Identified, Inherent Fraud Risks

Assessing the likelihood of each potential fraud risk is a subjective process that allows the organization to manage its fraud risks and design and implement anti-fraud measures rationally. It is one of the most difficult steps in performing a fraud risk assessment, especially when it is being done for the first time. The fraud risk assessment team should first consider fraud risks to the organization on an inherent basis, without consideration of known controls. By approaching the assessment in this manner, the team is better able to consider all relevant fraud risks and then evaluate and design controls to address those risks.

There are two common approaches to assessing the likelihood of a fraud risk:

1. The probability that the fraud will be attempted (normally within one year)
2. The frequency with which a fraud risk will occur (i.e., someone will attempt the fraud scheme)

The first approach – assessing the probability of the risk – is more common. However, for known risks experienced by the organization, frequency of occurrence can be more useful, especially for immaterial risks (i.e., those with an insignificant impact) for which the organization has accepted a certain level of tolerance.

Regardless of which approach is used, the likelihood should be assessed using a standard classification system agreed upon at the beginning of the assessment. Normally, three or more levels of likelihood should be used. For example, the likelihood of occurrence of each fraud risk can be classified qualitatively as *remote, reasonably possible*, or *probable*. Another example of a qualitative scale frequently used is *unlikely, possible*, or *likely*. If frequency is used in place of probability, an appropriate scale based on number of occurrences should be established.

In place of qualitative categories for assessing likelihood, some organizations elect to use a quantitative scale, with the least likely being a 1 and the most likely being a 3 or a 5.

The following is an example of a scale using both probability and frequency.

Rating	Based on Annual Probability of Occurrence		Based on Annual Frequency	
	Descriptor	Definition	Descriptor	Definition
5	Almost certain	>90% chance of occurrence	Very frequent	>20 times per year
4	Likely	66% to 90% chance of occurrence	Frequent	6 to 20 times per year
3	Reasonably possible	36% to 65% chance of occurrence	Reasonably frequent	2 to 5 times per year
2	Unlikely	10% to 35% chance of occurrence	Occasional	1 time per year
1	Remote	<10% chance of occurrence	Rare	<1 time per year

In assessing the likelihood of occurrence of each fraud risk, the fraud risk assessment team should consider the following factors:

- Past instances of the particular fraud at the organization
- Prevalence of the fraud risk in the organization's industry (based on industry statistics or other knowledge of the industry)
- Internal control environment of the organization
- Resources available to address fraud
- Support of fraud prevention efforts by management
- Ethical standards and culture of the organization
- Number of individual transactions involved (the greater the number of opportunities, the greater the likelihood that someone might attempt a fraud)
- The number of people involved (i.e., the more people an organization has in a position of trust, the greater the likelihood that one of them will attempt a fraud)
- Complexity of the fraud risk
- Unexplained losses
- Complaints by customers or vendors
- Information from fraud surveys and benchmarking reports such as the ACFE's *Report to the Nations on Occupational Fraud and Abuse*

Assess the Impact of the Inherent Fraud Risks to the Organization

The fraud risk assessment team should next consider the impact (sometimes referred to as *significance* or *consequence*) of identified fraud risks to the organization. As with likelihood, prior to starting the assessment of individual inherent fraud risks, the team should agree on an appropriate scale or classification system for measuring the impact of each risk. For instance, the impact of each potential fraud might be classified as *immaterial*, *significant*, or *material*. Another example of qualitative terms for impact is *problematic*, *disruptive*, and *catastrophic*. Alternatively, many organizations use a quantitative scale (e.g., 1–3 or 1–5) to measure the assessment of impact.

In assessing the impact of fraud risks, the fraud risk assessment team should consider both financial and nonfinancial factors, as fraud often has significant nonfinancial repercussions throughout an organization. For example, a particular fraud risk that might pose only an immaterial direct financial risk to the organization but that could greatly affect its reputation would likely be deemed a high risk in terms of potential impact to the organization. Certain frauds might be more prone to these nonfinancial impacts than others.

The following is an example of a scale for assessing a risk's impact to the organization:

Rating	Descriptor	Definition
5	Catastrophic	• Financial loss to company is more than $10 million. • International long-term media coverage • Widespread employee morale issues result, and multiple senior leaders leave. • Incident must be reported to authorities, and significant sanctions and financial penalties result.
4	Major	• Financial loss to company is between $100,000 and $10 million. • National long-term media coverage • Widespread employee morale problems and turnover • Incident must be reported to authorities, and sanctions against company result.
3	Moderate	• Financial loss to company is between $10,000 and $100,000. • Short-term regional or national media coverage • Widespread employee morale problems • Incident must be reported to authorities, and immediate corrective action is necessary.
2	Minor	• Financial loss to company is between $1,000 and $10,000. • Limited local media coverage • General employee morale problems • Incident is reportable to authorities, but no follow-up.
1	Incidental	• Financial loss to company is less than $1,000. • No media coverage • Isolated employee dissatisfaction • Event does not need to be reported to authorities.

In assessing the impact of each fraud risk, the team should consider the following financial and nonfinancial factors:

• Financial statement and monetary impact
• Financial condition of the organization
• Value of the threatened assets
• How critical the threatened assets are to the organization
• Revenue generated by the threatened assets
• Impact on the organization's operations, brand value, and reputation
• Whether employees would suffer any financial damages (i.e., whether the fraud would directly affect employees, such as by an employee using his position to steal from another employee)
• Whether any financial damages would be caused to third parties (e.g., customers)
• Criminal, civil, and regulatory liabilities
• Whether the fraud would result in required reporting to governmental authorities

- Reputational damage among stakeholders (customers, stockholders, etc.)
- Adverse media coverage
- Resulting competitive advantages to other companies
- Decline in employee morale
- Lost productivity
- Loss of key staff
- Whether the event would result in data loss
- Whether the event would result in a work stoppage
- Time spent investigating and following up on the fraud event

Evaluate Which Parties Are Most Likely to Commit Fraud

During the process of identifying potential inherent fraud risks, the risk assessment team evaluated the incentives and pressures on individuals and departments to commit fraud. The team should now use the information gained in that process to identify the individuals and departments most likely to commit fraud. This knowledge can help management tailor its fraud risk response, including establishing appropriate separation of duties, proper review and approval chains of authority, and proactive fraud auditing procedures.

In some cases, a fraud risk initially identified as a single risk ends up being treated as two risks after it is determined that one group of employees is more likely than another to engage in the fraudulent act, even though both have the potential to do so. For example, one inherent fraud risk identified by the company might be to use the company credit card to make unauthorized purchases. In theory, any employee holding a corporate credit card has the potential to engage in this act. However, the fraud risk assessment team might conclude that the company's sales personnel group is more likely than any other cardholder group to attempt this fraud. Such unauthorized purchases might be linked to providing inappropriate benefits to customers as an incentive to purchase the company's products, thereby generating commissions for the salesperson. As a result, the risk assessment team treats this risk as two separate risks – one related to making unauthorized purchases on the credit card and one related to giving inappropriate gifts to customers to boost commissions – each with potentially different risk responses.

Additionally, internal parties are not the only potential perpetrators of fraud against the organization. As noted in Chapter 1, various external parties can also perpetrate a fraud scheme. Thus, the fraud risk assessment must also consider who outside the organization has access and influence to defraud the organization.

Identify and Map Existing Internal Controls to the Relevant Inherent Fraud Risks

After identifying and assessing fraud risks for likelihood of occurrence and impact, the team should identify and map existing internal controls to the relevant fraud risks.

As internal controls are identified and matched with specific fraud risks, the team should indicate whether the control is designed to prevent or to detect the fraud. Further, with controls focused on detecting fraud, the timeliness of anticipated detection should be considered (e.g., is the detection control a monthly reconciliation or a real-time data monitoring technique?).

Additionally, in documenting the identified internal controls, the team should reference the specific policy or procedure document that supports the control. If the policy or procedure document has an identification number, the team should use that as a reference in the risk assessment documentation.

Evaluate Whether the Identified Controls Are Operating Effectively and Efficiently

Based on the controls identified in the previous step, the fraud risk assessment team must assess whether there are adequate controls in place, the controls are mitigating fraud risk as intended, and the benefit of the controls exceeds the cost. Depending on the control being evaluated, this might require:

- Reviewing the accounting policies and procedures
- Considering the risk of management's (or anyone else's) override of controls
- Interviewing management and employees
- Observing control activities in operation
- Testing samples of transactions subject to identified internal controls for compliance
- Conducting walk-throughs of transactions
- Reviewing previous audit reports
- Reviewing previous reports on fraud incidents, shrinkage, and unexplained shortages

The fraud risk assessment team members are rarely the ones who test the operating effectiveness of a company's internal controls. However, the team must collect information from the internal audit department, as well as from any others who might have this information, to understand the following aspects of the testing of internal controls:

- *Timing:* When was the last time the pertinent prevention and detection internal controls were formally tested?
- *Extent:* How many transactions were tested (out of a population of how many?), and which attributes of the internal controls were tested?
- *Results:* What were the results of those tests (were deviations from expected internal controls discovered)?

Based on the knowledge gained, the group might assign a formal control risk rating. The following table is an example of a scale that could be used for a control risk rating.

Control Risk Rating	Description
5	Very effective — reduces 81–100% of the risk
4	Effective — reduces 61–80% of the risk
3	Moderately effective — reduces 41–60% of the risk
2	Marginally effective — reduces 21–40% of the risk
1	Not effective — reduces 20% or less of the risk

Although such a scale is useful in that it assigns a number to the rating of a control's effectiveness, and each level corresponds to a percentage, this process inherently involves a certain degree of subjectivity. As such, it should be subjected to an open and fair discussion by the group, often in conjunction with input from the internal audit group or others who have been responsible for assessing the effectiveness of the controls in the past.

Identify, Evaluate, and Respond to Residual Fraud Risks

Any remaining risk that results after considering the effectiveness of internal controls, as aligned with the preliminary assessment of likelihood and impact of inherent fraud risks, represents residual risk. For example, consideration of the internal control structure might reveal certain residual fraud risks, including management's override of established controls, that have not been adequately mitigated due to:

- Lack of appropriate prevention and detection controls
- Noncompliance with established prevention and control measures

The fraud risk assessment team should then evaluate the likelihood and impact of occurrence of these residual fraud risks.

Fraud Risk Response

Based on the evaluation of the likelihood and impact of the identified residual fraud risks, the team – often in conjunction with management – should formulate a plan for responding to the remaining fraud risk.

Establishing an Acceptable Level of Risk

Because it is neither practical nor cost-effective for an organization to eliminate all fraud risk, management must establish an acceptable level of fraud risk based on the business objectives and risk tolerance of the organization. In responding to fraud risks identified during the fraud risk assessment, management must determine how the fraud risks affect business objectives and, using cost-benefit analysis, decide where to best allocate resources for fraud prevention and detection.

Ranking and Prioritizing Risks

As part of formulating the fraud risk response, the identified risks need to be prioritized. There are two basic frameworks for prioritizing risk:

1. Estimating the likely cost of a risk
2. Using a quadrant graph, called a *heat map*, to identify those risks that are both likely and significant

Estimating Likely Cost of a Risk

This approach involves determining a quantitative value for the expected loss based on the risk's likelihood of occurrence and potential cost (i.e., impact). Both of these factors are estimates and are far from objective, but, by engaging in a process to estimate and quantify these elements of risk, an organization can prioritize its risks from the highest to lowest expected cost and focus on the outcomes that would be the most expensive. Under this model, Risk = Likelihood × Cost.

Consider the following three risk scenarios:

1. Risk of lost business and reputation damage from a disruption in data processing:
    Likely cost (in lost revenue) = $100,000
    Likelihood of occurrence = 2%
    Potential loss = $2,000 (2% × $100,000)
2. Risk of lost revenues from losing a major client:
    Likely cost (in lost revenue) = $500,000
    Likelihood of occurrence = 15%
    Potential loss = $75,000 (15% × $500,000)
3. Risk of employee embezzlement:
    Likely cost = $150,000
    Likelihood of occurrence = 7%
    Potential loss = $10,500 (7% × $150,000)

This analysis could then be used to rank these three risks by listing them from highest to lowest potential loss:

Risk	Potential Loss
Loss of a major client	$75,000
Employee embezzlement	$10,500
Data processing disruption	$2,000

Based on this list, management could choose to allocate company resources accordingly to mitigate, share, or abandon the highest-cost risks.

Plotting Risks on a Heat Map

With a heat map, such as the one shown in Exhibit 3.1, the risk assessment team can easily see the risks that are the most likely and would have the greatest impact or significance. The team goes through the list of risks and places each risk on the heat map, based on its assessed likelihood and impact. The follow-on analysis prioritizes those risks that are in the darkest areas on the heat map.

This method is also useful in plotting the trajectory of a particular fraud risk as the risk assessment process progresses from measuring inherent risk to measuring residual risk. Ideally, risks starting out in the darkest area of the heat map on an inherent basis get pushed downward and leftward into the darkest areas once the operating effectiveness of internal controls is considered.

Exhibit 3.1   Heat Map

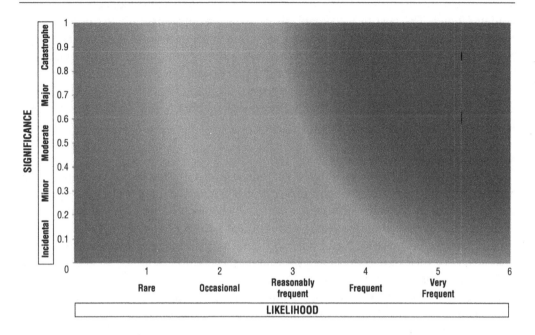

Responding to Residual Fraud Risks

Regardless of the framework used to conduct the fraud risk assessment, management must address the identified risks to ensure that the organization is within its established tolerance level for fraud risk. Management can use one or a combination of the following approaches to respond to the organization's residual fraud risks:

- Avoid the risk.
- Transfer the risk.
- Mitigate the risk.
- Assume the risk.

Avoid the Risk

For fraud risks assessed as having an extremely high likelihood or a very large impact (or both) to the organization, management might decide to avoid the risk completely by eliminating an asset or exiting an activity if the control measures required to protect the organization are too cost-prohibitive. This approach requires the fraud risk assessment team to complete a cost-benefit analysis of the value of the underlying asset or activity to the organization compared to the cost of implementing measures to protect the asset or activity. For example, a multinational conglomerate might choose not to conduct certain types of business in countries with a very poor ranking on the Transparency International Corruption Perception Index.

Transfer the Risk

Management might transfer some or all of a risk by purchasing fidelity insurance or a fidelity bond. The cost to the organization is the premium paid for the insurance or bond. The covered risk of loss is thereby transferred to the insurance company. Transferring risk through insurance coverage is not only a strategy to protect against employee frauds; it should be considered for certain third-party risks as well. For example, a financial institution, as part of its vendor management program, requires its outside systems analysts to have in place third-party fidelity coverage before allowing them to do work for the organization.

Mitigate the Risk

Management might choose to mitigate or reduce a risk by implementing appropriate countermeasures, such as prevention and detection controls. The fraud risk assessment team should evaluate each countermeasure to determine whether it is cost-effective and reasonable given the likelihood of occurrence and expected impact. For example, the accounting system administrator provides read-only access to managers responsible for authorizing transactions or reviewing transactions for accuracy and completeness; managers are not authorized to enter data or reconcile accounts.

Risk mitigation strategies should be linked to the specific aspect of the fraud risk assessment to be addressed. For example, most risk mitigation strategies tend to focus on one or both of the following:

- Reducing the likelihood of a fraud
- Reducing the impact of a fraud

Reducing the likelihood of fraud normally corresponds to enhancing the organization's fraud prevention measures. Improved fraud awareness training, employee counseling, a compensation system that is viewed as fair, and clarified fraud policies are examples of general controls that can reduce the likelihood of fraud. Improvements to an organization's separation of duties and certain information technology (IT) controls can also help prevent fraud, as these controls can be used to convince potential fraudsters that successfully perpetrating a particular scheme would be impossible.

For example, a company with high-resolution printing equipment might identify a risk that employees could use the equipment to print documents for personal purposes – perhaps even for outside business ventures. The risk assessment team determines that the likelihood for this risk is high, but that the impact is relatively low – likely only 2% more in printing expenses throughout the year. Thus, the company decides to mitigate this risk simply by requiring a login on the printer so that all print jobs can be tracked. This additional control can help discourage employees from using the equipment for nonbusiness purposes.

Of course, and perhaps most important, effective detection controls serve as the strongest deterrent to fraud. Simply put, when individuals think that an attempt at fraud will be detected, they are much less likely to attempt it.

Much of the focus in risk mitigation is on reducing the impact of a fraud event. The most common strategy for this is the implementation of controls designed to detect frauds sooner. For example, in addition to monthly account reconciliation, implementing a more frequent data mining procedure might result in earlier detection, thereby lowering the financial impact of the fraud.

Assume the Risk

Management can choose to assume or accept the risk if it determines that the likelihood of occurrence and the potential impact are low. Management might decide that it is more cost-effective to simply assume the risk than it is to eliminate the asset or exit the activity, buy insurance to transfer the risk, or implement countermeasures to mitigate the risk.

For example, the custodian of a petty cash fund has access to company funds, but the amount susceptible to embezzlement by the employee is limited to the amount in the fund, which is generally immaterial. And if the custodian is paid well, it is unlikely that she will be tempted by the small amount she could steal from the fund using bogus receipts. Consequently, management might choose to devote little, if any, effort to preventing such fraud.

Combination Approach

Management can also elect a combination of these approaches. For example, if the likelihood of occurrence and the impact of loss are high, management might decide both to transfer part of the risk through the purchase of insurance and to implement prevention and detection controls to mitigate the risk. In virtually all cases, some level of assumption (acceptance) of residual risk exists.

REPORTING THE RESULTS OF THE FRAUD RISK ASSESSMENT

The success of the fraud risk assessment process hinges on how effectively the results are reported and what the organization does with the results. A poorly communicated report can undermine the entire process and bring all established momentum to a halt. The report should be delivered in a style most suited to the language of the business. If management prefers reports to be given in succinct in-person presentations, the fraud risk assessment team should not deliver a 50-page printed document.

To maximize the effectiveness of the fraud risk assessment process, the team should remember several key points when developing the report of the results.

Report Objective, Not Subjective, Results

Much instinct and much judgment go into performing the fraud risk assessment. However, when reporting the results of the assessment, the team must remember to report only the facts and keep all opinions and biases out of the report. A report that includes the assessment team's subjective perspective dilutes and potentially undermines the results of the work.

Keep It Simple

The assessment results should be reported in a way that is easy to understand and that resonates with management. The reader of the report should be able to quickly view and comprehend the results. The goal of the report is to drive action, and a report that is overly complex or long risks being set aside or losing the reader – meaning no action is taken as a result of the assessment. For some readers, simple visuals, such as dashboards or heat maps, have the greatest effect.

Focus on What Really Matters

Less is often more when it comes to reporting the results of the fraud risk assessment. The team should take care not to turn the report into a laundry list of things that management has to sort through and prioritize. Instead, the report should focus on what really matters, clearly highlighting those points that are most important and that will make the most impact on the organization's fraud risk management efforts.

Identify Actions That Are Clear and Measurable

The report should include key recommendations for clear and measurable actions to address the organization's fraud risks. The actions should be presented in a way that makes apparent exactly what needs to be done. The report should not include vague recommendations or actions that will not reduce the risk of fraud. Additionally, management and those affected by the suggested actions should have vetted and agreed to them.

MAKING AN IMPACT WITH THE FRAUD RISK ASSESSMENT

To make the most of the fraud risk assessment process, management should not see the final report as the end of the process. The true value of a fraud risk assessment lies in how effectively and extensively management uses the results in its ongoing anti-fraud efforts.

Begin a Dialogue across the Company

The results of the fraud risk assessment can be used to begin a dialogue across the company that promotes awareness, education, and action aimed at reducing the risk of fraud. Engaging in an active dialogue is an effective way to further establish boundaries of acceptable and unacceptable behavior. Open communication about fraud risks also increases the chance that employees will come forward if they believe they witnessed fraud.

Look for Fraud in High-Risk Areas

An internal audit or investigative team within the organization can use the results of the fraud risk assessment to identify high-risk processes or activities and unusual transactions that might indicate fraud. This practice can also provide reassurance if the subsequent search for fraud reveals that, despite the assessed risk, fraud does not appear to be occurring at that point in time. Management should remember, however, that just because there is no evidence of current fraud, the risk that it could occur is not eliminated.

Hold Responsible Parties Accountable for Progress

It is often said that what gets measured gets done. To effectively reduce identified fraud risk, management must hold employees accountable for tracking and measuring progress against agreed-upon action plans. Publicly celebrating successes can be as (or more) effective at encouraging the right behaviors as providing negative consequences for failing to deliver results.

Keep the Assessment Alive and Relevant

Because there are so many factors that can affect an organization's vulnerability to fraud risk, management must ensure that the fraud risk assessment stays current and relevant. Someone within the organization should be assigned ownership of the fraud risk assessment process. That person or team should build processes to ensure that all changes in the business model, company operating environment, and personnel are considered relative to their impact on the company's risk of fraud.

Modify or Create the Code of Conduct, Ethics Policy, and Anti-Fraud Policy

The results of the fraud risk assessment can be extremely helpful in designing or redesigning the organization's code of conduct, ethics policy, and anti-fraud policy. By writing such policies with an eye toward the areas of the largest risk, management can be sure to include clear, appropriate guidance for employees who operate in those areas.

Monitor Key Controls

At the culmination of a fraud risk assessment, the organization should have a clear view of both the areas where the organization is susceptible to fraud and the controls that are designed and implemented to address those weak spots. To effectively manage the identified fraud risks, management should use the results of the fraud risk assessment to monitor the performance of key internal controls. Such proactive attention allows the identification and correction of deficiencies in control design or operation as quickly as possible.

NOTE

1. Committee of Sponsoring Organizations of the Treadway Commission and the Association of Certified Fraud Examiners, *Fraud Risk Management Guide*, 2016, p. 35.

CHAPTER 4

Preventing and Detecting Fraud

In all organizations, fraud will inevitably be attempted by one or more individuals, and in many organizations, at some point, at least one of those individuals will succeed. Thus, a holistic anti-fraud program includes mechanisms that address fraud before, during, and after it happens – that is, that prevent fraud from occurring, detect misconduct as soon as possible after it has been committed, and respond to any schemes that were perpetrated.

GOVERNANCE AND OVERSIGHT

The foundation for effectively fighting fraud lies in strong governance of the organization and its anti-fraud program. This includes the culture and tone set by management, as well as the organization's policies and the oversight thereof.

Creating an Anti-Fraud Culture

An organization's culture is embodied by how it operates – including its formal policies and procedures and whether those policies are taken seriously and are effectively enforced. An anti-fraud culture is rooted in ethics and compliance; it is a culture in which behavior and decision making at all levels (i.e., how things are done throughout the organization) are driven by the goal of doing the right thing. Consequently, a strong ethical culture is one of the most important anti-fraud mechanisms an organization can have, because it guides employees' responses to every organizational process or transaction. Additionally, employees are less likely to feel pressure to commit fraud or engage in misconduct in companies with a strong culture of ethics and compliance.

Hallmarks of an Effective Anti-Fraud Culture

A strong corporate culture is most often observed by its outcome, rather than by any individual component. Fostering an ethical culture runs deeper than just implementing a checklist of initiatives; similarly, a culture of corruption can exist even in companies that have policies that resemble good governance.

Nonetheless, cultures of ethics and compliance have certain hallmarks, such as:

- Open, transparent, and timely communication throughout the organization
- Management that:
  - Is held to a higher standard of ethics
  - Expects, models, prioritizes, and rewards ethical behavior and decision making

---

Portions of the material in this chapter also appear in the course material for the Association of Certified Fraud Examiners (ACFE) *Fraud Risk Management* and *Developing an Integrated Anti-Fraud, Compliance, and Ethics Program* seminars, as well as the *Internal Controls for Fraud Prevention* self-study course.

- Policies that are founded in the organization's core values
- Employees who feel comfortable and able to raise concerns or communicate bad news to management
- Certain, swift, and transparent responses to problems and violations

Warning Signs of an Unethical Culture

Conversely, the following are a few warning signs that might indicate that the organizational culture is not sufficiently ethics-focused and needs reevaluation:

- Disrespectful attitudes or bullying among peers
- Cliques, favoritism, or nepotism
- Low employee morale and lack of teamwork
- High absenteeism or turnover
- Large number of whistle-blower complaints, especially those reported anonymously
- Lack of response to employee questions, concerns, or suggestions about process improvements

Independent Oversight of Management

When management knows it is being overseen by a group (e.g., the board of directors and audit committee) that is actively watching for signs of fraud – such as management override of controls or inappropriate influence over the financial reporting process – it is less likely to engage in such acts. To reinforce the effectiveness of this function, those who compose the oversight body must be independent of management. An oversight body that consists of individuals who are beholden to management for any reason cannot effectively detect managerial misconduct.

Management Commitment

To help foster an anti-fraud culture, management should formalize its commitment to ethics in written form. This communication can be part of the organization's statement of values and principles, part of the foreword to the organization's code of conduct, or a separate short document, such as a letter provided to all employees, vendors, and customers. The statement of commitment should be disseminated widely (e.g., given to new hires during onboarding, published on the organization's website or in its newsletter) and should emphasize management's prioritization of the organization's ethical culture and anti-fraud program.

Tone at the Top

Executives must show not only through their words but also through their actions that dishonest or unethical behavior will not be tolerated. Accordingly, the board of directors and senior management must continuously display their commitment to ethics in their day-to-day actions and decisions. If an organization's leaders are unethical, lower-level employees are likely to exhibit the same type of behavior. Senior managers must know they are the foundation of the ethical culture within their organization; that is, they set the ethical tone for the entire organization, and the tone they set trickles down to all employees.

To ensure this ethical tone is effective, management must exude ethics and model the behavior that it expects from the staff. When members of management act as though they are above the law with respect to company policies, staff members are likely to resent the company's leaders and are less likely to follow the rules. However, when management acts ethically and openly follows organizational policies, the staff tends to respect and appreciate the behavior and emulate it. Additionally, executives should promote a strong organizational culture by projecting messages that reflect corporate responsibility and accountability.

Organizational leaders must also work to create an environment in which employees feel safe to challenge management's decisions or to speak up if they think something is wrong. Having a culture where people feel that management will listen to and address their concerns helps reduce the risk of fraud significantly because employees are able to deal with issues of stress or anger before they escalate to the point of misconduct or fraud.

Failure to set a proper tone at the top can have negative effects throughout the organization. If management rewards employees who get the job done regardless of how they do so, rather than ensuring they perform their job duties in an ethical manner, it sends the message that anything is acceptable to meet business goals.

Mood in the Middle

While a sound tone at the top is imperative to cultivating an ethical culture, in many organizations – especially large or geographically distributed companies – most employees rarely see the top executives. Consequently, middle managers play an important role in setting the proper ethical tone. Because they understand both the daily challenges faced by staff-level employees and the strategic and financial goals that the executives are charged with achieving, middle managers are the conduit between the upper and lower levels of the organization.

Just as the tone set by executives affects middle managers, actions by middle managers can have an impact on how their direct reports conduct themselves. If middle managers see that senior management has zero tolerance for unethical conduct, then they are more likely to display this same type of attitude, which then flows down to other employees. Thus, through their daily interactions with subordinates and each other, middle management's actions and attitudes are often among the most important factors in reinforcing – or undermining – the importance of ethics in the organization.

Buzz at the Bottom

Peer pressure can work in both positive and negative ways. Employees surrounded by peers committed to doing the right thing tend to follow suit; likewise, employees who witness their co-workers engaging in dishonest acts as a matter of business will be more likely to adopt the same approach. For example, if shipping employees are considering stealing merchandise from the warehouse, they are more likely to do so if they know that others in the organization are also behaving dishonestly. Similarly, if a senior salesperson regularly pays kickbacks to potential clients to land new sales contracts, then a junior salesperson who sees this practice will be more inclined to behave similarly.

Anti-Fraud Policy

As part of their overall corporate governance approach, most companies have an ethics policy or a code of conduct. However, having a separate anti-fraud policy makes these policies more robust, sends a strong message about management's intolerance of fraud, and allows employees to focus on what type of misconduct is permissible and what is not. Even though the specific contents of anti-fraud policies vary from company to company, every company should incorporate several key components to help ensure such policies are effective.

Policy Statement

An anti-fraud policy should formally define fraud and outline management's position or attitude toward fraud in the workplace. The message should be clear and concise, and senior management should strictly endorse it.

The policy statement might include straightforward messages, such as "Company executives, management, and the board of directors will not tolerate fraudulent behavior at any level within the organization. Anyone involved in a fraudulent act will face disciplinary action or termination."

Scope of the Policy

The anti-fraud policy should clearly state that it applies to everyone at all levels, from staff-level employees to executives.

Responsibility for Fraud Prevention and Detection

Management is ultimately responsible for fraud prevention and detection within the organization. However, management might delegate the day-to-day oversight of anti-fraud efforts to other individuals or bodies within the organization that have significant authority (e.g., the chief compliance officer or the director of internal audit). Consequently, the anti-fraud policy should clearly define oversight responsibility for fraud prevention and detection.

In addition, management must make employees aware that fraud prevention is a joint effort, and that everyone shares responsibility for preventing, detecting, and reporting instances of fraud. Where legally permissible, the policy should also include a statement informing employees that they are required to cooperate in any fraud investigations and that they have a duty to report any suspicious activity, and failure to do so could result in disciplinary action.

Actions Constituting Fraud

Anti-fraud policies should include specific examples of fraud. This helps prevent policies from being overly broad in nature, and thus difficult to enforce. The scope of fraud within an organization might range from internal theft of cash in small amounts to a third-party billing scheme worth millions. Regardless of the materiality of a fraud, management should include a high-level list of the types of fraud that could occur within the company. Doing so lays out specific guidance so employees can understand what actions constitute fraud, and provides management with the legal grounds to investigate and punish violators.

Examples of fraudulent offenses include:

- Personal use of company equipment (e.g., office supplies, company vehicles, cell phones, computers)
- Stealing company assets (e.g., cash, receivables, inventory)
- Inflating reported hours worked
- Forging or altering checks and other documents
- Disclosing proprietary information to competitors
- Accepting bribes from or paying bribes to vendors or customers
- Engaging in transactions in which the employee has an undisclosed conflict of interest
- Destroying company records with malicious intent
- Intentionally manipulating the financial statements

Management should assess the control environment within its own organization and identify specific areas and situations where fraud could occur. This assessment will help management determine which types of offenses to include in the anti-fraud policy.

Nonfraud Irregularities

In addition to explaining what acts constitute fraud, the anti-fraud policy can address allegations of personal improprieties or other irregularities – such as violations of company policy or interpersonal issues – and state which parties within the organization (e.g., departmental management or the human resources [HR] department) are responsible for resolving them.

Reporting Requirements and Procedures

The anti-fraud policy should state that if employees have concerns or observe suspicious activity, they should report it immediately through the proper channels so the appropriate parties can review the complaint and determine what further actions they should take. (See discussions on whistle-blower policy and whistle-blower helplines in the next section, "Whistle-Blower Policy," and later in this chapter for more information on creating and supporting reporting programs.)

Investigation Responsibilities

The anti-fraud policy should address who will investigate suspected irregularities, as well as to whom these irregularities should be reported (e.g., management, law enforcement, or legal counsel).

Authorization for Investigation

The policy should include a statement that whoever is in charge of the investigation has the authority to take control of and examine all records necessary to conduct the investigation. Management might want to consider including specific examples of items or documents that the fraud investigation team can search, review, or confiscate at any time during an investigation. Additionally, management should remind employees that their full cooperation is a requirement during an investigation.

Confidentiality

The anti-fraud policy should include a section describing the confidential nature of all fraud investigations undertaken. It should also state that neither management nor the fraud investigation team will disclose the investigation to outsiders except as required.

Disciplinary Action

To ensure an anti-fraud policy is effective, management should take a zero-tolerance stance and clearly state that it will not tolerate fraudulent conduct in any form. Employees should be aware of the disciplinary action they can expect for any fraudulent behavior.

If management defines the consequences of fraud, it is important that it follows through with disciplinary action. Any actions taken against employees should also be consistent. This will help dispel any feelings of partiality or favoritism among employees. This stance can have a significant deterrent effect. Employees with the opportunity to commit fraud might think twice before attempting to follow through with a scheme if they know what disciplinary action they will face; this can be especially true if they are aware that all previous perpetrators received the same punishment.

Whistle-Blower Policy

An effective anti-fraud program must also include a whistle-blower policy so employees, customers, vendors, and anyone else affiliated with the organization has a clear procedure for how to report suspected fraud and other forms of misconduct. Similar to the anti-fraud policy, having a specific whistle-blower policy conveys an important part of the message from the top. It can be a clause included in the anti-fraud policy or a separate policy altogether; many companies find that it is more visible as a separate policy and thereby demonstrates management's strong commitment. Regardless of the approach taken, documenting a whistle-blower policy communicates the importance management and the board place on the issue.

The policy should make clear that reporting unethical conduct is part of an employee's fiduciary duty. The policy should explicitly state that it applies to all employees, as well as outside parties, and should explain what actions these parties should take if they have knowledge of suspected fraud or misconduct.

The policy should also include information on:

- The available reporting mechanisms (e.g., helpline, online form, human resources, anonymous mailbox, etc.)

- The types of allegations individuals can and should report (e.g., suspected theft, non-compliance, violations of the code of ethics, etc.)
- Any incentives or rewards for reporting
- Information that is helpful or required when reporting (e.g., supporting documentation, names, dates of the alleged infractions, etc.)

Anti-Retaliation

The main purpose of the whistle-blower policy is to encourage reporting of unethical behavior without fear of retaliation. Employees are often concerned that if they report suspicious activities they will face repercussions. To encourage reporting of unacceptable behavior, these fears should be alleviated. Thus, the policy should clearly state that no employees will be retaliated against if they report an issue out of genuine concern, and that anyone who retaliates against them will be punished.

The provision should strictly ban any form of retaliation, including:

- Verbal abuse
- Denying raises or promotions
- Discharge
- Demotion
- Suspension
- Threats
- Harassment
- Failure to hire or rehire

A whistle-blower policy should explicitly state expectations for the treatment of whistle-blowers and the consequences for disobeying this policy. Punishment might include anything from conversational discipline to termination, depending on the severity of the behavior. This type of policy helps employees feel more comfortable sharing information that might otherwise be used against them, particularly when reporting unethical behavior of superiors. In addition, management should strictly endorse and enforce this policy. Employees who believe that anyone who retaliates against them will face punishment might be more comfortable raising their concerns.

Confidentiality of Reports

Management might also reassure employees that the information they report will remain confidential to the fullest extent possible. Even if the misconduct they report does not turn out to be fraud, employees should receive commendation for coming forward if they raised the issue out of genuine concern.

Good Faith Reporting

The policy should further explain that all reports of suspected misconduct must be made in good faith and based on reasonable grounds; allegations made maliciously or with knowledge of their falsity will not be tolerated.

RISK MANAGEMENT, INTERNAL CONTROLS, AND FRAUD

For many organizations, determining how to position the anti-fraud program within other organizational programs can be a challenge. The reality is that fraud overlaps with several other initiatives that organizations employ, such as risk management, internal controls, and compliance programs. While the anti-fraud program can benefit greatly from the resources and focus invested in these other areas, it's important for management to understand the similarities and differences among these programs.

Fraud and Risk Management

Following the 2008 recession, the public began to comprehend the negative effects of uncontained risk, which led to an increase in mainstream attention on the field of risk management. Among the numerous definitions of *risk management*, one of the most broadly recognized comes from the widely adopted suite of risk management standards published by the International Organization for Standardization (ISO), which defines risk management as "coordinated activities to direct and control an organization with regard to risk."[1]

Risk is the effect – positive or negative – of uncertainty on an organization's objectives. Risk management programs are generally designed to address several categories of risk:

- *Strategic risk* pertains to issues stemming from an organization's strategic plan and major initiatives, as well as resource-allocation risks associated with budgeting, business planning, and even organizational structure; this category also includes some external risks, such those related to competition, sociopolitical and technology changes, and macroeconomic factors.
- *Operational risk* focuses on hazards (e.g., natural disasters, etc.), information technology, physical assets, sales and marketing, sourcing distribution, and other value-chain matters, as well as risk pertaining to the organization's workforce, equipment and operational resources, and quality issues.
- *Financial risk* includes financial reporting risks (e.g., accounting, tax, etc.); risks involving market interest rate, foreign exchange, and other market risks; and issues involving liquidity and capital structure.
- *Compliance risk* includes all aspects of laws and regulations to which an organization is subject, such as trade and customs laws; health and safety, securities, environmental, and labor laws; as well as contractual issues, governance risks, and codes of conduct.
- *Reputation risk* manifests via market share and shareholder confidence.

While all risk cannot be avoided or controlled, it is beneficial to a company to mitigate as much risk as possible. Consequently, as part of its risk management program, management must gain a full understanding of the nature and extent of the organization's risks; determine what level and types of risks it is willing to accept, especially in light of the costs to control those risks; and implement countermeasures to address those it wants to mitigate. (Detailed information on the process for assessing and responding to fraud risks can be found in Chapter 3.)

What Type of Risk Is Fraud?

There is no universally correct way of including fraud within a risk classification system. Some organizations categorize fraud as a compliance risk, while others consider it a financial risk or an operational risk. There is one universally incorrect approach, however: completely omitting the risk of fraud from the organization's risk management process. Unfortunately, many risk management professionals tend to underestimate the role of fraud in – or even exclude fraud risks from – the scope of their professional duties.

Fraud Risk Management

As management teams increase their focus on risk, they should take the opportunity to consider, enact, and improve measures to detect, deter, and prevent fraud. This comprehensive approach – looking at fraud from a holistic perspective that includes proactive measures to assess the risk and address it before, during, and after it occurs – is embodied in the concept of fraud risk management. It's the natural evolution from fragmented programs that have focused on reacting to discovered incidents and ad hoc prevention programs based on past frauds.

The *Fraud Risk Management Guide*, published by the Committee of Sponsoring Organizations of the Treadway Commission (COSO) in collaboration with the Association of Certified Fraud Examiners (ACFE), describes fraud risk management as a process that involves five overarching principles:[2]

1. Establish a fraud risk management policy as part of organizational governance.
2. Perform a comprehensive fraud risk assessment.
3. Select, develop, and deploy preventive and detective fraud control activities.
4. Establish a fraud reporting process and coordinated approach to investigation and corrective action.
5. Monitor the fraud risk management process, report results, and improve the process.

When taken together, these five principles form a comprehensive framework for managing an organization's fraud risks.

Fraud and Internal Controls

As noted in the third principle in the COSO-ACFE fraud risk management framework outlined earlier, a significant part of an effective anti-fraud program is a system of internal control activities designed and implemented specifically to address the organization's fraud risks.

One of the most comprehensive definitions of internal control is found in the COSO *Internal Control – Integrated Framework*:

> *Internal control is a process, effected by an entity's board of directors, management, and other personnel, designed to provide reasonable assurance regarding the achievement of objectives relating to operations, reporting, and compliance.*[3]

According to this definition, the design of internal controls should be to assist management in meeting the following three categories of objectives:

1. Operations objectives, which pertain to the effectiveness and efficiency of the organization's operations
2. Reporting objectives, which pertain to the reporting of financial and nonfinancial information to internal and external parties
3. Compliance objectives, which pertain to the organization's adherence to applicable laws and regulations

As noted previously, fraud risk can affect each of these categories of objectives. Thus, an effective system of internal controls can and should greatly reduce an organization's vulnerability to fraud. No system of internal controls can fully eliminate the risk of fraud, but well-designed and effective internal controls can deter the average fraudster by reducing the opportunity to commit fraud.

Preventive versus Detective Controls

There are two main types of internal controls: preventive controls and detective controls. When designing internal controls, both types are needed in any organization since they attack errors and fraud from different perspectives.

Preventive controls are manual or automated processes, systems, policies, and procedures that are designed to prevent fraud before it occurs. Examples of these controls include:

- Employee fraud awareness training
- Background checks on employees (where permitted by law)
- Hiring policies and procedures
- Segregation of duties
- Dual authorization on transactions
- Security measures to limit access to physical assets or company data

Detective controls are designed and implemented to identify fraud that is occurring. Examples of detective controls include:

- A confidential reporting system, such as a whistle-blower helpline
- Independent account reconciliations, process reviews, and physical inspections and counts
- Data analysis and continuous monitoring techniques
- Surprise audits

Entity-Level versus Process- or Transaction-Level Controls

In addition to preventive and detective controls, organizations need both entitywide anti-fraud controls and targeted controls designed to prevent and detect specific fraud schemes within a certain process.

Entity-level controls apply across the organization, regardless of the process. Examples include a company's hiring practices, ethics and fraud awareness training, and general security features.

Process-specific controls focus on each activity vulnerable to a fraud risk. For example, controls implemented to control the risks within the procure-to-pay cycle (i.e., all the steps involved in making a purchase, from the purchase decision through reviewing and approving the vendor's invoices) represent process-specific controls.

Limitations of Internal Controls

Internal controls alone will not prevent and detect all fraud. Additionally, there are several inherent limitations that can reduce the effectiveness of even well-designed internal control systems:

- *Human error:* The effectiveness of preventive controls is limited by human error, which can result from errors in judgment, unclear or misunderstood instructions, distraction, incompetence, or carelessness.
- *Changes in operations or processes:* Changes in personnel or systems can result in breakdowns of internal controls. For example, downsizing might create a situation in which remaining employees are unaware of internal controls that were previously in place. Consequently, management might design internal controls that are effective initially, but it should ensure these controls are periodically updated to keep pace with a changing environment.
- *Circumvention:* Employees might look for ways to circumvent controls, particularly if the controls are new, cumbersome, or inconvenient.
- *Collusion:* Collusion occurs when an employee works with one or more other parties inside or outside the organization to circumvent controls. For example, an accounts payable clerk and an employee in charge of initiating electronic payments might collude to set up a fictitious vendor and then wire funds to that vendor's supposed bank account. According to the ACFE 2018 *Report to the Nations*, 49% of occupational fraud schemes involve multiple participants, and losses increase significantly as more people are involved in a scheme.
- *Management override:* Because management has primary responsibility for the design, implementation, and effectiveness of the internal control system, it is in a prime position to know how to manipulate the system to its advantage. That knowledge, combined with management's power to direct employees to carry out instructions, leaves the control system vulnerable to being overridden by management.

RESPONSIBILITIES FOR THE ANTI-FRAUD PROGRAM

Everyone in an organization plays a part in protecting the organization against fraud. However, the practical implementation of fraud risk management must start somewhere. To ensure the effectiveness of the anti-fraud program, the organization must have a team that is solely and explicitly responsible for executing, monitoring, and ensuring the success of the organization's anti-fraud initiatives. In assembling such a team, a cross-departmental approach is ideal because it incorporates a diverse skill set and holistic perspective into the team's initiatives. Thus, the team might consist of individuals from:

- Executive management
- The audit committee
- The investigations group
- The compliance function
- The controller's group
- Internal audit
- Information technology
- Security
- The legal department
- Human resources

However, the group should have a designated leader – such as the chief compliance officer or chief ethics officer – to guide the team and monitor achievement of its objectives.

Additionally, the team leader should clearly outline each member's role and responsibilities, and must set explicit expectations. Without clearly assigned fraud-related roles and responsibilities among parties overseeing the organization, the anti-fraud program runs the risk of being ineffective. The following discussion explores some of the specific responsibilities of various parties throughout the organization regarding fraud.

Board of Directors

For the anti-fraud program to be effective in both operation and design, it must be fully embraced by those charged with governing and overseeing the organization. If a board of directors exists, the board must be knowledgeable about the program and oversee its implementation. Specifically, the board of directors must recognize the organization's true and specific fraud risks, as well as their potential impact, and respond by:

- Setting an appropriate tone and realistic expectations of management to enforce an ethical anti-fraud culture
- Gaining a thorough understanding of the organization's activities and the environments in which it operates
- Developing a strategy to assess and manage fraud risks that aligns with the organization's risk appetite and strategic plans
- Ensuring fraud is a regular topic of discussion on the board's agenda
- Maintaining open communications with senior management and other personnel about the organization's fraud risks
- Making ethics a priority in decisions regarding hiring and firing members of the executive team (e.g., CEO, chief ethics and compliance officer [CECO], etc.)
- Proactively monitoring and evaluating the organization's anti-fraud, compliance, and ethics activities

Audit Committee

Many companies place their anti-fraud programs under the oversight of the audit committee. As a subgroup of the board of directors, the audit committee often oversees the organization's financial, accounting, and audit matters. As part of this responsibility, the committee must be active in assessing and monitoring the organization's fraud risks. This involves:

- Receiving regular updates on the status of reported or alleged fraud
- Being aware of fraud risks that are common in the organization's industry
- Meeting regularly with key internal parties (such as the chief audit executive or other senior financial staff) to discuss identified fraud risks and the steps being taken to prevent and detect fraud
- Understanding how internal and external audit strategies address fraud risk
- Providing external auditors with evidence of the audit committee's dedication to effective fraud risk management
- Engaging in candid conversations with external auditors about any known or suspected fraud
- Seeking advice of legal counsel whenever it deals with allegations of fraud

Executive and Senior Management

Senior management holds the primary responsibility for designing, implementing, monitoring, and improving the fraud risk management program. As part of this, management must:

- Be familiar with the organization's fraud risks:
  - o Perform a fraud risk assessment and update it regularly.
  - o Consider forming a risk management team within the organization to stay actively informed about emerging risks.
- Ensure that the organization has specific and effective internal controls in place to prevent and detect fraud.
- Set a tone at the top and monitor the company culture to ensure it appropriately supports the organization's fraud prevention and detection strategies. Senior management must exude ethics for staff to be inspired and feel obligated to follow suit.
- Clearly communicate, both in words and in actions, that fraud is not tolerated:
  - o Send regular communications to staff about the importance of ethics and controls.
  - o Conduct annual training on company policies and expectations.
  - o Discuss expectations at new-hire orientation to ensure that employees understand them from the beginning.
- Allocate adequate resources to anti-fraud initiatives and programs.
- Take seriously all reports of fraud, and undertake investigations for any such reports deemed reliable:
  - o Ensure open communication channels for reporting fraudulent activity.
  - o Ensure investigations are conducted for all allegations of fraud deemed reliable.
- Punish fraud perpetrators appropriately to reinforce the company's ethical culture and to emphasize the fact that fraud will not be tolerated.

- Take any steps necessary to remediate weaknesses that allowed frauds to occur.
- Report to the board of directors on a regular basis regarding the effectiveness of the organization's fraud risk management program.

Middle Management

While the tone senior management sets is important, in many cases – and especially in large or diverse organizations – employees follow the tone and the example set by their direct managers. Consequently, front-line management and middle managers are vital in creating a culture that supports the anti-fraud program. Specifically, middle managers can help ensure the effectiveness of the program by:

- Displaying ethical behavior and sound judgment
- Being approachable so their team members know they can turn to their supervisor with questions or concerns
- Helping conduct training
- Incorporating ethical considerations into performance goals and evaluations of team members
- Elevating issues to the executive management when appropriate

Internal Auditors

Part of the internal audit function's role is to evaluate and improve the effectiveness of the organization's risk management, control, and governance processes. Each of these organizational components – risk management strategies, internal controls, and governance processes – serves an important function in the fight against fraud.

According to the Institute of Internal Auditors' publication *IPPF – Practice Guide: Internal Auditing and Fraud*, during their audit engagements, internal auditors should:[4]

- Exercise professional skepticism – an attitude that includes a questioning mind and a critical assessment of audit evidence – in all audit work.
- Consider fraud risks in the assessment of internal control design and determination of audit steps to perform.
- Have sufficient knowledge of fraud to identify red flags indicating fraud might have been committed.
- Be alert to opportunities that could allow fraud, such as control deficiencies.
- Evaluate whether management is actively retaining responsibility for oversight of the fraud risk management program, whether timely and sufficient corrective measures have been taken with respect to any noted control deficiencies or weaknesses, and whether the plan for monitoring the program continues to be adequate for the program's ongoing success.
- Evaluate the indicators of fraud and decide whether any further action is necessary.
- Recommend an investigation when appropriate.

Additionally, depending on the organization's structure and the internal audit charter, the internal audit function might be explicitly responsible for investigating suspected fraud, analyzing factors that contributed to the occurrence of known fraud, recommending improvements to anti-fraud controls, monitoring incoming reports of suspected fraud, and providing ethics training for employees.

Risk and Control Personnel

Depending on a variety of factors (e.g., size and structure), an organization might have a separate risk and control group. In some cases, risk and control personnel report to each of the functional heads of the organization. Regardless of the reporting structure, when risk and control personnel are present, their responsibilities include identifying known and emerging fraud risks and assisting in the assessment of those risks. These personnel might also provide communication and education on fraud risks and responsibilities.

Staff Members

Fraud prevention and detection require the participation and commitment of every staff member. Employees at all levels need to understand that setting an example of appropriate behavior is not solely management's responsibility. Employees who regularly witness other employees exhibiting ethical behavior are less likely to go against the grain and commit violations – and are more likely to help maintain an ethical culture.

Consequently, all staff members should understand:

- What fraud is
- What red flags to watch for
- The expectation for ethical conduct
- Their roles within the organization's internal control and anti-fraud framework
- Potential compliance-, ethics-, and fraud-related issues regarding their specific positions
- How their job procedures help manage the organization's fraud risks
- How their own noncompliance with policies and procedures might create an opportunity for fraud to occur or go undetected
- How fraud affects everyone within the organization

In addition, staff at all levels, including management, should:

- Read, understand, and comply with all fraud-related policies and procedures (e.g., the anti-fraud policy, code of conduct, whistle-blower policy, procurement manuals, etc.).
- Act ethically and seek out guidance in making ethical decisions.
- Report any suspected or known incidences of fraud.
- Cooperate in investigations.

FRAUD CONTROL ACTIVITIES

As noted previously, one of the principles of effective fraud risk management is the implementation of preventive and detective fraud control activities. As discussed earlier, an effective anti-fraud program requires a balance of both preventive and detective controls, as well as entity-level and transaction-level controls.

The following discussion explores several best practices and common anti-fraud controls that help ensure the success of the organization's anti-fraud program. However, in determining which control activities should be included in the program, management must balance:

- Its understanding of the organization's fraud risks (i.e., the likelihood and impact) based on the fraud risk assessment
- Its risk appetite
- The resources (e.g., personnel, financing, technological) available to support the control
- Logistical, operational, or other limitations (e.g., geographic or regulatory challenges) to implementing the control
- The impact of the control on its operations

Personnel-Focused Controls

Some controls, such as the following, focus on supporting the organization's employees and providing programs that aim to mitigate the factors that can lead to fraud.

Whistle-Blower Program

A *whistle-blower* is a person who alerts someone in a position of authority to an instance of wrongdoing, such as unethical conduct, a legal violation, or fraud. An important gauge of the organization's ethical culture is how free employees feel to raise questions and concerns about the company's operations. Thus, a whistle-blower program that enables and encourages employees to submit information about known or suspected violations is an integral part of an anti-fraud program. According to the ACFE 2018 *Report to the Nations*, 40% of occupational frauds are uncovered by a tip, and more than half of those tips come from employees.

Consequently, an effective whistle-blower program:

- Helps proactively detect and address misconduct.
- Allows management to identify areas that might need improvement or areas where refresher training might be necessary.
- Provides evidence of a company's character and reinforces an ethical corporate culture.
- Enables management to uncover and address potential issues before regulators, the media, and/or law enforcement get involved.
- In some jurisdictions, ensures compliance with legal and regulatory requirements that require whistle-blower reporting mechanisms.

Reporting Mechanisms

When setting up a whistle-blower program, management should provide individuals with every possible means to report misconduct. The objective is to remove all possible barriers to reporting; a person with a concern should never feel as if there is no way to report it. Ideally, the whistle-blower program should include a variety of available reporting options that:

- Are free for the whistle-blower to use.
- Are easily accessible.
- Are available 24 hours a day, 365 days a year.
- Facilitate two-way communication with the reporting party.

The following are some common reporting methods organizations might provide:

- *Telephone:* A phone-based helpline or hotline is among the most popular reporting mechanisms used by organizations. According to the ACFE 2018 *Report to the Nations*, of the frauds uncovered by a tip made through a formal reporting mechanism, 42% were reported via a telephone hotline.
- *Email:* A dedicated email address provides a low-cost, easily accessible option for reporting concerns. Some individuals might prefer reporting their concerns using email so they have documentation to back up their claims if needed. However, whistle-blowers might also have concerns about confidentiality (due to the potential for tracing the sender's email address) and whether the recipient will forward their email reports.
- *Online form:* An online form is another relatively easy reporting option. Such a reporting mechanism can be managed internally or externally. If managed internally, the company must have security protocols in place so that no one within the company, such as the information technology group, can access the reports without the proper authority.
- *Postal mail:* A dedicated post office box or other mailing address can be another effective means for people to report concerns. If management includes mail as an option for reporting, a high-level independent party, such as the chief ethics and compliance officer or head of internal audit, should be responsible for opening all mail received to ensure uniform and appropriate handling of reports.
- *In-person reporting:* From an organizational perspective, management often prefers in-person reporting. Those responsible for receiving in-person reports can ask the whistle-blower specific questions to help determine how to proceed with the investigation. However, while this method provides the most information, it also is the most delicate; reporting parties are not always comfortable with in-person reporting because of confidentiality and sensitivity concerns. Consequently, all parties who might receive in-person reports must receive training to do so appropriately and sensitively, including instruction on whether and how to keep the reporter's identity as confidential as possible.
- *Suggestion box:* Many organizations provide employees a suggestion box for input about things that they believe the company should change or implement, such as

instituting flexible work options. Some employees might also see such a mechanism as an opportunity or means to report concerns related to potential acts of misconduct. While such a tool should not be the sole or primary whistle-blower reporting mechanism, the suggestion box might be helpful if used in conjunction with the other reporting methods mentioned.

Considerations in Implementation

Internally Managed versus Outsourced
Some companies use an outside vendor to manage the reporting mechanisms, while others manage the helpline using internal resources. Factors to consider in determining which approach is most effective include:

- Costs (e.g., training, operations, technology)
- Coverage (i.e., 24/7/365 or part-time)
- Accessibility
- Competency of individuals who staff the helpline
- Perception of trustworthiness and independence
- Desire and capability for anonymous reporting
- Effect on organizational processes

Support from Senior Management
To be effective, the whistle-blower program must be openly and fully supported by senior management. Company leadership should embrace whistle-blowers and understand what truly motivates them. While some whistle-blowers are bitter employees seeking revenge for some wrongdoing, most employees raise concerns because they are trying to do the right thing. The cost of ignoring reports from those acting ethically and responsibly is much greater than the cost of investigating reports from those acting vindictively. To help bolster the program, many organizations appoint someone on the executive management team to serve as a helpline champion; this individual has primary responsibility for overseeing the helpline's operation and setting up mechanisms to ensure incoming tips are appropriately acted upon.

Available to Internal and External Parties
Both internal and external parties should be able to access the helpline based on the mechanisms the company institutes. Some reporting mechanisms might be easier logistically for internal parties to access; nonetheless, external parties should have access to the helpline mechanisms established by the company (e.g., phone number, email, online reporting form, and mailing address).

Anonymity and Confidentiality
For the reporting mechanisms to be effective, whistle-blowers must have confidence that their reports will be handled sensitively. If potential whistle-blowers perceive that the information they want to report might be inappropriately communicated to others,

they will be less likely to report their concerns. Consequently, to the extent possible and legally permissible, whistle-blowers should have the following:

- The ability to file reports anonymously
- Assurance that their identity, if known, will be kept as confidential as possible

Publicizing the Helpline

Continued publicity of the helpline is critical to its success. To ensure all potential whistle-blowers are aware that the helpline exists and know how to use it, management should make proactive efforts to inform both employees and external parties (e.g., vendors, contractors, customers, competitors) about the helpline and related reporting resources.

The information conveyed should include:

- The importance of reporting improprieties
- How to make a report, including the types of mechanisms available to do so
- What happens when a person makes a report
- Assurance that anonymity will be respected, if desired (and where legally allowed)
- Assurance that all reports will be taken seriously and handled appropriately

Methods to publicize the helpline include:

- Posters, signs, and videos in common areas
- A dedicated website for information on the whistle-blower program
- Wallet cards for employees to carry with them
- Employee newsletters and communications from management
- Discussions during employee onboarding and ongoing training

Addressing International Differences

For companies with international operations, the whistle-blower program must accommodate issues that can arise regarding whistle-blowers in various jurisdictions. Considerations that might affect international whistle-blower programs include:

- *Legal and regulatory issues:* Some jurisdictions have legal and regulatory restrictions that can affect how the reporting program operates (e.g., those governing data privacy and prohibiting anonymous complaints).
- *Language barriers:* All employees, no matter where they reside, should be able to report misconduct in their native language. Those responsible for receiving inbound reports need to be fluent both in the whistle-blower's native language and in the language spoken by the parties who need the information provided in the report; thus, professional interpreters might be necessary to appropriately handle incoming tips. In addition, the helpline awareness and training efforts might need to be translated into all relevant languages.
- *Cultural differences:* Different cultures have different communication styles and behavioral nuances – even different interpretations of the concept of whistle-blowing.

Consequently, to help ensure cultural differences are effectively addressed in the whistle-blower program, management should work with program stakeholders in the relevant jurisdictions during the development of the program.

- *Accessibility of reporting mechanisms:* Infrastructure, technology, or other logistical issues might also present accessibility concerns in certain jurisdictions. For example, international phone calls might be cost-prohibitive, or Internet access might not be reliable, which can make reporting challenging or even impossible. If such factors are a concern in jurisdictions in which the company has operations, management might need to provide additional resources to support whistle-blowers in those regions.

Creating a Culture of Whistle-Blower Support

Many whistle-blowers report becoming ostracized, being fired or demoted, losing friends, damaging their professional reputation, and even suffering physical harm following their decision to provide information about potential fraud or misconduct. As a result, even in organizations with robust ethical cultures, most whistle-blowers still fear the risk of retaliation – whether real or perceived. To combat this apprehension, management must commit to fostering an environment where employees feel comfortable escalating concerns.

In support of such an environment, companies should have a standard approach or procedure once an employee reports a concern. One way to do this is to follow up with employees who did not report anonymously and let them know the outcome of the investigation. This shows that management takes whistle-blower reports seriously, which can help ease concerns about potential retaliation. Creating this type of culture within the organization not only reduces management's chances of liability, but also empowers employees to report instances of misconduct.

Anti-Retaliation Stance

The foundation of an effective whistle-blower program is a strong, clear, and meaningful stance by management against any form of retaliation. As discussed earlier in the section on the whistle-blower policy, this stance should be rooted in an anti-retaliation policy that assures employees and third parties that they can report their concerns about potential misconduct without fear of retaliation. However, like any policy, the anti-retaliation clause will be effective only if it is enforced. Consequently, management must make clear that there is zero tolerance for any form of retaliation against individuals who report concerns. If management discovers any retaliation, it must take swift action to address the situation in a transparent way. A whistle-blower program that does not immediately address retaliation concerns will fail.

Rewards for Whistle-Blowers

While many people report concerns because they feel it is the right thing to do, others are reluctant to come forward without some kind of acknowledgment or reward. As part of the whistle-blower program, management should consider whether and how best to provide incentives to individuals who supply information that leads to uncovering misconduct.

The appropriate incentive depends on the organization, the whistle-blower, and the allegation reported. Monetary rewards motivate some whistle-blowers. Some prefer a private, personal message of gratitude from management. For others, more public recognition, such as an appreciatory lunch with the CEO or acknowledgment at a company meeting, is sufficient.

To help prevent anyone from taking advantage of the incentive program by filing false reports, management must make it clear that anyone who reports wrongdoing will receive a reward only if an investigation reveals that an actual act of fraud or misconduct did occur.

Recognizing Known Whistle-Blowers

Publicly recognizing known whistle-blowers (if they consent) can illustrate a commitment to acknowledging and supporting whistle-blowers. By providing information about how it handled tips and the outcomes of the cases, management sends the message that it takes incoming reports seriously and responds transparently and appropriately. If the reporting party consents to revealing his identity, holding that individual out as a beacon of the organization's values can negate concerns of potential retaliation, and reinforces management's focus on ethics and support for whistle-blowers.

Open-Door Policy

An open-door policy that allows employees to speak freely about pressures can provide management with the opportunity to alleviate such pressures before they become acute, which helps prevent fraud and misconduct. If employees and others know they can speak freely to their supervisors, they might be more willing to discuss the personal and professional issues that could lead to illicit actions if not dealt with properly. Additionally, managers have more opportunities to understand the pressures employees face and might be able to eliminate them before they become acute.

Going a step further, rather than waiting for employees to come to them, managers might reach out to employees and ask them how their days are going. This can go a long way in putting employees at ease, which can help increase their comfort in sharing concerns and challenges with management without the fear of retaliation.

Support for Employees with Ethical Dilemmas

Some employees lie, cheat, and steal even when they know doing so is unethical, but many otherwise trustworthy employees can benefit from a program that provides guidance on what is right and wrong specific to the business activities of the organization.

Guidance on How to Solve Ethical Dilemmas

Since an organization's ethics policy and code of conduct cannot address every possible situation that might present a moral dilemma, it can be beneficial to provide resources to help employees determine whether an action is ethical. Some tools and resources include:

- An online portal dedicated to ethics and compliance issues
- A list of frequently asked questions (FAQ) regarding the code of ethics and other ethical situations employees commonly face
- A mechanism to contact someone on the compliance and ethics team for additional guidance or support
- An ethics checklist that can be used to walk through options in an ethically challenging situation, including questions such as:
  - What are the possible consequences of my choices?
  - What written rules govern my behavior?
  - Are the rules related to this action appropriate when applied to all people, all the time?
  - How does this decision affect the general balance of good versus evil?
  - What if everyone acted in this manner?
  - Does this action respect the rights of everyone involved?
  - Does this action represent the character strengths I value?
  - Would I be ashamed if others found out what I did?
  - Could I justify this action to my family?

Employees can use these resources to make assessments as they perform their jobs. Management should present these types of resources to employees during ethics training, and let them know that they can discuss any questions or concerns confidentially with an unbiased adviser through the company's helpline.

Employee Support Programs

Many progressive companies and agencies are realizing the benefits of employee support programs, such as assistance in dealing with alcohol and drug abuse, as well as counseling for gambling, family and marital problems, and for financial difficulties. Such programs provide employees with independent support for personal situations that might lead to ethical challenges or lapses. They are also an effective anti-fraud tool because they provide employees with the guidance necessary to help ease their personal burdens and redirect their energies toward more productive ways to solve their problems.

Hiring Processes

A successful anti-fraud program begins during the hiring process. Hiring just one unethical person can corrupt an entire team, process, or even the entire organization. While due diligence in hiring does not prevent all fraudulent acts by employees, it both communicates the company's ethical stance to hopeful job applicants and helps ensure that known thieves do not enter the organization through its front door.

Set Clear Expectations from the Start

The job posting is often the candidate's first exposure to the organization and the hiring process. This makes it an ideal time to set the ethical expectations for job candidates. Thus, the job posting should:

- Assert the organization's values and commitment to ethics.
- State that the company is looking for qualified candidates who embody these traits.
- Note openly that the organization conducts background and reference checks as a prerequisite for hiring.

Conduct Background Checks

Every position carries the risk of the employee engaging in fraud or other professional misconduct. Consequently, for virtually all employee positions, employers should conduct a pre-employment background check (where and to the extent permitted by law) on the final candidate for the job.

When assessing individuals for hire, employers should conduct as many of the following background checks as possible, applicable, and legally permissible:

- Work history
- Educational history
- Certification and license verification
- Criminal and civil records

Certain positions might merit additional screening. For example, candidates for positions involving access to cash, company bank accounts, credit card numbers, high-value inventory, or any other easily stolen or highly valuable assets should be subject to credit checks, where legally allowed. Management can use this information to compare the candidate's known debt to the expected salary for the position; large gaps between the individual's income and financial demands might result in a pressure to engage in unethical activities. Other potential types of screening management might consider, depending on the company and position, include drug screening and motor vehicle reports.

Check References

As part of the application process, most applicants supply professional references and provide permission for the hiring organization to contact them. If a candidate fails or refuses to provide such references when applying for a position, management should determine the reason; if the reason provided is lacking or questionable, it might be a warning sign against hiring the individual.

When checking a candidate's references, the hiring manager should speak directly to the candidate's previous direct supervisor if possible. In addition to confirming the applicant's employment details (e.g., dates of employment, job title, duties), where legally permissible, the person checking references should ask whether:

- The candidate had any disciplinary or performance issues, such as:
  - Dishonesty
  - Excessive tardiness or absenteeism
  - Discord with team members
  - Failure to follow directions or expected procedures
  - Violations of company policies or code of conduct
- The reference would recommend this individual for this position.
- The reference would hire this individual again.

For supervisory or management positions, the hiring manager might also request the names of previous direct reports to use as additional references. This can help provide information on the candidate's managerial style and the type of tone the candidate set for the team.

Consider Applicable Legal Requirements and Restrictions

While the previously discussed practices serve as important fraud prevention mechanisms, management must be mindful of the laws that govern the hiring process when determining which practices to incorporate into its processes. Some countries have stricter laws regarding what information companies can obtain about a potential hire. In addition, many jurisdictions have laws that prohibit discrimination against job candidates based on race, religion, gender, nationality, age, or disability; such laws also restrict the types of questions hiring managers can or should ask during candidate interviews. Consequently, the hiring manager should work closely with the human resources and legal teams to ensure that personnel follow proper procedures when hiring employees both locally and internationally.

Reasonable Performance Goals

Management must distinguish performance goals that motivate employees to push themselves from those that are so aggressive that the only way employees can meet them is to perpetrate fraud. When employee compensation, bonuses, or job security is tied to unachievable performance goals, employees often think up creative – or fraudulent – approaches to meeting them.

Moreover, including ethics-based metrics – those that focus on how employees perform their duties, not just how much business they do – as a component of performance goals and evaluation can be an effective way to foster ethical behavior and reinforce the importance of ethics as the guiding factor in making business decisions.

Employee Anti-Fraud Training

Properly trained employees are one of the best defenses against fraud. Preventing fraud requires ensuring that employees, managers, and those charged with governance understand how fraud affects the organization and their roles in fighting it. Consequently, the anti-fraud program must include robust, comprehensive anti-fraud training.

Developing the Training Content

To be successful, anti-fraud training must connect with the entire audience. While it might be tempting to purchase an off-the-shelf training package from an outside provider, generic training is typically less effective in improving employees' ethics or commitment to helping prevent and detect fraud than content customized for the organization. The training program should also do more than just inform employees about the specific rules they must comply with. If the goal of the program is to reinforce the anti-fraud program, it must provide employees with information on how and why to engage in honest and ethical behavior.

Additionally, those charged with developing the training content should work closely with the individuals responsible for the success of the anti-fraud program to ensure the training reflects the organization's specific fraud risks, operations, and circumstances.

Identifying the Target Audience

Employee training is expensive, and selecting the right participants is important to the program's success. It would be unwise to implement an organizationwide training effort that does not concentrate resources where they are needed most.

As a rule, participation in the training program should be requisite for every employee within the organization. No individuals – regardless of their positions – should be exempt from receiving an initial orientation and ongoing anti-fraud education. However, to conduct this training in the most cost-effective manner, management should consider which portions of the training are best for every person in the organization, and which portions are most appropriate for specific, targeted groups.

Organizationwide Training
Management should deliver some anti-fraud training content uniformly to employees throughout the organization. Generally, this includes material on:

- Management's overall stance and emphasis on workplace ethics
- Information about the organization's ethics and anti-fraud policies
- What fraud is and what it is not
- How fraud hurts the organization
- How fraud hurts employees
- How to identify fraud and red flags to watch for
- How to report suspected wrongdoing
- The punishment for dishonest acts
- Sources of additional information about or help with ethical decisions

Ensuring every staff member receives the same information on these topics helps form a solid foundation for the other material presented as part of the training program.

Segmented or Targeted Training

While some training content is appropriate and necessary for all employees, other forms of training might benefit only employees whose positions might require such knowledge. Likewise, management should present certain portions of organizationwide content in a way that connects the information to the specific circumstances faced by employees in different positions and areas. For example, educating warehouse employees about financial statement fraud would not be effective because their exposure to this risk is likely minimal. Providing training on irrelevant topics not only wastes organizational time, but can also reduce the overall impact of the training because employees might lose interest in the messaging or feel as though the training program does not apply to their roles.

Depending on the audience, the targeted training might include sections discussing:

- Conflicts of interest
- Bribery, corruption, gifts, and gratuities
- Protecting company information and data
- Cybersecurity
- Antitrust and competition issues
- Insider trading
- Government contracting issues and fraud risks
- Compliance with specific laws and regulations (e.g., anti-money-laundering regulations)

Management can also incorporate some ethics and anti-fraud training topics into other company training sessions. For example, training about the vendor contracting process should also include information about unacceptable practices such as bribery and about compliance with the relevant anti-corruption regulations.

Training for Executives and Managers

In addition to the information presented to all employees, managers and executives should receive special training that addresses the additional fraud prevention and detection responsibility – and ability – provided by their positions of authority.

Executives typically have the power to commit the most devastating frauds. According to the 2018 *Report to the Nations*, frauds committed by executives are more than five times larger than those committed by managers, and 17 times larger than those committed by employees. Further, dishonesty and unethical conduct displayed by those in executive positions can cause a ripple effect throughout the organization, leading to a breakdown in the corporate culture. To help protect against these damaging circumstances, executives should receive specialized – and disproportionate – ethics and anti-fraud training. This training should cover any executive-specific policies, as well as the crucial role and specific responsibilities those in leadership positions have for building, reinforcing, and publicizing the organization's commitment to ethics and an anti-fraud culture. Additionally, having the executive team be the first employees to complete the training sends a strong message about the training program's importance to the rest of the staff.

Middle managers also deserve special attention when it comes to anti-fraud training. Department managers should be trained in the specific warning signs and prevention and detection methods pertinent to their department's functions. For example, purchasing managers should be well versed in the red flags of bribery schemes, while controllers should understand just how important their vigilance is in preventing and detecting fraudulent disbursements.

Choosing Appropriate Training Methods

Formal anti-fraud training can take many forms, including live, in-class instruction; recorded video or animated courses; or interactive self-study programs. Of these options, a live class is preferable because it allows employees the opportunity to participate, interact with other employees, discuss fraud risks at the organization, and seek and provide feedback regarding the fraud risk management program overall. Integrating games and role-playing exercises into the training curriculum can make the course more enjoyable – and thus more effective – for participants.

As messages from an employee's direct supervisor often carry the most weight with an employee, the concept of cascading training can be an effective means of anti-fraud education. In cascading training, managers are tasked with and specifically educated on how to provide anti-fraud training to their own staff. This allows training to be customized to each team's respective needs, and for the message to come directly from the team's leader.

Perhaps most important is that the training be based on the realities of the organization rather than on generic anti-fraud messages. While providing general information is good and necessary, doing so without addressing the specific concerns of the company or providing employees with practical knowledge and ideas to apply will render the training program ineffective.

Determining the Training Frequency

Like any educational efforts, frequent exposure is the key to ensuring that employees absorb and apply the information provided during the anti-fraud training. Rather than a one-time exercise, the training program should be an ongoing process that begins at the time of hire. Employees should also participate in refresher training at least annually to help keep the program alive and ingrained in their minds. In addition, management should provide additional training for employees when there is a policy change or in response to a real or potential breach.

Considering Other Factors

Other factors in designing the training program include language and culture, education levels, exposure to potential fraud, timing, and geographic considerations. Because employee training should be tailored to the ethical culture and anti-fraud stance of the organization, it is best to have local managers – those within the organization's specific jurisdiction(s) – either conduct the training or have input into the training program.

Reinforcing the Training

Repetition aids learning. Continual exposure to anti-fraud messaging reinforces the information presented during the formal training program. Management should use informal means – such as periodic newsletters, posters in break rooms, postings on the company intranet, and other casual reminders – to reinforce its anti-fraud stance and keep fraud prevention and detection at the front of employees' minds.

Mandatory Time Off and Rotation of Job Duties

Many fraud schemes flourish because the same person is responsible for the same part or parts of a process. Staff members who frequently work long hours and rarely take time off might be diligent employees; however, they might also be doing something that they do not want anyone else to be aware of. Requiring that an employee take her annual leave time allows another employee to take over for a short period. This can present an opportunity to uncover any procedures that are not being followed properly – whether erroneously or as a part of a fraud scheme. Similarly, periodically rotating job functions of key employees is another anti-fraud measure employers can take – and it comes with the added benefit of having cross-trained employees who can fill in when needed.

Exit Interviews

Exit interviews are an opportunity for employees to give honest feedback as they are departing the company. Consequently, they provide a valuable opportunity for management to obtain candid information about ethical issues, blind spots, and areas vulnerable to fraud.

During exit interviews, the party conducting the interview (e.g., HR) should ask the employees:

- Why they are leaving the company
- Whether they received adequate training regarding the company's ethics and anti-fraud policies
- Whether their co-workers, supervisors, and management adhered to the company's ethics and anti-fraud policies
- Whether they know where and how to report any suspected or known fraud or other misconduct
- Whether there are any unresolved ethical issues related to the positions they are leaving
- Whether they have knowledge about any unresolved ethical issues in general

The interviewer should also follow up with additional questions on any responses that indicate potential issues. If conducted effectively, exit interviews can provide management with a wealth of knowledge that can help assess the culture – and the related fraud risks – of specific departments and the organization as a whole.

Process- and Policy-Focused Controls

Other controls focus on creating processes and setting policies that address the factors that can lead to fraud.

Separation of Duties

The premise behind separation of duties (also called *segregation of duties*) is that more than one person should be required to fully complete a task within the organization. In other words, critical functions of a key process should be dispersed to more than one person or one department. Because multiple individuals have visibility into transactions, separating duties prevents any one person from having the ability to both commit and conceal fraud, and helps ensure that errors, noncompliance, and fraud are caught quickly.

Effective separation of duties involves dividing the following functions among different parties:

- Authorization
- Recording or record keeping
- Custody of assets
- Reconciliation

Properly separating these duties can help reduce the opportunity for fraud. For example, if one employee has custody of an asset as well as responsibility for the related record keeping of that asset, that person has an opportunity to both steal the asset and cover up the crime in the records. Likewise, the individual responsible for setting up new employees in the payroll system should be independent of the person who processes payroll; if one person were responsible for both duties, it would be easy for that individual to create a fictitious employee and issue fraudulent paychecks to the fraudster's own account.

Separation of duties can be a challenge for smaller companies with strained resources and a limited number of personnel. Greater day-to-day involvement and additional review by management, the board of directors, or third parties (e.g., an external auditor) can serve as a compensating control in such situations. Rotation of duties among existing personnel can also help compensate for inadequate separation of duties.

Physical Security

Physical safeguards should be in place to protect the assets of an organization from theft or destruction. The types and extent of controls needed to physically protect an asset are driven by the value of the asset and its susceptibility to theft or loss. Examples of physical access controls include the use of safes, lockboxes, locks on doors and filing cabinets, security guards, security alarms, employee ID badges, and surveillance cameras.

Electronic Access Controls

Just as safeguards are important for protecting physical assets, electronic safeguards should be used to protect both data and electronic access to company funds. Such security measures can guard access to overall systems or specific applications. Examples of electronic security controls include:

- Passwords and security questions
- Access restriction based on employee role or profile
- File transfer restrictions and monitoring

Proactive Audit Policy

A proactive audit policy means that the organization's auditors aggressively seek out possible fraudulent conduct instead of waiting for reports to come to their attention. As part of this approach, the audit team might incorporate the following into their audit plans:

- Use targeted analytical reviews designed to identify red flags of fraud.
- Ask employees specifically about fraud.
- Conduct surprise audits where possible.

Reviews and Reconciliations

Regular reviews and reconciliations can be a timelier method of detecting fraud than audits. Monthly reviews of certain accounts enable management to examine unusual balances or activity, which might lead to identifying potential red flags of fraud.

Reconciliations between records and assets should be performed as often as possible, taking into account the risk profile of the asset involved. For example, low-activity bank accounts are frequently reconciled monthly, while some organizations perform daily reconciliations of payments from high-activity accounts. Similarly, while it can be cost-prohibitive to perform a full inventory count more than once a year, certain inventory items (e.g., those of high value or those more susceptible to theft) might be reconciled more frequently.

Proactive Data Monitoring and Analysis

According to the ACFE 2018 *Report to the Nations*, 37% of organizations use proactive data monitoring and analysis as part of their anti-fraud programs. Additionally, organizations that proactively monitor or analyze their data for warning signs of fraud catch frauds more than twice as quickly and suffer fraud losses that are 52% less than organizations that do not use such an initiative.

As part of a system of anti-fraud controls, data analytics and continuous monitoring should focus on identifying anomalies that might reveal one or more of the following:

- The perpetration of a fraud scheme (the initial steps taken when an individual commits a fraud)
- The concealment of a fraud scheme (often, steps taken to conceal a fraud are distinct from those taken to commit the fraud, and may occur subsequent to the perpetration)
- The override or improper application of a preventive or detective internal control (e.g., analytics aimed at identifying whether a particular control is functioning as intended, such as a manager's review and approval of transactions)
- The effect of a fraud (e.g., an inventory shortage, a discrepancy in an account balance, etc.)

A library of anti-fraud data analytics tests that can be used to help identify various fraud schemes is available at www.acfe.com/fraudrisktools-tests.aspx. While the specific analytic tests that can be performed are dependent on the availability of the data, the format of the data, and the functionality of the software used, many data analysis software programs are robust enough that tests for the majority of identified fraud risks can be designed and continuously run to help identify potential fraud.

To be most effective, any data monitoring or analysis initiatives should be based on the results of the fraud risk assessment. In other words, the organization should design data analytics tests and monitoring procedures to support their targeted, risk-based approach to fighting fraud. Running various tests on different data without connecting the tests to a specific fraud risk – and thus identifying what specific data is related to that risk and what types of anomalies to look for – can result in not only wasted resources, but also missed red flags that might indicate a fraud scheme.

Perception of Detection

For most individuals, the fear of getting caught is enough to deter crossing the line into fraud; even individuals who feel sufficient pressure and have rationalized the act in their minds will likely not cross the line if they believe they cannot do so without being noticed. Consequently, increasing the perception of detection might well be the most effective fraud prevention method. Controls do little good in preventing theft and fraud if potential perpetrators are unaware of the presence of controls in an organization. For example, the internal audit team routinely conducts targeted reviews of employee expense reports for signs of fraud, but employees are not aware of this scrutiny; such a control might be helpful in detecting falsified expense reports but will likely not prevent employees from attempting to defraud the company. In contrast, visible surveillance cameras aimed at a retail operation's point-of-sale registers – regardless of whether they are actively recording – can help deter theft from the registers.

Examples of Scheme-Specific Control Activities

The anti-fraud program should include targeted control activities to help mitigate the fraud risks identified as part of the fraud risk assessment. The following are some examples of scheme-specific controls that might be used to prevent and detect various fraud risks.

Internal Controls to Address the Risk of Theft of Incoming Cash

Controls to help prevent and detect schemes involving the theft of incoming cash (i.e., skimming and cash larceny) include the following:

- Post signs offering a discount to any customers who do not receive a receipt for their purchase.
- Use surveillance cameras or other monitoring mechanisms in areas where handling of cash takes place.
- Perform surprise cash counts.
- Require management approval for voids, refunds, and other no-sale transactions.
- Deposit cash daily and itemize deposit slips.
- Place any cash funds in a time-lock safe.

- Do not keep excessive amounts of cash on hand.
- Use point-of-sale registers that have adequate security features, such as access controls and a management override key for voids and returns.
- Require unique logins for each person who can access the register.
- Mail monthly customer statements.
- Require mandatory vacations and rotation of duties for personnel in accounts receivable functions, and cross-train employees so someone else can fill in.
- Require management approval for:
  ○ Changes to the accounts receivable master file.
  ○ Write-offs and discounts to accounts receivable.
  ○ All accounts to be sent to a collection agency.
- Periodically scan journal entries for illogical debits used to balance accounts receivable.
- Monitor accounts receivable for an unusually high number of write-offs, debits, or overdue accounts.

Internal Controls to Address the Risk of Accounts Payable and Cash Disbursement Fraud

Accounts payable and cash disbursement schemes are occupational frauds in which the perpetrator illegally or improperly causes the distribution of funds in a way that appears to be legitimate. Common variations of these schemes include billing schemes and payment tampering schemes. The following are some examples of controls for preventing and detecting these schemes:

- Separate the duties of accounts payable processing, vendor master file maintenance, vendor payment, and bank reconciliation.
- Separate the requisition, purchasing, and receiving functions.
- Require mandatory vacations of employees in the purchasing and accounts payable functions, and cross-train others to fill in for these positions.
- Use physical and software controls to restrict access to the accounts payable and cash disbursements systems, including access to banking software.
- Restrict access to the vendor master file, and flag any changes to the file.
- Periodically purge the vendor master file to maintain only active approved vendors.
- Periodically cross-check the vendor master file against the employee master file to identify matching addresses or other contact information.
- Maintain an approved vendor list independent of the purchasing department.
- Use a payables system that checks for duplicate payments or multiple payments to the same vendor in one day.
- Require proper authorization of all transactions.
- Require original invoices and other documentation for all payments; do not pay from summary statements alone.
- Require that invoices be matched to purchase orders and receiving reports prior to issuing payment.
- Request bank notification if a duplicate payment on an organizational account is pending posting.
- Require dual approval when a new vendor is set up for electronic payment.

Internal Controls to Address the Risk of Payroll Fraud

The following are examples of controls that can help address the risk of payroll fraud:

- Separate payroll functions from human resources functions (e.g., hiring and maintaining personnel records), general accounting functions (e.g., payroll bank account reconciliation), and treasury functions (e.g., funds transfers from the general account to the payroll account).
- Separate the functions of timekeeping, approval of time cards, payroll preparation, direct deposit authorization, and funds transfers.
- Use physical and software controls to prevent unauthorized access to payroll applications and data files.
- Use physical and software controls to prevent unauthorized access to personnel files.
- Require mandatory vacations of employees in the personnel and payroll functions, and cross-train others to fill in for those positions.
- Ensure that adequate authorization, approval, and documentation procedures are followed regarding changes in employment, salaries and wage rates, and payroll deductions.
- Match the payroll against personnel files every pay period to ensure there are no unauthorized names.
- Require supervisors to verify the time worked by each of their employees.
- Require authorization in advance for overtime and paid time off.

Internal Controls to Address the Risk of Expense Reimbursement Fraud

The following are examples of controls that can help prevent and detect expense reimbursement fraud:

- Establish clear policies and procedures regarding travel and entertainment expenses, including the types of expenses that are reimbursable and limits on reimbursable expenses.
- Require that expense reports be submitted within a certain amount of time from the date on which the expense was incurred.
- Require original receipts for all expense reimbursements, including items paid for by credit card.
- Require the submission of detailed expense reports before issuing any reimbursement. At a minimum, require the following information:
  - An explanation for the expense, including the specific business purpose
  - The time and date of the expense
  - The location of the expenditure
  - A list of attendees for any meals or entertainment expenses
  - The amount of the expense
- Require supervisors' review and approval of expense reports before they are paid. A direct supervisor will be most familiar with the employee's work and travel schedules and, therefore, will be in the best position to spot fraud.

Internal Controls to Address the Risk of Misappropriation of Physical Noncash Assets

The following are examples of controls that can help to prevent and detect the theft or misuse of the organization's inventory or fixed assets:

- Maintain physical security over high-value items.
- Secure the perimeter of buildings containing at-risk assets, and install surveillance cameras in vulnerable areas.
- Implement access controls over computerized inventory and accounting systems.
- Perform surprise inventory counts.
- Require approval for adjustments to inventory records, including write-downs.
- Require authorization for scrap sales.
- Ensure proper separation of record keeping, custody, and authorization functions.
- Require mandatory vacations for employees with inventory responsibilities, and cross-train others to fill in for those positions.
- Test for unusual inventory shrinkage using analytical procedures, ratios, and other types of relationship tests.
- Create and communicate a policy on personal use of company fixed assets.
- Attach identification tags to fixed assets, and track them in an up-to-date list.
- Require authorization for fixed asset purchases, improvements, and retirements, and for additions to and deletions from fixed asset accounts.
- Update access codes and locks when employees resign or are terminated.
- Perform a periodic fixed asset count, and reconcile it to the fixed asset records.

Internal Controls to Address the Risk of Misappropriation of Investment Assets

Examples of controls that can help address the risk of investment schemes include:

- Hold securities in the organization's name, when possible.
- Maintain a current list of all investments held by the organization, including a record of expected income payments.
- Require authorization by the board of directors, or other appropriate party for investment transactions.
- Implement proper separation of duties by separating the authorization of transactions, the execution of transactions, the record keeping function, and the custody function.
- Maintain proper access controls over investment accounts and accounting and banking software.
- Perform periodic reconciliations of investments.

Internal Controls to Address the Risk of Corruption

Because many bribery and corruption schemes are similar to payables and disbursements schemes, the controls discussed previously relating to payables and disbursements fraud are often also effective in preventing and detecting these corruption schemes.

In addition, the International Organization for Standardization (ISO) created a standard for anti-bribery management systems, ISO 37001.[5] The framework described in

ISO 37001 is designed to help organizations establish, implement, maintain, and improve anti-bribery compliance programs across borders. Compliance with ISO 37001 is voluntary; to fully comply with ISO 37001, an organization must take the following steps:

- Implement an anti-bribery policy and program, communicating these to all relevant personnel and business associates (including joint venture partners, subcontractors, suppliers, and consultants).
- Appoint a compliance manager to oversee the policy and program.
- Provide anti-bribery training and guidance to employees.
- Perform an assessment of bribery risks, including conducting necessary due diligence on third parties.
- Ensure controlled organizations and third parties implement anti-bribery controls.
- Verify that personnel will comply with the policy and program.
- Control benefits provided to individuals and third parties – such as hospitality, gifts, and donations – to ensure they do not serve a corrupt purpose.
- Implement financial, procurement, and other commercial controls to help mitigate the potential for bribery.
- Implement whistle-blower procedures, and investigate and address any suspected or actual bribery.

Internal Controls to Address the Risk of Financial Statement Fraud

Examples of internal controls to address the risk of financial statement fraud include the following:

- Thoroughly review all post-financial-statement-date transactions, such as accounts payable increases and decreases, to detect omitted liabilities in financial statements.
- Have an internal auditing staff review financial statement information throughout the year.
- Engage independent auditors to conduct annual external audits of financial statements.
- Thoroughly review the appropriateness of capitalization procedures.
- Thoroughly review the entity's loan covenants for any financial ratio requirements, paying special attention to areas where a financial statement fraud could have helped the entity meet the lending requirements. For example, the misclassification of long-term assets as current assets can be used to maintain a desirable current ratio.
- Search for and investigate changes that were made to original inventory count documents. Ensure that the original inventory count matches the inventory reported in the financial statements.
- Review the company's methods for estimating financial statement values. Check the estimates for reasonableness, and ensure that the estimates were actually calculated according to the company's established procedures. For example, ensure that estimated liabilities for bad debt are reasonably stated by reviewing the company's standards for estimating bad debt, and review the computations for accuracy.
- Review disclosures for completeness and accuracy, and tie to the financial statements where necessary.

Internal Controls to Address the Risk of Fraud Involving Vendors

Examples of controls to prevent or detect vendor fraud include:

- Enforce an exhaustive process for approving new vendors, including verification of address, phone number, and tax identification number; review of company websites; contacting references; requiring audited financial statements; and other similar checks.
- Issue internal conflict of interest questionnaires and address any potential conflicts.
- Reconcile goods and services received from vendors against purchase documentation (e.g., purchase orders, contracts) to ensure they meet stated requirements.
- Perform vendor compliance audits.
- Carefully review and approve invoices prior to payment.

FRAUD RESPONSE

How management responds to discovered fraud is an important part of a comprehensive anti-fraud program. A swift, certain, and transparent response reinforces management's anti-fraud stance and thus helps deter other acts in the future.

The investigation of alleged fraud is covered in detail in Chapter 5, but responding to fraud involves much more than simply conducting an investigation. Management must also be proactive and consistent in how it disciplines perpetrators, identifies and remedies the issues that allowed the fraud to be committed and concealed, and communicates the situation to various parties.

Disciplining the Perpetrator(s)

Enforcing an anti-fraud program means adhering to a system of disciplinary actions for rule breakers. Employees must know that if they commit fraud, they face punishment or termination. The opportunity to engage in misconduct is psychologically more acceptable when employees believe misconduct normally goes undetected and unprosecuted.

Examples of disciplinary action include:

- Reporting to law enforcement for criminal prosecution
- Pursuit of civil legal action
- Report to an outside organization (e.g., licensing organization)
- Termination
- Requiring reimbursement of losses or damages
- Suspension
- Probation
- Demotion (e.g., reduction in job responsibilities and title change)
- Verbal or written warning or reprimand
- Loss of benefits
- Salary reduction
- Denial of a promotion or disqualification from certain positions

- Disqualification from bonus eligibility
- Reassignment
- Mandatory training

Creating and Enforcing a Consistent Set of Disciplinary Guidelines

Any action taken against the perpetrator(s) should be appropriate under the circumstances and applied consistently to all levels of employees, including senior management. To ensure fairness and consistency of punishments for misconduct, management might create a disciplinary action committee made of up key stakeholders (e.g., general counsel, human resources, and compliance officer) to oversee the development and enforcement of the organization's disciplinary policies. Depending on the organization, the committee might either make its own determinations regarding disciplinary action or make recommendations to the CEO or senior management for final action. Those on the committee must be able to remain objective and reasonable; one way to help address potential favoritism or bias is to have committee deliberations conducted as a "blind" process, whereby no individuals or departments involved in the violations are identified during the deliberations.

Additionally, the organization might create a separate set of guidelines or an additional clause in the disciplinary policy for responding to misconduct by parties with increased authority in the organization.

Consulting with Legal Counsel

In both determining company disciplinary policies and applying those policies to punish specific individuals, management must work closely with legal counsel – whether in-house counsel or outside employment law experts – to ensure discipline is in strict compliance with all applicable laws and regulations. Failing to consider the legal requirements and implications can open the organization up to wrongful termination or other legal claims.

Disciplining Managers Who Fail to Prevent or Detect Misconduct

Part of managers' responsibility for overseeing staff members is preventing and detecting fraud and misconduct committed by those reporting to them. If violations recur in the same department, it might be necessary to discipline the manager for failing to meet this responsibility.

Identifying and Remedying the Underlying Issues

After determining that a fraud has occurred, management should seek to understand the issues that led to the misconduct and then take action to prevent similar offenses in the future. Remediation efforts in the wake of a fraud might include:

- Reassessing the fraud risk in the area where the issue occurred
- Examining how and why it happened (i.e., what situational opportunities, pressures, and rationalizations were present that led to the fraud)

- Identifying and implementing process or program modifications to reduce the factors that contributed to the fraud
- Identifying internal control weaknesses or breakdowns (including those due to collusion or override of the controls) and implementing measures to strengthen the related controls
- Implementing additional monitoring procedures to ensure any other changes made have the desired effect

In determining the appropriate remediation steps, management should consider:

- How long the fraud had been happening and why it was not discovered sooner
- Whether any red flags were missed by parties who should have noticed and reported them
- Whether the occurrence of the fraud has implications regarding the organization's ethical culture (e.g., did the fraud involve members of upper management or a large group of individuals at a lower level?)

Communicating about the Fraud

Beyond the official investigation report, management has several considerations when it comes to communicating the occurrence of the fraud, the results of the investigation, and any related issues. Some of these might be a matter of protocol. For example, it might be necessary to report any findings of actual or potential material impact to the board, the audit committee, and the external auditor if they are not receiving investigation reports directly. Other potential communications, however, present opportunities to improve the organization's anti-fraud stance and fraud prevention and detection activities.

Specifically, executive management should ensure that midlevel management and supervisors in areas that were directly and indirectly affected by a fraud are informed about the situation – even if just in general terms – and about any associated process, policy, or control changes that have been made as part of the remediation efforts. This can help ensure that these midlevel managers understand the reason for and importance of any modifications to the operations in their areas.

In addition, management should consider whether and how to communicate any of the information about the fraud to employees throughout the organization. Some companies use actual fraud cases, with details redacted, as part of their anti-fraud training programs. Others keep a "blotter" of egregious violations and the associated disciplinary actions on their company intranet or in company newsletters. While publicizing information about cases can be uncomfortable, doing so can also help raise awareness that management is looking for fraud and will punish anyone found to have engaged in fraudulent conduct.

Before communicating information about the fraud to any parties, management should consult with legal counsel to ensure that all legal and regulatory requirements are met and that any potential legal issues with such communication are identified and considered.

NOTES

1. www.iso.org/obp/ui/#iso:std:iso:31000:en
2. Committee of Sponsoring Organizations of the Treadway Commission and the Association of Certified Fraud Examiners, Fraud Risk Management Guide, 2016, p. 4.
3. Committee of Sponsoring Organizations of the Treadway Commission, Internal Control – Integrated Framework Executive Summary, May 2013, p. 3 (www.coso. org/Documents/990025P-Executive-Summary-final-may20.pdf).
4. https://na.theiia.org/standards-guidance/recommended-guidance/practice-guides/ Pages/Internal-Auditing-and-Fraud-Practice-Guide.aspx
5. www.iso.org/iso-37001-anti-bribery-management.html

CHAPTER 5

Fraud Investigation

Conducting a fraud investigation in any jurisdiction can be a difficult task. Investigations tend to involve accusations of wrongdoing against employees within the organization and can be disruptive, costly, distracting, and time-consuming. Furthermore, by their very nature, fraudulent acts are purposefully concealed, leaving the fraud examiner at a particularly difficult starting point.

METHODOLOGY

Fraud examination methodology requires that all fraud allegations be handled in a uniform, legal fashion and be resolved on a timely basis. Fraud investigations can lead to a variety of legal problems and other unexpected complications if they are not conducted with the utmost care and confidentiality. Consequently, fraud examiners should approach each fraud investigation with the proposition that the case will end in litigation. This assumption must be maintained and considered throughout the investigation. If fraud examiners assume litigation will follow each investigation, they are more likely to conform their conduct to the relevant rules of evidence and remain well within the applicable legal guidelines.

Further, unlike with other offenses, an inherent part of the methodology of committing fraud is to conceal its existence. For example, a bank robber's modus operandi is the use of threats or force, while a bank embezzler's operations involve not only stealing money but also covering up the theft. The element of concealment often increases the difficulty in detecting whether a crime has been committed. The methods for concealing fraud are so numerous and sometimes ingenious that almost anyone – even the fraud examiner – can be defrauded. As a result, *no opinion should be given to any person that fraud does or does not exist within a specific environment.* Expressing opinions undermines the investigation and leaves the fraud examiner personally vulnerable to legal action.

Because investigations of fraud often involve an extensive array of information, the fraud examiner can lose sight of the objectives. However, the examiner must remember that the purpose of the fraud examination is to prove or disprove the legal elements of the offense, which can differ subtly or significantly from country to country. The key to successful fraud examinations lies in effective planning, in terms of both an organizational fraud response plan that establishes a basic framework for responding to fraud-related incidents and an investigation plan specific to the incident or allegation in question.

Portions of the material in this chapter also appear in the following Association of Certified Fraud Examiners (ACFE) publications: *Issues in Conducting International Investigations*, *Report Writing*, and the "Investigation" section of the *Fraud Examiners Manual*.

CREATING A FRAUD RESPONSE PLAN

Because time is critical during the initial phase of an investigation – when evidence of misconduct first arises – management must respond promptly and appropriately. To help ensure that the organization responds to potential fraud-related activity efficiently, management should have a response plan in place that outlines how to address such issues.

This allows management to respond to suspected and detected incidents of fraud in a consistent and comprehensive manner, and sends the message that management takes fraud seriously. Organizations without a fraud response plan might not be able to respond to issues efficiently, and will likely expend more resources and suffer greater harm than those that have such a plan in place. Having a response plan puts an organization in the best position to respond promptly and effectively.

A fraud response plan outlines the actions an organization will take when suspicions of fraud arise. Because every fraud is different, the response plan should not outline how a fraud examination should be conducted. Instead, it should help the organization manage its response, optimize its resources, and create an environment to minimize risk and maximize the potential for success. More specifically, the fraud response plan should guide an organization's actions when fraud is alleged or identified.

The actions in the plan might include notification of the investigation and establishing an investigative team to identifying factors that determine the course of the investigation or documentation procedures. Additionally, because the appropriate response will vary based on the event, management should include a range of scenarios in the response plan.

To create a fraud response plan, management should form a committee of internal and potentially external personnel to determine the organization's vulnerability to fraud. To assess vulnerabilities, the committee should consider common occurrences of fraud specific to the organization's industry as well as any history of fraud within the organization itself.

The plan should feature means to prevent, detect, and react to instances of fraud and the important information that will steer the organization's course of action in the event fraud is discovered. It should also cover the following questions:

- Who should be informed if a violation is suspected?
- Who should investigate the incident?
- Who will determine what action to take against the violator, and how will such action be determined?
- Who will be responsible and accountable for improving identified control weaknesses?

All organizational policies – including a fraud response plan – should be anchored in organizational values and based on the organization's operational realities. While the substance of any policy is important, so are the format, length, and writing style. These aspects help ensure that the policies are not ambiguous but have a clear and implementable message. The fraud response plan should be as short and concise as possible, using simple vocabulary and definitions when necessary.

ASSESSING THE NEED FOR AN INVESTIGATION

Before beginning an investigation, fraud examiners should work with management to determine whether an investigation is appropriate or necessary. The need for an investigation can arise in a number of circumstances. For example, when management suspects an employee of wrongdoing, an internal investigation should be conducted before dismissing that employee. Investigations might also be necessary to determine the source and amount of any losses caused by fraudulent activity. A thorough investigation in these circumstances can enable a company to reduce its losses, identify the perpetrator, gather evidence for a criminal prosecution or civil trial, and recapture some or all of its losses.

An investigation can also shed light on weaknesses in the company's control structure, thereby helping shore up the organization's internal defenses against future employee misconduct.

There are many reasons why organizations choose to conduct fraud investigations. In particular, a well-executed fraud investigation can address a number of organizational objectives, including:

- Identifying improper conduct
- Stopping fraud
- Sending a message throughout the organization that fraud will not be tolerated
- Determining the extent of potential liabilities or losses that might exist
- Stopping future losses
- Mitigating other potential consequences

There are also certain instances in which an organization might be required to conduct an internal investigation. For example, management might have a legal duty to investigate alleged wrongdoing if it consists of a criminal offense.

Additionally, regulatory agencies often require accurate financial reporting by the companies they oversee, compelling companies to conduct internal investigations to ensure that all relevant facts are known and reported.

PREPARING FOR THE INVESTIGATION

Establishing Predication

Before launching a fraud investigation, a fraud examiner must determine if there is sufficient predication. For predication to be sufficient, the totality of circumstances must be such that a reasonable, well-trained professional would believe that a fraud has occurred, is occurring, or will occur. The origin of predication might be generated by an employee tip, an audit, or any number of other situations that merit further analysis.

Beginning with the process of scrutinizing a tip or other indicator and continuing with every subsequent step of the investigation, the examiner must consider whether sufficient predication exists to proceed further with the inquiry.

Developing a Plan

Investigative planning should be conducted at the very beginning of the fraud examination process, taking into account any circumstances unique to jurisdictions in which the examination will take place, including governing laws or regulations that might affect the collection of evidence and information. As the examination progresses, the plan will have to be modified, amended, and expanded.

Because fraud examinations are inherently adversarial in nature, fraud examiners should expect their work to be scrutinized and challenged on form, content, and technique. The best way to withstand such scrutiny is to have an organized investigative plan prior to beginning the examination. This plan should be based on the organization's fraud response plan but should also address the specific circumstances of the incident(s) or allegation(s) in question.

As part of that plan, the investigation of fraud should be approached from two perspectives. In order to prove that fraud occurred, the proof must include attempts to prove that it did *not* occur. The reverse is also true. In attempting to prove fraud did *not* occur, the proof must also attempt to prove it *did*. The reason is that both sides of fraud must be examined. *Under many jurisdictions' laws, proof of fraud must preclude any explanation other than guilt.*

In developing the investigative plan, the fraud examiner should specifically consider the following information:

- Knowledge necessary to complete the process, such as:
  - Knowledge of the industry
  - Knowledge of the organization
  - Knowledge of the jurisdiction
- Skills necessary to complete the investigation, such as:
  - Document collection and analysis
  - Interview techniques
  - Observation
  - Report writing

The fraud examiner should also consider the goal or purpose of the examination or investigation. More often than not, if a fraud examiner is involved in the investigation, one or more allegations of wrongdoing are present. The goal of the investigation will be to determine whether wrongdoing occurred and, if so, who might be involved. It is necessary to plan the investigation so the evidence will answer these questions. The basic plan developed at this stage will be built upon and finalized later.

Assembling the Investigation Team

Most investigations require the involvement of individuals beyond just the fraud examiner(s), each with different specializations or experience. Once it is determined that an allegation or issue will be investigated, management must determine who will lead the investigation, and who should be involved in the investigation.

The findings and observations that emerge from the efforts up to this point should be the primary factors used to determine who should be involved in the investigation, including both internal and external resources.

Team Composition

A typical investigation team might include the following types of professionals:

- *Certified Fraud Examiners (CFEs):* A CFE is trained to conduct a fraud investigation from inception to conclusion. Fraud investigations frequently present special problems because they require an understanding of complex financial transactions, as well as traditional investigative techniques. A CFE has training in all aspects of a fraud investigation and, therefore, can serve as a valuable cornerstone to the investigation team, tying together the financial examination and the more traditional investigative techniques.
- *Legal counsel:* It is often crucial to have legal counsel involved in and, in most cases, directing the investigation, at least as far as the legal aspects are concerned. An internal investigation can generate an array of legal questions. The investigation team must have legal counsel on hand to address these questions. Otherwise, the investigating organization risks exposing itself to greater danger than just the threat that it is investigating. In addition, by having an attorney directing the investigation, or overseeing an investigation conducted at the attorney's request, management might be able to protect the confidentiality of its investigation under privileges such as the legal professional privilege (known as attorney-client privilege in the US or legal advice privilege in the UK) and litigation privileges (including the work-product doctrine in the US). Fraud examiners working on international investigations or investigations spanning multiple jurisdictions should consult with lawyers in each jurisdiction or legal counsel familiar with the legal issues in all relevant jurisdictions.
- *Accountants or auditors (internal or external):* Because accounting and audit knowledge is necessary to most fraud investigations, a team might include accountants or auditors, whether internal or external. A forensic accountant can provide various services, including examinations of financial documents for signs of fraud, misconduct, or violations of industry standards. Moreover, these experts can mine and analyze large amounts of data to identify potentially irregular transactions and high-risk relationships. Auditors can also support the investigation with information on company procedures and controls. Internal auditors are often used to review internal documentary evidence, evaluate tips or complaints, calculate estimated losses, and provide assistance in technical areas of the company's operations. Additionally, auditors can help design procedural methods to identify the perpetrators and help determine the extent of the fraud. For investigations in unfamiliar jurisdictions, enlisting the support of a local auditor or accountant can provide important information.
- *Security personnel:* Security department investigators are often assigned the investigation's fieldwork responsibilities, including interviewing outside witnesses and obtaining public records and other documents from third parties. It is crucial that their work be integrated with the financial side of the investigation so that the team

does not devolve into two de facto investigations – one for financials and one for fieldwork. The process works best when all aspects of the investigation are coordinated and focused on the same goal. Furthermore, investigations might require fieldwork in jurisdictions that would benefit from security personnel's advice or presence.

- *Human resources (HR) personnel:* The HR department should be consulted to ensure that the local laws governing the rights of employees in the workplace are not violated. Such involvement will lessen the possibility of a wrongful discharge suit or other civil action by the employee. Advice from an HR specialist might also be needed, but normally this person would not directly participate in the investigation. Moreover, HR can help the team understand office procedures or cultural differences in a particular jurisdiction and, if needed, can help place suspect employees on paid leave.

- *Management representatives:* Representatives of management or, in significant cases, the audit committee of the board of directors should be kept informed of the progress of the investigation and be available to lend the necessary assistance. A sensitive employee investigation has little hope of success without strong management support.

- *Information technology (IT) personnel:* In most cases, IT department personnel will need to be part of an investigation to help identify what data is available and where it is located, as well as to help safeguard the data until it can be analyzed. Additionally, if an investigation involves more than cursory analysis of electronic evidence, the team should include someone with computer forensics expertise. With the majority of communication being conducted electronically, emails or other electronic correspondence can be used as evidence in most cases and might require the assistance of IT personnel to identify or recover it. Computer forensic experts can uncover a large amount of data that relates to the use of a computer, what is or has been stored on it, and the details about the computer's users. Additionally, computer forensic experts might be able to recover evidence that a nonexpert cannot.

- *Outside consultants:* In some cases, especially those involving powerful employees or foreign jurisdictions, it might be useful to employ outside specialists who are relatively immune to the company's politics or to threats of reprisals. An employee suspected of fraudulent activity might try to influence the investigation by limiting a fraud examiner's access to necessary information or by discouraging other employees from cooperating with the investigation. Additionally, it might be more difficult for an internal fraud examiner to carry out the investigation objectively due to the expressed or perceived threats of repercussions stemming from investigating a powerful or well-liked employee. An outside specialist will not be subject to any intimidation, and the outside specialist's involvement can discourage an alleged perpetrator from attempting to influence the investigation. Outside experts might also have more subject matter experience, local familiarity, and investigative contacts than insiders. It might also be necessary to include an individual with deep industry knowledge. Industry specialists can use that knowledge and experience to help develop the investigation plan, evaluate technical documents, and identify potential misstatements by interviewees.

Additional Considerations

When organizing the team, it is important to consider all the implications that might arise from an investigation. These include the business, legal, human resources, and operational factors that arise when an investigation commences. Addressing these potential issues up front ensures that significant factors (e.g., the team members' abilities, the leading executives, and the assurance of independent action and reporting) are considered.

A successful fraud investigation depends not only on the knowledge and skills of individual team members but also on each member's interpersonal skills that facilitate team productivity and functioning. These characteristics are especially critical for teams that require a significant amount of coordination.

Management should also consider the size of the team and any potential conflicts of interest between internal and external team members in terms of how they might affect the investigative team's ability to succeed. The success of the team should be the driving factor in all decisions regarding selection of the team members, rather than any personal motivations such as repaying a favor or selecting a friend.

Identifying the Investigation Leader

When assembling the team, management must designate someone to lead the investigation. To be effective, the leader should:

- Have sufficient investigative experience.
- Understand the legal and compliance requirements regarding the specific issues involved.
- Be independent of the activity surrounding the alleged fraud.
- Have the means to recruit any resources necessary to conduct the investigation.
- Have sufficient authority and access to gather any necessary information.
- Have the ability to communicate effectively with senior management.

Additionally, the investigative leader should be determined based on the seriousness of the allegation. For example, an allegation of skimming by a low-level employee might leave more options for team leadership since the investigation should be relatively straightforward. Management should also consider whether to appoint an internal party (if available) or an external third party to lead and oversee the investigation. An allegation of major financial statement fraud that has serious implications for the company might be a situation in which it is beneficial to bring in a third party with expertise in financial statement fraud and no prior relationship with the accused or the company. In some jurisdictions, having a local legal professional lead an investigation may be advisable to ensure that the investigation complies with all local laws.

Roles and Responsibilities

If the organization does not have a pre-established line of authority in its fraud policy or investigation protocols, management should, during the investigation planning process,

147

define the team's level of authority, responsibilities for action, and reporting lines. All team members must clearly understand their specific roles and responsibilities and how those relate to the goals of the investigation. This allows for efficient and effective coordination across the team and gives team members purpose and checkpoints for measuring success.

Without clear roles, the team might waste time and money, experience gaps in the investigation process, or conclude the investigation with incomplete or faulty results.

Delineating the team members' roles can be difficult because fraud investigations often are conducted in an unstable and high-pressure atmosphere that disrupts communication. Even so, the team must coordinate and share information associated with members' respective roles and responsibilities.

Management should also define the line of authority to help avoid conflicts between departments and team members. Additionally, roles and responsibilities and line-of-authority protocols should be regularly reviewed and adapted as necessary over the course of the investigation. As new information is discovered, the scope and course of the investigation might necessitate alteration of team members' roles and responsibilities in order to pursue new leads or allegations. In other words, the roles initially established should not be considered permanent.

Further Defining the Goal or Purpose of the Investigation

After selecting the investigation team, the team leader should again consider the goal or purpose of the investigation and define it or refine it in terms that help the team achieve it. The goal or purpose helps keep the investigation team focused and on task and can serve as an energizer. To be effective, the investigation's goals should be:

- *Specific:* A specific goal is more likely to be achieved than a general goal.
- *Well defined:* If goals are not well defined, the team cannot expect to reach them.
- *Realistic:* The goals must be realistic within the availability of resources, knowledge, and time.
- *Measurable:* Measurable goals will allow the team to determine attainability, estimate a time line, and know when the goals have been achieved.

The primary goal for most fraud investigations is to determine whether fraud occurred and, if so, who perpetrated it. However, fraud investigations might also have secondary goals, such as:

- Prevent further loss or exposure to risk.
- Establish and secure evidence necessary for criminal or disciplinary action.
- Minimize and recover losses.
- Review the reasons for the incident and determine any action needed to strengthen future responses to fraud.
- Promote an anti-fraud culture.

Once the goals are defined, the team can design the investigation to uncover evidence that answers the questions necessary to satisfy the goals.

Notifying Relevant Parties

Once the decision has been made to proceed with an investigation, relevant parties inside the organization should be notified about the allegations in question as well as the investigation, regardless of whether those parties' authorization is necessary. Additionally, legal or regulatory requirements might dictate that parties outside the organization be notified, depending on the jurisdiction. For example, an investigation into serious criminal wrongdoing might require immediate notification of law enforcement, or an allegation of tax-related fraud might need to be reported to the agency responsible for collecting taxes in that jurisdiction.

Confidentiality Concerns

Fraud investigations must maintain a balance between complying with both internal and external notification requirements and keeping critical details confidential. Failure to do so could compromise the investigation and make employees reluctant to report future incidents. In general, as few people as are necessary should be kept informed. Factors to consider when determining who should be kept informed include the severity of the incident under investigation, the suspect's role in the organization, and the tasks necessary to conduct the investigation.

The investigation leader should explicitly outline the expectations related to confidentiality when the team investigative team first meets, and then should reinforce these expectations throughout the investigation. If appropriate and allowable in the relevant jurisdiction, management might require participants to sign a confidentiality agreement vowing not to divulge any information regarding the investigation.

Depending on the jurisdiction, there could be evidentiary privilege, such as legal professional privilege or attorney work-product privilege, available to the investigation team. The team leader or management should check with legal counsel to determine confidentiality options and requirements in the relevant jurisdiction(s).

Additional information can be found in the "Legal Work Privileges" section in Chapter 2, Legal Issues Pertaining to Fraud.

Internal Notifications

When beginning an investigation, the team should determine the internal members of the organization who need to know about the situation. In-house legal counsel should be among the first informed. Almost every investigation will require that key decision makers within the organization are notified of the impending investigation, as well as when it will begin and how it might affect regular operations. The manager of a suspect, a whistle-blower, or the divisions involved might need to be alerted about the investigation, especially if the evidence gathering and interviewing phases might disrupt normal work flow in the department. Additionally, depending on the circumstances, the investigation team might notify:

- Compliance department or officer(s)
- Board of directors or audit committee

- Human resources
- Corporate security
- Information technology

This list is purely subjective, and there might be strong reasons for excluding or including people depending on the specific facts of the case. For example, a tip might allege that a fraud suspect's direct supervisor was involved in the scheme. If this supervisor is informed of the investigation prematurely, it could compromise the integrity of the investigation.

Every organization should have a written policy for making the determinations included in the fraud response plan.

External Notifications

Management should determine whether, and at what stage of an investigation, it might be required to notify outside parties. For example, in certain regulated industries, such as banking, management might need to inform a government agency or a central branch of the company when it begins a fraud investigation.

Additionally, some jurisdictions might require organizations to report specific instances of suspected illegal conduct. For example, if an organization uncovers evidence of bribes paid by one of its employees to a government official, it is typically required to inform the appropriate government agency.

The determination of whether and when to notify law enforcement hinges on a number of factors, the most important being whether it is required under local law. If it is not required, then it is a decision that management must make regarding whether to pursue the fraudster through law enforcement, civil action, or both. If, at the beginning of the investigation, management determines that it will make a formal referral to law enforcement or a prosecuting agency, then it typically must notify the authorities before the investigation commences to determine whether law enforcement personnel should participate in the examination. Working with law enforcement is discussed later in this chapter.

Fraud examiners should be familiar with the specific language of relevant notification requirements, because notification is required upon commencement of some investigations, whereas in others notification might not be required until after confirmation that fraud occurred.

If insurance might cover some or all of the damages caused by a fraud, the examiner should understand the notification requirements in the insurance policy. Coverage under the policy might depend upon timely notification.

Further, in some cases, management might need to notify customers or vendors (e.g., if the fraud compromised customer data). Even if there is no legal requirement, management should always consider whether it would be appropriate to notify vendors or customers who might be affected by the fraud.

If the investigation team includes external personnel such as contractors or consultants, a decision should be made regarding the extent of the detail included in reports to their external management.

Developing a Fraud Theory

In order to determine the direction of the investigation before having complete evidence, it is necessary for the fraud examiner to make certain assumptions. This is not unlike the scientist who postulates a theory based on an observation and then tests it. In the case of complex frauds, use of the fraud theory is almost indispensable. The fraud theory begins with the assumption, based on the known facts, of what might have occurred. Then that assumption is tested to determine whether it is provable. Among the important questions to consider in developing the fraud theory are:

- Who might be involved?
- What might have happened?
- Why might the allegation be true?
- Where are the possible concealment places or methods?
- When did (or will) this likely take place (e.g., past, present, or future)?
- How is the fraud likely being perpetrated?
- Where is the evidence likely to be?
  - On-book versus off-book
  - Direct or circumstantial
- Who are the potential witnesses?
  - Neutral third party witness(es)
  - Corroborative witness(es)
  - Victim(s)
- What evidence might be necessary to prove intent?
  - Number of occurrences
  - Other areas of impropriety
  - Witnesses

After carefully developing a fraud theory, the fraud examiner should revise and amend it as necessary. New information discovered at various stages of the investigation will likely impact the fraud theory, perhaps disproving it, revealing additional individuals involved, or increasing the scope of related misdeeds. As a result, the fraud examiner might need to change the investigation plan and seek out new evidence from different sources, interview additional subjects, or obtain further legal counsel.

Depending on the complexity of the fraud theory, it might be useful at this point to prepare a chart or graph to more clearly link people and evidence. Any visual aids should be prepared with the expectation that they could be presented to a court and should therefore not contain any presumptions of guilt or inappropriate content. A well-prepared visualization can help highlight key relationships or areas in which questions remain unanswered and on which investigative efforts should be focused.

In the final phase of the fraud theory development, fraud examiners should analyze possible defenses to the allegations and determine how those possible defenses could impact the investigation. The possible defenses might be easily debunked with a particular document or piece of evidence, and the investigation plan should feature efforts to secure that evidence. If the possible defenses are credible and supported by their own piece of information or evidence, the investigation team should revisit the fraud theory and make any appropriate changes.

Determining the Scope of the Investigation

The team and management must determine the scope of the investigation. An investigation might be limited to the subject matter, the department, or the geographic area at issue.

The scope of an investigation depends on a number of factors. To help determine the scope, those responsible should use the following guidelines:

- Consider the ultimate goals of the investigation.
- Develop a list of key issues raised in the development of the fraud theory.
- Determine the level of discretion that is required.
- Determine whether there are any constraints (e.g., time, resource, authority, procedural, legal, practical, etc.). Identifying such limitations helps ensure that the team can meet realistic objectives and develop alternative strategies.
- Consider the quality of the organization's anti-fraud program and policies.
- Consider the organization's actual culture of compliance.
- Determine the extent to which mid- and senior-level management is involved in the suspected misconduct.
- Determine whether the issue is widespread or isolated to a particular area.
- Ascertain whether the suspected misconduct was prohibited by the company's compliance program.
- Consider broadening the scope if the allegations indicate a failure in the company's compliance program.
- Consider what the government expects.

The team and management should also consider how the issue became known (i.e., what prompted the investigation). Fraud issues can stem from different sources, and different sources prompt different responses. If, for example, the issue arose out of a government investigation, the company's investigation might shadow the government's actions.

Some common sources of allegations include:

- Whistle-blower allegations from known or anonymous sources
- Concerns from the board of directors, executives, or management
- Internal audit findings or concerns
- Complaints from vendors, contractors, subcontractors, customers, competitors, or other outside parties
- Regulator inquiry
- Government investigators or officials
- Media sources (e.g., newspapers, websites)
- Prospective purchasers

As part of defining the scope of the investigation, the team should also focus on what information needs to be gathered. To determine what evidence it should gather and how to gather it, the team might consider some or all of the following questions regarding the different areas of investigation:

The Allegation

- What is the nature of the suspected fraud?
- How long has the issue existed?
- Does the issue predate any of the key players?
- Did the suspected fraud occur in an industry or location that has a history or culture of fraud?
- What period is under review?

The Subjects

- Who are the targets?
- Does the organization perform background checks on employees as a precondition of employment?
- What other entities, departments, or jurisdictions might be involved?
- Has there been a recent acquisition, and, if so, is former management still in place?
- Who is the contact at the location?

The Location(s)

- Where are the relevant locations?
- What other locations might be involved?
- Have any related fraud investigations ever been conducted at the relevant location?

The Organization

- What is the culture of the department, industry, and jurisdiction(s) at issue?
- Has the organization been in compliance with the reporting and regulatory requirements for all relevant jurisdictions?
- What is the profitability of the unit or organization at issue in the investigation?
- Does the organization's level of growth make sense in light of its industry and peers?
- Does the organization have a fraud policy?

Logistics

- What type of report (written or oral) does the client or management expect?
- What is the budget?

The time frame of the investigation will also need to be established so that the team members understand how quickly they will need to gather information and process it, and can adjust accordingly. There might be a deadline imposed by management or resulting from external requirements that will dictate expediency. Even if there is not a strict deadline, the team should consider obtaining the dates of upcoming earnings releases and audit committee meetings, if relevant and appropriate.

A quick and appropriate response can help avoid future legal disputes and minimize adverse impact on employee morale. However, some circumstances might require extensive investigations of multiple allegations that make a quick resolution impossible. Assessing the time requirements up front so as to establish a realistic investigation time frame helps the team members structure their plans.

Finalize the Case Plan

Once a fraud theory is developed, but before the investigation begins in earnest, the investigation team should finalize the case plan to ensure that it addresses every relevant issue. The plan should include an outline of the specific course of action the team expects to take throughout the investigation. Having a case plan for the client, management, and team helps outline the investigation and streamline tasks before they begin, and keeps the team focused on the issues key to the investigation.

The case plan should outline what the team will investigate, and it could encompass the previously covered matters, such as:

- The overall approach to conducting the investigation
- The goals of the investigation
- The scope of the investigation
- Resources needed
- Task assignments
- Time parameters

Additionally, the case plan should, among other things, outline how and in what order the team will proceed. Thus, it should identify the information that is necessary to complete the investigation and include the investigative activities to be performed, such as:

- Documents and evidence that should be located, obtained, and examined
- A list of witnesses and subjects to interview and the preferred order of the interviews
- The reporting time line, including any required progress reports
- Matters that need supervisory review and approval

When finalizing the investigation plan, the team should consider:

- How to most efficiently achieve the goals of the investigation
- How to accomplish the goals of the investigation on a timely basis, with appropriate confidentiality and fairness to all parties

- How to ensure that the investigation's results are thorough and accurate, and that they are documented appropriately
- How to ensure compliance with the law and the organization's policies and procedures

The procedures performed during an investigation will vary from case to case, and they might include any number of measures. As circumstances change and new information emerges over the course of an investigation, the team and management should continually refine and modify the plan throughout the investigation.

Each stage of the investigation should be documented. Documenting the planning process demonstrates preparation and forethought. Documentation also indicates thoroughness, which can counter accusations that the investigation was inadequate.

APPLYING THE FRAUD EXAMINATION METHODOLOGY

Fraud examinations typically involve the following steps:

- Collecting and analyzing evidence
- Interviewing witnesses and suspects
- Reporting the case
- Working with law enforcement (when applicable)

The following section covers each step of the fraud examination methodology in depth.

Collecting and Analyzing Evidence

The value of an investigation rests on the credibility of the information obtained. Thus, the team must take care to properly collect, preserve, store, and use evidence relevant to an investigation. And, once the collection process is under way, it is important to ensure that the evidence is not damaged, altered, lost, or spoiled. Evidence of fraud can take the form of data, electronic communications, documents, or statements by witnesses. Accordingly, the fraud examiner must know how to properly and legally obtain, document, and store all types of evidence.

As a rule, documents and other evidence should be examined before interviews commence. This allows the investigation team to understand the potential evidentiary value of the case, protect the security of documents, and build a strategy for the interviewing phase. The evidence collection phase can include many methods of collection, sources of information, and analysis techniques, depending on the circumstances of the allegation or incident. This could also be referred to as the *building of knowledge phase*, and it is often when the fraud examiner first recognizes many of the tasks that will be necessary to complete the investigation.

When initiating this phase of the process, the fraud examiner should realize that many times, documents and other evidence are hidden, and that the perpetrator hid them hoping no one would ever find them. The fraud examiner should always be on the alert for documents or other pieces of evidence that should be there but are not.

During the evidence collection phase of the examination, there are many tasks that will become apparent based on the information contained in the documents, data, or electronic evidence. In determining how to approach the collection of evidence, the fraud examiner should consider the following:

- The location of any documents and data necessary to complete the examination, including both internal and external sources of evidence
- A list of information needed from witnesses
- A list of witnesses who can confirm or refute the information contained in the evidence
- Other experts who might examine or analyze the evidence
- Defenses that a potential suspect might use to refute the allegation (whether valid or not)

Sources of Information

To perform almost any fraud-related task, fraud examiners must be knowledgeable about what information to look for, what information is available, and where to look for it.

Fortunately, the world is full of information. Fraud examiners can access a vast variety of information to assist in an assortment of tasks, such as:

- Locating individuals or verifying their identities
- Researching assets or financial positions
- Documenting lifestyles and background information
- Discovering banking or creditor relationships
- Identifying business affiliations or associates
- Uncovering litigation history

Finding the right sources of information can be difficult. Even though the world is full of information, not all of it is legally accessible, useful, relevant, or accurate. Rules governing accessibility differ from jurisdiction to jurisdiction, as well. Additionally, information can come from virtually anywhere – company data and documents, interviews, news sources, social media, personal experiences, expert opinions, Internet sources, and so on – and different information requires different evidence-collection tasks.

To conduct a successful fraud investigation, examiners must be knowledgeable about laws and regulations restricting access to information, the relevant sources of information for certain types of searches, and the types of records specific to different types of fraud schemes. The examiner should make a list of potential internal and external sources of documentary evidence or other tangible information, such as:

- File cabinets
- Potential suspect's office
- Trash
- Third-party sources (e.g., vendors, public records, creditors)
- Personnel department

The examiner should also identify potential sources of electronic evidence, such as:

- Files or data stored on hard drives, memory cards, USB drives, or other physical storage devices
- Files or data stored in the cloud
- Files or data stored on servers and backup drives
- Files or data on mobile devices
- Deleted files
- Surveillance footage
- Email and other electronic communications
- Evidence obtained from Internet sources

Internal Sources

Sources of information within the victim organization are useful for various reasons. They can provide a more in-depth look at specific facts and information. They can provide the framework necessary to prove fraud allegations or for continued investigation from other sources. Also, internal sources are often the only resource for certain types of documents, such as accounting and business tax records or employee personnel files.

Unfortunately, obtaining information from internal sources might be complicated. Most organizations maintain an extremely voluminous amount of data and process millions of transactions every day; the sheer size is a major challenge. Also, the larger an organization gets, the more data it has to store. And, as an entity attains additional organizational units and opens new branches, its data is dispersed even further.

Often, some organizations are run by different departments that lack adequate channels or inclination to share information; such environments can hinder the identification of fraud and decrease the efficiency with which examiners can respond to ongoing frauds. That is, in such environments, fraud examiners might not have access to potentially valuable data, or the amount of time required to access the data can be prohibitive.

A fraud examiner's access to internal sources might also be hindered because the examiner lacks information about what is available and where it is stored, which makes obtaining relevant information difficult because data might be stored in large volumes and in different locations.

Common internal sources of information can be grouped by organizational department, such as:

Accounting and Finance

- Bank account records
- Vendor master file
- General ledger records
- Travel and entertainment expense records
- Corporate credit card and purchasing card records
- Accounts receivable records
- Accounts payable records

- Purchase orders and invoices
- Customer lists with revenue amounts for relevant periods
- Customer account files
- Payroll records
- Chart of accounts
- Financial reports for relevant period
- Check register or payment files
- Budget reports
- Fixed asset records

Legal

- Legal files
- Contracts with third parties
- Rental agreements
- Purchase contracts
- Leasing documents

Human Resources

- Personnel or human resources files
- Written policies and procedures
- Training records
- Ethics and compliance certifications or questionnaires
- Financial disclosures, which include the source, type, amount, or value of the incomes of certain employees
- Conflict-of-interest disclosure forms
- Conflict-of-interest waivers
- Communication records (e.g., email, call logs, etc.)

Operations

- Inventory records
- Purchasing requisitions
- Shipping and receiving reports

Internal Audit and Compliance

- Risk assessments
- Hotline complaints
- Information regarding internal investigations
- Prior internal audit reports

Information Technology

- Servers
- Email and other internal communications

- Event logs
- System registry
- Internet activity
- Deleted files
- System search history
- Hash values
- Metadata
- Shortcuts

External Sources

External sources of information are numerous and vary widely in terms of availability, applicable regulations, and format. The three main categories of external sources of information that can be useful for fraud examiners are public records, nonpublic records, and online or Internet sources.

Public Records

Whether certain types of records relating to an individual or organization are publicly available depends on the jurisdiction, and policies can vary widely among jurisdictions. Fraud examiners should always check with local legal counsel or investigative professionals to ensure they are aware of what information related to the investigation might be publicly available and how to obtain it. The following types of information are often made available to the public and can reveal key details about subjects in an investigation:

- Property records
- Business or corporate filings
- Commercial filings
- Tax records
- Court records

In jurisdictions where these types of records are public, they are frequently maintained by the government and made available or searchable in online databases hosted by the agency responsible for maintaining them. There are often costs associated with accessing these records, and, depending on the jurisdiction, the records might be spread among numerous agencies and levels of government, making them difficult to find.

In most jurisdictions, there are vendors who offer wide access to public records. Such vendors essentially aggregate public records and make them available in a searchable database. Unlike public databases available through governmental websites, public record vendors generally offer a broad range of information from different government agencies. These vendors compile public records and summarize the information contained therein.

Fraud examiners often mistakenly treat a search through a vendor's database as the complete search, when in fact they have completed only a portion of the process. Basically, when conducting a search through a public record vendor, fraud examiners need to confirm the legitimacy of the vendor and the information obtained from the vendor by reading reviews, articles, and so forth. Also, because not all records are available through vendors, fraud examiners should pull public records from original sources when possible.

Nonpublic Records

Nonpublic records include information about a person or business that is considered private and confidential. Nonpublic records might be needed to prove fraud or to provide leads in a fraud investigation.

Nonpublic records are not available to everyone, and because fraud examiners do not have an absolute right to see them, obtaining access might be difficult or impossible. However, fraud examiners might be able to access such records by obtaining consent from the individual the records pertain to. Additionally, if the company is involved in a civil suit, legal counsel might be able to obtain certain records through the discovery process. In criminal cases, law enforcement often uses search warrants to obtain nonpublic information.

Examples of nonpublic records that can be valuable to investigations include:

- Banking records
- Tax records
- Consumer credit records
- Phone records
- Credit card account records
- Personal health care records

Fraud examiners should be wary of any vendors or parties that claim to be able to provide nonpublic data, and should exercise caution in obtaining and using such information as it could result in legal complications with the case or liability for the examiner.

Online Sources

A great deal of information is accessible through the Internet for little or no cost. The most basic way to find information on the Internet is to use search engines such as Google or Baidu, but there are numerous tools that fraud examiners should use while collecting evidence:

Search and Metasearch Engines　*Search engines* are programs that comb through websites and documents for specified keywords and return a list of sites and documents where the keywords were found. *Metasearch engines* are programs that send keyword requests to multiple search engines simultaneously and display the results.

Search engines are most useful when the user is investigating a topic or website the person is not familiar with or when the user wants to cast a wide net. However, fraud examiners should not rely on them exclusively.

Search Operators　*Search operators* are symbols that help search engines better understand exactly what the user is looking for, and they return relevant links faster. Search operators help conduct more effective searches, although different engines use different operators.

Most search engines support using the words AND, OR, and NOT to connect keywords and phrases together for a logical search. Placing AND between two words will return pages containing both terms. Placing OR between two or more words will return pages containing either one, several, or all of the search terms. Placing NOT before a word will return pages that do not contain the term.

Most search engines also allow users to place quotation marks around a word or set of words to search for pages containing the text in quotations. This provides a more limiting search than those using connectors.

Other search operators include proximity connectors, which allow users to indicate that they want a keyword or phrase to appear in close proximity to another keyword or phrase, and "wildcard" symbols such as an asterisk (*) that serve as placeholders for any unknown or wildcard terms.

The Deep Web   The *deep Web* (also known as the *invisible Web*) refers to Web content that is not indexed by standard search engines. There are many reasons the deep Web exists. For one thing, there are places where Web-crawling robots cannot enter. These deep Web resources include websites without any links pointing to them, certain file formats that search engines cannot process, sites that have been blocked from crawler access, password-protected sites, and information stored in databases. The Tor browser is the most popular method of accessing the deep Web, but it can be blocked by many organizations' information security protocols.

Internet Archives   Fraud examiners can also search the Internet archives – archived versions of Web pages that have since been updated or are no longer available online.

The most popular tool for searching Internet archives is the Wayback Machine, located at archive.org/web. The Wayback Machine allows users to access archived versions of Web pages from 1996 to the present. As of 2017, the Wayback Machine's archive includes more than 300 billion indexed Web pages.

When fraud examiners are researching archived sites, they should always search for what is not there – this is what is important. They should also look for any evidence of unusual activity and compile it for analysis.

Social Media   There is a growing trend of investigators mining social media for evidence. Social networking websites use software to build online social networks for communities of people with shared interests. The popularity of social sites makes it easy for fraud examiners to find information about individuals who use them.

The data available on social networking sites is basically whatever personal information the user is willing to share. Relevant social media evidence about an individual can include photographs, status updates, location at a certain time, friends, political beliefs, work history, social schedules, hobbies, music and movie tastes, vacation destinations, and typical hangouts. Fraud examiners might also find information about businesses on social networking sites.

While LinkedIn, Facebook, Twitter, and Instagram are the most popular and recognizable social media sites, the landscape is constantly evolving, and new sites emerge regularly. It might not be enough to simply search the top social media sites for information. Accordingly, fraud examiners must keep current with emerging technologies and sites.

Media Databases   Newspapers, periodicals, and journals can be excellent sources of information, particularly when searching for background information on an individual or a business. Many media outlets publish stories online for anyone to see, and such resources are accessible through search engines or by going to the site directly. However, some publications are not so readily available, and many specialized publications limit access to those with a membership or subscription. Some researchers might benefit from using media databases to access more exclusive resources.

There are a number of online databases that deal specifically with news and media resources. These databases compile different media resources and allow the user to search for a specific topic, returning articles, or transcripts that pertain to that topic.

Organization of Evidence

Since fraud cases often involve many pieces of evidence, it is also necessary that they be organized in a manner that will allow an item to be located quickly. The examiner should log the evidence and, when appropriate, enter the information into a database, which makes the evidence easy to access, sort, and analyze.

Segregation of Documents

In general, the fraud examiner should segregate the documents by person or transaction. In the former method, the examiner takes the list of names, whether employee, associate, or witness, and begins assembling collected documents by person. Alternatively, the fraud examiner might find it easier to organize the information by grouping evidence of the same or similar transactions together. Chronological organization of documents is the least preferred method, as that system will make it difficult to find documents specific to a certain person or event.

Key-Document File

To help organize documents, the examiner should keep a key-document file for easy access to the most relevant documents. A *key-document file* is a separate file that contains copies of certain important pieces of information for quick access. In addition, the examiner should periodically review the key-document file and move the less important documents to backup files, keeping only the most relevant documents in the main file.

Establish a Database

In every internal investigation, the examiner should establish a database early and code all documents, especially if there is a large amount of information to process. This database will likely be computerized and accessed by keywords or a comprehensive numerical identification system. The coding system should provide meaningful and comparable data; therefore, the database should, at a minimum, include the following fields of information:

- Date of the document
- Individual from whom the document was obtained
- Date the document was obtained
- Brief description of the contents
- Subject the document pertains to

Chronology of Events

The fraud examiner should also start a chronology of events early in the investigation to establish the chain of events leading to the proof. The chronology might or might not be included in the formal report; at a minimum, it can be used for analysis of the case and placed in a working-paper binder. The examiner should keep the chronology brief and include only information necessary to prove the case. If the chronology is too detailed, the examiner defeats its purpose. The chronology should be revised as necessary by adding new information and deleting the irrelevant.

Preserving Evidence

Management must take action to preserve evidence as soon as the decision to investigate is made and collection efforts begin, especially given the impermanence of electronic evidence, which will likely be critical to any investigation.

Electronic Evidence

The proliferation of digital technologies has created new opportunities for technology to be used in perpetrating almost every type of fraud. Consequently, fraud examiners will gather some type of electronic evidence in almost all fraud investigations. Electronic evidence can be found in emails, website postings, text messages, social media activities, chat room messages, stored computer records and databases, digital photographs, voice mails, instant messages, documents, spreadsheets, databases, file fragments, metadata, digital images, and digital diagrams. Additionally, electronic evidence can be stored on all types of electronic media, including hard drives, flash drives, computers, printers, mobile phones, tablets, MP3 players, the Internet of Things (IoT) devices, and optical disks.

Electronic evidence can change with use and undergo alteration by improper or purposeful mishandling and storage. People can also deliberately remove or alter electronic evidence. As a result, fraud examiners should be mindful of authentication issues (i.e., showing that the data has not been altered or changed from the time it was collected through production in court) throughout the process of obtaining electronic evidence.

The destruction of electronic evidence through improper handling can raise questions about the alteration of evidence by the opposing party, weakening a case or investigation.

Further, if digital evidence cannot be satisfactorily authenticated, the judge may rule that it is inadmissible as evidence.

Examiners should never assume that a website or a social media post that was available yesterday day will be there tomorrow. Capturing information as they find it is essential for examiners because subjects of an investigation often delete websites and social media profiles. Individuals can preserve Web pages by selecting Print Screen and pasting the screen capture into a document.

When possible, examiners should capture the time, date, time zone, or any other information that proves when or where they captured the data. Not doing so can lead to time line inconsistencies, alibi contradictions, and dismissed evidence due to inaccuracies. It could also affect the examiner's credibility and could negatively impact the case if brought to trial.

Physical Evidence

The physical evidence collected in most investigations will primarily consist of documents. When collecting documentary evidence, investigators must handle all documents carefully and store them in a sealed, initialed, and dated paper folder or envelope to avoid damage or contamination. When possible or feasible, the original versions of documents should be obtained, with working copies made for review and the originals kept separately.

The originals should be handled as little as possible, as the documents might have to undergo forensic analysis later and could be compromised through being handled too much. Original documents and their copies should be stored in a secure location to ensure they are not tampered with.

Legal Considerations for Evidence

As examiners gather documentary evidence, they must keep in mind the legal requirements related to collecting and maintaining documents in all jurisdictions pertaining to the investigation. This will typically require consultation with legal professionals in each jurisdiction.

In addition, the examiner must always be aware of the potential for litigation in any investigation. Because documents make up so much of the evidence in fraud cases, it is important to understand the appropriate way of handling them so that they will be admissible in court. These considerations primarily relate to the authentication of evidence, the chain of evidence custody and litigation holds.

Additional information can be found in the "Admissibility of Evidence" section in Chapter 2, Legal Issues Pertaining to Fraud.

Reviewing and Analyzing the Evidence

After collecting as much relevant evidence as possible or reasonable within time constraints, the fraud examiner should review the documents or other pieces of information to test the fraud theory and narrow the scope of the investigation. There are a variety of quantitative and qualitative analysis techniques that might be appropriate depending on the circumstances of the fraud under investigation or the nature of the information collected.

Data Analysis

Before conducting interviews, examiners should perform data mining and other electronic analysis of relevant information. This enables them to analyze substantial amounts of data without the subject or anyone else becoming aware that an investigation is under way. Data analysis helps guide the investigation plan by identifying patterns, trends, and anomalies that correspond to transactions for which supporting documentation should be reviewed.

Performing data analysis techniques, including the necessary data extraction and cleansing, requires a combination of fraud investigation skills and technological savvy, in addition to relevant industry knowledge. If fraud examiners do not possess the specific technological savvy or industry knowledge, they should consider bringing in a consultant or subject matter expert. Fraud examiners should also assess the integrity of the data they gather before performing analysis.

Data analysis helps the fraud examiner quickly and thoroughly examine large volumes of data to find anomalies. After identifying these anomalies, the fraud examiner can focus on them to identify areas for further investigation. If the fraud examiner has access to large volumes of relevant data, data analysis tools and software can save time and greatly increase the efficiency of investigative efforts. However, because no single software tool can satisfy all user purposes, the fraud examiner must consider the applications with respect to the client's, organization's, or investigation's particular needs.

Data analysis tests will likely reveal many potential areas of exploration. After executing the desired tests, the fraud examiner will need to determine how to respond to the findings and how to watch for future anomalies.

Additional information can be found in the "Proactive Data Monitoring and Analysis" section in Chapter 4, Preventing and Detecting Fraud.

Document Analysis

Forged, altered, fabricated, and other suspicious documents are regularly encountered in fraud cases. Fraud examiners are not expected to be document experts. They should, however, be aware of ways to spot counterfeit documents and have knowledge of the capabilities and limitations of forensic examinations. Fraud examiners should consider consulting with experts early in their investigation or inquiry if they suspect that significant documents are counterfeit or have been forged, altered, or otherwise manipulated.

Evaluating the Impact of the Evidence

In addition to the more technical process of data analysis, fraud examiners should evaluate collected evidence to determine whether it is relevant, accurate, unaltered, and admissible to court if the investigation leads to litigation. Once the bulk of the evidence is collected and examined in the context of the fraud theory, fraud examiners should be able to determine which pieces of information, data, or documents are relevant to the investigation and which are not.

Additionally, during the evidence collection and analysis phase of the examination, many tasks will become apparent based on the information contained in the gathered documents. When analyzing collected documents, the fraud examiner should continue developing the investigation plan and should consider whether any changes made to the investigation plan warrant notifying any internal or external parties.

Interviewing Witnesses and Suspects

Almost every investigation will require the fraud examiner to conduct interviews. Investigative interviews help fraud examiners gather additional information; corroborate physical evidence with accounts of the event given by the victim, suspect, and witnesses; and potentially obtain a written confession. The interviewing process, like the fraud investigation itself, requires advanced planning and preparation. Chapter 6, Interviewing Witnesses and Suspects, provides detailed information on how to prepare for and conduct successful interviews.

Reporting the Case

After obtaining the necessary evidence and interviewing the appropriate witnesses, the fraud examiner is responsible for writing a clear, accurate and unbiased report reflecting the fraud examination results. This report might ultimately be used by management, attorneys, prosecutors, and others to determine the facts.

A strong fraud examination report conveys all the evidence and gives credibility to the fraud investigation and to the examiner. It forces fraud examiners to consider their actions during the investigation by requiring documentation of the evidence gathered and omitting irrelevant information, thereby allowing readers to clearly understand the facts pertinent to the investigation. An exemplary written report is based on an exemplary, well-planned examination, and proper preparation entails analyzing what is expected of the end product.

Planning the report requires reviewing all the documents and evidence accumulated to ensure familiarity with the parties and facts before writing a first draft.

Additionally, it might be helpful for the fraud examiner to first create a time line to help focus on the critical events and the sequence in which they occurred. Likewise, if there are numerous people involved, a list and a brief description of each individual's identity and role can aid in planning the report.

The examiner should begin the report during the investigation and complete it as soon as possible thereafter to mitigate the risk of omitting or distorting important data.

Purpose of the Report

Fraud examiners must record their specific activities and findings to comply with professional policies and procedures and, in some cases, to satisfy the courts. The records or reports must be accurate and understandable so that readers can determine what transpired without needing to speak to the report's author. In other words, the report should speak for itself.

The primary purpose of a fraud examination report is to communicate the results of a fraud examination and document the work performed. The fraud examiner should take care not to deviate from this goal while writing the report, and should remember that an investigation is often judged not by what was uncovered, but by the way in which the information is presented.

Characteristics of a Well-Written Report

A fraud examination report should stand on its own and answer the classic questions of who, what, when, where, why, and how. If it is prepared properly, the reader should not have to refer to any other documents to understand the issues contained in the report.

The fraud examiner should complete the following steps to ensure the accuracy of the report:

- Reconfirm all dates and supporting information before the report is written, not after.
- Provide a full description of all attachments to the report, if any.
- Check for errors in dates, amounts, spelling, and even seemingly unimportant facts or details. Fraud examination reports are frequently used as a basis for litigation and prosecution; defense attorneys can cite the smallest error as evidence that the entire document is inaccurate.
- Record in a memorandum of interview each contact made over the course of the investigation. Although testimony does not need to be recorded word for word, the fraud examiner should include all facts of possible relevance to ensure accuracy.

Additionally, reports should convey pertinent information in the clearest possible language to avoid various interpretations. If necessary, the examiner should quote the respondent directly (provided the quotation does not distort the context). The report should include only the facts – it should not editorialize or include judgments. The fraud examiner should use complex or technical terms only in their proper contexts and, where necessary, explain their meaning. Similarly, the fraud examiner should avoid the use of jargon because the report might be read by people who are not familiar with esoteric or technical terminology.

The fraud examiner must report all facts without bias. The report should include everything relevant, regardless of which side the findings favor or what they prove or disprove. At the outset of a fraud investigation, the examiner should determine exactly what information is needed to prove the case and include only matters that are relevant to the investigation. However, almost every investigation yields much information whose relevance is not immediately known. In such cases, the examiner should opt for completeness.

At the end of the investigation, the fraud examiner must submit a thorough, professional-looking report that is worth its cost. A well-composed report will likely indicate to the reader that the expert is a methodical person, which will bolster the expert's credibility and be more likely to persuade the reader.

Legal Considerations

Both the information included in a report and the parties who read it can have legal consequences for the company and possibly the investigators. These consequences are primarily related to the legal concepts of privilege, privacy, and disclosure.

Additional information can be found in the "Investigations in Private Actions" section in Chapter 2, Legal Issues Pertaining to Fraud.

Impartiality of the Report

The fraud examiner is a gatherer of evidence – not the ultimate judge thereof. The existence of fraud is solely the purview of the courts and legal fact finders (e.g., judges and juries). Consequently, opinions in fraud examination matters are generally avoided. In resolving fraud issues, the examiner must postulate a theory – guilt or innocence – in order to attempt to prove that theory. Any discussion of guilt or innocence is only a part of that theory; the examiner must not make statements that could be construed to be conclusive of that theory.

When writing a report, fraud examiners should be familiar with the standards of reporting as set forth in the Certified Fraud Examiner (CFE) Code of Professional Standards. It is quite common for fraud examiners to be questioned by an opposing attorney about the standards and their specific requirements.

The CFE Code of Professional Standards states the following with regard to reporting:

> *General*
> *Fraud examination reports may be oral or written, including fact witness and/or expert witness testimony, and may take many different forms. There is no single structure or format that is prescribed for a CFE's report; however, the report should not be misleading.*
>
> *Report Content*
> *Certified Fraud Examiners' reports shall be based on evidence that is sufficient, reliable and relevant to support the facts, conclusions, opinions and/or recommendations related to the fraud examination. The report shall be confined to subject matter, principles and methodologies within the member's area of knowledge, skill, experience, training or education.*
>
> *No opinion shall be expressed regarding the legal guilt or innocence of any person or party.*[1]

In a report-writing context, conclusions and opinions are similar, but not identical. Conclusions are based on observations of the evidence, whereas opinions call for an interpretation of the facts.

In most situations, the conclusions from the fraud examination should be self-evident and should not need to be pointed out in the body of the report. If the conclusions are not obvious, the examiner should clarify the report.

Evidence presented in the fraud examination report might constitute a convincing case pointing to the guilt or innocence of a person. The report should essentially say, "Here is the evidence," rather than "This person is guilty of this offense" or "This person is inno-cent." The ultimate question of guilt or innocence rests solely with the judicial system.

Expert Reports

A slightly different rule applies for expert reports. Opinions regarding technical matters are permitted if the fraud examiner is qualified as an expert in the matter being consid-ered, or is acting as an expert witness in a trial. Depending on the specific engagement, the expert might be hired either to draw a conclusion or to express an opinion based on a given set of facts. For example, a permissible expert opinion might be in regard to the adequacy of an entity's internal controls. Another opinion might discuss whether finan-cial transactions conform to generally accepted accounting principles.

Organizing the Information in the Report

Because of the amount of information and the number of documents that might be col-lected during a fraud investigation, the examiner should plan early and plan well. If circum-stances permit, the examiner should establish an information database in the early phases of the case. The information can be presented in chronological order or by transaction.

Chronological

This method presents facts in the order in which they were uncovered. For example, if the fraud investigation was prompted by an anonymous tip, the information received in the tip would be presented first in the report. Thereafter, the reader would follow the development of each step as the case progressed.

Information from each witness should be presented in a chronological manner. If interviewing an associate of the target, for example, the fraud examiner should present the information from the point the associate first met the target, then proceed through the course of pertinent events that lead to the present.

By Transaction

If a multitude of documents support several instances of fraud, this information should be presented by separating individual transactions. For example, in a case of six differ-ent instances of internal embezzlement, the documents and related interviews might be best understood if presented as a group, and then the remaining transactions would be detailed chronologically.

Report Format

Reporting formats vary widely. Some organizations, especially governmental investi-gative bodies, use standard report forms so examiners can provide case information in a consistent manner. However, because fraud examination reports are not universal, no format can cover every case, company, or situation. A standard format is a good place to start.[2] As a general guideline, the following sections should be included in most reports.

Background

The background section generally should be approximately two paragraphs long. It should succinctly state the reason for the fraud investigation (e.g., an anonymous tip was received, an anomaly was discovered during an audit, or money or property was missing). It might also state who called for the investigation and who assembled the investigation team.

Executive Summary

For a simple fraud investigation, the executive summary should be no more than four or five paragraphs long. For a more complex case, the summary might reach a page in length.

This section should summarize what actions were performed during the investigation, such as reviewing documents, interviewing witnesses, or conducting analyses or tests. It provides the reader with an overview of what was done during the investigation process.

The end of this section should contain a summary of the outcome of the investigation. For example, "€50,000 in checks was deposited into an account owned by Henrik Jansen. When confronted with this information, Jansen stated that he had only borrowed the money and meant to pay it back."

Scope

The scope section should consist of only one paragraph explaining the scope of the fraud investigation. For example, "Determine whether inventory was misappropriated from the warehouse," or "Determine why money is missing from the bank account."

Approach

The approach section provides a brief description of the following items:

- Fraud investigation team members
- Procedures (generally, what documents or data were reviewed or what tests were conducted)
- Individuals interviewed

Findings

The findings section contains the details of the fraud investigation and generally consists of several pages. It should describe what tasks were performed and what was found. The fraud examiner should provide enough details so the reader understands what occurred, but not so much detail that the reader begins to lose interest or becomes bogged down in the details. A reader might want to know, for example, how many invoices were forged, who was involved, how it was done, and what proof is available.

If the findings section is long, the fraud examiner should use subheadings for particular topics or specific individuals to make it easier for the reader to keep track of information. As mentioned, the fraud examiner can present the information either chronologically or by topic – whichever makes it easier for the reader to follow.

Summary

The summary should be one or two paragraphs long, succinctly summarize the results of the fraud investigation, and be similar to the outcome stated at the end of the executive summary section.

Impact

The impact section should describe how the fraud affected the victim organization. It can include an estimated amount of losses or any other tangible or intangible damage already suffered or that might occur in the future.

Follow-Up and Recommendations (If Necessary or Requested)

A follow-up section is generally optional. This section identifies any aspect of the investigation that remains outstanding, usually because it is outside the mandate of the fraud examiner. This could include the recovery of property that is in the hands of third parties or the collection of information held by vendors or suppliers.

If requested, the examiner might also identify and make any recommendations related to procedures and controls; however, the examiner might want to convey recommendations related to flawed internal controls and other failings of the organization to management in person or in a separate document. If included in the primary report, this information could potentially be seized upon by the accused or his representatives to steer blame away from the suspect's actions and toward the organization's shortcomings.

The follow-ups or recommendations should state what action is necessary or recommended, including remedial measures such as a review of internal controls, the introduction of a hotline, or an increase in security.

Working with Law Enforcement

In the event criminal conduct is uncovered during a fraud investigation, those responsible should determine whether the case should be presented to local law enforcement or government authorities. In some jurisdictions, local law requires such reporting. In certain situations, organizations might have a legal duty to notify law enforcement prior to beginning the investigation, and doing so can demonstrate that the organization is responding appropriately. Also, if notified, law enforcement can provide additional resources and experience. But if law enforcement becomes involved after receiving notice, management might lose control over the investigation.

When a fraud investigation uncovers criminal conduct and the underlying organization is not required by law to report the fraud to local authorities, data protection laws might restrict the organization's freedom to report the fraud to government authorities.

Again, some countries have data privacy laws that restrict employers from reporting personal information to government authorities.

Working with Foreign Governments

When the issue at hand crosses jurisdictional lines, those responsible should determine whether to notify local or foreign law enforcement about the issue. Generally, management should consider engaging foreign law enforcement when evidence is located abroad, it is seeking the prosecution of a foreign national abroad, or it is seeking to recover losses from a party whose assets are stored abroad. Engaging foreign law enforcement, however, is not without disadvantages. Foreign officials might be corrupt, and providing notice might result in the target being tipped off about the investigation or unwanted publicity.

When an organization faces a fraud-related incident in which a foreign government also commences an investigation, management must respond to the government's actions appropriately. Investigations by a foreign government can initiate reporting obligations, interrupt business operations, and result in an issue being made public.

Although the appropriate response will vary depending on the case, there are some basic principles organizations should comply with when responding to investigations by foreign governments. First, management should consult with legal counsel before responding to a government investigation. Second, management must be truthful in all communications with government agents. Finally, management must ensure that its employees and agents do not engage in any actions that might impede the government's investigation (e.g., destroying, hiding, or altering evidence).

ISSUES IN CONDUCTING CROSS-BORDER FRAUD INVESTIGATIONS

The globalization of the world's economy in recent decades has resulted in companies that are not simply located in one building, one city, or even one country. Many of today's companies employ a global workforce, often with vendors, suppliers, subsidiaries, or entire operations based in other parts of the world.

As such, the need for organizations that operate abroad to prevent and detect fraud has never been greater, and, because of a heightened awareness of this need, more organizations are conducting fraud investigations that cross national borders. Many markets, especially emerging ones, have inadequate commercial infrastructures, weak legal systems, unstable political systems, and a high-risk business environment; these factors all combine to complicate fraud investigation efforts in international cases.

Domestic fraud investigations can be complicated enough, but conducting an investigation that ventures into foreign jurisdictions can create an additional set of challenges that fraud examiners must address. For examiners conducting cross-border investigations, the capacity to prepare for and respond to these challenges in an efficient, defensible, and cost-effective way is critical.

Because cross-border fraud investigations present their own unique challenges, fraud examiners cannot simply retool their domestic investigation processes for the international context. Rather, they must develop an approach that is appropriate to the needs of the investigation at issue and complies with applicable local and foreign laws, cultures, and practices.

Among the challenges that a fraud examiner's approach must address are high costs, language differences, cultural differences, legal differences, high-risk regions, and lack of access to information.

Cost

Cross-border fraud investigations involve costs not typically associated with domestic investigations. Matters that can quickly and dramatically drive up costs include hiring outside counsel and local counsel, travel expenses, costs for analyzing and navigating foreign laws (e.g., data privacy laws), and hiring foreign language reviewers, translators, security providers (especially in high-risk locations), or locally credentialed investigators. A cross-border fraud investigation can end up being exponentially more expensive than a domestic investigation.

Fraud examiners should make every effort to come up with an accurate estimate of the costs associated with a cross-border fraud investigation, and present those costs in an organized fashion to management before proceeding. It is possible that management would be unwilling to pay the associated costs or would significantly limit the fraud examiner's budget for the case. Estimates in which each cost is accompanied by an explanation of its necessity or prioritized can help a fraud examiner justify the costs or adjust the plan based on the resources made available by management.

Language Differences

Conducting an international investigation that includes a jurisdiction where a different language is spoken can be a source of significant complications. While the aspect of investigations most affected by a language barrier is the interviewing phase, it will also affect virtually all investigation tasks carried out in the foreign jurisdiction(s).

It is always a good idea to learn basic phrases and greetings in the destination country's most common language. Even when speaking the language poorly, efforts by the interviewer to learn the language can be endearing to others and demonstrate an interest in the local culture. Furthermore, use of the local language might provoke others into using their own second language skills to ease communication.

The most obvious and effective way to mitigate the issues caused by differing languages is to hire an interpreter or translator to assist with all parts of the investigation occurring in a jurisdiction where a different language is spoken.

The use of an interpreter is likely unavoidable if the interviewer and interview subject speak two different languages. Even the most advanced bilingual individuals can rarely articulate themselves as well in their second language as they can in their first. For this reason, it might also be necessary to use an interpreter even when interviewing a bilingual person whose second language is the same as that of the interviewer's first.

When selecting an interpreter, the fraud examiner should ensure that the person's skills are sufficient for the task and the person is an interpreter rather than a translator.

While the skills required for both are similar, translators deal primarily with the written word, whereas interpreters deal with the spoken word.

The interviewer should spend time with the interpreter prior to the interview to achieve some familiarity and to ensure that the interpreter understands the relevant subject matter before bringing in an interview subject. The interviewer must also be mindful of and discuss industry-specific jargon that might be difficult to translate. Any visual aids, documents, or other props that the interviewer might use must be discussed with the interpreter beforehand to avoid surprise or confusion.

Additionally, it is important to set expectations for the interpreter prior to beginning the interview. Expectations should be set for the amount of speech to be translated in each increment (e.g., three sentences). Another expectation should be that the interpreter will translate everything that each party says and agree not to answer any questions on the interviewer's behalf. Seating arrangements are also important in this situation and should be determined beforehand with consideration given to the culture or jurisdiction of the involved parties.

When scheduling an interview involving an interpreter, examiners must recognize that the interview will take significantly longer because everything is said twice, first by the speaker and then by the interpreter. While this might impact the amount of time available to conduct the interview, the interviewer must always show patience and allow the interpreter to finish translating without interruption.

During the interview, the fraud examiner must be sure to speak directly to the interview subject rather than the interpreter. Building rapport remains crucial, and the use of an interpreter can impede the process if too much attention is focused on the interpreter rather than the interview subject. The interviewer must maintain eye contact and show interest in what the subject is saying regardless of whether the interviewer understands what is being said.

Additionally, humor should be avoided because jokes often do not translate well. Similarly, idioms and devices such as hyperbole and metaphors are unlikely to translate successfully and should be avoided. And rather than using acronyms for organizations, state their full names.

Interviewers must never assume that the subject is incapable of understanding the language being interpreted. People are often hesitant to admit limited second language capabilities. Consequently, the fraud examiner should refrain from making any comments to another party in the room with the assumption that the interviewee will not understand.

Cultural Differences

Culture refers to a common set of standards, traditions, and beliefs that are characteristic of a particular group of people. People from different cultures see and perceive things differently, and such differences can complicate investigatory efforts. For example, many cultures view the cultural group as more important than the individual, and polite behavior in one culture might be considered impolite in another.

It is important that fraud examiners learn the cultural intricacies of the places where they conduct investigations, and they must be familiar with cultural differences when collecting information to avoid reaching incorrect or incomplete conclusions. Seemingly minor details, such as whether to shake an interviewee's hand, could significantly impact the fraud investigation.

Certain cultural aspects such as dress, food, and language likely come to mind easily, but cultures are far more complex than they appear. Less obvious differences should be considered, potentially involving more extensive research or consultation than the fraud examiner might be used to in domestic investigations.

These less obvious cultural challenges might include traditions, morals, beliefs, and societal norms. Outsiders often view these facets only in superficial terms; a deep understanding of another culture typically requires full immersion and participation. And while these deeper aspects exist in all cultures, people typically take them for granted when considering their own culture. Gaining further understanding of another culture permits examiners to more accurately gauge how others might react to particular questions or behaviors, and better exhibit respect for cultural values.

Part of a fraud examiner's planning process for an international investigation should involve becoming familiar with how local culture and customs might affect the process. Resources for this information could include local branches of the fraud examiner's organization, open source and Internet research, consultation with local clients, or in conjunction with arranging local services such as translators, transportation, or investigators.

Differing Laws

Different countries have different laws, and in some jurisdictions, different laws apply to different categories of people. As mentioned, differences in laws often occur in areas such as collecting evidence, protecting the privacy of people, protecting the confidentiality of information, and employment rights and protections. Thus, before commencing international investigations spanning multiple jurisdictions, examiners must become familiar with such laws. The failure to account for the differences between relevant countries' legal requirements in fraud investigations can cause significant problems for the investigation, a fraud examiner's organization, or the fraud examiner personally. It is for this reason that fraud examiners must consult with legal counsel in all applicable jurisdictions before taking any investigative actions so as to ensure compliance.

Some countries have laws that place restrictions on who can conduct investigations into illegal conduct, and fraud examiners must consider these restrictions before conducting investigations abroad. The criminal procedure laws in some of these jurisdictions prohibit private (nongovernmental) parties from conducting an investigation. These laws are based on the rationale that private parties should not intrude on the investigatory powers of law enforcement.

High-Risk Regions

In some situations, an organization might need to conduct an investigation in a high-risk region, but doing so can be perilous. High-risk regions include countries that are characterized by high degrees of political, economic, legal, operational, or security risks. Typically, high-risk regions have immature or volatile political systems, weak legal systems, poor business environments, or high levels of corruption. These regions also include remote, unfamiliar, and hostile regions and countries with geopolitical unrest and turmoil.

The following resources provide information about the risk climates of foreign countries:

- The Economist Intelligence Unit (EIU) is an independent business that provides information services for companies establishing and managing operations across national borders (www.eiu.com/home.aspx).
- The *World Factbook*, which is a reference resource produced by the US Central Intelligence Agency (CIA), provides an extensive summary of the social, demographic, political, and economic conditions of countries worldwide (www.cia.gov/library/publications/the-world-factbook).
- Transparency International's Corruption Perception Index (CPI), which ranks countries by the degree of corruption perceived to exist among its public officials and politicians, can also provide insight into the level of risk in a particular country or region (www.transparency.org/research/cpi/overview).
- UNdata is a portal for extracts of data compiled by various United Nations agencies (data.un.org).
- The World Bank Group's annual "Doing Business" reports is a series of annual reports that aim to measure the costs of doing business in countries around the world (www.doingbusiness.org).
- Nationmaster provides a compilation of data from prominent international statistics sources (www.nationmaster.com).
- Penn World Tables provide data on the national accounts for all countries (cid.econ. ucdavis.edu/pwt.html).

Most, if not all, countries in the world receive credit ratings that provide valuable insight into the country's economic and political climate. Generally, it is safe to assume that the higher the credit rating, the lower the risk.

Lack of Access to Information

Lack of access to information is a common problem examiners face during cross-border investigations. In many countries, fraud examiners must obtain consent from the data subjects before accessing information stored abroad. In some countries, data cannot be exported outside the jurisdiction in which it was obtained. Often, the resources available domestically are not similarly searchable in foreign jurisdictions. In addition, many countries have restrictions on foreigners accessing information about both individuals and businesses. Thus, examiners must understand the rules and regulations regarding collecting, accessing, transporting, and storing data across national borders.

Logistical Issues with Cross-Border Investigations

Disorganization

Disorganization can plague international fraud investigations, and the complexities of coordinating such investigations can be daunting. Often, in international investigations, the fraud examiner must build a team composed of individuals from different countries who must work together toward a common goal. Without a common goal, the team will not be effective. But building a collaborative team for international investigations can be difficult when the members have different backgrounds, speak different native languages, and work in different business cultures.

Distance

Distance is a critical factor in international fraud investigations. The farther an investigation is from the examiner's home base, the more complex the planning and management of the engagement will be. Also, for fraud investigations conducted abroad, costs related to the distance are a factor. The greater the distance, the greater the costs, and because of the time and expense involved, investigations in foreign countries must often be performed on a compressed schedule.

Transportation

Similarly, transportation is a logistical issue for many international investigations. This is especially true if the relevant operations are in developing economies, remote locations, or areas with a higher risk of security-related incidents. Lack of access to an automobile or adequate public transit can hinder transportation. When investigations are to be conducted in high-risk areas, management must evaluate the quality of the available transportation before selecting a transportation provider. Additionally, the transportation of any necessary equipment to the investigation site can present logistical issues that vary depending on the type of gear being transported (e.g., laptops, mobile phones, computer forensics hardware, reference books, travel router, camera, cable locks, external storage drives, travel adapter, portable projector, universal translator, portable scanner, etc.). The examiner must make sure that the equipment arrives on time and undamaged.

Safety

In some investigations, especially those in areas with a higher risk of security-related incidents, safety can be an issue. In such cases, special security precautions (e.g., arranging bodyguards for security details or making other efforts to provide personal protection) might be necessary. When investigations are to be conducted in high-risk areas, management must develop an exit strategy before commencing the investigation. The exit strategy must identify the on-ground leaders who are in charge when needed.

Immigration

Some jurisdictions require foreign fraud examiners to have visas or, in some situations, work permits to perform investigatory activities; therefore, fraud examiners should obtain the appropriate immigration documents for all countries in which they plan to conduct investigations. For example, if fraud examiners plan to travel to China to engage in business-related activities, they must obtain a business visa (M visa). In countries where visas are required, fraud examiners must familiarize themselves with any relevant work restrictions. For example, some countries prohibit individuals with business visas from conducting interviews or digital forensics. Because obtaining the appropriate visas can take weeks, examiners should begin the process as soon as they reasonably believe they might be required to travel abroad.

Infrastructure Limitations

Infrastructure refers to the fundamental structures, facilities, and systems necessary for a country or region to sustain and support economic development. Many countries and regions do not have the basic infrastructure needed to function properly, which can complicate international investigations. Whether there are poor electrical grids, weak communication systems, or other factors, infrastructure limitations can affect an examiner's ability to gather the information needed to determine whether fraud has occurred. Poor communication, energy, and transportation infrastructures in particular can hinder cross-border investigations. For example, poor communication infrastructures are especially problematic because locating, and communicating with people across the globe – via email or otherwise – on a 24-hour basis is often important to an investigation, but might not always be possible in countries with weak infrastructures. Also, power supply is unreliable in countries with weak energy infrastructures, and power outages can drive up the cost of cross-border investigations. Additionally, in many countries inadequate transportation infrastructures hamper the movement of people and goods, which can also negatively impact international investigations.

Technology Differences

Countries and individuals across the globe use different technologies to communicate, and fraud examiners must consider such differences when conducting international investigations. Furthermore, the ways in which people use technology might vary among cultures, and not all technologies are acceptable in all cultures. For example, some countries might not allow the use of encryption in hardware or software, and some countries might not tolerate photography of government buildings.

Additionally, some countries are known to access foreign travelers' electronic devices without permission. Fraud examiners preparing to travel abroad for an investigation should check the travel advice of their home country or the foreign travel policies of their organization to determine what devices they should or should not take, as well as any security precautions for those devices.

NOTES

1. www.acfe.com/uploadedFiles/ACFE_Website/Content/documents/Code-of-Standards-2014.pdf
2. A sample fraud examination report can be found at www.acfe.com/samplereport.

CHAPTER 6

Interviewing Witnesses and Suspects

Interviews are an integral part of most fraud investigations. They serve to help the fraud examiner corroborate information already gathered, obtain additional information and evidence, and secure a signed confession. As part of a fraud investigation, an *interview* is a structured face-to-face question-and-answer session designed to elicit specific information. It differs from an ordinary conversation in that it is structured as opposed to free-form. An interview can consist of one question or a series of questions.

Interviewing is a much broader concept than interrogating. The term *interrogating* is often associated with oppressive tactics; consequently, the term *interviewing* has largely taken its place to describe the task of obtaining information from witnesses, victims, and suspects. Being able to gather information through interviews could be the most important skill that a fraud investigator ever develops.

A fraud examiner's interview skills must encompass more than eliciting a statement from a subject or suspect. Strategic planning of the entire interview process – from the order of the interviews to the goals and methodology for each interview to the analysis of the subjects' statements – is crucial and could determine the investigation's success or failure.

PLANNING AND PREPARING FOR AN INTERVIEW

Planning and preparation constitute one of the most important phases in effective interviewing. The interviewer should plan and prepare for each interview, regardless of whether it is an information-seeking interview with a witness or victim, or an admission-seeking interview with a suspect. Planning and preparation ensure that the interviewer is well equipped to conduct effective and ethical interviews.

There are a number of points the interviewer must consider during the planning and preparation phase of all interviews. The specific circumstances of each fraud investigation case determine the importance of each of these points and how they impinge on one another. For example, the need to have an adult guardian or an interpreter present might affect when and where the interview takes place. Additionally, interviewers should consider each point in relation to the others.

Understanding the Interview's Role in the Investigation

To appropriately plan and prepare for interviews, fraud examiners must review and consider the evidence gathered, and determine how the interviews will contribute to the goals of the investigation. Interviewers must prepare every interview with the needs of the whole investigation in mind. They must also consider how they might use the information or evidence gathered during each interview to establish the truth of the

Portions of the material in this chapter also appear in the following Association of Certified Fraud Examiners (ACFE) publications: *Issues in Conducting International Interviews, Interviewing Witnesses and Suspects*, and *Analyzing Written Statements*.

matter under investigation. The following questions help ensure that the interviewer obtains relevant and useful information from the interviews to support the investigation:

- Who needs to be interviewed and in what order?
- Why is a particular interviewee's viewpoint important?
- What information do I now need to obtain?
- When should the interview take place (e.g., now or after obtaining more information about the circumstances)?

Understanding the Interviewee

For an interview to be effective, the interviewer needs to understand the interviewee as an individual. This requires having background knowledge about both the individual and the alleged fraud. The amount of background information needed will depend on the interviewee's relationship to the overall investigation; an investigator probably will not need to know as much about a witness as about a suspect. Developing a profile of the interviewee can help the investigator determine how to approach the interview based on the following factors.

Age

Knowing the interviewee's age helps determine the most appropriate time for each interview to avoid interviewees' scheduling conflicts (e.g., a juvenile subject's school schedule) or whether an interview will require the presence of an adult guardian.

Beyond scheduling considerations, knowing the age of the subject can help the interviewer determine an effective approach or communication strategy for each interviewee. For example, subjects in their 60s will likely prefer more formal language or attire and use of titles such as Mr. or Mrs., while also being less familiar with technical jargon. Conversely, subjects in their 20s might be more comfortable with slang or laid-back approaches to the interview.

Gender

In certain violations, it is important to consider the gender of the interviewee and the interviewer. For example, it is not uncommon for employment fraud allegations to exist in tandem with claims of sexual harassment or similar issues. In such situations, it might be appropriate to have someone of the same gender conduct the interview; for example, a female witness or suspect might be more willing to speak openly with a female interviewer.

Domestic Circumstances

Knowledge of an interviewee's domestic circumstances might indicate to the interviewee that the interviewer conducted thorough research prior to the interview. To obtain such information, the interviewer should consider speaking to members of the interviewee's immediate family, relatives, associates, colleagues, and neighbors. However, depending on the circumstances, interviewing those close to the subject could reveal the investigation's existence and negatively impact the process. Interviewers might be able to effectively develop a profile of the subject's domestic circumstances through human resources files, public records, or social media research.

Cultural and Language Background

An interviewee's culture and native language might affect the way the interviewer should address the individual and how formal the verbal and physical approach needs to be. Does the interviewee's culture frown upon eye-to-eye contact? Does the interviewee have a strong regional dialect? Do the interviewee and interviewer speak the same language? If not, the interviewer should enlist the services of an interpreter.

Educational Background and Intellectual Ability

Knowing a person's educational background and intellectual ability can help provide information about potential areas of vulnerability. For example, interviewees who have certain intellectual disabilities might not understand the significance of the questions or the implications of their answers.

Physical and Mental Health

Some interviewees might be vulnerable because of physical or mental health conditions. The interviewer should be alert to signs and symptoms of health problems when planning and preparing for the interviews. If the interviewer does not feel comfortable making informed decisions about matters related to interviewees' potential health issues, the interviewer should consult a medical expert.

Knowledge of the Incident

An interviewee's knowledge of the incident and details of what information the interviewer has might indicate whether the interviewee is likely to be cooperative or hostile. Previous contact with the investigator is useful to anticipate cooperation.

Previous Contact with Interviewers

Knowledge about the subject's previous interviews can provide insight into a subject's potential attitude and behavior toward the interviewer. However, previous attitude and behavior might have been in response to the specific situation at that time. Also, background checks might reveal information about any offenses committed by a suspect and the methods used. Interviewers should always consider liaising with interviewers who have previous knowledge of the interviewee.

Traumatic Experience

The interviewer should consider not only the background and personal characteristics of the interviewee, but also any experiences the interviewee recently underwent or is undergoing, whether as a witness, victim, or suspect. This might affect the timing of the interview because of the interviewee's need for treatment, counseling, or social support.

For example, a suspect might be dealing with an addiction problem, a medical emergency, or serious personal issues like divorce or foreclosure.

Legal Considerations

There are a number of legal problems that might arise as a result of an interview if the interviewer is unaware of the relevant rules. However, if interviewers understand and follow basic legal concepts, use common sense, and consult legal counsel as needed, they and the organization should emerge from the interviews unscathed.

Because some countries have laws that impose restrictions on conducting employee interviews, an organization's management and legal counsel should confirm that it is legal under local law to conduct such interviews. Some countries prohibit private employers from conducting employee interviews in internal investigations that are criminal in nature. These laws prevent private parties from encroaching on law enforcement's exclusive authority to exercise police power.

Some jurisdictions have laws that prevent an employer from coercing its employees to participate in interviews. If, in a jurisdiction with this type of law, an employee refuses to participate in an interview or answer questions during an interview, the employer may not compel the employee to cooperate, and the employee's refusal might not provide sufficient grounds for disciplinary action. Interviewers must also be aware of whether employees have a right to remain silent.

In many countries, employees have interview representation rights. Local labor laws might require that an employer consult with or notify labor unions or works councils before interviewing employees. Similarly, an employee who is a member of a union may have the right to have a union representative present during an interview.

Some countries have laws that impose restrictions on using information gathered during employee interviews as evidentiary support for decisions to take disciplinary actions against the employees.

The legal considerations of a fraud investigation vary depending on the specific circumstances involved and the jurisdiction in which it is conducted. Additionally, the misunderstanding or misapplication of legal concepts can cause fatal consequences to an otherwise well-run fraud examination. Therefore, if interviewers are uncertain or have any specific questions regarding the rules of a particular jurisdiction, they should seek the advice of legal counsel before conducting any interviews.

Offenses and Points to Prove or Disprove

Fraud examiners must clearly identify all the possible offenses they are investigating as part of their planning and preparation. They should use this information to determine the points to prove and should anticipate any defense that might be offered. The main areas to consider are:

- The intent (*mens rea*): What was in the suspect's mind at the time?
- The motive: Why did the suspect commit the fraud?
- The action (*actus reus*): What did the suspect do?
- The method (*modus operandi*): How did the suspect commit the fraud?

However, while it is important in all interviews to know the points necessary to prove the possible offense or offenses in question, the need to cover these points should not dominate the interview by controlling the flow of information, nor should they artificially constrain or distort the account of events given by an interviewee. Therefore, the interviewer should encourage the interviewee to provide a full explanation of the events before being asked specific questions that are relevant to the proof of the alleged offenses.

Practical Arrangements

Practical arrangements are an important consideration in the planning and preparation for an interview. These practical issues apply to the planning of witness, victim, and suspect interviews. The following factors should be considered.

Venue

The term *venue* refers to the physical location where the interview takes place. When possible, the interview should be held in a location where the subject will feel comfortable and secure, but in an environment that the interviewer can control.

The interview room should be quiet and free from distractions, comfortably lit, and well ventilated. There should be no locks on the doors or any physical barriers placed between the subject and the exit. If the interview location causes the subject to feel that his freedom is restricted, this can inhibit communication and might subject the interviewer or the company to liability for false imprisonment.

The interview should not take place in a venue that the subject is overly familiar with. However, forcing the subject to meet somewhere inconvenient or difficult will adversely affect the interview. Communication requires cooperation, and effective interviewers understand that they need the subject's cooperation; therefore, they should do what they can, within reason, to accommodate the subject's needs.

The interviewer should consider whether the location of the interview makes a statement to the subject, the subject's associates, or the subject's co-workers. The interviewer should be aware that tightening or loosening the level of privacy for an interview might signal to others that there is something unique about a particular interview, and might therefore create an implication about the subject's involvement in the conduct that is under investigation. Consequently, the level of confidentiality should remain constant for all interviews, from the most tangential witness to the prime suspect. It is preferable to maintain a single location for all interviews; however, when this is not possible, alternate locations should be comparable in terms of security and atmosphere. Reserving a meeting room in advance can save time and prevent awkward or problematic interview conditions resulting from a poorly chosen interview venue.

Remote Interviews

Technology has advanced to the point that a video interview conducted via the Internet is a valid alternative if schedules, travel costs, or other obstacles preclude an in-person interview. However, while video interviews are often effective for information-seeking interviews, they are less effective for admission-seeking interviews and should be avoided for this purpose if possible.

The selection of a reliable and widely available videoconferencing service is of paramount importance when conducting a video interview. The interviewer should test the service before conducting an interview to ensure that it works as needed and to gain familiarity with the service. The interviewer should also verify that the microphone works correctly and the volume is set to an appropriate level. Performing these actions ensures that the interviewer can devote full attention to the interview without being distracted by the technology.

Interviewers should have a backup plan in case the service provider fails or some other technological problem occurs. A backup plan might be using another videoconferencing service or simply resorting to a telephone interview.

When scheduling a video interview, examiners must be mindful of time zones and other factors, such as daylight saving time, to ensure that both parties join the conference at the same time. While one should attempt to avoid scheduling the interview late at night, this might be unavoidable depending on the time difference. In this case, it is preferable that the interviewer experience any inconvenience that might occur, not the interview subject.

When conducting a video interview, the interviewer should dress appropriately and act as professionally as if the interview were taking place in person. Also, poor posture, leaning back in a chair, or other casual behaviors might plague an interviewer who is at home and feels more relaxed; such unprofessional behavior should be avoided.

Multiple Interviewers

There can be advantages when two interviewers are able to conduct interviews together; however, it is important that they work together in planning and preparing for the interview. The interviewers should each consider and agree upon their respective roles and responsibilities before the interview. Thorough preparation helps avoid the possibility of the second interviewer interrupting or breaking planned silences or pauses between questions. Consequently, the interview plan should include when the second interviewer is going to ask questions. This might be at the end of each topic or when the first interviewer has finished asking all his questions in relation to all the topics. There might be occasions when the interview needs to be suspended so that the interviewers can revise the plan.

Time

The interviewers must always ensure they allow sufficient time to conduct the interview. Legal requirements and the availability of interview rooms might affect suspect interviews. The interviewer might have to plan a witness interview around the subject's work schedule and domestic responsibilities, as well as local religious or official holidays.

Recording Interviews

Recording an interview can be a significant obstacle to full cooperation. Many people are hesitant about being recorded. This can be overcome in many cases by explaining that the recording will be an accurate record of the interview and that it is in the best interests of the witness. However, there might be restrictions on whether an interview can be recorded, depending on the jurisdiction in which the interview occurs or the policies of an organization. Before asking for permission from the subject, interviewers will have to determine what is or is not allowed regarding recording interviews, what they might need to seek approval for, and who has the approval authority.

If recording is allowed and appropriate, the best practice is to control the recording outside of the interview room, when possible, to minimize disruption. Typically, if the recorder is invisible to the witness, it is usually soon forgotten and the interview progresses in a free-flowing way. However, if the recording must occur in the interview room, the interviewer should make it as unobtrusive as possible, and avoid having to visibly interact with the recording device.

Note Taking

In a professional setting, most subjects understand the critical nature of notes. Very few subjects will say that it is not acceptable for the interviewer to take notes, regardless of how they feel about it. If they are absolutely opposed to note taking, the interviewer should find out why, concentrate on what the subject says, and reduce the interview to notes as quickly as possible after the interview. With a hostile subject who opposes note taking, the interviewer can ask for approval to make selected notes regarding dates or things the interviewer might not remember later. The interviewer can explain that it is important that he understand the subject's position or communication correctly. If the subject is adamant that the interviewer not take notes, it should be documented in the interviewer's report.

When notes are not taken during the interview, they should be taken immediately after, when results are still fresh in the interviewer's mind. If notes are going to be taken, the interviewer should begin each interview on a clean page, and should note the date, time, and place of the interview, as well as all the individuals present. The interviewer should also initial and date the notes. In addition, the following suggestions might be helpful:

- Obtain biographical data for the subject, including full name, government identification number if available, and means of contacting the subject (e.g., telephone numbers, email addresses), including alternate contact information of family and friends.
- Document the questions that were asked.
- Ensure the notes are adequate to prepare the investigation report.
- Do not document conclusions or interpretations, as such notes can cause problems with the interviewer's credibility if they are later produced in court.
- Document any unusual change in body language in an objective manner.
- Document changes in body language and tone, if applicable, in conjunction with notes of what the subject or interviewer said at the time the body language or tone changed.

Equipment

Preparation should include making sure that all the necessary equipment is on hand. Interviewers should check in advance that all the equipment – such as digital recording devices and devices necessary to display exhibits – is working correctly.

185

Exhibits and Property

Some exhibits and property might be too large to show in an interview room or at the home, such as allegedly misappropriated tangible items. Examiners might need to make alternative arrangements, such as using photographs or video recordings of the items. All property should be clearly marked and identified to assist in the interview.

TYPES OF INTERVIEWS

Many investigations will require a series of interviews, with each interview differing either by the type of interviewee or by the strategy employed. During the planning and preparation phase, investigators should categorize each interviewee and decide on a strategy to use for each individual interview. These determinations will also influence the order in which the interviewer should schedule the interviews.

Typically, the interviews should start with neutral, third-party witnesses in which the investigator needs to determine or confirm facts. The order of interviews usually proceeds from least likely to most likely to be involved. The last subject to be interviewed will almost always need to be the main suspect, or the accused, in an admission-seeking interview that ideally results in a confession.

Interviews by Subject

Neutral, Third-Party Witnesses

In a typical fraud examination, the interviewer should first interview neutral third-party witnesses – individuals not involved in the specific instance of fraud under investigation but who have information relevant to the situation. These might include vendors, clients, contractors, or co-workers from another department.

Corroborative Witnesses and Victims

Next, the interviewer should interview corroborative witnesses. *Corroborative witnesses* are those who can confirm facts relating to a specific offense. These witnesses might be either cooperative or uncooperative.

Additionally, the fraud examiner should meet with the victim(s) of the crime. The victim in a fraud case will often be an organization or other entity, but in some cases victims include one or more people, and their accounts of what happened to them are valuable to the investigation.

Co-Conspirators

Those suspected of complicity should be next on the list of interviewees, from the least culpable to the most culpable. In criminal investigations, law enforcement and prosecutors can frequently promise leniency in return for cooperation if appropriate. However, fraud examiners outside of law enforcement should be aware that they cannot promise the same type of leniency; this is beyond the scope of their duties.

Suspect(s)

The main suspect, or the accused, of the investigation is generally interviewed last, after obtaining all the facts necessary to resolve the allegation. Even if it is unlikely that the subject will confess, an interview is usually scheduled; in many instances, it can be used for later impeachment – the process in which the accused's testimony in a trial or administrative proceeding is contradicted by their previous statements. An interview might also give the examiner a good idea of what defenses the subject might raise. If there are multiple suspects, the interviewer should interview them in order of likely culpability, from least to most.

Interviews by Purpose

Information Seeking

Information-seeking interviews are typically the first interviews conducted; they should be nonconfrontational and nonthreatening, and should encourage open communication. Adopting an objective approach that is highly oriented toward obtaining accurate information is usually the most appropriate strategy for this type of interview.

Admission Seeking

Admission-seeking interviews are reserved specifically for individuals whose culpability is reasonably certain. An interviewer might base an assessment of culpability on verbal and nonverbal responses to interview questions, as well as documents, physical evidence, and other interviews.

The interviewer poses admission-seeking questions in an exact order designed to clear an innocent person or encourage a culpable person to confess. These questions must not violate the rights and privileges of the interviewee.

Interviewers should schedule the admission-seeking interview when they can control the situation. Normally, they should not conduct an admission-seeking interview in the accused's office or an area where the accused feels a sense of comfort. Additionally, the interview is best conducted by surprise, if possible, so that the accused does not have time to prepare potential dishonest responses or to undertake further concealment efforts.

The choice of when to conduct an admission-seeking interview of a suspect is critical. Before conducting one, examiners should ensure that all other reasonable investigative steps have been completed; as much information as possible has been developed from other sources; and the interviewer can reasonably control the place, time, and subject matter of the interview.

INTERVIEWING STRATEGIES

The degree to which a prospective witness is either willing or required to meet and speak with an interviewer should have no bearing on the approach the interviewer takes. Whether the prospective witness is an employee required to meet with the interviewer or a reluctant witness the interviewer has been trying to interview for several months, the same basic elements of courtesy, building rapport, and professionalism apply.

Interviewers should recognize that they need all the information witnesses might have. Investigators also need the full and complete cooperation of witnesses, not only for the current interview, but also for potential follow-up interviews.

One of the most important factors in interviewers' preparation before making contact is their perception of the witness. In other words, how does the interviewer see, perceive, view, or consider the witness?

If the interviewer is prejudiced, predisposed in any fashion, or in any way less than fully interested in the interview, the effectiveness of the interview will be significantly reduced. Each subject is the most important person in the interviewer's professional life during all contact with that person.

If the interviewer considers that each witness might have the key information needed to solve the case, then the interviewer can better prepare for the meeting. The interviewer needs the witness; the witness does not need the interviewer.

Every word used in the phrasing of a question, the interviewer's tone and body language, and even the setting of the interview send signals to the subject. By retaining an objective demeanor, asking questions that reveal little about what they already know, choosing a private setting, and interviewing one subject at a time, interviewers keep the integrity of the interview intact to the best of their abilities.

Types of Questions

When conducting an interview, there are five general types of questions an interviewer can ask:

- Introductory questions
- Informational questions
- Assessment questions
- Admission-seeking questions
- Closing questions

The purpose of the first interviews is to gather information. In these routine interview situations, interviewers will normally ask only three of the five types of questions: introductory, informational, and closing questions. If they have reasonable cause to believe the respondent is not being truthful, they can ask assessment questions. Finally, if they decide with reasonable cause that the respondent is responsible for misdeeds, they can pose admission-seeking questions.

Introductory Questions

One of the most difficult aspects of an interview is getting started. In many instances, the interview is the first meeting between the interviewer and the respondent. The interviewer needs to accomplish the following objectives: provide an introduction, establish necessary rapport, state a reason for the interview to establish its theme, and get information through the subject's answers and reactions.

The way to accomplish the introduction is through questions, as opposed to statements, that allow the interviewer to assess feedback from the respondent. If the respondent is resistant to an interview, that fact will come out through the subject's responses to the introductory questions.

Providing the Introduction

The interviewer should indicate his name and company, but avoid using titles. As a general proposition, the more informal the interview, the more relaxed the respondent will be. This leads to better communication.

Making physical contact helps break down psychological barriers to communication; therefore, the interviewer should also shake hands with the subject when appropriate. The interviewer must remember that the practice and acceptability of touching when greeting or conversing differs considerably from one culture to the next. The interviewer should avoid invading the respondent's personal space, however, as this might make the person uncomfortable. The definition of personal space will differ from culture to culture, and interviewers should become familiar with jurisdictional norms during the planning phase.

One of the goals of the introduction is to create a comfortable climate for the subject – one that will encourage open communication. Once the subject is seated, it is a good idea to ask the subject if he would like something to drink, needs to take off his coat or jacket, and so on. It is best to take care of these matters before beginning the interview to avoid delays and interruptions.

Establishing Rapport

It is important to establish rapport – a relationship of common understanding or trust and acquiescence between people – during the introductory phase of an interview. In other words, there must be some common ground established before questioning begins. Engaging in small talk, or informal conversation with the subject for a few minutes can usually accomplish this. Interviewers should avoid overdoing this, but should use it to break the ice and establish a flow of communication between themselves and subjects.

Establishing the Interview Theme

The interviewer must state the purpose of the interview in some way before asking serious questions. The interview theme might be related only indirectly to the actual purpose of the interview. The goal of the theme is to get the respondent to buy in to assisting in the interview. The theme for the interview should be logical for the respondent to accept and easy for the interviewer to explain. At this stage of the interview, less specific, open-ended inquiries are generally more effective than narrow, closed questions; both types of questions are discussed later in this chapter. One of the most effective interview themes is that the interviewer is seeking the subject's help. Nearly all human beings get satisfaction from helping others. Throughout the interview, it is important to include the subject as part of the process, as opposed to making the person feel like a target or less than a full participant in the process. During this phase of the interview, the respondent must not feel threatened in any way.

Observing Reactions

The interviewer must be adept in interpreting the respondent's reactions to questions. Most communication between individuals is unspoken; subjects will provide clues about what they know – consciously or subconsciously – with their body language, tone of voice, and attitudes. The interviewer must therefore systematically observe the various responses the subject gives during the course of the conversation.

The interviewer can do this by first posing nonsensitive questions while establishing rapport. By observing the subject's reactions to the nonsensitive questions, the interviewer can establish a baseline for the subject's verbal and nonverbal behavior. Later, when asking more sensitive questions, the interviewer will observe the respondent's reactions. If the respondent's verbal and nonverbal behavior significantly changes as the interviewer poses particular questions, the interviewer must attempt to determine why.

Informational Questions

Once the proper format for the interview is set, the interviewer should turn to the fact-gathering portion. Again, informational questions should be nonconfrontational and nonthreatening, and should elicit unbiased factual information. The great majority of the interviewer's questions will fall into this category.

Three Types of Questions

There are essentially three types of questions: open, closed, and leading. Each type of question is used in a logical sequence to maximize the development of information.

Open Questions
Open questions are worded in a way that makes it difficult to answer "yes" or "no." The typical open question calls for a monologue response and can be answered in several different ways. During the informational phase of the interview, the interviewer should endeavor to ask primarily open questions. This is to stimulate conversation and allow the subject to convey as much information as possible.

An open question does not restrict the subject's response. So instead of asking, "You are in charge of posting expenses, aren't you?," which directs the subject's response to one particular area, the investigator might ask, "Would you tell me about your job?" The latter example allows a broad response that will yield more information. Later, the interviewer can go back and draw out more information about a particular topic.

Closed Questions
Closed questions are those that require a precise answer, usually "yes" or "no." Interviewers use closed questions to deal with specifics, such as amounts, dates, and times. Generally, interviewers should avoid closed questions in the informational part of the interview. They are used extensively in the closing phase.

Leading Questions

Leading questions contain the answer as a part of the question. They are usually used to confirm facts that are already known. An example of a leading question is: "There have been no changes in the operation since last year, have there?" This type of question gives the subject much less room to maneuver than an open or closed question.

Notice how the leading question directs the subject to answer in a particular way – that there have not been any changes. It implies that the interviewer already knows the answer, and asks the subject to confirm what is already known. The open question allows more latitude for subjects to make any comments they want about changes in the operation. The closed question narrows the subject's options a bit, but it still allows the subject to confirm or deny that changes have been made. Leading questions can be particularly effective in obtaining confessions or getting subjects to make unpleasant admissions.

Informational Question Techniques

The following are suggestions to improve the quality of the interview during the information-gathering phase:

- Begin by asking questions that are not likely to cause the respondent to become defensive or hostile.
- Ask the questions in a manner that will develop the facts in the order of their occurrence, or in some other systematic order.
- Ask only one question at a time, and frame the question so that only one answer is required.
- Ask straightforward and frank questions; generally avoid shrewd approaches.
- Keep interruptions to a minimum, and do not stop the subject's narrative without good reason.
- Give the respondent ample time to answer; do not rush.
- Try to help the respondent remember, but do not suggest answers; be careful not to imply any particular answer through facial expressions, gestures, methods of asking questions, or types of questions asked.
- Repeat or rephrase questions, if necessary, to get the desired facts.
- Be sure the answers are understood; if they are not perfectly clear, have the respondent clarify them at the time instead of asking for more explanation later.
- Give the subject an opportunity to qualify answers.
- Separate facts from inferences.
- Have the subject give comparisons by percentages, fractions, estimates of time and distance, and other such methods to ensure accuracy.
- After the respondent gives a narrative account, ask follow-up questions about every key issue that was discussed.
- Upon conclusion of the direct questioning, ask the respondent to summarize the information given. Then summarize the facts as they are understood, and have the respondent verify that these conclusions are correct.

If the interviewer has reason to believe that the respondent is being untruthful, then the interviewer can pose assessment questions. Otherwise, the interview is brought to a logical close at the end of the informational phase.

Assessment Questions

If the interviewer has reason to believe that the respondent is being deceptive, the interviewer should begin asking assessment questions. These are questions specifically designed to establish the respondent's credibility. When assessing credibility, the interviewer must observe the subject's verbal and nonverbal responses. By making such observations, the interviewer can assess the respondent's credibility with some degree of accuracy. That assessment will form the basis of the interviewer's decision about whether to pose admission-seeking questions to obtain a legal admission of wrongdoing.

If the subject answered all the informational questions about the event and the interviewer has reason to believe the subject is being deceptive, the interviewer must establish a theme to justify additional questions. This theme can ordinarily be put forth by saying, "I have a few additional questions." The interviewer should not indicate in any way that these questions are for a different purpose than seeking information.

Norming or *calibrating* is the process of observing behavior before critical questions are asked, as opposed to doing so during questioning. Norming should be a routine part of all interviews. For example, the interviewer can ask questions regarding how long subjects have been employed by the organization, how long they have lived in their residences, or where they went to school – questions that should elicit honest and easily verifiable responses. The mannerisms the subject displays while responding to these norming questions establish a baseline for the rest of the interview. Any departures from the baseline later in the interview could indicate that the subject is being deceptive or untruthful.

People with truthful attitudes will answer questions one way; those with untruthful attitudes will generally answer them differently. Assessment questions ask the subject to agree with matters that go against the principles of most honest people. In other words, dishonest people are likely to agree with many of the statements, whereas honest people will not. The primary purpose of assessment questions is to get a verbal or nonverbal reaction from the respondent. The interviewer will then carefully assess that reaction.

Admission-Seeking Questions

The choice of when to conduct an admission-seeking interview of a suspect is critical. Admission-seeking interviews are reserved specifically for situations in which:

- The respondent's culpability is reasonably certain.
- All other reasonable investigative steps have been completed.
- As much information as possible has been developed from other sources.
- The interviewer can reasonably control the place, time, and subject matter of the interview.

The interviewer must be careful when asking these questions not to violate the rights and privileges of the person being interviewed.

Admission-seeking questions serve at least three purposes. The first purpose is to distinguish the innocent from the culpable. A culpable individual will frequently confess during the admission-seeking phase of an interview, while an innocent person will not do so unless threats or coercion are used. In some instances, the only way to differentiate the culpable from the innocent is to seek an admission of guilt.

The second purpose is to obtain a valid confession. Confessions, under the law, must be voluntarily obtained. The importance of a valid and binding confession to wrongdoing cannot be overstated.

The third purpose of admission-seeking questions is to convince the person making a confession to sign a written statement acknowledging the facts. Although oral confessions are as legally binding as written ones, the written statement has greater credibility. It also discourages a person from later attempting to recant.

Closing Questions

In routine, informational interviews, closing the interview on a positive note is a must. Beyond maintaining good will, closing questions serve the following purposes: to reconfirm facts, to gather additional facts, and to conclude the interview.

Reconfirm Facts

It is not unusual for the interviewer to have misunderstood or misinterpreted one or more of the respondent's statements. Therefore, to ensure that the interviewer has understood the information that the witness provided, the interviewer should review the key facts during the closing phase of the interview.

It is a good technique to pose leading questions at this phase of the interview. This allows interviewers to state what they understood the subject to have said, and it gives the subject a chance to confirm or deny the interviewer's interpretation. For example, the interviewer might ask, "You knew Ms. Jones had some financial problems – is that right?"

Gather Additional Facts

The closing phase also seeks previously unknown facts. It provides subjects further opportunity to say whatever they want about the matter at hand. The interviewer should make it a point to ask subjects if they know of any other evidence or witnesses that would be helpful to the investigation. This information is not always volunteered, and the interviewer should not promise confidentiality. The theme of the closing phase should be to provide the subject with an opportunity to furnish any relevant facts or opinions that might have been overlooked.

Conclude the Interview

Concluding the interview properly is important because doing so helps maintain good-will and ensure future cooperation. The interviewer should ask the subject if there is anything else the subject would like to say. This gives the correct impression that the interviewer is interested in all relevant information, regardless of which side it favors. It can be helpful to involve the respondent in solving the case.

In addition, asking a witness if there is anything else the witness would like to say gives the respondent an opportunity to assist the interviewer, and it makes the respondent feel like a vital part of the interview. It also opens the door for the respondent to provide additional information that was not specifically asked for. Similarly, asking subjects if they know of someone else whom the interviewer might talk to can be helpful and lead to other potential sources of information.

Interview Methodologies

While interviewers might apply different strategies for each subject, there are frameworks for most situations. Ideally, interviewers should have a variety of strategies in their repertoire that they can adjust to different subjects and situations. However, organizations' rules or the laws of their jurisdictions might limit some interviewers in their use of techniques.

Frequently, interviews with witnesses and victims should involve information-gathering techniques, where the examiner seeks cooperation and uses cognitive techniques to learn what the interviewee knows. Information-gathering interviews can also be useful with suspects. Accusatory interviews are most often used with suspects in admission-seeking interviews. However, the investigator might find that victims and witnesses also have motivations for being dishonest, such as when they are partially culpable for the offense in question or when they are trying to protect someone else. In these cases, accusatory interviewing might be used with victims and witnesses. If the witness or victim is reluctant to reveal information, motivational interviewing might also be useful.

The PEACE Framework

Information-seeking interviews adopt an objective approach that is highly oriented toward obtaining accurate information. One of the most popular international information-seeking techniques is the PEACE framework, originally developed in the UK but adopted in many jurisdictions.

In this framework, PEACE stands for:

- Planning and preparation for interviews
- Engage and explain
- Account, clarification, compare, and contrast (formally challenge)
- Closure
- Evaluation

The PEACE framework can be used effectively in interviews of witnesses, victims, and suspects, although there might be differences in strategy for each.

The Planning and Preparation Phase

Interviewers need to decide the order in which they will conduct the interviews, with a view to maximizing their effectiveness. They should carefully manage the timing of the interviews within an investigation and clearly define the objectives of each interview. First, interviewers should decide whether an interview with a specific person is immediately necessary or there are more important priorities to which they need to attend.

The method and the effectiveness of a suspect's interview are influenced by the amount and quality of the information the interviewer has previously obtained from other sources. For instance, if the interviewer hopes to obtain a confession from the suspect, it is important to develop substantial evidence beforehand.

Investigators should consider interview requirements and strategy, as well as where the interview will take place. All of these decisions constitute the planning and preparation phase of the interview.

The Engage and Explain Phase

Once the interview begins, the investigator should strive to engage and explain. At the earliest opportunity, the interviewer should establish a relationship with the interviewee, and should seek to maintain it throughout the interview. This is what is meant by *engage*. Also, at the beginning of an interview, the investigator needs to explain the purpose of the interview, the rights of the individual, the ground rules, and any relevant procedures.

The Account, Clarification, Compare, and Contrast Phase

This phase is where the investigator obtains the interviewee's full account of events. The interviewer might need to clarify or compare and contrast the interviewee's account because of inconsistencies in what the interviewee said or inconsistencies with other evidence in the investigator's possession.

The Closure Phase

In the closure phase, the investigator needs to bring the interview to a conclusion by confirming what the interviewee said and explaining what happens next.

The Evaluation Phase

After an interview, the interviewer should evaluate its significance within the framework of the entire investigation. In the final step of the PEACE framework, the evaluation phase, the investigator must consider the following questions:

- What information has been obtained?
- How does the interview match other available evidence?
- What action needs to be taken?

- What further inquiries now need to be made?
- How did the investigator perform?
- How could the investigator further develop his skills?

The investigator's previous investigation plan might need revising. Information obtained during the interview could suggest the need for an urgent reassessment of priorities. Sometimes there might seem to be insufficient time for evaluation, or even for planning and preparation, but the investigator should always spend time on these two phases.

Motivational Interviewing

Motivational interviewing is a strategy that originally developed out of clinical interviewing, where health practitioners counsel patients or clients to change their behavior by exploring and resolving ambivalence. However, motivational interviewing techniques can also be successful in interviews within the field of fraud examination.

The key theory behind motivational interviewing is *cognitive dissonance*, or the psychological discomfort of having two conflicting thoughts at the same time or engaging in behavior that goes against one's beliefs. Under the theory, most people have a desire to resolve this conflict, but they often use rationalization or repression to escape it.

In the case of fraud examination, most subjects who committed fraud experience cognitive dissonance when they discuss information related to their offense, either because they are lying to the interviewer or because of the guilt surrounding their actions. The interviewer seeks to put the subject in an emotional state through questioning and presenting evidence. The interviewer then helps the subject resolve the internal conflict by cooperating.

Accusatory Model

Another common interview strategy is the accusatory model, which is primarily used for admission-seeking or suspect interviews (although interviewers might also use such methods when witnesses appear to have something to hide). As the name suggests, the purpose of this interview is to eventually confront the subject directly with accusations to obtain a confession.

Accusatory interviews often start similarly to information-seeking interviews such as the PEACE method, by encouraging rapport. The interviewer begins by asking objective, open questions. Then, the interviewer shifts to a norming process to note changes in the subject's behavior based on different questioning. The purpose of the norming process is to look for behavioral changes that might indicate deceptive behavior.

Eventually, the interviewer begins an admission-seeking process, which involves presenting the subject with evidence that contradicts earlier statements and then firmly accusing the subject of guilt. The goal is to make the subject feel that the violation is already proven and that cooperation is the best course.

During most admission-seeking interviews, the interviewer should take the following steps.

Make a Direct Accusation

The accusation should be in the form of a statement rather than a question. Additionally, the accusatory process should not include emotive words, such as *steal, fraud,* and *crime.* The interviewer should phrase the accusation so that the accused is psychologically trapped, with no way out.

Observe the Suspect's Reaction

When accused of wrongdoing, the typical guilty person reacts with silence. If the accused does deny culpability, those denials are usually weak. In some cases, the accused almost mumbles the denial. It is common for culpable individuals to avoid outright denials. Rather, they give reasons why they could not have committed the act in question.

In contrast, the innocent person might react with genuine shock or anger at an accusation. As opposed to the guilty person, the innocent person usually strongly denies carrying out the act in question.

Repeat the Accusation

If the accused does not strenuously object after the interviewer makes the accusation, the interviewer should repeat it with the same degree of conviction and strength. For example, an interviewer might say, "As I said, our examination has concluded that you are the responsible person. So, now it is not so much a question of what you did, but why you did it."

Interrupt Denials

In instances in which the subject attempts to deny the allegations and the examiner is convinced of the subject's guilt, the examiner must interrupt the denial. An innocent person is unlikely to allow the interviewer to prevail in stopping the denial. Additionally, a guilty person is more likely than an innocent person to stop short of an outright denial (e.g., "I didn't do it"), and is also more likely to furnish the interviewer with explanations as to why the accused is not the responsible party.

Additionally, the interviewer must prevent the subject from making an outright denial, because it becomes extremely difficult to change a denial once it is uttered. If the person denies the accusation and later admits it, the individual is admitting to lying, and this type of admission is hard to make. Therefore, the interviewer's job is to prevent the subject from making an outright denial, thereby making it easier for the subject to eventually confess to the act.

Examiners can use several techniques to stop or interrupt denials:

- *Delays:* One of the most effective techniques to stop or interrupt a denial is to delay the respondent's ability to speak. When using this tactic, the interviewer should not argue with the accused, but rather attempt to delay the outright denial. The innocent person often refuses to wait or to let the interviewer continue talking.

- *Repeating interruptions:* Occasionally, it might be necessary to interrupt the accused's attempted denial repeatedly. Because this stage of the interview is crucial, interviewers should be prepared to increase the tone of the interruptions to the point when they are prepared to say: "If you keep interrupting, I am going to have to terminate this conversation." Guilty individuals will find this threatening, since they want to know the extent of any incriminating evidence the interviewer has.
- *Reasoning:* If the use of delays and interruptions is unsuccessful, the interviewer can attempt to reason with the accused. While appealing to the suspect's logic, the examiner should present the accused with implicating evidence. However, the interviewer should not normally disclose all the facts of the case, but rather small portions here and there.

Establish a Rationalization

Once the interviewer makes and repeats the accusation and stops the suspect's denials, the interviewer should establish a morally acceptable rationalization that allows the accused to square the misdeed with his conscience. It is not necessary that this rationalization be related to the actual underlying causes of the misconduct. It is common and acceptable for the accused to explain away the moral consequences of the action by seizing onto any plausible explanation other than being a "bad person."

If the accused does not seem to relate to one theme, the interviewer should go on to another until one seems to fit. Thereafter, the interviewer should fully develop that theme. Note that the theme development explains away the moral – but not the legal – consequences of the misdeed. The interviewer should take care not to make any statements that would lead the accused to expect to be excused from legal liability by cooperating.

Rather than being confrontational, questions posed should constantly seek agreement from the accused. The interviewer must strike a balance between being in control of the interview and appearing compassionate and understanding. Again, no matter what act the accused has supposedly committed, the interviewer should not express shock, outrage, or condemnation.

Diffuse Alibis

Even if the interviewer presents the accused with an appropriate rationalization, the accused might continue denying culpability. When the interviewer successfully stops denials, the accused often turn to various reasons why he could not have committed the act in question. If this occurs, the interviewer should attempt to convince the accused of the weight of the evidence against him. Guilty individuals usually have a keen interest in evidence that tends to implicate them. Alibis are diffusible by displaying physical evidence, discussing the testimony of other witnesses, or discussing the suspect's deceptions.

Display Physical Evidence
It is common for most guilty individuals to overestimate the amount of physical evidence against them. Interviewers should aim to reinforce this notion by the way they

present the evidence to the accused. The interviewer should generally display physical evidence – usually documents in fraud matters – one piece at a time, in reverse order of importance. In this way, the full extent of the evidence is not immediately known by the accused. When the accused no longer denies culpability, the interviewer should stop displaying evidence.

Each time the interviewer lays out a document or piece of evidence to the accused, the interviewer should note its significance. During this phase, the accused is trying to accept having been caught. The interviewer should therefore expect that the accused will attempt to lie to get out of the situation. Like denials, the interviewer should stop the alibis and other falsehoods before they are fully articulated. After diffusing the alibis, the interviewer should return to the rationalization theme being developed.

Discuss Witnesses

Another technique for diffusing alibis is to discuss the testimony of witnesses. The objective is to give enough information about what other people have said without providing too much. Ideally, the interviewer makes the accused think that many people can contradict the accused's story.

The interviewer should take care not to furnish so much information that the accused can identify witnesses. To do so might place the witnesses in a difficult position; the accused might contact them in an effort to influence testimony. Alternatively, the accused could take reprisals against potential witnesses.

Discuss Deceptions

The final technique is to discuss the accused's deceptions. If physical evidence or witness testimony against the perpetrator is lacking, this technique might be the only one available. The purpose of this approach is to appeal to the accused's logic, not to scold or degrade. As with other interview situations, the interviewer should avoid the word *lying*.

Present an Alternative Question

After the accused's alibis have been diffused, the accused might become quiet and withdrawn. Some individuals in this situation might cry. If this happens, the interviewer should be comforting and should not discourage the accused from showing emotion.

At this stage, the accused is likely deciding whether to confess. To help the person decide, the interviewer should present an alternative question to the accused. The alternative question forces the accused to choose one of two answers. One alternative allows the accused a morally acceptable reason for the misdeed; the other paints the accused in a negative light. Regardless of which answer the accused chooses, he is acknowledging guilt. For example, the interviewer might ask, "Did you plan this, or did it just sort of happen?" or "Did you simply want extra money, or was there a serious financial need that led you to do this?"

The interviewer can also construct the questions for the admission as leading questions so they can be answered "yes" or "no"; the interviewer should not construct them so that the answer requires some type of explanation. Either way the accused answers the question – yes or no – the accused has made a culpable statement, or benchmark admission. Once the accused makes a benchmark admission, the suspect has made a subconscious decision to confess.

In cases in which the accused answers the question in the negative, the interviewer should press further for a positive admission. The interviewer's follow-up questions might be: "Then it just happened on the spur of the moment?" or "Then you did it to take care of your financial problems?"

Obtain a Benchmark Admission

If the accused still does not respond to the interviewer's questions with the benchmark admission, the interviewer should repeat the questions or variations thereof until the accused makes the benchmark admission. It is important for the interviewer to get a response that is tantamount to a commitment to confess.

Reinforce the Rationalization

Once the accused makes the benchmark admission, the interviewer should reinforce the suspect's decision to confess. The interviewer should then make the transition to the verbal confession, where the interviewer obtains the details of the offense. Reinforcing the rationalization developed earlier helps those who have confessed feel comfortable and believe that the interviewer does not look down on them.

RECOGNIZING SIGNS OF DECEPTION

Individuals typically lie for one of two reasons: to receive rewards or to avoid punishment. In most people, lying produces stress. The human body attempts to relieve this stress (even in practiced liars) through verbal and nonverbal clues. A practiced interviewer is able to draw inferences from subjects' behavior about the honesty of their statements.

Conclusions concerning behavior must be tempered by a number of factors:

- The physical environment in which the interview is conducted can affect behavior. Respondents who are comfortable might exhibit fewer behavioral quirks.
- The more intelligent the respondent, the more reliable verbal and nonverbal clues will be.
- If the respondent is biased toward the interviewer, or vice versa, this will affect behavior.
- People who are mentally unstable or are under the influence of drugs will be unsuitable to interview.
- Behavioral symptoms of juveniles are generally unreliable.
- Ethnic and economic factors should be carefully noted. Some cultures, for example, discourage looking directly at someone. Other cultures use certain body language that might be misinterpreted.
- Because pathological liars are often familiar with advanced interview techniques, they are less likely to furnish observable behavioral clues.

The interviewer must take all the relevant factors into account before drawing any conclusions about the meaning of the verbal and nonverbal signals that a subject demonstrates.

An Important Caveat

When evaluating signs of deception, it is possible to draw the wrong conclusions. The fraud examiner must understand that no single sign is an absolute indicator of deception. Therefore, no single behavior should be isolated and no conclusion should be drawn from it; behaviors must be considered together. Furthermore, the signs of deception are not necessarily universal, and might differ from culture to culture.

Verbal Signs of Deception

Interview subjects, whether witnesses or suspects, divulge more than they intend when making a statement. While nonverbal communication in an interview setting can reveal a subject's level of stress, the subject's choice of words, and the way in which the subject constructs a statement can provide clues to its veracity.

Most people cannot maintain deception throughout the length of an interview or story without raising a red flag. One lie begets another, often resulting in an unbalanced narrative and a subject who tries to convince the interviewer that a story is true, rather than plainly communicating information.

Verbal clues are those behaviors relating to wordings, expressions, and responses to specific questions. Verbal responses include spoken words and gestures that serve as word substitutes, including nodding or shaking the head to indicate "yes" or "no." The following are some examples of verbal clues of deception.

Changes in Speech Patterns

Deceptive people often speed up or slow down their speech, or speak louder. There might be a change in the voice pitch; as a person becomes tense, the vocal cords constrict. Deceptive people also tend to cough or clear their throats during times of deception.

Repetition of the Question

Repeating the question is a means for a deceptive respondent to gain more time to think of what to say. The respondent might repeat the question verbatim or might frame the answer with a request to repeat the question (e.g., "What was that again?" or similar language). Conversely, truthful subjects usually do not have to contemplate their answers.

Comments Regarding the Interview

Deceptive people will often comment on the physical environment of the interview room (e.g., complaining that it is too hot, too cold, etc.). As they come under increasing stress, they might frequently ask how much longer the interview will take.

Selective Memory

In some cases, a deceptive person will have a fine memory for insignificant events, but will claim to be unable to remember important facts.

Making Excuses

Dishonest people frequently make excuses about things that look bad for them, such as "I'm always nervous; don't pay any attention to that."

Oaths

Dishonest individuals frequently use expressions such as "I swear to God," "honestly," "frankly," or "to tell the truth" to try to add credibility to their lies.

Character Testimony

A dishonest person will often request that the interviewer "Check with my spouse" or "Talk to my minister." This tactic is often used to try to add credibility to a false statement.

Answering with a Question

Rather than deny allegations outright, a deceptive person frequently answers a question with a question, such as "Why would I do something like that?" As a variation, the deceptive person sometimes will question the interview procedure by asking, "Why are you targeting me?"

Increasingly Weak Denials

When accused of something they did not do, honest people are likely to become angry or forceful in making denials. The more the innocent person is accused, the more forceful the denial becomes. The dishonest person, in contrast, is likely to make a weak denial, and upon repeated accusations, the dishonest person's denials become weaker, to the point that the person is silent.

Failure to Deny

Honest people are more likely than dishonest people to deny an event directly. An honest person might offer a simple and clear "no," while the dishonest person will qualify the denial: "No, I did not steal $43,500 from the company on June 27." Other qualified denial phrases include "to the best of my memory," "as far as I recall," or similar language.

Avoidance of Emotive Words

A deceptive person will often avoid emotionally provocative terms such as *steal*, *lie*, and *crime*. Instead, the dishonest person frequently prefers soft words such as *borrow* and *it* (referring to the deed in question).

Refusal to Implicate Other Suspects

Regardless of their involvement (or lack thereof) in potential misconduct, interviewees are often reluctant to name others who could be involved. Even the dishonest respondent will frequently refuse to implicate possible suspects – no matter how much pressure the interviewer applies. This is because the culpable person does not want the circle of suspicion to be narrowed.

Tolerant Attitudes

Dishonest people typically have tolerant attitudes toward criminal conduct. The interviewer in an internal theft case might ask, "What should happen to these people when they are caught?" The honest person will usually say, "They should be fired and prosecuted." The dishonest individual is much more likely to reply, "How should I know?" or "Maybe they are good employees who got into a bad situation. Perhaps they should be given a second chance."

Reluctance to Terminate Interview

Dishonest people will generally be more reluctant than honest ones to terminate the interview. Dishonest individuals want to convince the interviewer that they are not responsible so the investigation into their actions will not continue. The honest person generally has no such reluctance.

Feigned Unconcern

The dishonest person will often try to appear casual and unconcerned, will frequently adopt an unnatural slouching posture, and might react to questions with nervous or false laughter or feeble attempts at humor. The honest person, conversely, will typically be very concerned about being suspected of wrongdoing, and will treat the interviewer's questions seriously.

Nonverbal Signs of Deception

Nonverbal clues to deception include various body movements and postures accompanying the verbal reply. Some of these are discussed next.

Full-Body Motions

When asked sensitive or emotive questions, the dishonest person will typically change posture completely – as if moving away from the interviewer. The honest person will frequently lean forward – toward the interviewer – when questions are serious.

Anatomical Physical Responses

Anatomical physical responses are those involuntary reactions by the body to fright, such as increased heart rate, shallow or labored breathing, or excessive perspiration. These reactions are typical of dishonest people accused of wrongdoing.

Illustrators

Illustrators are the motions made primarily with the hands to demonstrate points when talking. During nonthreatening questions, dishonest people often use the illustrators at one rate. During threatening questions, their use of illustrators might increase or decrease.

Hands over the Mouth

Frequently, dishonest people will cover their mouths with their hands or fingers during deception. It is typically done subconsciously to conceal the statement.

Manipulators

Manipulators are habitual motions like picking lint from clothing, playing with objects such as pencils, or holding one's hands while talking. Manipulators are displacement activities that reduce nervousness.

Fleeing Positions

During the interview, dishonest people will often posture themselves in a fleeing position. While the head and trunk might be facing the interviewer, the feet and lower portion of the body might be pointing toward the door in an unconscious effort to flee from the interviewer.

Crossing the Arms

Crossing one's arms over the middle zone of the body is a classic defensive reaction to difficult or uncomfortable questions. A variation is crossing the feet under the chair and locking them. These crossing motions occur mostly when a person is being deceptive.

Reaction to Evidence

While trying to be outwardly unconcerned, the guilty person will have a keen interest in implicating evidence. The dishonest person will often look at documents presented by the interviewer, attempt to be casual about observing them, and then shove them away as though wanting nothing to do with the evidence.

Fake Smiles

Genuine smiles usually involve the whole mouth; false ones are confined to the upper half. People involved in deception tend to smirk rather than to smile.

ADDITIONAL INTERVIEW STEPS

Near the conclusion of the interview, there might be certain tasks that interviewers should undertake to ensure they accomplish the goal of the interview. For all interviews, the investigator should review, point by point, the notes taken with the subject. The interviewer should repeat areas critical to the investigation, asking the subject to confirm the information.

Sensitive Issues and Questions

There are almost always issues or subjects that are more sensitive than others. It is best to delve into the sensitive areas later in the interview for several reasons. First, the interviewer will have had the opportunity to build rapport with the subject, increasing the odds that the subject will open up. Also, less sensitive questions can lay the groundwork for more sensitive issues. Finally, in the event the sensitive issue causes the subject to resist or become defensive, the interviewer will have most of the questions already answered.

Here are some examples of ways to approach the topic of fraud within a company. The questions are posed in a hypothetical way to avoid being accusatory.

- "Part of my job is to prevent and uncover waste, fraud, and abuse. You understand that, don't you?"
- "Please tell me where you think the company is wasting assets or money."
- "Where do you think the company is vulnerable to an employee abusing his or her position?"

Obtaining Confessions

In admission-seeking interviews, one of the final tasks is obtaining a confession from the subject in the form of either a verbal confession or a signed statement, or both. A confession is the ideal outcome of an admission-seeking interview, but is not guaranteed by any means.

Verbal Confessions

The transition to the verbal confession is made when the accused furnishes the first detailed information about the offense. Thereafter, it is the interviewer's job to probe gently for additional details – preferably including those that only the accused would know.

There are three general approaches to obtaining the details during a verbal confession: chronologically, by transaction, or by event. The interviewer should base the choice of approach on the circumstances of the case.

When taking a verbal confession, interviewers should first confirm the general details of the offense – for example, the accused's estimates of the amounts in question, who else was involved, and the location of physical evidence. After confirming these basic facts, the interviewer can delve into the specifics of how the accused committed the crime.

Because of the psychological nature of confessions, most people confessing lie about one or more aspects of the offense, even though they confirm overall guilt. When this happens during the verbal confession, interviewers should make a mental note of the discrepancy and proceed as if they accepted the falsehood as truth.

The interviewer should save such discrepancies until the accused provides all other relevant facts. If the discrepancies are material to the offense, then the interviewer should either resolve them at the end of the verbal confession or wait and correct them in the written confession. If not material, there is no need to include such information in the written confession.

The interviewer should obtain the following information during the verbal confession:

- Confirmation that the accused knew the conduct was wrong
- Estimate of the number of instances and amounts
- A motive for the offense
- When the offense commenced
- Whether and when the offense was terminated
- Any other parties involved
- Authorization for access to physical evidence
- Information about the disposition of proceeds
- The location of residual assets
- Specifics of each offense

During the verbal confession, it is imperative that the interviewer obtain an early admission that the accused knew the conduct in question was wrong. This confirms the essential element of intent, which is requisite in all matters involving fraud. That is, the person confessing must have committed the act intentionally, rather than accidentally or by mistake.

Once the question of intent is resolved, the questioning can turn to those facts known only to the person making the confession. These facts include, at a minimum, the accused's estimates of the number of instances of wrongful conduct, as well as the total amount of money involved. The interviewer should not phrase the questions in a way that the accused can answer "yes" or "no."

Signed Statements

The interviewer should then reduce the verbal confession to a concise written statement, and ensure that the person making the confession signs it before leaving the interview. Rarely should the statement exceed two or three handwritten pages.

The information to include in the signed statement is essentially the same as that which the interviewer should obtain in the verbal confession. However, in addition to the information obtained in the verbal confession, a written confession should include:

- *Language expressly stating that the confession is being made voluntarily:* This can be important if an organization pursues legal action. Many courts examine whether an accused confessed voluntarily.
- *Language indicating the subject knowingly and intentionally committed the act, and knew the act was wrong (intent):* Most crimes require, as part of the elements of proof, the fact that the person making the confession knew the conduct was wrong and intended to commit the act. The presence of intent can best be addressed by using precise language in the statement that clearly describes the act (e.g., "I wrongfully took assets from the company that weren't mine" versus "I borrowed money from the

company without telling anyone"). As a general rule, the statement should not include strong emotive words such as *lie* and *steal* because the confessing person might balk at signing a statement that contains such terms. Still, the wording must be precise. The word *lied* could be replaced with "knew the statement was untrue," and the word *stole* could be replaced with "wrongfully took ____'s property for my own benefit."

- *The approximate dates of the offense:* The signed statement should also include the approximate dates of the misconduct. If the exact dates of the offense are unknown, the word *approximately* must precede any dates given. If the person making the confession is unsure about the dates, the statement should include language to that effect.

- *The approximate amounts of losses:* The signed statement should include the approximate losses, with any listed amount specifically labeled as *approximate* or *an estimate*. Including a range is also acceptable (e.g., "probably not less than $____ or more than $____").

- *The approximate number of instances:* The signed statement should include the approximate number of instances of occurrence, or a range thereof, as this helps establish intent by showing a repeated pattern of activity.

- *Language indicating the subject's willingness to cooperate:* People are more likely to sign a written confession if the language in the statement portrays them in a favorable light. Therefore, the statement should emphasize their cooperation and willingness to make amends.

- *The subject's moral excuse:* The statement should mention the moral excuse of the person making the confession. However, the interviewer should ensure that the excuse clause wording does not diminish legal responsibility.

- *An acknowledgment that the subject read the statement:* People confessing should overtly acknowledge that they read the statement and initialed all the pages of the statement.

- *An explicit acknowledgment that the statement is true:* The written statement should state specifically that it is true. This adds weight to it. However, the language should also allow for mistakes (e.g., "to the best of my knowledge").

There is typically no legal requirement that a statement must be in the handwriting or wording of the person making the confession, but investigators should check with legal counsel to make sure. The wording of the confession should be precise, and because the examiner usually knows how to draft a valid statement, it is generally not a good idea to let the subject draft it.

The confessing person should read and sign the statement without undue delay. Instead of asking the subject to sign the statement, the interviewer should say, "Please sign here." Although there is no legal requirement to have a witness present when the subject signs a statement, it is a good idea to have two people witness the signing of a statement and the subject's declaration of having read the statement and having confirmed that it is correct.

Additionally, there should not be more than one written statement for each offense. If errors are identified after the subject signed the document, the interviewer should cross out the incorrect information, insert a correction, and have the subject initial the insertion. If facts are inadvertently omitted, the interviewer can add them to the original statement later as an addendum. For legal purposes, the interviewer should prepare separate statements for unrelated offenses. This rule applies because the target might be tried separately for each offense.

The interviewer should preserve all notes taken during an interview, especially those concerning a confession. Having access to pertinent notes can aid in a cross-examination regarding the validity of a signed statement. After obtaining a confession, the fraud examiner should substantiate it through additional investigation, if necessary.

Follow-up Interviews

The interviewer should advise the subject that it might be necessary for them to be in contact again with any follow-up questions. The interviewer should also ask where and when it would be most convenient to contact the subject. The examiner might learn some of the most critical and important information in subsequent interviews, especially after the subject has grown to respect and trust the interviewer.

PART II

Fraud-related laws and investigative resources differ greatly from country to country, and finding the relevant information for every jurisdiction can be a challenge. Accordingly, this book was designed to serve as a comprehensive resource to help fraud examiners find the information they need to prevent and detect fraud, no matter where it occurs.

Part II of this book consists of country-specific information divided by geographic region and country. The topics covered include general fraud trends for the region, sources of information commonly used by local investigators, the country's legal system and relevant laws, and cultural and other considerations.

To gather the information in Part II, questionnaires were sent to Association of Certified Fraud Examiners (ACFE) chapters and members throughout the world. ACFE members from more than 35 countries generously contributed their time and expertise to complete these questionnaires. The names of the contributors are listed before each country's entry, as well as in the Acknowledgments section in the front of the book. All information included for each country comes directly from these contributors; omitted responses indicate that no information was provided regarding that question. Once again, the ACFE would like to thank all of the contributors who made this book possible.

CHAPTER 7

Asia-Pacific Region

REGIONAL FRAUD TRENDS

The 2018 *Report to the Nations on Occupational Fraud and Abuse* issued by the Association of Certified Fraud Examiners (ACFE) includes 220 cases from the Asia-Pacific region that were investigated between January 2016 and October 2017. These cases caused a median loss of US $236,000 per case.

As noted in Exhibit 7.1, corruption is the most common form of occupational fraud committed in the Asia-Pacific region; 51% of the cases analyzed involved some form of corruption, which is more than twice as frequent as any other type of fraud scheme. Theft of noncash assets is the second most common category of occupational fraud, occurring in one-quarter of the cases in the region. In addition, fraud schemes in the Asia-Pacific region are almost three times more likely to be detected by a tip than by any other means (see Exhibit 7.2).

The 2018 *Report to the Nations* also examines the anti-fraud controls that were present at victim organizations at the time the frauds being analyzed were committed. Exhibit 7.3 shows that external audits of the financial statements are the most commonly implemented anti-fraud controls among victim organizations in the Asia-Pacific region, followed by a formal code of conduct. On the other end of the spectrum, only 16% of these organizations had a mandatory vacation or job rotation policy in place, and just 11% provided rewards to whistle-blowers.

Exhibit 7.1   Scheme Types – Asia-Pacific Region

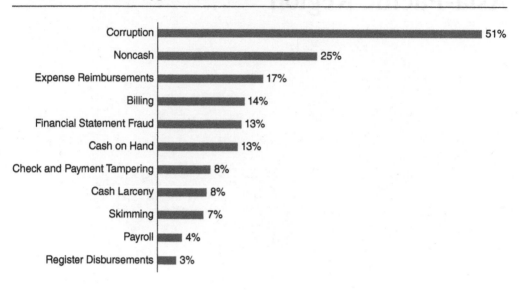

Exhibit 7.2   Initial Detection Method – Asia-Pacific Region

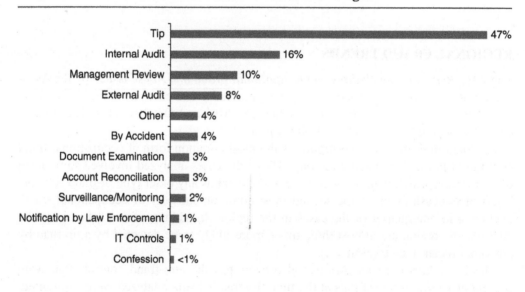

Exhibit 7.3 Frequency of Anti-Fraud Controls – Asia-Pacific Region

Control	% of Cases
External Audit of Financial Statements	93%
Code of Conduct	87%
Internal Audit Department	80%
Management Certification of Financial Statements	79%
Hotline	74%
External Audit of Internal Controls over Financial Reporting	73%
Management Review	71%
Independent Audit Committee	69%
Anti-Fraud Policy	60%
Fraud Training for Employees	59%
Fraud Training for Managers/Executives	57%
Employee Support Programs	49%
Dedicated Fraud Department, Function, or Team	42%
Formal Fraud Risk Assessments	37%
Surprise Audits	34%
Proactive Data Monitoring/Analysis	32%
Job Rotation/Mandatory Vacation	16%
Rewards for Whistle-Blowers	11%

The following discussions provide jurisdiction-specific information pertaining to the legal, investigatory, and general anti-fraud environment for several countries in the Asia-Pacific region.

AUSTRALIA

Contributors

Melbourne Chapter:

Roger Darvall-Stevens, MBA, MA, CFE

Perth Chapter:

Dom Blackshaw, CFE
Chris Porteous

Sydney Chapter:

Tony Prior, MBA, CFE, CAMS

Sources of Information

1. What types of information about individuals are available to the public?

In Australia, the following resources contain free information about individuals:

- Electoral rolls: Names and addresses are available, but only by visiting Australian Electoral Commission locations to search their computer records (not available via the Internet).
- White pages: Registered telephone numbers are available through websites such as www.whitepages.com.au.
- Social media: Facebook, LinkedIn, and others.
- Data.gov.au is a government website containing a range of public data for free or for a search fee.

The following information and resources are available on a subscription or fee-per-inquiry basis:

- Criminal record checks can be conducted, with the consent of the subject, through:
  - Any Australian police force, such as the Australian Federal Police (www.afp.gov. au/what-we-do/services/criminal-records/national-police-checks)
  - The Australian postal service, known as the Australian Post (auspost.com.au/ police-checks)
  - The Australian Criminal Court Records website (www.criminal-court-records. com.au), which has limited information from official daily records of criminal court attendances. (Note: These records are publicly available on the date of publication but not thereafter.)
- There are different land title registries in Australia's various states and territories. Land title registry searches can be conducted for a fee and will confirm the current owners of property and show any registered interests, such as mortgages. There is no national, countrywide database; searches must be conducted for each relevant state and territory.
- Credit checks generally require the subject's consent and may be conducted for a fee by commercial services, such as Equifax and Experian (or Dun & Bradstreet for businesses).
- Bankruptcy data from the Australian Financial Security Authority (www.afsa.gov.au).
- Personal Property Securities Register (www.ppsr.gov.au).
- Birth, deaths, and marriage records.
- Government-issued licenses (e.g., to practice a particular trade or profession).

2. What types of information about businesses are available to the public?

In addition to the resources listed in the response to Question 1, the following resources contain information about businesses:

- Australian Securities and Investments Commission (ASIC) (asic.gov.au) is a government website that contains a wide range of information about Australian companies, such as the names of officers and directors and organizational documents; a fee is required for searches and alerts.

- Australian Business Register (ABR) (abr.business.gov.au) enables one to look up a company's Australian Business Number, Australian Company Number, or name (free service).
- The company's website.

In some circumstances, additional information about a company may be obtained by making a freedom of information request to the government.

3. Are court records available to the public? If so, explain what types of civil and criminal records can be obtained by the public.

Generally, civil and criminal court records are not available to the public. However, some civil court records are available via the Australian Legal Information Institute's online database (www.austlii.edu.au). Criminal records and convictions generally cannot be accessed without the subject's consent (see response to Question 1 for more information), but court schedules and attendance lists might be available online and can contain useful information. Court transcripts can sometimes be obtained by making a freedom of information request.

4. What other resources or types of information are regularly used by investigators in your country?

- Witness interviews
- Surveillance from public locations
- Accounting records
- Banking records
- Electronic data (e.g., emails)

5. What are some of the most useful Internet or online sources regularly used in fraud investigations?

- Internet search engines
- Social media

Legal and Regulatory Environment

6. What are the major data privacy laws in your country, and how do these affect most fraud investigations?

- Australian Privacy Act 1988
- Local laws governing surveillance devices, workplace surveillance, or similar issues

7. What type of legal system does your country have (e.g., civil law system, common law system, religious law system, hybrid)?

Australia has a common law system based on the English model.

8. What laws governing the rights of individuals are of primary concern to investigators?

In Australia, there are a range of principles of natural justice and procedural fairness that come from statutory and common law and govern the rights of individuals when interacting with investigators. Investigators should consult a local CFE or lawyer for advice. The laws relating to accessing information, gathering evidence, and conducting interviews vary by state and territory.

9. Is bribery a criminal offense in your country? If so, does it include payments to both government officials and private businesses?

Bribery is a crime in Australia, and it includes payments to both government officials and private businesses.

10. What are the primary financial and investment regulatory bodies in your country?

- Australian Prudential Regulation Authority (APRA) (www.apra.gov.au) oversees banks, credit unions, building societies, general insurance and reinsurance companies, life insurance, private health insurance, friendly societies, and most members of the superannuation (retirement/pension) industry.
- Australian Securities and Investments Commission (ASIC) (www.asic.gov.au) is Australia's corporate, markets, and financial services regulator.
- Australian Stock Exchange (ASX) (www.asx.com.au) is Australia's financial market exchange.
- Australian Taxation Office (ATO) (www.ato.gov.au).
- Foreign Investment Review Board (FIRB) (firb.gov.au) is a nonstatutory body established in 1976 to advise the government on Australia's foreign investment policy.
- Reserve Bank of Australia (RBA) (www.rba.gov.au) conducts monetary policy, works to maintain a strong financial system, and issues the nation's banknotes.
- Australian Transaction Reports and Analysis Centre (AUSTRAC) (www.austrac.gov.au) is a financial intelligence agency with responsibility for anti-money-laundering and counterterrorism financing.

11. What are the most significant pieces of fraud-related legislation in your country?

The most significant pieces of fraud-related legislation in Australia are the Criminal Code Act 1995 and the criminal laws in states and territories that prohibit fraud.

12. Does your country have laws in place to protect whistle-blowers? Please describe.

- Australian Corporations Act 2001 protects whistle-blowers in the private sector.
- Public Interest Disclosure Act 2013 protects whistle-blowers in the public sector.
- Other laws: States and territories have their own laws protecting whistle-blowers in the public sector.

Anti-Fraud Programs

13. What foundational frameworks for internal controls, risk management, corporate governance, and so on are commonly used by organizations in your country when designing or assessing their anti-fraud programs (e.g., Committee of Sponsoring Organizations of the Treadway Commission [COSO] frameworks, specific International Organization for Standardization [ISO] standards, Organisation for Economic Co-operation and Development [OECD] guidance)?

- Commonwealth Fraud Control Framework 2017 and Australian Government Investigations Standards 2011, both of which apply only to fraud control and investigation work within or for the Australian Commonwealth Government
- Australian Standard AS 8001 on Fraud and Corruption Control
- Australian Standard AS 8004, Whistleblower Protection Programs for Entities
- Australian/New Zealand standard AS/NZS ISO 31000, Risk Management
- ISO 37001, Anti-Bribery Management Systems
- COSO Enterprise Risk Management Integrated Framework
- Association of Certified Fraud Examiners (ACFE) *Fraud Examiners Manual* (International Edition), *Report to the Nations on Occupational Fraud and Abuse*, and other ACFE publications and leading practices
- *Fraud Risk Management Guide*, a joint publication of COSO and the Association of Certified Fraud Examiners

14. What types of background checks, if any, are commonly run on prospective employees in your country (e.g., criminal, civil, credit, employment, educational)?

Records that are private or maintained by the government (such as criminal records, credit records, or educational qualifications) require consent from the subject. Some other records are publicly available or accessible from commercial databases for a fee.

Considerations in Fraud Investigations

15. Are there any special legal considerations that individuals from outside your country should be aware of when they are working on an investigation in your country? Examples might include licenses needed, special laws governing information gathering, or restrictions on transmitting personal data outside the country.

Generally, any person who conducts investigations (including surveillance) in any state or territory of Australia must hold an Investigator or Inquiry Agent License. Australia's National Privacy Principles govern the collection, use, disclosure, and storage of personal information.

16. Are there any special cultural considerations that individuals from outside your country should be aware of when they are working on an investigation in your country? Examples might include who is present during an interview, how to address or greet individuals, inappropriate dress, and so on.

Australia is extremely culturally diverse; as such, the customs and traditions of the individual to be interviewed should always be researched beforehand.

CHINA

Contributors

Edward J. Epstein, LLB, LLM
Caoyu Xu

Sources of Information

1. What types of information about individuals are available to the public?

Certain personal credit failure records are publicly available, such as judgment debtors in default. Some litigation and regulatory records are also available online, such as parties to civil cases, some judgments and business registration information (e.g., shareholdings and directorships).

2. What types of information about businesses are available to the public?

Generally, business registration information is publicly available, including business scope, registered capital, shareholdings, directors and officers, registration dates, and past registration changes. All business registration authorities operate online databases, but there is no central registry and the information available varies.

3. Are court records available to the public? If so, explain what types of civil and criminal records can be obtained by the public.

For civil cases, most national-, provincial-, and municipal-level court records are available online, but they are usually incomplete. Criminal records are not available to be searched, but they are frequently published in the media.

4. What other resources or types of information are regularly used by investigators in your country?

Proprietary databases storing personal and corporate information are used by investigators (see response to Question 5).

5. What are some of the most useful Internet or online sources regularly used in fraud investigations?

The websites Qichacha (www.qichacha.com) and Tianyancha (www.tianyancha. com) are often used for business information. Other sites are used for personal credit failure checks.

Business information is also collected by local registries. Most registries have search capabilities for basic information, such as the names of officers, directors, and shareholders. Lawyers can obtain additional information by searching the physical records, but sometimes a court order is required.

Legal and Regulatory Environment

6. What are the major data privacy laws in your country, and how do these affect most fraud investigations?

China's Cybersecurity Law, which took effect on June 1, 2017, is now the country's primary data privacy law. It contains legal requirements for the collection, use, and protection of electronic personal information. Before the Cybersecurity Law, the legal protection of personal data was spread among a vast number of laws and regulations relating to different types of personal data, such as real estate ownership records, business information, telecommunications data, and data concerning personal identity and cross-border movements. These laws and regulations are still in force, but some of their provisions have been subsumed by the Cybersecurity Law when data is obtained or stored by electronic means. Like the EU's General Data Protection Regulation, China's Cybersecurity Law generally requires informed consent by data subjects, mandates data security, and limits cross-border transfers of personal information. The law also requires personal information collected by "critical information infrastructure operators" to be stored in China.

See the response to Question 8 for other Chinese data protection laws.

7. What type of legal system does your country have (e.g., civil law system, common law system, religious law system, hybrid)?

Mainland China, Taiwan, and Macau all have civil law systems, although they have different historical roots. Hong Kong has a common law system.

8. What laws governing the rights of individuals are of primary concern to investigators?

- Criminal Law: Various provisions prohibit fraud, bribery, embezzlement, and corruption.
- Cybersecurity Law is a 2017 law that governs the collection, use, and protection of personal information (see response to Question 6).
- Article 253 of the Criminal Law provides that it is a crime to sell or illegally provide to others the personal information of Chinese citizens.
- Provisions on Employment Services and Employment Management require employers to keep their employees' personal information confidential.
- State Secrets Law prohibits the transfer of state secrets out of the country; the definition of *state secrets* is broad and subject to interpretation.
- Law on Residents' Identity Cards (2011; 2012) and Passport Law (2006) protect personal identity information.
- Law on the Administration of Exit and Entry (2013) protects information concerning cross-border movements.

- Measures on the Investigation of Registered Company Files (2003) protect registered information in physical files of business entities.
- For whistle-blower protections, see response to Question 12.

9. Is bribery a criminal offense in your country? If so, does it include payments to both government officials and private businesses?

China's Anti-Unfair Competition Law and the Criminal Law prohibit both the bribery of government officials and commercial bribery. Penalties for bribery range from monetary fines and the confiscation of property to the death penalty in serious cases.

10. What are the primary financial and investment regulatory bodies in your country?

- China Banking Regulatory Commission
- China Insurance Regulatory Commission
- China Securities Regulatory Commission
- China Financial Stability and Development Committee
- People's Bank of China
- Ministry of Commerce
- National Development and Reform Commission

11. What are the most significant pieces of fraud-related legislation in your country?

- Criminal Law
- Anti-Unfair Competition Law
- Anti-Money Laundering Law
- Contract Law
- Law on Tendering and Bidding
- Securities Law

12. Does your country have laws in place to protect whistle-blowers? Please describe.

China has laws protecting whistle-blowers who report corruption by government officials. In 2016, the Chinese government issued regulations called Several Provisions on Protecting and Rewarding Whistleblowers for Reporting Duty Crimes. These regulations provide confidentiality and financial rewards for whistle-blowers who report corruption by government officials, as well as prohibiting retaliation against such whistle-blowers.

Under Chinese criminal law, government officials who retaliate against whistle-blowers may be subject to criminal penalties, including imprisonment.

Anti-Fraud Programs

13. What foundational frameworks for internal controls, risk management, corporate governance, and so on are commonly used by organizations in your country when designing or assessing their anti-fraud programs (e.g., COSO frameworks, specific ISO standards, OECD guidance)?

Chinese organizations commonly use the Basic Standard for Enterprise Internal Control (also known as China SOX), which was issued in 2008 and updated in 2010. The Basic Standard and its supporting guidelines contain internal control requirements for listed companies, as well as guidelines for establishing, evaluating, and auditing such controls.

Although China has anti-money-laundering laws, there are no specific guidelines on how to detect or prevent money laundering.

14. What types of background checks, if any, are commonly run on prospective employees in your country (e.g., criminal, civil, credit, employment, educational)?

Common background checks include criminal, credit, employment, educational, and license verification. These background checks are voluntary because employers have no means to search most of the relevant databases.

Considerations in Fraud Investigations

15. Are there any special legal considerations that individuals from outside your country should be aware of when they are working on an investigation in your country? Examples might include licenses needed, special laws governing information gathering, or restrictions on transmitting personal data outside the country.

China's Cybersecurity Law, which took effect on June 1, 2017, restricts the collection and use of electronic personal data, except for "big data" that cannot identify individuals. Geolocation data is also considered confidential.

16. Are there any special cultural considerations that individuals from outside your country should be aware of when they are working on an investigation in your country? Examples might include who is present during an interview, how to address or greet individuals, inappropriate dress, and so on.

Due to the ongoing anti-corruption campaign in China, sources may be reluctant to accept interviews, and it might be necessary to explain that the investigation is not being conducted on behalf of any government body. Interviewees might be more comfortable working with investigators who can speak Chinese.

JAPAN

Contributors

Makito Hamada, CFE, CPA
Ayumi Uzawa, CFE, CPA
Daisuke Yuki, CFE
Sachie Tsuji, CFE, CPA
Toshiaki Yamaguchi, CFE

Sources of Information

1. What types of information about individuals are available to the public?

- The Official Gazette, telephone directory, and directory of government officials (blue book) are available to the public.
- The national government maintains the Family Register System, and local governments maintain the residence certificates system. These systems are basically non-public, but individuals can request access.
- Criminal background checks can be requested from the National Police Agency.
- There is public information available about owners of real estate and individuals who have a registered automobile.

2. What types of information about businesses are available to the public?

- Corporation Registration System: A company's trade name, location, and representative's name are available at the Registry Office.
- Electronic Disclosure for Investors Network (EDINET): The names of board members, auditors, and executive officers of listed companies are available on EDINET, maintained by the Financial Service Agency.
- Annual securities reports, quarterly securities reports, and reporting on internal controls as required by the Financial Instruments and Exchange Act.
- Corporate accounting documents, business reports, and Notices of Calling of Shareholders Meeting as required by the Companies Act.
- Timely disclosed information, including a brief announcement of the most recent financial statement following the end of the fiscal year as required by the code of conduct of companies listed on the Tokyo Stock Exchange.
- Company websites.

3. Are court records available to the public? If so, explain what types of civil and criminal records can be obtained by the public.

Generally, civil court records are available only to interested parties. Criminal court records are generally not available to the public, but they can be requested. Some civil and criminal judgments are available on court websites, or published in legal journals, with personal information redacted.

4. What other resources or types of information are regularly used by investigators in your country?

- Corporate credit agencies, such as Teikoku Data Bank and Tokyo Shoko Research
- Paid commercial databases
- Research companies that compile public news articles
- White papers released by government agencies or private organizations
- Attorney Act, Article 23 (request for information)

5. What are some of the most useful Internet or online sources regularly used in fraud investigations?

- Google and other search engines
- Social media (Facebook, LinkedIn, Twitter)

Legal and Regulatory Environment

6. What are the major data privacy laws in your country, and how do these affect most fraud investigations?

Under Japan's Act on the Protection of Personal Information, companies generally must obtain an employee's consent before collecting the employee's personal information or providing the information to a third party.

7. What type of legal system does your country have (e.g., civil law system, common law system, religious law system, hybrid)?

Japan has a civil law system.

8. What laws governing the rights of individuals are of primary concern to investigators?

- The Constitution of Japan (right of privacy, dignity of an individual, etc.)
- Act on the Protection of Personal Information
- Labor and employment laws
- The Penal Code (e.g., defamation)

9. Is bribery a criminal offense in your country? If so, does it include payments to both government officials and private businesses?

Bribery is a crime in Japan, and it includes payments to both government officials and private businesses. Article 198 of the Penal Code prohibits the bribery of public servants. Article 967 of the Company Act prohibits company officers and directors from giving or accepting bribes. A company employee who accepts a bribe from a business associate is guilty of embezzlement in violation of Article 253 of the Penal Code.

10. What are the primary financial and investment regulatory bodies in your country?

- Financial Service Agency
- Securities and Exchange Surveillance Commission
- National Taxation Agency

11. What are the most significant pieces of fraud-related legislation in your country?

- Financial Instruments and Exchange Act (financial reporting fraud)
- Corporation Tax Act (financial reporting fraud)

- Income Tax Act (financial reporting fraud)
- Penal Code Article 235 (theft)
- Penal Code Article 246 (fraud)
- Penal Code Article 198 (public bribery)

12. Does your country have laws in place to protect whistle-blowers? Please describe.

Japan's Whistleblower Protection Act prohibits retaliation against public and private employees who report illegal conduct.

Anti-Fraud Programs

13. What foundational frameworks for internal controls, risk management, corporate governance, and so on are commonly used by organizations in your country when designing or assessing their anti-fraud programs (e.g., COSO frameworks, specific ISO standards, OECD guidance)?

- Listed companies use the Standards and Practice Standards for Management Assessment and Audit Concerning Internal Control over Financial Reporting issued by the Financial Service Agency.
- Overseas listed companies use the COSO framework.
- Corporate Governance Code of Japan.
- Internal control reporting system under the Financial Instruments and Exchange Act.

14. What types of background checks, if any, are commonly run on prospective employees in your country (e.g., criminal, civil, credit, employment, educational)?

Background checks are generally not permitted. However, an indirect background check can be conducted by requesting a copy of the applicant's diploma, academic transcript, residence certificates, and recommendations. Companies cannot contact previous employers without the applicant's consent, but previous employment can be confirmed with retirement certificates, withholding certificates, or employment insurance certificates. Criminal background checks are generally prohibited.

Considerations in Fraud Investigations

15. Are there any special legal considerations that individuals from outside your country should be aware of when they are working on an investigation in your country? Examples might include licenses needed, special laws governing information gathering, or restrictions on transmitting personal data outside the country.

Under the Act on the Protection of Personal Information, companies generally must obtain an employee's consent before collecting the employee's personal information or providing the information to a third party.

16. Are there any special cultural considerations that individuals from outside your country should be aware of when they are working on an investigation in your country? Examples might include who is present during an interview, how to address or greet individuals, inappropriate dress, and so on.

There is no attorney-client privilege in Japan, and Japanese law generally does not require parties to disclose evidence. Also, many Japanese people do not speak English, so interpreters may be necessary.

MALAYSIA

Contributors

Maheswari Kanniah, CFE
Siti Zeenath Shaik Ibrahim
Zulhisham Osman
Wong Siew Jiuan, CFE

Sources of Information

1. What types of information about individuals are available to the public?

- Bankruptcy status (official assignee search)
- Credit information, civil cases (credit reporting agencies search)
- Travel blacklist

2. What types of information about businesses are available to the public?

- Winding up or company liquidation status (official assignee search)
- Credit information, civil cases (credit reporting agencies search)

3. Are court records available to the public? If so, explain what types of civil and criminal records can be obtained by the public.

Court records are generally not available to the public, unless the case number is available to conduct a file search in the court registry and a fee is paid. Criminal records are generally not available to the public.

Legal and Regulatory Environment

6. What are the major data privacy laws in your country, and how do these affect most fraud investigations?

Malaysia's Personal Data Protection Act 2010 requires the subject's authorization before personal information is accessed or disclosed. However, the act generally does not apply to government investigations.

S133 Financial Services Act 2013 (FSA) and Islamic Financial Services Act 2013 (IFSA) protect client information held by financial institutions. Under S134 FSA and IFSA, disclosures are allowed only when one of the Schedule 11 conditions in the FSA and IFSA has been met. These conditions are likely to take time. Fraud investigations usually require immediate attention. Therefore, these laws can hinder the progress of a fraud examination.

7. What type of legal system does your country have (e.g., civil law system, common law system, religious law system, hybrid)?

Malaysia has a common law system. In addition, Shariah courts have been developed to resolve disputes regarding Shariah matters (e.g., marriage, divorce, child adoption, child custody).

8. What laws governing the rights of individuals are of primary concern to investigators?

- In private investigations, an individual's right to confidentiality/privacy is protected by the Personal Data Protection Act 2010, the Financial Services Act 2013 (regarding banking transactions and customer information), and the Securities Industry Central Depositories Act (regarding securities transactions).
- Theft of information is a criminal offense under the Penal Code.
- There is a common law claim for trespass.

9. Is bribery a criminal offense in your country? If so, does it include payments to both government officials and private businesses?

Bribery is a crime in Malaysia, which includes payments to both government officials and private businesses, under Sections 21 and 22 of the Malaysian Anti-Corruption Commission Act 2009 and the Malaysian Anti-Money Laundering, Anti-Terrorism Financing, and Proceeds of Unlawful Activities Act 2001.

10. What are the primary financial and investment regulatory bodies in your country?

- Bank Negara Malaysia
- Securities Commission Malaysia
- Bursa Malaysia Berhad

11. What are the most significant pieces of fraud-related legislation in your country?

- Penal Code
- Financial Services Act 2013
- Islamic Financial Services Act 2013
- Anti-Corruption Commission Act 2009
- Anti-Money Laundering, Anti-Terrorism Financing, and Proceeds of Unlawful Activities Act 2001

12. Does your country have laws in place to protect whistle-blowers? Please describe.

Malaysia's Whistleblower Protection Act 2010 protects whistle-blowers who voluntarily report information about corrupt activities. The identity of the whistle-blower and the information provided are kept confidential. Whistle-blowers are also given immunity from any civil, criminal, or disciplinary action due to revealing the act of corruption.

The Malaysian Anti-Corruption Commission Act 2009 and the Malaysian Anti-Money Laundering, Anti-Terrorism Financing, and Proceeds of Unlawful Activities Act 2001 protect any person who reports a suspicion of money laundering or terrorism financing. All information related to the report must be kept confidential. The reporting person is given immunity from any civil, criminal, or disciplinary action due to submitting the report, so long as it was made in good faith.

Anti-Fraud Programs

13. What foundational frameworks for internal controls, risk management, corporate governance, and so on are commonly used by organizations in your country when designing or assessing their anti-fraud programs (e.g., COSO frameworks, specific ISO standards, OECD guidance)?

Organizations use the COSO framework, which includes the newly added pillar on fraud risk management.

14. What types of background checks, if any, are commonly run on prospective employees in your country (e.g., criminal, civil, credit, employment, educational)?

- For the banking industry, comprehensive checks such as credit, financial, employment, educational, civil, and criminal are used.
- For other nonregulated industries, background checks include employment, credit, and educational; the extent of the checks depends on the level of seniority.

NEW ZEALAND

Contributors

Several New Zealand ACFE Chapter members and committee members contributed to the survey.

Sources of Information

1. What types of information about individuals are available to the public?

- Births, deaths, and marriages information (www.govt.nz/organisations/births-deaths-and-marriages) is maintained by the Department of Internal Affairs.

- Companies Register (companies-register.companiesoffice.govt.nz) can reveal whether an individual is a shareholder or director of a company, as well as other information about companies, such as the names of officers and directors, legal form, and company documents.
- Land Online (www.linz.govt.nz/land/landonline) contains information on real property ownership, including mortgages, sales, purchases, and pricing.
- Terranet (Terranet.co.nz) is a commercial database containing information on real property ownership.
- Personal Property Security Register (www.ppsr.govt.nz/cms) covers security interests in personal property.
- Motor Vehicle Register (nzta.govt.nz/vehicles) contains motor vehicle ownership records.
- Association records – various associations governing particular professions, such as lawyers and accountants, or particular industries.
- Debt collectors' databases.
- Social media (LinkedIn, Facebook, Twitter).

2. What types of information about businesses are available to the public?

Many of the resources listed in the response to Question 1 can also be used to obtain information about businesses.

3. Are court records available to the public? If so, explain what types of civil and criminal records can be obtained by the public.

For most civil actions, a statement of claim is available, or sometimes the whole file. Significant cases are posted online. Other reported cases are available through commercial databases (e.g., LexisNexis). It is also possible to submit an application to a particular court to access court records.

Criminal records must be applied for in writing, with reasons for the information included in the application. Such applications are granted at the discretion of the court.

4. What other resources or types of information are regularly used by investigators in your country?

- Data sets held by government agencies can be accessed for the purpose of preventing and detecting serious crime.
- Bank records can be obtained via court order or by consent of the affected party.
- Credit inquiries can be made.

5. What are some of the most useful Internet or online sources regularly used in fraud investigations?

In addition to the resources listed in the response to Question 1, the following websites are commonly used in fraud investigations:

- Infolog provides a one-stop information management tool for organizations to search across multiple information sources: Infolog-info.co.nz
- Google New Zealand: www.google.co.nz

Legal and Regulatory Environment

6. What are the major data privacy laws in your country, and how do these affect most fraud investigations?

The New Zealand Privacy Act restricts how individuals and organizations can collect, store, use, and disclose personal information. In addition, there are other laws governing the powers of investigative agencies, which can make information sharing difficult.

7. What type of legal system does your country have (e.g., civil law system, common law system, religious law system, hybrid)?

New Zealand's legal system relies on both civil law and common law.

8. What laws governing the rights of individuals are of primary concern to investigators?

- New Zealand Privacy Act
- New Zealand Human Rights Act
- New Zealand Official Information Act

9. Is bribery a criminal offense in your country? If so, does it include payments to both government officials and private businesses?

Bribery is a crime in New Zealand and it includes payments to both government officials and private businesses. Part 6 of the Crimes Act 1961 contains criminal bribery offenses involving public officials. The Secret Commissions Act 1910 deals with bribery in relation to private businesses.

10. What are the primary financial and investment regulatory bodies in your country?

- Reserve Bank is responsible for formulating and implementing monetary policy, promoting a sound and efficient financial system, and monitoring and regulating registered banks.
- Financial Markets Authority (FMA) is responsible for enforcing securities and financial reporting laws and regulating securities exchanges, financial advisers and brokers, auditors, trustees, and issuers of superannuation (retirement/pension) schemes.
- Department of Internal Affairs supervises casinos, non-deposit-taking lenders, non-bank credit card providers, stored value card providers and cash transporters, and any other reporting entities not supervised by the Reserve Bank or the Financial Markets Authority.
- Commerce Commission enforces legislation that promotes competition in New Zealand markets and prohibits misleading and deceptive conduct by traders.
- New Zealand Police provide law enforcement and crime prevention and rely on a range of partner organizations to support them.
- Serious Fraud Office investigates and prosecutes serious and complex fraud so that New Zealand is a safe place to invest and do business.

11. What are the most significant pieces of fraud-related legislation in your country?

The laws of New Zealand that set out crimes and offenses are scattered over a number of Acts of Parliament; however, all crimes are set out on the Crimes Act 1961, which covers the majority of fraud-related offenses.

12. Does your country have laws in place to protect whistle-blowers? Please describe.

New Zealand's Protected Disclosures Act 2000 protects whistle-blowers from civil, criminal, or disciplinary proceedings for making a protected disclosure. The Act generally requires the whistle-blower's identity to be kept confidential, although there are exceptions. The Act also provides that an employee can institute a personal grievance proceeding under the Employment Relations Act in cases involving employer retaliation.

It is unlawful under the Human Rights Act to treat whistle-blowers or potential whistle-blowers less favorably than others in the same or similar circumstances. Legal remedies are available under the Human Rights Act.

Anti-Fraud Programs

13. What foundational frameworks for internal controls, risk management, corporate governance, and so on are commonly used by organizations in your country when designing or assessing their anti-fraud programs (e.g., COSO frameworks, specific ISO standards, OECD guidance)?

- ISO 31000: 2009 Risk Management – Principles and Guidelines applied to fraud management (previously AS/NZ standard 4360)
- COSO Enterprise Risk Management Conceptual Framework
- COSO Internal Control – Integrated Framework
- International Standards on Auditing
- FMA Principles for Corporate Governance

New Zealand is a signatory to a number of international agreements, but the Financial Action Task Force and the Organisation for Economic Co-operation and Development (OECD) remain key.

14. What types of background checks, if any, are commonly run on prospective employees in your country (e.g., criminal, civil, credit, employment, educational)?

Depending on the industry, a combination of all the types mentioned may be used; however, none are very common.

Considerations in Fraud Investigations

15. Are there any special legal considerations that individuals from outside your country should be aware of when they are working on an investigation in your

country? Examples might include licenses needed, special laws governing information gathering, or restrictions on transmitting personal data outside the country.

Investigators from overseas must be licensed under the Private Security Personnel Licensing Act. Operating without a license is a criminal offense. In addition, investigators must comply with the requirements of the Privacy Act in relation to information gathering, retention, and disclosure.

16. Are there any special cultural considerations that individuals from outside your country should be aware of when they are working on an investigation in your country? Examples might include who is present during an interview, how to address or greet individuals, inappropriate dress, and so on.

Individuals should be aware of the cultural significance of the Treaty of Waitangi (i.e., how it shaped New Zealand history and acknowledged the customs and greetings of the indigenous Maori people).

Under New Zealand law, interviewers have certain obligations when interviewing persons who are suspected of committing a crime. In addition, interviewers should be aware of the rules regarding interviewing children under the age of 17. There are also restrictions on investigators taking photographs and video.

PHILIPPINES

Contributors

Dante T. Fuentes, CFE, CPA, CAMS
Mario B. Demarillas, CFE, CPISI, CRISC, CISM, CISA, CIA
Atty. Laureano L. Galon Jr., CFE, CPA
Raymond A. San Pedro, CPA, CICA

Sources of Information

1. What types of information about individuals are available to the public?

Personal information is available through social media (e.g., Facebook, LinkedIn, Twitter) and Internet search engines (e.g., Google, Yahoo).

2. What types of information about businesses are available to the public?

Information about corporations and partnerships is considered part of the public record and is available upon request from the Securities and Exchange Commission of the Philippines (SEC) (www.sec.gov.ph). Such information might include copies of the company's certificate of registration, articles of incorporation or partnership, bylaws, and audited financial statements. This information must be updated regularly through a General Information Sheet (GIS). The GIS includes the company's name and business address, as well as the names, addresses, and contributions of the company's incorporators, stockholders, and directors.

3. Are court records available to the public? If so, explain what types of civil and criminal records can be obtained by the public.

Although the right to a public trial is enshrined in the Constitution, court records are strictly confidential and are available only to the parties, subject to court approval. Final judgments of the Supreme Court are published and available to the public, but trial court decisions are not.

4. What other resources or types of information are regularly used by investigators in your country?

Informal channels of information are regularly used by investigators in the Philippines.

5. What are some of the most useful Internet or online sources regularly used in fraud investigations?

- Internet search engines (e.g., Google, Yahoo)
- Social media (e.g., Facebook, LinkedIn, Twitter)
- Dun & Bradstreet Philippines (www.dnb.com.ph)
- Dow Jones (www.dowjones.com)
- Company websites

Legal and Regulatory Environment

6. What are the major data privacy laws in your country, and how do these affect most fraud investigations?

- Data Privacy Act (R.A. No. 10173)
- Bank Secrecy Law (R.A. No. 1405)
- Foreign Currency Deposit Act (R.A. No. 6426)

7. What type of legal system does your country have (e.g., civil law system, common law system, religious law system, hybrid)?

The Philippines has a civil law system.

8. What laws governing the rights of individuals are of primary concern to investigators?

There are a variety of individual rights that must be considered during an investigation, including the right to privacy and the right against self-incrimination, which are both part of the Bill of Rights of the Constitution.

9. Is bribery a criminal offense in your country? If so, does it include payments to both government officials and private businesses?

Bribery is a criminal offense under the general criminal/penal law (Revised Penal Code, Act No. 3815) and the special law commonly known as the Anti-Graft and

Corrupt Practices Act (R.A. No. 3019), which in effect is a further predicate offense of the crime of plunder under R.A. No. 7080.

Generally, only payments made to government officials are considered bribery. However, private individuals may be implicated and charged under the bribery laws if they conspire with public officials or employees.

10. What are the primary financial and investment regulatory bodies in your country?

- Department of Trade and Industry and its agencies, such as the Board of Investment
- Bangko Sentral ng Pilipinas
- Department of Finance and its agencies, such as the Bureau of Internal Revenue, the Bureau of Local Government Finance, and the Bureau of Customs
- Intellectual Property Office
- Securities and Exchange Commission of the Philippines
- Local governments

11. What are the most significant pieces of fraud-related legislation in your country?

- Anti–Money Laundering Act (R.A. No. 9160)
- Terrorism Financing Prevention and Suppression Act (R.A. No. 10168)
- Data Privacy Act (R.A. No. 10173)
- Philippine Competition Act (R.A. No. 10667)
- Cybercrime Prevention Act (R.A. No. 10175)
- Anti-Plunder Law (R.A. No. 7080)
- Electronic Commerce Act (R.A. No. 8792)
- Government Procurement Reform Act (R.A. No. 9184)
- Anti-Graft and Corrupt Practices Act (R.A. No. 3019)
- Some of the laws forming part of the general penal or criminal law (Revised Penal Code, Act No. 3815) that includes *estafa*, theft, and others

12. Does your country have laws in place to protect whistle-blowers? Please describe.

There are no laws protecting whistle-blowers, but such laws are under discussion.

Anti-Fraud Programs

13. What foundational frameworks for internal controls, risk management, corporate governance, and so on are commonly used by organizations in your country when designing or assessing their anti-fraud programs (e.g., COSO frameworks, specific ISO standards, OECD guidance)?

The Securities and Exchange Commission of the Philippines requires all registered corporations to adopt a corporate governance framework that follows OECD guidance. The following frameworks and standards are also commonly used:

- COSO Enterprise Risk Management – Internal Control Framework
- COBIT 5 Framework
- Basel II Framework

- ISO 31000 Risk Management
- ISO 27000 Information Security Management System
- ISO 22301 Business Continuity Management System
- ISO 9000 Quality Management System
- ISO 38500 IT Governance
- ISO 2000 IT Service Management
- Payment Card Industry Data Security Standards (PCI–DSS)
- Health Insurance Portability and Accountability Act (HIPAA)
- ITIL Framework (formerly Information Technology Infrastructure Library)
- PMBOK/PRINCE 2
- Open Source Security Testing Methodology Manual (OSSTMM)
- Open Web Application Security Project (OWASP)

14. What types of background checks, if any, are commonly run on prospective employees in your country (e.g., criminal, civil, credit, employment, educational)?

For purposes of hiring an employee, an employer merely asks for the submission of government clearances, such as police clearance or National Bureau of Investigation (NBI) clearance. A background investigation is conducted only when there are suspicions.

Considerations in Fraud Investigations

15. Are there any special legal considerations that individuals from outside your country should be aware of when they are working on an investigation in your country? Examples might include licenses needed, special laws governing information gathering, or restrictions on transmitting personal data outside the country.

As in other jurisdictions, the Philippines has existing laws that may restrict the gathering of data, such as:

- National Defense Act (CA No. 1)
- Data Privacy Act (R.A. No. 10173)
- Secrecy of Bank Deposits Act (R.A. No. 1405)
- Foreign Currency Deposit Act (R.A. No. 6426)
- Revised Non-Stock Savings and Loan Association Act of 1997 (R.A. No. 8367)
- Philippine Competition Act (R.A. No. 10667)
- Human Security Act (R.A. No. 9372)
- The privileges afforded to certain individuals such as the marital and attorney-client privileges

SINGAPORE

Contributor

Sherlyn Yeo

Sources of Information

1. What types of information about individuals are available to the public?

- Business interests
- Bankruptcy
- Litigation history
- Marriage records

2. What types of information about businesses are available to the public?

- Particulars of business
- Principal activities
- Capital and shareholdings
- Particulars of officers/authorized representatives
- Financial records, profile, and ratios
- Compliance rating status
- Audit opinion in auditors' report
- Directors' opinion in Statement by Directors
- Litigation history

3. Are court records available to the public? If so, explain what types of civil and criminal records can be obtained by the public.

There are publicly available records for upper-level civil courts, which may include the case type, file date, case number, name of court, name of plaintiff, name of defendant, and disposition.

4. What other resources or types of information are regularly used by investigators in your country?

- Credit reports
- Criminal records

5. What are some of the most useful Internet or online sources regularly used in fraud investigations?

- Social media
- Online email

Legal and Regulatory Environment

6. What are the major data privacy laws in your country, and how do these affect most fraud investigations?

- Personal Data Protection Act restricts the collection, use, and disclosure of personal information.

- Computer Misuse and Cybersecurity Act prohibits unauthorized access to or modification of computer material and contains requirements to ensure cybersecurity.

7. What type of legal system does your country have (e.g., civil law system, common law system, religious law system, hybrid)?

Singapore has a common law system.

8. What laws governing the rights of individuals are of primary concern to investigators?

- Penal Code and Criminal Procedure Code contains general provisions that may be relevant to an investigation (e.g., an individual's right to counsel, trespassing, harassment).
- Common law: There are various common law principles, such as the right against self-incrimination (subject to statutory exceptions).
- Employment laws are relevant when companies investigate their employees.

9. Is bribery a criminal offense in your country? If so, does it include payments to both government officials and private businesses?

Bribery is a crime in Singapore, and it includes payments to both government officials and private businesses.

10. What are the primary financial and investment regulatory bodies in your country?

- Monetary Authority of Singapore (MAS)
- Singapore Stock Exchange
- Commercial Affairs Department of the Singapore Police Force (not a regulatory body but works together with MAS on investigations of white-collar crime)

11. What are the most significant pieces of fraud-related legislation in your country?

- Penal Code
- Securities and Futures Act
- Prevention of Corruption Act
- Corruption, Drug Trafficking, and Other Serious Crimes Act

12. Does your country have laws in place to protect whistle-blowers? Please describe.

Singapore has no general laws protecting whistle-blowers. However, the Prevention of Corruption Act has provisions protecting informers during investigations of offenses under the Act.

Anti-Fraud Programs

13. What foundational frameworks for internal controls, risk management, corporate governance, and so on are commonly used by organizations in your

country when designing or assessing their anti-fraud programs (e.g., COSO frameworks, specific ISO standards, OECD guidance)?

- COSO frameworks
- General and industry-specific local regulatory guidelines

14. What types of background checks, if any, are commonly run on prospective employees in your country (e.g., criminal, civil, credit, employment, educational)?

Criminal, civil, credit, employment, and educational background checks are commonly conducted.

Considerations in Fraud Investigations

15. Are there any special legal considerations that individuals from outside your country should be aware of when they are working on an investigation in your country? Examples might include licenses needed, special laws governing information gathering, or restrictions on transmitting personal data outside the country.

The Private Investigation and Security Agencies Act provides for the licensing and regulation of private investigators.

The Personal Data Protection Act restricts the collection, use, and disclosure of personal information, including the transfer of such information outside the country.

16. Are there any special cultural considerations that individuals from outside your country should be aware of when they are working on an investigation in your country? Examples might include who is present during an interview, how to address or greet individuals, inappropriate dress, and so on.

Singapore is a multiracial and multicultural society. There are various cultural considerations that may be relevant, depending on the investigation.

SOUTH KOREA

Contributors

Dong Woo Seo, CFE
Hyeon Kang, CFE
Kwang Jun Kim
Jun Ho Lee
Sun Hee Cho
Umaer Khalil
Tae Kyung Sung, PhD, CFE

Sources of Information

1. What types of information about individuals are available to the public?

Except for the personal information that an individual voluntarily discloses through social media such as Facebook, Twitter, or Instagram, an individual's personal information can be collected and used only with the prior agreement and consent of the individual. Therefore, there is no resource that allows public access to personal information without the consent of the individual, with the exception of information that is released to the public in connection with crimes of a sexually violent nature.

2. What types of information about businesses are available to the public?

Information regarding listed corporations is publicly available through the Financial Supervisory Service's electronic disclosure system (dart.fss.or.kr), which includes information such as quarterly reports, audit reports, and the results of general shareholders' meetings, among other things.

3. Are court records available to the public? If so, explain what types of civil and criminal records can be obtained by the public.

Most court decisions are publicly available on the Supreme Court's website (eng. scourt.go.kr). These decisions can be accessed using the case number or other identifiers, such as the issuing court and the date of the decision. Among other things, these decisions provide information regarding the progress of the case, including past and prospective court dates for the case. Even though the courts' decisions are publicly available, personal information within the decisions is redacted or made anonymous to maintain the privacy of the individuals involved. Other parts of the case record, such as evidence, complaints, and memoranda, are not disclosed through this system. Some decisions are not published because the Supreme Court determines that they are unsuitable for publication.

4. What other resources or types of information are regularly used by investigators in your country?

In order to detect the illegal flow of funds, officials conducting investigations often use information available from the Financial Supervisory Service, the Korea Financial Intelligence Institute, and the National Tax Service. There are no special licenses or access privileges for private investigators in South Korea. Therefore, private investigators must rely on publicly available information from bodies such as the Financial Supervisory Service.

5. What are some of the most useful Internet or online sources regularly used in fraud investigations?

In addition to filing an official request for investigation with the relevant authorities, investigators can obtain basic corporate information (e.g., financial statements, names of directors, licenses, etc.) from the Financial Supervisory Service's electronic disclosure system (dart.fss.or.kr).

Legal and Regulatory Environment

6. What are the major data privacy laws in your country, and how do these affect most fraud investigations?

In South Korea, the Personal Information Protection Act is the general law that governs the protection and processing of personal information. There are also various special laws that may be relevant, such as the Act on Promotion of Information and Communications Network Utilization and Information Protection, Etc. (IT Network Act), which regulates the protection of personal information for users of information technology (IT) and communication services. As noted in the response to Question 1, investigators can obtain an individual's personal information only with the consent of the individual or through special provisions in the law. If the individual does not consent, the information can be obtained only by a court-issued warrant.

7. What type of legal system does your country have (e.g., civil law system, common law system, religious law system, hybrid)?

South Korea has a civil law system.

8. What laws governing the rights of individuals are of primary concern to investigators?

The primary concern for most investigators is obtaining personal information within the bounds of the various data and information protection laws applicable in South Korea, such as those mentioned in the response to Question 6.

9. Is bribery a criminal offense in your country? If so, does it include payments to both government officials and private businesses?

The Criminal Act of Korea makes the payment of bribes to both government officials and private businesses a criminal offense. Under the Act, it is a crime for public officials to receive, demand, or promise to accept a bribe in connection with their duties. It is also a crime for any person (working for or representing a business) to request a bribe or offer to bribe another person in relation to business duties.

10. What are the primary financial and investment regulatory bodies in your country?

The main regulatory bodies in South Korea for financial and investment matters are the Financial Supervisory Service and the Bank of Korea. The Financial Supervisory Service is a quasi-governmental statutory body charged with the supervision of financial and capital markets. The Bank of Korea is South Korea's central bank.

11. What are the most significant pieces of fraud-related legislation in your country?

In principle, all fraud-related offenses are covered by the Criminal Act and the Act on the Aggravated Punishment of Specific Economic Crimes. In addition, South Korea has the Improper Solicitation and Graft Act, effective since 2016, under which it is an offense for public officials to receive from any one person money, gifts, or other items that are valued in excess of KRW 1 million in any instance (approximately $900) or that cumulatively exceed KRW 3 million in a fiscal year (approximately $2,700). Prior to this law, in order to prove that an official had accepted a bribe, it was necessary to establish that the official had received a benefit in exchange for granting a favor. However, under the Improper Solicitation and Graft Act, the offense of receiving benefits is not contingent on whether the benefits are received in connection with the official's duties or are provided with the intent of influencing the official. This Act also prohibits improper solicitations made directly or through a third party to public officials by stipulating 15 types of acts that may hinder the fair performance of a public official's duties and that therefore constitute offenses.

12. Does your country have laws in place to protect whistle-blowers? Please describe.

Whistle-blowers against corruption or public interest violations are defined and protected under the Act on the Protection of Public Interest Whistleblowers, which was enacted in 2011. The supervisory body empowered to administer the Act and perform the various functions thereunder is the Anti-Corruption and Civil Rights Commission. The Commission protects and rewards whistle-blowers who report corruption in the public sector. The Improper Solicitation and Graft Act also provides similar protection for individuals who report violations of that Act.

Anti-Fraud Programs

13. What foundational frameworks for internal controls, risk management, corporate governance, and so on are commonly used by organizations in your country when designing or assessing their anti-fraud programs (e.g., COSO frameworks, specific ISO standards, OECD guidance)?

In South Korea, the basic framework of internal control regimes differs between general companies and financial institutions. The details of the regimes themselves differ in certain ways from the various international standards. Broadly, however, general companies adopt internal control regimes that are similar to the US Sarbanes-Oxley Act of 2002 (SOX), while financial institutions adopt regimes based on the COSO frameworks and the Framework for Internal Control Systems in Banking Organizations 1998 (from the Basel Committee on Banking Supervision).

14. What types of background checks, if any, are commonly run on prospective employees in your country (e.g., criminal, civil, credit, employment, educational)?

South Korean employers commonly check candidates' educational backgrounds, criminal records, family relationships, and credit standing.

Considerations in Fraud Investigations

15. Are there any special legal considerations that individuals from outside your country should be aware of when they are working on an investigation in your country? Examples might include licenses needed, special laws governing information gathering, or restrictions on transmitting personal data outside the country.

In general, a special license is not necessary to acquire an individual's personal information. In connection with the transfer of personal information outside the country, contracts for the transfer of personal information in violation of the Personal Information

Protection Act and the IT Network Act are impermissible. In order to provide an individual's personal information to a third party outside the country, a party must obtain the consent of the individual. In addition, if a party wishes to transmit information from another country to South Korea, the law of the country from which the information is being transmitted applies. However, where a party knows that certain information has been obtained illegally but still receives the information with the intent of using it for profit or for any unlawful purpose, the party receiving such information is subject to criminal liability.

16. Are there any special cultural considerations that individuals from outside your country should be aware of when they are working on an investigation in your country? Examples might include who is present during an interview, how to address or greet individuals, inappropriate dress, and so on.

The dress code in South Korean workplaces is often conservative. Most employees, including interns and entry-level employees, wear formal professional attire such as business suits. Special attention should be paid to the seniority of staff members. At first meetings, it is possible to identify the most senior staff member by the fact that he or she will be the first to shake hands, while the junior members traditionally bow upon introduction. The same practice is followed at the end of a meeting or upon departure (the practice is reflective of Confucian tradition). The hosts are likely to indicate seating positions for the individuals present. Once seated, it is important to maintain proper posture, including not crossing one's legs or feet when seated in front of a senior or elderly person.

TAIWAN

Contributors

Shun Hsiung Hsu, CFE, CPA
Dr. Sheree S. Ma, CPA

Sources of Information

1. What types of information about individuals are available to the public?

Generally, information about individuals is not publicly available due to restrictions imposed by the Personal Information Protection Act. However, some personal information is available through the news, regulatory databases, disciplinary sanctions, and court judgments.

2. What types of information about businesses are available to the public?

- Database maintained by the Ministry of Economic Affairs (findbiz.nat.gov.tw/fts/query/QueryBar/queryInit.do) contains information about businesses, such as business name, ID number, address of the company, status as active or dormant, amount of registered capital, total paid-in capital, location of capital providers, date of original registration and most recent modification, and names of representatives, directors, supervisors, and managers.

- Market Observation Post System (emops.twse.com.tw/server-java/t58query) contains information about public companies, such as financial statements, annual reports, and other material information.

3. Are court records available to the public? If so, explain what types of civil and criminal records can be obtained by the public.

Court judgments are publicly available (including civil and criminal courts, administrative proceedings, and disciplinary sanctions of public functionaries).

4. What other resources or types of information are regularly used by investigators in your country?

- Books of the company
- Financial statements
- Income tax returns and value-added tax (VAT) returns
- News and media

5. What are some of the most useful Internet or online sources regularly used in fraud investigations?

In addition to the websites listed in the response to Question 2, the following online sources are regularly used by fraud examiners:

- Laws and Regulations Database of the Republic of China (law.moj.gov.tw/ENG/index.aspx)
- The Judicial Yuan database (jirs.judicial.gov.tw/FJUD/FJUDQRY01M_1.aspx)
- Statistics published by Directorate-General of Budget, Accounting, and Statistics, Executive Yuan (www.dgbas.gov.tw)

Legal and Regulatory Environment

6. What are the major data privacy laws in your country, and how do these affect most fraud investigations?

- Personal Information Protection Act
- Trade Secrets Act
- Civil Code

7. What type of legal system does your country have (e.g., civil law system, common law system, religious law system, hybrid)?

Taiwan has a civil law system.

8. What laws governing the rights of individuals are of primary concern to investigators?

The Code of Criminal Procedure is of primary concern to investigators.

9. Is bribery a criminal offense in your country? If so, does it include payments to both government officials and private businesses?

The bribery of government officials is a criminal offense. The bribery of a private business is a criminal offense only when loss or damage results from the bribery.

10. What are the primary financial and investment regulatory bodies in your country?

- Financial Supervisory Commission
- Investigation Bureau, Ministry of Justice
- Prosecutors Office, Ministry of Justice
- Agency against Corruption, Ministry of Justice

11. What are the most significant pieces of fraud-related legislation in your country?

- Criminal Code of the Republic of China
- Code of Criminal Procedure
- Civil Code
- Taiwan Code of Civil Procedure
- Anti-Corruption Act
- Money Laundering Control Act

12. Does your country have laws in place to protect whistle-blowers? Please describe.

Taiwan has no laws protecting whistle-blowers.

Anti-Fraud Programs

13. What foundational frameworks for internal controls, risk management, corporate governance, and so on are commonly used by organizations in your country when designing or assessing their anti-fraud programs (e.g., COSO frameworks, specific ISO standards, OECD guidance)?

- COSO frameworks (internal control)
- Act to Implement United Nations Convention against Corruption
- OECD guidance (Principles of Corporate Governance)

14. What types of background checks, if any, are commonly run on prospective employees in your country (e.g., criminal, civil, credit, employment, educational)?

Employment and educational background checks are common.

Considerations in Fraud Investigations

15. Are there any special legal considerations that individuals from outside your country should be aware of when they are working on an investigation in your country? Examples might include licenses needed, special laws governing information gathering, or restrictions on transmitting personal data outside the country.

Most investigations are conducted by CPAs and law firms.

CHAPTER 8

Canada

REGIONAL FRAUD TRENDS

The 2018 *Report to the Nations on Occupational Fraud and Abuse* issued by the Association of Certified Fraud Examiners (ACFE) includes 82 cases from Canada that were investigated between January 2016 and October 2017. These cases caused a median loss of US $200,000 per case.

As noted in Exhibit 8.1, corruption is the most common form of occupational fraud committed in Canada; 40% of cases in the region involved some form of corruption, which is twice as frequent as any other type of fraud scheme. Billing schemes are the second most common category of occupational fraud, occurring in 20% of the cases in Canada. In addition, nearly one-third of fraud schemes in Canada are detected by tip, making this the most frequent form of fraud detection in the region (see Exhibit 8.2).

The 2018 *Report to the Nations* also examines the anti-fraud controls that were present at victim organizations at the time the frauds being analyzed were committed. Exhibit 8.3 shows that a formal code of conduct is the most commonly implemented anti-fraud control among victim organizations in Canada, followed by external audits of the financial statements, internal audits, and employee support programs. On the other end of the spectrum, only 15% of these organizations had a mandatory vacation or job rotation policy in place, and just 10% provided rewards to whistle-blowers.

Exhibit 8.1 Scheme Types – Canada

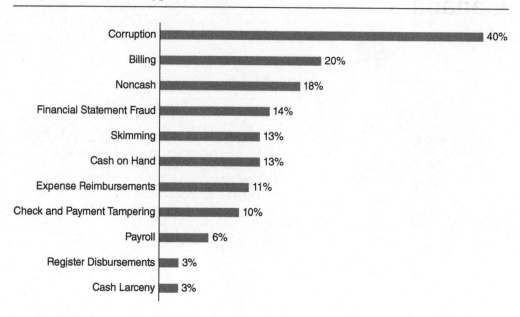

Exhibit 8.2 Initial Detection Method – Canada

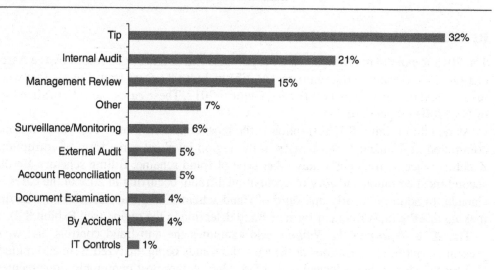

Exhibit 8.3 Frequency of Anti-Fraud Controls – Canada

Control	% of Cases
Code of Conduct	80%
External Audit of Financial Statements	72%
Internal Audit Department	71%
Employee Support Programs	71%
Management Review	68%
Management Certification of Financial Statements	67%
Independent Audit Committee	61%
Hotline	57%
External Audit of Internal Controls over Financial Reporting	54%
Fraud Training for Managers/Executives	51%
Fraud Training for Employees	51%
Anti-Fraud Policy	44%
Proactive Data Monitoring/Analysis	38%
Formal Fraud Risk Assessments	35%
Dedicated Fraud Department, Function, or Team	33%
Surprise Audits	28%
Job Rotation/Mandatory Vacation	15%
Rewards for Whistle-Blowers	10%

The following discussion provides country-specific information pertaining to the legal, investigatory, and general anti-fraud environment for Canada.

CANADA

Contributor

Andrew H. Kautz, CFE

Sources of Information

1. What types of information about individuals are available to the public?

Apart from what is available on social networking Web sites, access to personal information about individuals is very limited in Canada. Birth and death records fall under provincial jurisdiction and cannot be accessed by the public.

2. What types of information about businesses are available to the public?

- Corporate filings, which include names and addresses of directors
- Annual reports for publicly traded companies

3. Are court records available to the public? If so, explain what types of civil and criminal records can be obtained by the public.

Access to court records depends on whether the case is a civil or criminal matter and on the province. Technically, most of the information is available to the public, but locating the information is a challenge. For civil courts, the Web site for the Canadian Legal Information Institute (www.canlii.org) contains many reported cases, but not all of them.

British Columbia has an online database of civil, criminal, and highway traffic cases. However, Ontario has no online access to court records. To access court records in many provinces, investigators must know the name of the court and the date the case was heard.

4. What other resources or types of information are regularly used by investigators in your country?

Property searches are commonly performed by investigators, but there is no nation-wide database, so investigators must know the jurisdiction.

5. What are some of the most useful Internet or online sources regularly used in fraud investigations?

- Social networking websites (Facebook, Twitter)
- Sales-related websites (eBay, Craigslist, Kijiji)
- Web sites of regulatory bodies that post licensing and disciplinary information about professionals (e.g., lawyers, accountants, insurance dealers, medical professionals)
- Google Street View

Legal and Regulatory Environment

6. What are the major data privacy laws in your country, and how do these affect most fraud investigations?

Canadian privacy laws often prevent private investigators from gaining access to personal information without a court order.

The Personal Information Protection and Electronic Documents Act (PIPEDA) restricts the collection, use, and disclosure of personal information. The law applies to all businesses in Canada unless the relevant province has enacted a substantially similar law. Although PIPEDA contains many exceptions, including an exception for fraud investigations, these exceptions are not commonly known or understood, even by lawyers. Therefore, PIPEDA can cause problems when investigating fraud or attempting to recover stolen funds.

The Privacy Act governs the collection and disclosure of personal information by the federal government.

The Freedom of Information Act (FOIA) allows individuals to request information from federal government agencies. There are similar laws for provinces and municipalities.

7. What type of legal system does your country have (e.g., civil law system, common law system, religious law system, hybrid)?

The Canadian legal system is based on common law and civil law. Criminal law is based on the Criminal Code and applies to all provinces. Quebec civil law is based on the Civil Code; civil law in other provinces is based on common law.

8. What laws governing the rights of individuals are of primary concern to investigators?

- Personal Information Protection and Electronic Documents Act (applies to both government and private investigators)
- Canadian Charter of Rights and Freedoms (applies to government investigators)
- Provincial human rights laws (apply to private investigators)
- Provincial laws governing licensed private investigators

9. Is bribery a criminal offense in your country? If so, does it include payments to both government officials and private businesses?

Bribery is a crime in Canada, and it includes payments to both government officials and private businesses. The Corruption of Foreign Public Officials Act and the Criminal Code apply to government officials. The offense of secret commissions in the Criminal Code applies to private businesses.

10. What are the primary financial and investment regulatory bodies in your country?

- Office of the Superintendent of Financial Institutions regulates all federally regulated banks, trust companies, insurance companies, and pension plans.
- Provincial laws: Each province has its own regulators that regulate provincial credit unions, some trust and mortgage companies, and investment dealers (national self-regulating associations also regulate investment dealers).

11. What are the most significant pieces of fraud-related legislation in your country?

The Criminal Code of Canada is the most significant legislation.

12. Does your country have laws in place to protect whistle-blowers? Please describe.

Canada has laws protecting whistle-blowers, including:

- Criminal Code protects employees who provide information to law enforcement.
- Public Servants Disclosure Protection Act protects federal employees.
- Provincial laws: Various provinces have laws protecting government employees.

There is minimal protection for private-sector employees, although there is some whistle-blower protection in provincial labor and securities laws.

Anti-Fraud Programs

13. What foundational frameworks for internal controls, risk management, corporate governance, and so on are commonly used by organizations in your country when designing or assessing their anti-fraud programs (e.g., COSO frameworks, specific ISO standards, OECD guidance)?

COSO frameworks are commonly used for anti-fraud programs.

14. What types of background checks, if any, are commonly run on prospective employees in your country (e.g., criminal, civil, credit, employment, educational)?

Regulated companies generally require criminal record checks, credit checks, and, in some situations, employment verification. There are usually no requirements for civil, employment, or educational checks.

The practices of nonregulated companies vary widely. Some do not perform any background checks.

Considerations in Fraud Investigations

15. Are there any special legal considerations that individuals from outside your country should be aware of when they are working on an investigation in your country? Examples might include licenses needed, special laws governing information gathering, or restrictions on transmitting personal data outside the country.

Information that is available in other countries may not be available in Canada. If it is available, it can be difficult to access, or a fee might be required to obtain it. Some examples include property records, criminal convictions, marriage records, and bankruptcy records. The availability of such information varies by province.

Privacy legislation restricts what can be collected, stored, and distributed.

Quebec has specific rules related to language. In particular, employees have the right to speak French at work. That includes work-related interviews.

CHAPTER 9

Eastern Europe and Western/Central Asia

REGIONAL FRAUD TRENDS

The 2018 *Report to the Nations on Occupational Fraud and Abuse* issued by the Association of Certified Fraud Examiners (ACFE) includes 86 cases from Eastern Europe and Western/Central Asia that were investigated between January 2016 and October 2017. These cases caused a median loss of US $150,000 per case.

As noted in Exhibit 9.1, corruption is the most common form of occupational fraud committed in Eastern Europe and Western/Central Asia; 60% of the cases analyzed involved some form of corruption, which is twice as frequent as any other type of fraud scheme. Theft of noncash assets is the second most common category of occupational fraud, occurring in 30% of the cases in the region. In addition, fraud schemes in Eastern Europe and Western/Central Asia are twice as likely to be detected by a tip as by any other means (see Exhibit 9.2).

The 2018 *Report to the Nations* also examines the anti-fraud controls that were present at victim organizations at the time the frauds being analyzed were committed. Exhibit 9.3 shows that external audits of the financial statements are the most commonly implemented anti-fraud control among victim organizations in Eastern Europe and Western/Central Asia, followed by an internal audit department. On the other end of the spectrum, only 17% of these organizations had a mandatory vacation or job rotation policy in place, and just 5% provided rewards to whistle-blowers.

Exhibit 9.1 Scheme Types – Eastern Europe and Western/Central Asia

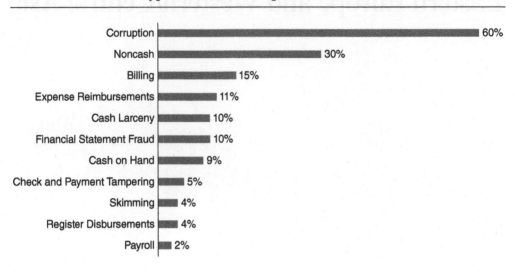

Exhibit 9.2 Initial Detection Method – Eastern Europe and Western/Central Asia

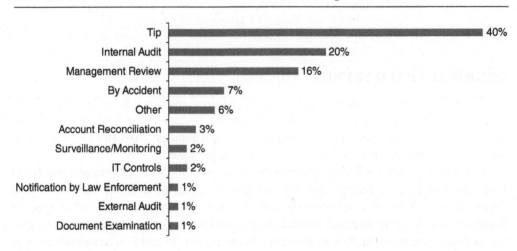

Exhibit 9.3   Frequency of Anti-Fraud Controls – Eastern Europe and Western/Central Asia

Control	% of Cases
External Audit of Financial Statements	95%
Internal Audit Department	91%
Code of Conduct	83%
Management Certification of Financial Statements	79%
Management Review	76%
Hotline	75%
External Audit of Internal Controls over Financial Reporting	75%
Independent Audit Committee	73%
Anti-Fraud Policy	66%
Fraud Training for Employees	58%
Dedicated Fraud Department, Function, or Team	57%
Fraud Training for Managers/Executives	56%
Formal Fraud Risk Assessments	46%
Surprise Audits	40%
Proactive Data Monitoring/Analysis	36%
Employee Support Programs	27%
Job Rotation/Mandatory Vacation	17%
Rewards for Whistle-Blowers	5%

The following discussions provide jurisdiction-specific information pertaining to the legal, investigatory, and general anti-fraud environment for several countries in Eastern Europe and Western/Central Asia.

BULGARIA
Contributor

Vladimir Ikonomov, CFE

Sources of Information

1. What types of information about individuals are available to the public?

The identification numbers of individuals might be available if they are registered in connection with a company in the commercial register, known as the BULSTAT Register.

2. What types of information about businesses are available to the public?

The BULSTAT Register contains information about businesses, such as ownership data, date of incorporation, business activities, and audit reports. Basic information is available to everyone. More detailed information (e.g., reports, declarations) is available with an electronic signature.

3. Are court records available to the public? If so, explain what types of civil and criminal records can be obtained by the public.

The results of court cases are generally available to the public on the website of the appropriate court.

4. What other resources or types of information are regularly used by investigators in your country?

Publicly available information and targeted searches for particular individuals are used by investigators.

5. What are some of the most useful Internet or online sources regularly used in fraud investigations?

- APIS (www.apis.bg/en) is a resource for legal information (registration required).
- Daxy (www.daxy.com) contains information about companies (commercial website).
- BULSTAT Register (psc.egov.bg/en/psc-starting-a-business-bulstat) is a commercial register.
- Central Credit Register of the Bulgarian National Bank (www.bnb.bg) has credit information.
- Registry Agency (www.registryagency.bg/bg) has information about property.

Legal and Regulatory Environment

6. What are the major data privacy laws in your country, and how do these affect most fraud investigations?

Bulgarian and EU data protection laws restrict the collection and transfer of personal information.

7. What type of legal system does your country have (e.g., civil law system, common law system, religious law system, hybrid)?

Bulgaria has a civil law system.

8. What laws governing the rights of individuals are of primary concern to investigators?

See response to Question 6.

9. Is bribery a criminal offense in your country? If so, does it include payments to both government officials and private businesses?

Bribery is a criminal offense in Bulgaria, and it includes payments to both government officials and private businesses.

10. What are the primary financial and investment regulatory bodies in your country?

The Financial Supervision Commission is the primary financial and investment regulatory body.

11. What are the most significant pieces of fraud-related legislation in your country?

- Civil Convention on Corruption
- OECD Convention on Combating Bribery of Foreign Public Officials in International Business Transactions

12. Does your country have laws in place to protect whistle-blowers? Please describe.

Bulgaria has laws that protect whistle-blowers in the public sector, but not in the private sector.

Anti-Fraud Programs

13. What foundational frameworks for internal controls, risk management, corporate governance, and so on are commonly used by organizations in your country when designing or assessing their anti-fraud programs (e.g., COSO frameworks, specific ISO standards, OECD guidance)?

Most companies follow ISO standards, such as 9001 and 27001. Large companies use COSO.

14. What types of background checks, if any, are commonly run on prospective employees in your country (e.g., criminal, civil, credit, employment, educational)?

Employers sometimes require applicants to submit their criminal records for review.

Considerations in Fraud Investigations

16. Are there any special cultural considerations that individuals from outside your country should be aware of when they are working on an investigation in your country? Examples might include who is present during an interview, how to address or greet individuals, inappropriate dress, and so on.

Nodding means no, and head shaking means yes. Two people should be present in an interview – one to ask questions, and one to take notes (and be a witness).

CZECH REPUBLIC

Contributor

Pavla Hladká, CFE

Sources of Information

1. What types of information about individuals are available to the public?

- Names and addresses of individuals who own businesses that are recorded in the Public Register
- Names and addresses of individuals who are members of boards or statutory bodies, or owners of companies that are recorded in the Public Register

2. What types of information about businesses are available to the public?

Generally, the Public Register contains the following information about businesses:

- Business name
- Registered office
- Names of directors
- Registered capital
- Business type or activities
- Legal form of the business
- Identification number
- Names and addresses of owners of the company (with the exception of shareholders of joint-stock companies)
- Memorandum or articles of association
- Documents concerning the appointment or removal of directors
- Financial statements
- Other documents filed in specific situations, such as mergers and controlling agreements

The Public Register is available to the public free of charge via a Web portal (or. justice.cz/ias/ui/rejstrik). It can be searched by entity name or by identification number.

3. Are court records available to the public? If so, explain what types of civil and criminal records can be obtained by the public.

Criminal records are maintained at the Criminal Records Office in Prague, which is part of the Ministry of Justice. Individuals can request copies of their own criminal records from the Penal Register. Corporate criminal records are accessible by the general public.

The decisions of the Constitutional Court, Supreme Court, and Supreme Administrative Court are published periodically in official reports. These decisions are also available for free on each court's website, but most of them are not available in English.

The following commercial legal databases are available on a subscription basis:

- Lexgalaxy (www.lexgalaxy.cz)
- Automated legal information system (ASPI) (www.lib.cas.cz/en/db/aspi)
- Beck-Online (www.beck-online.cz)
- Codexis Academia (www.mup.cz/en/library/online-sources/codexis-academia)

4. What other resources or types of information are regularly used by investigators in your country?

Useful resources include various local and international business and financial databases, as well as social media and adverse media information or negative news. In addition, the following website contains a list of useful online resources: akms.cz/information-sources-2.

5. What are some of the most useful Internet or online sources regularly used in fraud investigations?

Investigators use commercial and trade registers, cadastres (land registers), media information, and the sources mentioned in the response to Question 4.

Legal and Regulatory Environment

6. What are the major data privacy laws in your country, and how do these affect most fraud investigations?

EU Directive 95/46/EC and Czech Act No. 101/2000 Coll., on the Protection of Personal Data, restrict the collection and transfer of personal information. On May 25, 2018, these laws will be replaced by the more restrictive EU General Data Protection Regulation.

7. What type of legal system does your country have (e.g., civil law system, common law system, religious law system, hybrid)?

The Czech Republic has a civil law system.

8. What laws governing the rights of individuals are of primary concern to investigators?

See the response to Question 6 regarding data privacy laws.

9. Is bribery a criminal offense in your country? If so, does it include payments to both government officials and private businesses?

Bribery is a criminal offense in the Czech Republic, and it includes payments to both government officials and private businesses.

10. What are the primary financial and investment regulatory bodies in your country?

The primary financial regulator is the Czech National Bank (*Česká národní banka* or CNB), which supervises financial markets, sets monetary policy, and issues currency.

11. What are the most significant pieces of fraud-related legislation in your country?

Investigators conduct investigations into alleged breaches of, among others, the Civil and Criminal Codes; Codes of Criminal, Civil, and Administrative Procedure; Labor Law; Intellectual Property Law; Act on Criminal Liability of Legal Entities and Their Prosecution; Tax Law; bank regulations under the Czech Anti-Money Laundering Act; Act on Capital Markets; and Public Procurement Act.

12. Does your country have laws in place to protect whistle-blowers? Please describe.

The Czech Republic has no laws specifically designed to protect whistle-blowers, although such laws are under discussion. The Act on Banks, the Act on Savings and Credit Cooperatives, the Capital Market Undertakings Act, and the Civil Service Act contain some protections for employees who report illegal or unethical practices.

Anti-Fraud Programs

13. What foundational frameworks for internal controls, risk management, corporate governance, and so on are commonly used by organizations in your country when designing or assessing their anti-fraud programs (e.g., COSO frameworks, specific ISO standards, OECD guidance)?

The Czech Corporate Governance Code is based on OECD principles, but most of its provisions are not mandatory. Large and midsize companies adopt international standards for internal controls and risk management, such as the COSO frameworks, OECD guidance, specific ISO standards (e.g., ISO 37001 – Anti-bribery Management Systems), the US Federal Sentencing Guidelines, and guidance on the UK Bribery Act and German Compliance Management Systems requirements.

14. What types of background checks, if any, are commonly run on prospective employees in your country (e.g., criminal, civil, credit, employment, educational)?

Czech employers often require applicants to provide proof of a clean criminal record, a certificate of good standing, and a medical certificate or drug test results. Only information directly related to employment may be requested. Employers must treat applicants equally and avoid discrimination. Also, employers must comply with applicable data privacy laws (see response to Question 6).

Considerations in Fraud Investigations

15. Are there any special legal considerations that individuals from outside your country should be aware of when they are working on an investigation in your country? Examples might include licenses needed, special laws governing information gathering, or restrictions on transmitting personal data outside the country.

Private fraud investigators do not need a license or special training in the Czech Republic. The CFE designation can be an advantage in some cases. Data privacy laws restrict the transmission of personal data outside the country (see response to Question 6).

16. Are there any special cultural considerations that individuals from outside your country should be aware of when they are working on an investigation in your country? Examples might include who is present during an interview, how to address or greet individuals, inappropriate dress, and so on.

Investigators from abroad should consult with the local ACFE chapter.

POLAND

Contributors

Piotr Chmiel, CFE, CISA, CIA
Agata Kamińska, Master in International Relations

Sources of Information

1. What types of information about individuals are available to the public?

The Polish Personal Data Protection Act significantly limits the personal information that is available to the public. Generally, personal information can be gathered from social networks.

Business-related information about certain individuals may be available from the Registry Court and the Central Registry of Enterprises (see response to Question 2).

2. What types of information about businesses are available to the public?

Generally, business records are publicly available and free of charge. Business information can be obtained from the Registry Court (*Krajowy Rejestr Sądowy* or KRS), and such information might include:

- Business name and address
- Type of legal entity
- Information about ownership and management
- Representation rules
- Information about any changes of legal structure
- Tax Identification Number (NIP)
- Registration number (REGON)
- Information about capital
- Financial reports

The Central Registry of Enterprises (*Centralna Ewidencja i Informacja o Działalności Gospodarczej or* CEIDG) also contains information about businesses and related individuals.

3. Are court records available to the public? If so, explain what types of civil and criminal records can be obtained by the public.

In general, civil records are publicly available. Criminal records are not publicly available, except in limited cases where such information is required by law (e.g., when a job requires a criminal background check).

4. What other resources or types of information are regularly used by investigators in your country?

Standard sources include general Internet searches and social networks analysis.

5. What are some of the most useful Internet or online sources regularly used in fraud investigations?

Wolters Kluwer (wolterskluwer.pl) offers an online tool called LEX Informator Prawno-Gospodarczy, which contains data from KRS and CEIDG.

Legal and Regulatory Environment

6. What are the major data privacy laws in your country, and how do these affect most fraud investigations?

The Polish Personal Data Protection Act regulates the privacy of personal information. It will be replaced by the EU's General Data Protection Regulation on May 25, 2018.

7. What type of legal system does your country have (e.g., civil law system, common law system, religious law system, hybrid)?

Poland has a civil law system (based on continental law, mostly French and German).

8. What laws governing the rights of individuals are of primary concern to investigators?

Private investigators must obtain a license. Licenses are not required for fraud investigators; however, it is advisable to have some sort of formal certification.

9. Is bribery a criminal offense in your country? If so, does it include payments to both government officials and private businesses?

Bribery is a criminal offense in Poland, and it includes payments to both government officials and private businesses. However, most enforcement focuses on government officials rather than private businesses.

10. What are the primary financial and investment regulatory bodies in your country?

The primary financial regulatory body is the Polish Financial Oversight Commission (*Komisja Nadzoru Finansowego* or KNF), which oversees the financial sector, including banks, insurance companies, and investment companies. Banks have an additional regulatory body called the Banking Oversight Commission (*Komisja Nadzoru Bankowego* or KNB).

11. What are the most significant pieces of fraud-related legislation in your country?

There is no legislation dedicated solely to fraud; however, the Penal Code, the Civil Code, the Trade Code, the Accounting Act, and banking regulations all contain anti-fraud provisions.

12. Does your country have laws in place to protect whistle-blowers? Please describe.

Banks are legally required to implement whistle-blower programs and ensure that whistle-blowers are protected. Polish law also protects individuals who denounce market cartels. There are no other dedicated laws that protect whistle-blowers. However, some companies implement internal programs that include whistle-blower protection.

Anti-Fraud Programs

13. What foundational frameworks for internal controls, risk management, corporate governance, and so on are commonly used by organizations in your country when designing or assessing their anti-fraud programs (e.g., COSO frameworks, specific ISO standards, OECD guidance)?

ISO standards, especially ISO 27001, are the most popular frameworks. Public-sector organizations use Polish versions of ISO standards. COSO is also used.

14. What types of background checks, if any, are commonly run on prospective employees in your country (e.g., criminal, civil, credit, employment, educational)?

The Polish Personal Data Protection Act strictly limits what can be verified or asked during the employment process. Generally, employers cannot check an applicant's credit or criminal history. There are exceptions for certain jobs, mostly in the public sector. During interviews, employers can ask about information on the applicant's curriculum vitae (CV). If the applicant consents, employers can question the applicant's references.

Considerations in Fraud Investigations

15. Are there any special legal considerations that individuals from outside your country should be aware of when they are working on an investigation in your country? Examples might include licenses needed, special laws governing information gathering, or restrictions on transmitting personal data outside the country.

Private investigators must obtain a license. However, there is no license requirement for investigators involved in corporate fraud investigations or when the investigation is based on a formal contract.

Usually, transferring personal data outside of Poland requires a dedicated data transfer agreement.

16. Are there any special cultural considerations that individuals from outside your country should be aware of when they are working on an investigation in your country? Examples might include who is present during an interview, how to address or greet individuals, inappropriate dress, and so on.

In some situations, workers are permitted to request the assistance of a union representative during an interview.

SLOVENIA

Contributors

Sandra Damijan, PhD, CFE
Mojca Koder, CFE
Mihael Kranjc

Sources of Information

1. What types of information about individuals are available to the public?

General information about individuals is available through Google and other Internet search engines, as well as social media such as Facebook. Data on individuals who own companies, or serve as officers or directors of companies, is available from the Agency of the Republic of Slovenia for Public Legal Records and Related Services (AJPES) in the Slovenian Business Register. AJPES also contains information about insolvency proceedings and other information. All of this information is free of charge. The website of AJPES is www.ajpes.si.

Information about the owners of real estate, including property values, is available for free from the Surveying and Mapping Authority of the Republic of Slovenia (www.gu.gov.si/en and www.e-prostor.gov.si). Additional information on real estate, including legal status and mortgage values, is available for free from the Land Register (www.sodisce.si/javne_knjige/zemljiska_knjiga).

2. What types of information about businesses are available to the public?

Through AJPES (www.ajpes.si), individuals can obtain free information about businesses, such as:

- Company name
- Address
- Subscribed capital
- Names of officers and directors
- Open accounts in Slovenian banks
- Annual reports, statements, and disclosures
- Court disputes
- Blocked bank accounts
- Bankruptcy proceedings

Commercial services, such as Gvin.com (www.gvin.com), offer access to additional information about businesses, such as days of blocked bank accounts, changes in company data, involvement in court proceedings, and benchmarking against competitors.

3. Are court records available to the public? If so, explain what types of civil and criminal records can be obtained by the public.

For civil and criminal cases, anonymized rulings of high and supreme courts are available on the Slovenian Courts website (www.sodisce.si).

4. What other resources or types of information are regularly used by investigators in your country?

The paid commercial website IUS-Info (www.iusinfo.si) contains useful information regarding legislation, court decisions, and related materials.

5. What are some of the most useful Internet or online sources regularly used in fraud investigations?

See responses to Questions 1–4.

Legal and Regulatory Environment

6. What are the major data privacy laws in your country, and how do these affect most fraud investigations?

The primary data privacy law in Slovenia is the Personal Data Protection Act (Official Gazette of the Republic of Slovenia No. 86/2004). The privacy of financial information is also governed by the Banking Act (Official Gazette of the Republic of Slovenia No. 25/15) and the Insurance Act (Official Gazette of the Republic of Slovenia No. 93/15).

7. What type of legal system does your country have (e.g., civil law system, common law system, religious law system, hybrid)?

Slovenia has a civil law system.

8. What laws governing the rights of individuals are of primary concern to investigators?

The Personal Data Protection Act is of primary concern.

9. Is bribery a criminal offense in your country? If so, does it include payments to both government officials and private businesses?

Bribery of both government officials and private businesses is a criminal offense in Slovenia.

10. What are the primary financial and investment regulatory bodies in your country?

- Insurance Supervision Agency (*Agencija za zavarovalni nadzor*)
- Bank of Slovenia (*Banka Slovenije*)
- Securities Market Agency (*Agencija za trg vrednostnih papirjev*)
- Office for Money Laundering Prevention (*Urad za preprečevanje pranja denarja*)
- Slovenian Competition Protection Body (*Javna agencija Republike Slovenije za varstvo konkurence*)

11. What are the most significant pieces of fraud-related legislation in your country?

- Criminal Code (*Kazenski zakonik*)
- Criminal Procedure Act (*Zakon o kazenskem postopku*)

12. Does your country have laws in place to protect whistle-blowers? Please describe.

Slovenia has laws that protect whistle-blowers, including the Integrity and Prevention of Corruption Act.

Anti-Fraud Programs

13. What foundational frameworks for internal controls, risk management, corporate governance, and so on are commonly used by organizations in your country when designing or assessing their anti-fraud programs (e.g., COSO frameworks, specific ISO standards, OECD guidance)?

- COSO frameworks
- Specific ISO standards
- OECD guidance
- Corporate Integrity Guidelines (www.korporativna-integriteta.si/Smernice/Smernice (SSKI).aspx)
- Corporate Governance Code (www.ljse.si/cgi-bin/jve.cgi?doc=8377)

14. What types of background checks, if any, are commonly run on prospective employees in your country (e.g., criminal, civil, credit, employment, educational)?

Criminal, civil, employment, and reputational background checks are commonly conducted on prospective hires.

Considerations in Fraud Investigations

15. Are there any special legal considerations that individuals from outside your country should be aware of when they are working on an investigation in your country? Examples might include licenses needed, special laws governing information gathering, or restrictions on transmitting personal data outside the country.

Investigators must be aware of legal limitations related to data privacy. The Information Commissioner's website (www.ip-rs.si/en) contains legislation and other relevant information.

CHAPTER 10

Latin America and the Caribbean

REGIONAL FRAUD TRENDS

The 2018 *Report to the Nations on Occupational Fraud and Abuse* issued by the Association of Certified Fraud Examiners (ACFE) includes 110 cases from Latin America and the Caribbean that were investigated between January 2016 and October 2017. These cases caused a median loss of US $193,000 per case.

As noted in Exhibit 10.1, corruption is the most common form of occupational fraud committed in Latin America and the Caribbean; 51% of the cases analyzed involved some form of corruption, which is more than twice as frequent as any other type of fraud scheme. Theft of noncash assets is the second most common category of occupational fraud, occurring in 22% of the cases in the region. In addition, almost half of the fraud schemes in Latin America and the Caribbean are detected by a tip, making this the most likely method of detection by far (see Exhibit 10.2).

The 2018 *Report to the Nations* also examines the anti-fraud controls that were present at victim organizations at the time the frauds being analyzed were committed. Exhibit 10.3 shows that an internal audit department is the most commonly implemented anti-fraud control among victim organizations in Latin America and the Caribbean, followed by external audits of the financial statements. On the other end of the spectrum, only 26% of these organizations had a mandatory vacation or job rotation policy in place, and just 6% provided rewards to whistle-blowers.

Exhibit 10.1   Scheme Types – Latin America and the Caribbean

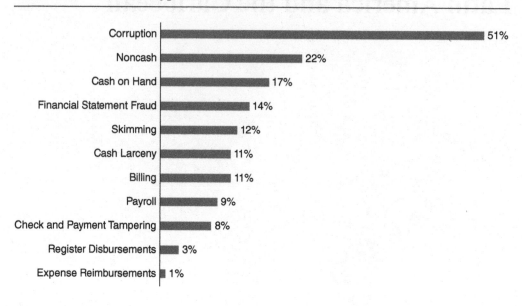

Exhibit 10.2   Initial Detection Method – Latin America and the Caribbean

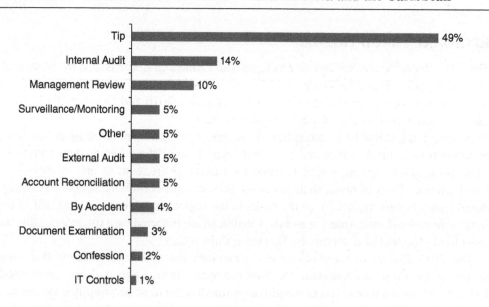

Exhibit 10.3   Frequency of Anti-Fraud Controls – Latin America and the Caribbean

Control	% of Cases
Internal Audit Department	89%
External Audit of Financial Statements	86%
Code of Conduct	81%
Management Certification of Financial Statements	73%
Management Review	71%
External Audit of Internal Controls over Financial Reporting	70%
Hotline	68%
Independent Audit Committee	61%
Employee Support Programs	51%
Anti-Fraud Policy	50%
Fraud Training for Employees	50%
Fraud Training for Managers/Executives	48%
Dedicated Fraud Department, Function, or Team	44%
Formal Fraud Risk Assessments	40%
Surprise Audits	35%
Proactive Data Monitoring/Analysis	32%
Job Rotation/Mandatory Vacation	26%
Rewards for Whistle-Blowers	6%

The following discussions provide jurisdiction-specific information pertaining to the legal, investigatory, and general anti-fraud environment for several countries in Latin America and the Caribbean.

BRAZIL

Contributor

Marco Antonio E. Fernandes

Sources of Information

1. What types of information about individuals are available to the public?

- Confirmation of name, address, and date of birth
- Credit information and pending financial issues with national coverage
- Criminal record when accessed by a lawyer

2. What types of information about businesses are available to the public?

- Address, location, and shareholder information
- Credit scoring and pending financial issues with national coverage
- Financial statements depending on the type of entity

3. Are court records available to the public? If so, explain what types of civil and criminal records can be obtained by the public.

Brazil is in the process of digitizing all data from all tribunals and registrars (*cartórios*) in the country. The goal is to create a website that provides access to information on legal proceedings, statistical data on the judiciary, real estate records, divorce proceedings, and more. The National Center for Procedural and Extra-Procedural Information (*Central Nacional de Informações Processuais e Extraprocessuais* or CNIPE) will provide information regarding whether a person or company is being criminally prosecuted, has any type of dispute pending in court, or has property in dispute. Currently, to obtain procedural information online, an individual must access the individual website of one of the 91 different courts in the country, which have different requirements and levels of data access.

4. What other resources or types of information are regularly used by investigators in your country?

Credit bureaus, such as Serasa, Experian, and LexisNexis, are used by investigators.

5. What are some of the most useful Internet or online sources regularly used in fraud investigations?

Court records and credit agencies are online sources used in fraud investigations.

Legal and Regulatory Environment

6. What are the major data privacy laws in your country, and how do these affect most fraud investigations?

Brazil does not have a general law concerning the protection of personal data. Such a law is currently under consideration.

Article 5, Sections X and XII of the federal Constitution protect privacy and private life. They also guarantee the secrecy of correspondence and of telegraphic data and telephone communications.

7. What type of legal system does your country have (e.g., civil law system, common law system, religious law system, hybrid)?

Brazil has a civil law system based on European civil codes, especially Portuguese legal codes.

8. What laws governing the rights of individuals are of primary concern to investigators?

The Brazilian Constitution treats privacy and data protection as fundamental rights. The Brazilian Civil Code (Law No. 10,406/02), the Consumer Protection Code (Law No. 8,078/9), and the Internet Act (Law No. 12,965/14) are the most important statutes governing the use, collection, and processing of personal data.

9. Is bribery a criminal offense in your country? If so, does it include payments to both government officials and private businesses?

Brazilian law prohibits the bribery of government officials and private businesses.

10. What are the primary financial and investment regulatory bodies in your country?

- The Central Bank of Brazil is responsible for ensuring the stability of the currency's purchasing power by controlling inflation and maintaining a sound and efficient financial system.
- The Securities Commission (CVM) regulates the securities market.

11. What are the most significant pieces of fraud-related legislation in your country?

Under the Clean Company Act 2014 (Law No. 12,846), companies are strictly liable for the corrupt acts of their employees. The law contains civil and administrative penalties, but it has no criminal penalties for companies.

12. Does your country have laws in place to protect whistle-blowers? Please describe.

Brazil's Anti-Corruption Law (Law No. 12,846/2013) requires companies to adopt compliance programs with whistle-blower protections.

Anti-Fraud Programs

13. What foundational frameworks for internal controls, risk management, corporate governance, and so on are commonly used by organizations in your country when designing or assessing their anti-fraud programs (e.g., COSO frameworks, specific ISO standards, OECD guidance)?

- ISO 37001
- ISO 19600 (Compliance Management Systems – Guidelines)
- ISO 31000
- COSO 2013
- *Cadastro Nacional de Empresas Comprometidas com a Ética e a Integridade* (Pro-Ethics Company), Initiative of the Ethos Institute and the Ministry of Transparency, Inspection, and Comptroller General of the Union

14. What types of background checks, if any, are commonly run on prospective employees in your country (e.g., criminal, civil, credit, employment, educational)?

Criminal, civil, credit, and employment background checks are commonly conducted on prospective hires.

Considerations in Fraud Investigations

15. Are there any special legal considerations that individuals from outside your country should be aware of when they are working on an investigation in your country? Examples might include licenses needed, special laws governing information gathering, or restrictions on transmitting personal data outside the country.

Brazil does not have a general, unified law concerning the protection of personal data. However, there are laws requiring companies to inform consumers about how their data will be used. The Internet Act provides that Internet service providers may collect information only for justified reasons and that they must retain the least possible amount of personal data.

CHILE

Contributors

Stefano Bordoli
Andrea Rondot, CFE
Pedro Trevisan, CFE
Rodrigo Yáñez

Sources of Information

1. What types of information about individuals are available to the public?

In Chile, the following information about individuals is available from free public databases:

- **National ID numbers:** There is a private and nonofficial database named Rutificador (chile.rutificador.cl) that provides information on the national ID numbers of adults (people who are over 18 years old).
- **Marital status:** If an individual's national ID number is known, it is possible to view the individual's marital status in the database of the Civil Registry and Identification Service of Chile (www.registrocivil.cl).
- **Litigation history:** The Judicial Branch of the State of Chile has a public litigation database (www.pjud.cl) that includes records of court proceedings regarding bankruptcy, civil and commercial actions, labor disputes, and social security debt recovery, and benefits actions from 2005 to present.

- **Bankruptcies:** The Superintendence of Insolvency and Entrepreneurship (www. superir.gob.cl) provides a public database called the Insolvency Bulletin (www.boletinconcursal.cl/boletin/getListaPublicaciones), which contains information regarding bankruptcy proceedings.
- **Real estate:** In Chile, the real estate registration is managed by several Real Estate Registries (*Conservadores de Bienes Raíces*) that are responsible for safeguarding and updating real estate records in order to maintain the history of property and to give full publicity to restrictions that may affect the real estate. The registries usually cover either a district or a group of them. Only some registries have online databases (i.e., Santiago at www.conservador.cl). At all registries, it is possible to request information in their offices.
- **Tax information:** Tax information is available on the website for the Internal Revenue Service of Chile (zeus.sii.cl/cvc/stc/stc.html).
- **Government contracts:** The websites Chile Proveedores (www.chileproveedores.cl) and Mercado Público (www.mercadopublico.cl) provide information on contracts with government entities, as well as assigned contracts to certain parties.
- **Other information:** The Official Gazette of the Republic of Chile (www.doe.cl) is an online publication that provides information from the prior two years about adoptions, name changes, presumed deaths, rulings from various courts, and other information. It also provides information on the creation, modification, and dissolution of companies from March 31, 2011, to the present. Free searches are available only by date and not by national ID number. Information about individuals is also available through search engines (e.g., Google), international and national media, and social media.

The following commercial services also provide information about individuals:

- DiCom is a commercial database used to evaluate the financial situations of individuals, including credit ratings. Consumer debts are deleted five years after they become due, even if unpaid. Currently, DiCom stores information about commercial banking (checks, credit cards, and consumer loans); university (student) loans (including monthly payments); commercial loans (supermarkets, retailers, and pharmacies); and any economic transactions, as well as debt defaults, unless the debts were paid, renegotiated, or canceled (by the ruling of a civil court or a five-year statute of limitation). This database provides useful information to banking and financial institutions to minimize their risks. The use of DiCom is regulated in Chile, and anyone other than financial institutions must request proper authorization. DiCom is managed in Chile by Equifax.
- Other subscription-based financial and legal databases provide information about individuals, such as Servicio Interactivo de Informes, S.A. (SIISA), Sistema Nacional de Comunicaciones Financieras (SINACOFI), and TransUnion.
- Subscription-based online databases such as World-Check and Dow Jones Risk and Compliance Databases contain information on companies and individuals who are politically exposed persons (PEPs), or are listed on sanction and embargo lists, including those of the Office of Foreign Assets Control, UN Oil for Food Program, the UK HM Treasury, European Union, Office of the Superintendent of Financial Institutions,

Financial Action Task Force, the Australian Department of Foreign Affairs and Trade, and others. Other similar databases are Compliance Tracker (Chilean database covering PEPs, sanctions, and adverse media), Dun & Bradstreet, Hoovers, and Factiva.

2. What types of information about businesses are available to the public?

Most of the resources listed in the response to Question 1 can also be used to obtain information about businesses. In addition, the following information about businesses is publicly available:

- **Shareholders:** The Superintendence of Securities and Insurance (www.svs.cl) has a free public database of public companies (*Sociedades Anónimas Abiertas*) and their current shareholders. For limited liability companies, the names of the current partners can be obtained by looking at the public records regarding the constitution or modification of companies in the Real Estate Registries or their online databases, if any, or the summaries of such public records published in the Official Gazette of the Republic of Chile, which extends back to March 31, 2011.
- **Companies convicted of anti-union practices:** The Government's Labor Bureau (*Dirección del Trabajo*) (www.dt.gob.cl) maintains an updated list of companies that have been convicted of anti-union practices by the labor courts. Such companies are prohibited from entering into government contracts for two years.
- **Other information:** The Official Gazette of the Republic of Chile (www.doe.cl) has a private, paid database that provides information regarding the creation and modification of companies. This service can be used to discover the ultimate beneficial owner of legal entities. It has several tools that facilitate research (e.g., filtered by year or keywords). While the public database is limited to the prior two years, the private database goes back to 1985.

3. Are court records available to the public? If so, explain what types of civil and criminal records can be obtained by the public.

Court records are generally available to the public. However, access to records of criminal and family proceedings may be limited to parties to the proceeding. Nevertheless, in some cases, it is possible to gain access to official records of administrative and agency proceedings to find information related to opinions, judgments, or other dispositions associated with a party's identification number (*rol único tributario* or RUT). This information is usually redacted and limited to the docket and written disposition of the court.

4. What other resources or types of information are regularly used by investigators in your country?

For private investigations, the following resources or types of information are regularly used by investigators:

- Forensic data collection
- On-site investigation

- Company internal accountability records, such as bank records and other supporting documentation for transactions
- Company policies and procedures, such as the Designation of Authorities (DOA)
- Interviews with key employees or related persons

Public investigations must be carried out by the Public Prosecutor's Office (*Ministerio Público*), according to Chapter VIII of the Political Constitution of the Republic of Chile, the Organic Constitutional Public Prosecutor's Office Law No. 19,640, and the Criminal Procedure Code. In these cases, the Prosecutor's Office can use any means previously authorized by the guarantee judge (*juez de garantía*). Also, the Law No. 19,913, which created the Financial Intelligence Unit (UAF), lists the means it may use for the investigation of financial crimes.

5. What are some of the most useful Internet or online sources regularly used in fraud investigations?

See responses to Questions 1 and 2.

Legal and Regulatory Environment

6. What are the major data privacy laws in your country, and how do these affect most fraud investigations?

Privacy is a major concern in Chilean law, with constitutional status. Article 19 of the Chilean Political Constitution of 1980 ensures to all persons (1) the respect and protection of private life and the honor of the person and his family, and (2) the inviolability of homes and all forms of private communication. The law limits home searches and the interception and inspection of private communications and documents. The fundamental right to privacy has a great impact in the investigation of fraud, even by government agencies.

The Law No. 19,628 on the Protection of Private Life (issued in 1998), along with the Law No. 20,575, which reformed it, limits the investigation and collection of information. Article 5 states, "When a request for personal data is made through an electronic means it must be recorded. The record of such request of information includes: (a) The individualization of the applicant; (b) The purpose of the request; and (c) The type of data that is transmitted. The admissibility of the request will be evaluated by the person in charge of the data bank who receives it, but the responsibility for that request will be of whoever does it." For example, when accessing credit rating information available in databases such as Equifax, SIISA, or TransUnion, the search will be recorded and available to the person or legal entity investigated.

Despite the efforts made by the Chilean lawmakers in 1999 to regulate this subject, the Law No. 19,628 is currently considered obsolete because it does not meet international standards regarding personal data processing, or the guidelines of the Organisation for Economic Co-operation and Development (OECD), or the challenges that a digital economy entails. Because of this, there have been recent efforts to amend the law.

7. What type of legal system does your country have (e.g., civil law system, common law system, religious law system, hybrid)?

Chile has a civil law system.

8. What laws governing the rights of individuals are of primary concern to investigators?

- The Chilean Political Constitution of the Republic (1980)
- Criminal Code (1874)
- Criminal Procedure Code (2000)
- Corporate Criminal Liability Act (CCLA; Law No. 20,393) (2009)
- Decree in Force of Law No. 1 of the Ministry of Economy, Promotion, and Reconstruction of 2005, establishing the consolidated, coordinated, and systematized text of the Competition Decree, Law No. 211 (1973)
- Law No. 19,628 on the Protection of Private Life (1999)
- Labor Code, in particular its 5th book about Labor Jurisdiction, which was reformed by Law No. 20,087 (2006)

9. Is bribery a criminal offense in your country? If so, does it include payments to both government officials and private businesses?

According to Articles 248–251 of the Chilean Criminal Code, the bribery of local and foreign government officials is a criminal offense and may lead to imprisonment for up to five years.

Law No. 20,393, which applies to all Chilean corporate entities, states that companies can be investigated, charged, prosecuted, and convicted for financing of terrorism, money laundering, and bribery of public officials in Chile or other countries. When a corporation violates the Law No. 20,393, it may be forbidden from entering into contracts with governmental entities and agencies, lose government benefits, face fines, and be forced to surrender profits resulting from the bribery. It is also at risk of dissolution.

Bribery is also forbidden under laws that regulate the activity of local public officials, such as the Law No. 18,575 on Public Administration and the Law No. 18,834 on Statute of Public Officials. These laws, as well as the Criminal Code, forbid public officials from receiving or requesting greater fees or rights than those they are legally entitled to according to their position, or an economic benefit in consideration for performing an act intrinsic to their position for which no payment is due.

In Chile, there is no law prohibiting commercial bribery. However, there may be a civil claim for damages under general tort law or under Law No. 20,169 on Unfair Competition. Laws prohibiting commercial bribery have been introduced and are currently under discussion.

10. What are the primary financial and investment regulatory bodies in your country?

- Central Bank of Chile
- Superintendence of Securities and Insurance (SVS)
- Superintendence of Banks and Financial Institutions (SBIF)

- Financial Intelligence Unit (UAF)
- Internal Revenue Service (SII)
- Superintendence of Pensions (SP)
- Superintendence of Insolvency and Entrepreneurship

11. What are the most significant pieces of fraud-related legislation in your country?

- Criminal Code (Articles 233–237, Misappropriation of Assets; Article 239, Taxation Fraud; Articles 248–251, Bribery; Articles 246–247, Violation of Secrets)
- Corporate Criminal Liability Act (CCLA; Law No. 20,393) (2009)
- Decree in Force of Law No. 1 of the Ministry of Economy, Promotion, and Reconstruction of 2005, which establishes the consolidated, coordinated, and systematized text of the Competition Decree, Law No. 211 (1973)
- Securities Market Law No. 18,045 for Insider Trading and other securities fraud

12. Does your country have laws in place to protect whistle-blowers? Please describe.

The protection of whistle-blowers depends on the context, crime, or offense and the relevant branch of law, as follows:

Criminal Law

Neither the Chilean Criminal Procedure Code nor the Criminal Code has any safeguards to protect private employees who report offenses. The Law No. 20,393, which established criminal liability for companies, has led some companies to establish whistle-blower procedures as a means to detect and deter corruption. In addition to this law, foreign regulations and international standards have led a number of corporations doing business in Chile to introduce whistle-blower procedures as part of their compliance programs.

Administrative Law

In 2007, the Chilean Congress passed the Law No. 20,205, which amended the following laws: the Organic Constitutional Law No. 18,575 on the General Rules of the State's Administration; Law No. 18,834 on Statute of Public Officials; and Law No. 18,883 on Administrative Statute of Municipal Officials. It introduced the duty for public officials to report criminal offenses, faults, and lack of integrity of Chilean officials, as well as protecting whistle-blowers from retaliation such as administrative punishment, dismissal, suspensions, relocation, and relegation. However, this protection lasts for only 90 days.

According to the local law, civil servants and public officials must report cases of corruption to the Public Prosecutor's Office (*Ministerio Público*) or to the police or competent authority. It is the responsibility of the Public Prosecutor's Office to handle the complaint. Public officials who report unfounded or false allegations with the mere intention to denigrate a person may be removed from office.

Fair Competition Law

Under Article 39 bis of the Competition Act for the Defense of Competition, individuals who inform government authorities that they are part of a cartel may qualify for a reduced fine or an exemption from fines. However, strict conditions must be met.

Anti-Fraud Programs

13. What foundational frameworks for internal controls, risk management, corporate governance, and so on are commonly used by organizations in your country when designing or assessing their anti-fraud programs (e.g., COSO frameworks, specific ISO standards, OECD guidance)?

Chile joined the OECD in 2010, and this resulted in efforts to elevate the local standards regarding transparency and corporate governance as part of the OECD requirements for membership. Chilean law and local stock exchanges impose corporate governance rules on public companies. Large companies with business activities abroad are likely to make use of international frameworks, such as the COSO Internal Control Framework and ISO standards.

14. What types of background checks, if any, are commonly run on prospective employees in your country (e.g., criminal, civil, credit, employment, educational)?

The types and intensity of background checks normally depend on the job grade (blue collar/white collar), but the typical procedures are as follows:

- Identification: Validate prospective employee's ID.
- Previous employment: Verify CV history with previous employers (e.g., employment dates, positions occupied, functions in positions, etc.).
- Education: Verify academic degrees and other certificates.
- Criminal history: Criminal records can be requested for all individuals, but only with the individual's authorization.
- Professional references: Verify previous employers and schools.
- Work permits: Check that the applicant has the required work permits.
- Independence: Ensure that the applicant has no conflicts of interest (sometimes required for management positions).
- Credit history: Check the applicant's credit history, bankruptcies, foreclosures, and so on (requires the individual's authorization).

Considerations in Fraud Investigations

15. Are there any special legal considerations that individuals from outside your country should be aware of when they are working on an investigation in your country? Examples might include licenses needed, special laws governing information gathering, or restrictions on transmitting personal data outside the country.

See response to Question 6 regarding privacy laws.

16. Are there any special cultural considerations that individuals from outside your country should be aware of when they are working on an investigation in your country? Examples might include who is present during an interview, how to address or greet individuals, inappropriate dress, and so on.

- **Language:** Language is one of the factors to be considered in working on an investigation in Chile. Middle or top management being interviewed may not speak English. To avoid language barriers and misunderstandings, native speakers should be considered to manage interviews.
- **Relationships:** Personal relationships and networks are a key aspect of doing business in Chile. It is important to establish rapport and conduct some light conversation before getting down to business.
- **Hierarchy:** Organizations tend to have a vertical structure of decision making.
- **Informal communications:** Although at times Chile may seem like a traditional and formal country, communications can easily be less formal among co-workers and even with supervisors, especially when discussing sports and current events (excluding politics or religion).
- **Informality around schedules and time:** Do not be surprised if a meeting does not start on time or if it takes longer than was originally scheduled. This may result in business interactions taking longer than in other regions. Follow up on scheduled activities and plans. Always get written confirmation of agreements.
- **Avoid confrontation in communication:** Confrontation is generally avoided in order not to jeopardize relationships or another's reputation; therefore, it may be necessary to read between the lines to fully understand what is really meant. Chileans are generally indirect in their communication styles, but they can be very animated and assertive when they get emotional. Pay attention to hand movements; gestures have different meanings across cultures. Avoid openly criticizing anyone.

MEXICO

Contributor

Muna D. Buchahin, PhD, CFE, CFI, CGAP, CRMA

Sources of Information

1. What kind of information about people is available to the public?

- Information related to movable or immovable property is available – as long as it is in one of the public registries that exist in the country.
- Ministry of Public Education contains information about individuals' professions.
- Public Registry of Property and Commerce contains information related to all properties (owners, locations, neighborhoods and structural changes, as well as commercial acts that have affected the property, such as sales, foreclosures, mortgages, etc.).

- National Public Maritime Registry contains information on people from shipping companies, their operators, acquisition contracts, alienation or assignment processes, the constitutive rights of property, transfer or extinction of property, modalities, mortgages, and levies on Mexican vessels.
- Public Registry of Mining records information on individuals and companies regarding mining concession contracts, extensions, declarations of nullity or cancellation thereof; titles of mining assignment; and transfer of ownership of concessions or mining rights, levies, or obligations and contracts.
- Mexican Aeronautical Registry keeps records of acquisitions, transmissions, modifications, encumbrances, or extinctions of ownership, possession, and other rights over Mexican or foreign aircraft, as well as the concessions and permits that cover the air transport service, its modifications, and extinctions.

2. What kind of information about companies is available to the public?

In addition to the information and resources discussed in the response to Question 1, the following information about businesses is publicly available:

- General information that is publicly available includes information related to a company's creation, denomination, or corporate name, and all commercial acts related to the company and related to the movable and immovable property in its possession, provided it is in a public record of the country as indicated by Article 120, Section I of the General Law on Transparency and Access to Public Information.
- Public Registry of Property and Commerce contains information related to the company's properties, as well as information linked to the creation of the company, such as corporate name, trade name, date of creation, corporate purpose, and names of shareholders.
- National Agrarian Registry contains the original operations and modifications suffered by land ownership and legally constituted rights over community-owned farmlands and communal property (*ejidos* are considered moral persons).

3. Are the judicial records available to the public? If so, explain what types of civil and criminal records the public can obtain.

The only way to obtain judicial records is through the judicial bulletins issued by state courts, provided that the court's name or number is known, from which the names of the parties and the file number can be discovered. The following are the websites for some of the judicial bulletins:

- Mexico City: www.poderjudicialcdmx.gob.mx/boletin
- Mexico State: notificacion.pjedomex.gob.mx/notificacion/vista/php/ConsultaBoletin.php
- Guadalajara City: cjj.gob.mx/consultas/boletin

There are no judicial bulletins for criminal matters.

At the federal level, there is an electronic tool available on the website for the Judicial Branch of the Federation: www.dgepj.cjf.gob.mx/paginas/serviciosTramites.htm?pageName=servicios%2FlistaAcuerdos.htm. This tool can be useful when combined with other information about the case.

The parties involved in a case may ask the court not to disclose their personal data. In addition, the public versions of case resolutions may delete the parties' data.

4. What other resources or types of information are regularly used by researchers or investigators in your country?

In private investigations, the legal system generally shields information related to individuals and companies, making the work of investigators difficult.

In government-directed investigations of public servants, investigators can obtain a wide range of information regarding the public servant's finances, taxes, judicial history, property, family, and so forth.

5. What are some of the most useful Internet or online sources that are regularly used in fraud investigations?

- National Electoral Institute (listanominal.ine.mx) – to verify the validity of voters' credentials
- Ministry of Public Education (www.cedulaprofesional.sep.gob.mx/cedula/presidencia/indexAvanzada.action) – to verify professional cards
- Secretariat of Public Function (directoriosancionados.funcionpublica.gob.mx/SanFicTec/jsp/Ficha_Tecnica/SancionadosN.htm) – sanctioned suppliers
- Tax Administration Service (www.sat.gob.mx/informacion_fiscal/Paginas/notificacion_contribuyentes_operaciones_inexistentes.aspx) – in relation to the list of persons or companies with nonexistent operations at present
- Courts of Justice (www.siat.sat.gob.mx/PTSC/index.jsp?opcion=4)

Legal and Regulatory Environment

6. What are the main data privacy laws in your country, and how do they affect most fraud investigations?

- General Law on Transparency and Access to Public Information
- Federal Law on Transparency and Access to Public Information
- General Law on the Protection of Personal Data in the Possession of Obliged Subjects
- Federal Law on the Protection of Personal Data Held by Individuals
- Similar state laws

7. What type of legal system does your country have (e.g., civil law system, customary law system, religious law system, hybrid)?

Mexico has a civil law system.

8. Which laws that govern the rights of individuals are of primary interest to researchers?

- The Political Constitution of the United Mexican States, especially regarding human rights (Articles 1–25)
- The General Law on the Protection of Personal Data in the Possession of Obliged Subjects
- The Federal Law on the Protection of Personal Data Held by Individuals
- The international legislation that governs in Mexico

9. Is bribery a crime in your country? If so, does it include payments to government officials and private companies?

The bribery of public servants is a crime in Mexico. There is no law prohibiting the bribery of private companies.

10. What are the main financial and investment regulators in your country?

- Ministry of Finance and Public Credit (SHCP) (www.gob.mx/hacienda)
- Bank of Mexico (BANXICO) (www.banxico.org.mx)
- National Banking and Securities Commission (CNBV) (www.gob.mx/cnbv)
- National Insurance and Bonding Commission (CNSF) (www.gob.mx/cnsf)
- National Commission for the Retirement Savings System (CONSAR) (www.gob.mx/consar)

11. What are the most significant parts of the fraud-related legislation in your country?

- Federal Criminal Code
- State Penal Codes
- Federal Law for the Prevention and Identification of Operations with Resources of Illicit Origin
- Law on Supervision/Prosecution and Accountability of the Federation
- Law of Acquisitions, Leases, and Services of the Public Sector
- Law on Public Works and Related Services

12. Does your country have laws in place to protect whistle-blowers? Please describe.

The Federal Law for the Protection of Persons Involved in Criminal Procedure protects whistle-blowers.

Anti-Fraud Programs

13. What are the key frameworks for internal controls, risk management, corporate governance, and so on commonly used by organizations in your country when designing or evaluating your anti-fraud programs (COSO frameworks, specific ISO standards, OECD guidance)?

The COSO system is usually applied.

14. What types of background checks, if any, are commonly performed on future employees in your country (criminal, civil, credit, employment, education)?

- Letter of no criminal record
- Letter of non-disqualification in the case of public servants
- Credit bureau reports
- Evidence of studies
- Letters from previous jobs

Considerations in Fraud Investigations

15. Are there any special legal considerations that individuals from outside your country should be aware of when they are working on an investigation in your country? Examples might include licenses needed, special laws governing information gathering, or restrictions on transmitting personal data outside the country.

Laws concerning the treatment of confidential information are relevant. There are no licenses or diploma requirements for research or investigative activities in Mexico.

16. Are there any special cultural considerations that individuals from outside your country should be aware of when they are working on an investigation in your country? Examples might include who is present during an interview, how to address or greet individuals, inappropriate dress, and so on.

In Mexico, there are several indigenous peoples who are governed by mores and customs; investigators must adjust their behavior according to the traditions of each of these communities. An example is the prohibition against taking photographs of people or places in particular locations.

PERU

Contributors

Tomasita Pazos Aurich, CFE, CRISC
Nereyda López Canales
Luis Navarro Pizarro

Sources of Information

1. What types of information about individuals are available to the public?

The following information about individuals is available to the public:

- Debt information is available from the credit bureau Infocorp.
- Property ownership information is available from the public registry Sunarp.
- Tax information: Custom and tributary information is available from SUNAT.

- Participation in business: Information regarding shares held by individuals is available from Sunarp.
- ID numbers are available from the National Registry of Identity and Marital Status (RENIEC).

2. What types of information about businesses are available to the public?

Most of the resources listed in the response to Question 1 can also be used for business information. For example, SUNAT and Sunarp contain information about businesses.

3. Are court records available to the public? If so, explain what types of civil and criminal records can be obtained by the public.

Only criminal and police records are available to the public. Information regarding legal processes can only be granted to the lawyers for the parties.

4. What other resources or types of information are regularly used by investigators in your country?

- Investments
- Information available on social media
- Migratory movement
- Financial information and transactions (but Peru has a bank secrecy law)
- Information regarding communications (but Peru has a telecommunications secrecy law)

5. What are some of the most useful Internet or online sources regularly used in fraud investigations?

- SUNAT (www.sunat.gob.pe) – tax information
- Infocorp (www.infocorp.com.pe) – credit bureau
- Sunarp (www.sunarp.gob.pe) – property ownership information
- RENIEC (www.reniec.gob.pe) – identity and marital status

Legal and Regulatory Environment

6. What are the major data privacy laws in your country, and how do these affect most fraud investigations?

- **Bank secrecy law regarding the privacy of financial information:** This law is contained in Article No. 2 of Peru's political Constitution. Its content and scope are developed by Article No. 140 of the General Law of the Financial and Insurance System from the Superintendency of Banking, Insurance, and Private Pension Funds, Law No. 26702.
- **Communication secrecy law regarding the privacy of communications:** This right is granted in Article No. 2 of Peru's political Constitution. It protects the freedom to communicate with other people without limits and includes the content of the communication as well as its existence and the identity of the participants. It includes postal, telegraphic, telephone, informatic (email) communications, and

other mechanisms used to transmit information between parties. Article No. 13 of the Regulation of the Telecommunications Law, approved by Supreme Decree No. 020-2007-MTC, as well as the Ministry Resolution No. 111-2009-MTC/03, prescribes the inviolability and secrecy of communications.

- **Law regarding the privacy of personal information:** The Law of Personal Data Protection, Law No. 29733, and its regulation state that users have the right to determine how their personal information is used by a private or public entity institution.

7. What type of legal system does your country have (e.g., civil law system, common law system, religious law system, hybrid)?

Peru has a civil law system.

8. What laws governing the rights of individuals are of primary concern to investigators?

- Bank Secrecy Law
- Telecommunications Secrecy Law
- Personal Data Protection Law
- Labor regulations, which may affect the preferred procedures for conducting interviews, such as choosing a physical space with glass walls, formally communicating to interviewees that they are under investigation, and conducting interviews during working hours
- Company norms

9. Is bribery a criminal offense in your country? If so, does it include payments to both government officials and private businesses?

Bribery is a criminal offense in Peru, and it includes payments to both government officials and private businesses.

10. What are the primary financial and investment regulatory bodies in your country?

- Central Reserve Bank of Peru (www.bcrp.gob.pe): Peru's political Constitution establishes that the bank's main objective is to preserve monetary stability.
- Superintendency of Banking, Insurance, and Private Pension Funds (www.sbs.gob.pe): The agency is in charge of regulating and supervising the financial, insurance, and pension funds systems, as well as preventing and detecting money laundering and terrorist financing. Its primary objective is to preserve the interests of depositors, insurance holders, and pension funds affiliates.
- Securities Market Superintendency (www.smv.gob.pe): The agency's primary objectives are to protect investors and to ensure market transparency and efficiency of the markets under its supervision.
- Financial Intelligence Unit: The agency is in charge of receiving, analyzing, and transmitting information for the detection of money laundering or terrorist financing. It was incorporated into the Superintendency of Banking, Insurance, and Private Pension Funds through the Law No. 29038, June 2007, and it has both technical and functional autonomy.

11. What are the most significant pieces of fraud-related legislation in your country?

Law No. 30096, Cybercrime Law, modified by Law No. 30171, is designed to prevent and impose sanctions against illicit conduct that affects computer systems, data, and other assets that could be vulnerable to crime.

12. Does your country have laws in place to protect whistle-blowers? Please describe.

- Law No. 27378, Regulation Regarding Protection Measures for Justice Collaborators, Victims, Witnesses, and Appraisals: The prosecutor is in charge of adopting protection measures contemplated by the law and should control the correct execution of the measures, implementing the corrective measures if needed. Article No. 9 lists protection measures that can be adopted, including:
  - Police protection
  - Concealing the identity of the person being protected in the course of the legal process
  - Guaranteeing that the person being protected cannot be identified during audiences and adopting any procedure that guarantees the impossibility of identifying the person visually
  - The use of technology such as videoconferences
  - Establishing the prosecution headquarters as the address of the person being protected for notification purposes
  - Facilitating documents that contain a new identity
  - Placing collaborators in jail in an environment that guarantees their security
  - Protection of labor rights in accordance with the law
- Law No. 28008, Regulation Regarding Customs Crime: Article No. 29 protects the identities of whistle-blowers. A whistle-blower is a person who informs a competent authority of the commission of a crime. Authorities should put in place appropriate measures to ensure the protection of the whistle-blower's identity.
- Regulation from Legislative Decree No. 1327 approved by Supreme Decree No. 010-2017-JUS, published on the official daily *El Peruano* on April 14, 2017: The regulation establishes protection measures for whistle-blowers who denounce acts of corruption, and imposes sanctions against allegations made in bad faith.
- Article No. 6, Principle of Reserve: The whistle-blower's identity must be protected until the legal process is concluded. An official who negligently fails to comply with this law may be sanctioned (i.e., disciplined).

Anti-Fraud Programs

13. What foundational frameworks for internal controls, risk management, corporate governance, and so on are commonly used by organizations in your country when designing or assessing their anti-fraud programs (e.g., COSO frameworks, specific ISO standards, OECD guidance)?

The most commonly used framework for internal controls, risk management, and corporate governance is COSO. This is mainly because the COSO framework is adopted by firms that issue shares in the stock exchange; thus, companies must comply with COSO's Principle No. 8, which incorporates the concept of fraud within the risk analysis.

In terms of the fight against corruption, in April 2017 the Peruvian Technical Norm (NTP) ISO 37001, regarding the "anti-bribe management system," was approved. The norm's objective is to specify the requisites and provide a guide to establishing, implementing, maintaining, assessing, reviewing, and improving an anti-bribe management system within organizations regardless of their size or industry.

14. What types of background checks, if any, are commonly run on prospective employees in your country (e.g., criminal, civil, credit, employment, educational)?

- Curriculum vitae (CV) of the applicant: The information contained in the document is confirmed by contacting previous employers and references.
- Records: criminal, judicial, police, and credit.

CHAPTER 11

Middle East and North Africa

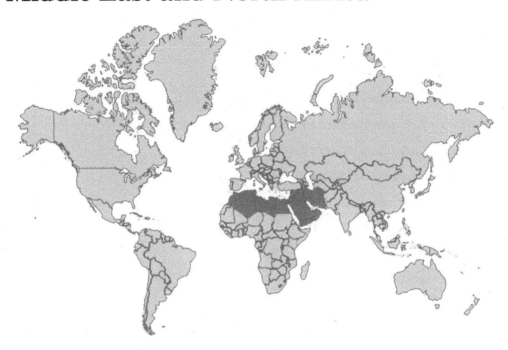

REGIONAL FRAUD TRENDS

The 2018 *Report to the Nations on Occupational Fraud and Abuse* issued by the Association of Certified Fraud Examiners (ACFE) includes 101 cases from the Middle East and North Africa that were investigated between January 2016 and October 2017. These cases caused a median loss of US $200,000 per case.

As noted in Exhibit 11.1, corruption is the most common form of occupational fraud committed in the Middle East and North Africa; 49% of the cases analyzed involved some form of corruption, which is more than twice as frequent as any other type of fraud scheme. Theft of cash on hand is the second most common category of occupational fraud, occurring in 23% of the cases in the region. In addition, fraud schemes in the Middle East and North Africa are almost twice as likely to be detected by a tip as by any other means (see Exhibit 11.2).

The 2018 *Report to the Nations* also examines the anti-fraud controls that were present at victim organizations at the time the frauds being analyzed were committed. Exhibit 11.3 shows that external audits of the financial statements are the most commonly implemented anti-fraud control among victim organizations in the Middle East and North Africa, followed by an internal audit department. On the other end of the spectrum, only 23% of these organizations had a mandatory vacation or job rotation policy in place, and just 9% provided rewards to whistle-blowers.

Exhibit 11.1   Scheme Types – Middle East and North Africa

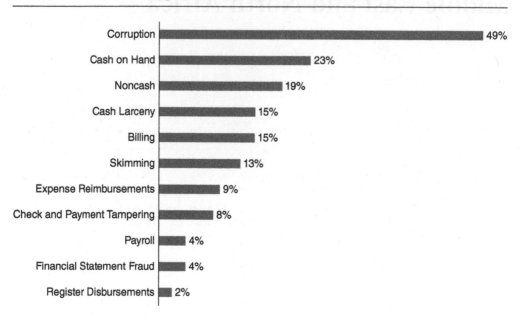

Exhibit 11.2   Initial Detection Method – Middle East and North Africa

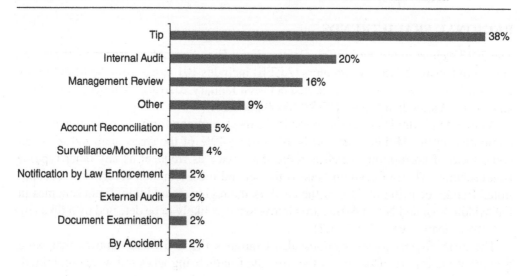

Exhibit 11.3   Frequency of Anti-Fraud Controls – Middle East and North Africa

Control	% of Cases
External Audit of Financial Statements	93%
Internal Audit Department	85%
Management Certification of Financial Statements	81%
Code of Conduct	78%
External Audit of Internal Controls over Financial Reporting	69%
Management Review	68%
Independent Audit Committee	67%
Hotline	59%
Surprise Audits	59%
Anti-Fraud Policy	54%
Fraud Training for Managers/Executives	47%
Fraud Training for Employees	47%
Dedicated Fraud Department, Function, or Team	44%
Formal Fraud Risk Assessments	40%
Proactive Data Monitoring/Analysis	40%
Employee Support Programs	33%
Job Rotation/Mandatory Vacation	23%
Rewards for Whistle-Blowers	9%

The following discussions provide jurisdiction-specific information pertaining to the legal, investigatory, and general anti-fraud environment for several countries in the Middle East and North Africa.

CYPRUS

Contributors

George Rostantis, CFE
Agis Taramides, CFE, FCA
George Yiallouros, CFE

Sources of Information

1. What types of information about individuals are available to the public?

Only the Bankruptcy Archive at the Registrar of Companies is available to the public.

2. What types of information about businesses are available to the public?

- Corporate documents (e.g., date of incorporation, directors and secretary, shareholders, registered office address)
- Financial statements
- Legal structure
- Value-added tax (VAT) liability (through financial statements)

3. Are court records available to the public? If so, explain what types of civil and criminal records can be obtained by the public.

The majority of civil and criminal records are publicly available after a final judgment.

4. What other resources or types of information are regularly used by investigators in your country?

- Police investigators have unlimited access to any kind of information, subject to court order or to attorney general permission.
- Private investigators' access to information is available only upon approval or consent of the individual or business involved.

5. What are some of the most useful Internet or online sources regularly used in fraud investigations?

- Registrar of Companies (www.mcit.gov.cy/mcit/drcor/drcor.nsf/index_en/index_en)
- Cyprus Law (www.cylaw.org)
- World-Check (risk.thomsonreuters.com/en/products/world-check-know-your-customer.html)
- World Compliance (risk.lexisnexis.com/global/en/products/worldcompliance-online-search-tool-global)
- LexisNexis (www.lexisnexis.com)
- Social media (Facebook, LinkedIn, Twitter, etc.)

Legal and Regulatory Environment

6. What are the major data privacy laws in your country, and how do these affect most fraud investigations?

Generally, the Processing of Personal Data (Protection of the Individual) Law prohibits the processing of an individual's personal information without the individual's consent. However, the law contains a number of exceptions.

7. What type of legal system does your country have (e.g., civil law system, common law system, religious law system, hybrid)?

The Republic of Cyprus has a common law system.

8. What laws governing the rights of individuals are of primary concern to investigators?

- Processing of Personal Data (Protection of the Individual) Law
- Prevention and Suppression of Money Laundering Activities Law

9. Is bribery a criminal offense in your country? If so, does it include payments to both government officials and private businesses?

Bribery is a crime in the Republic of Cyprus, and it includes payments to both government officials and private businesses.

10. What are the primary financial and investment regulatory bodies in your country?

- Central Bank of Cyprus
- Unit for Combating Money Laundering (for anti-money-laundering purposes only)
- Cyprus Securities and Exchange Commission
- Insurance Companies Control Service
- Institute of Certified Public Accountants of Cyprus
- Cyprus Bar Association

11. What are the most significant pieces of fraud-related legislation in your country?

The most significant piece of fraud-related legislation in the Republic of Cyprus is the Prevention and Suppression of Money Laundering Activities Law.

12. Does your country have laws in place to protect whistle-blowers? Please describe.

The Republic of Cyprus does not have laws in place to protect whistle-blowers. However, there are provisions in the Prevention and Suppression of Money Laundering Activities Law regarding tipping off. Also, the Cyprus Securities and Exchange Commission issued a circular regarding the procedures for the receipt and investigation of reports of market abuse.

Anti-Fraud Programs

13. What foundational frameworks for internal controls, risk management, corporate governance, and so on are commonly used by organizations in your country when designing or assessing their anti-fraud programs (e.g., COSO frameworks, specific ISO standards, OECD guidance)?

Large organizations (especially banks) use COSO frameworks and OECD guidance when designing or assessing their anti-fraud programs.

14. What types of background checks, if any, are commonly run on prospective employees in your country (e.g., criminal, civil, credit, employment, educational)?

Criminal, civil, credit, employment, and educational background checks are commonly run on prospective employees.

Considerations in Fraud Investigations

15. Are there any special legal considerations that individuals from outside your country should be aware of when they are working on an investigation in your country? Examples might include licenses needed, special laws governing information gathering, or restrictions on transmitting personal data outside the country.

There have been recent developments regarding transfers of personal data between EU countries and the US; the consent of the Cyprus Data Commissioner is required to proceed with such transfers. The appropriate practice for the time being is to proceed with a notification to the Data Commissioner in accordance with the practice of Model Contracts for the transfer of personal data to third countries. This can be achieved via the adoption of the standard contractual clauses for transfers from data controllers to data controllers established outside the EU/European Economic Area (EEA) and for the transfer to processors established outside the EU/EEA provided by the European Commission.

EGYPT

Contributors

Mahmoud Elbagoury, GRCA, CPFA, CICA, CACM
Hossam Elshafie, CFE, CRMA, CCSA, CFCI
Ahmed Mokhtar, CFE, CRMA
Hazem Abd Eltawab

Sources of Information

1. What types of information about individuals are available to the public?

Social and career information about individuals is available to the public.

2. What types of information about businesses are available to the public?

General information in media and press releases about businesses is available to the public.

3. Are court records available to the public? If so, explain what types of civil and criminal records can be obtained by the public.

Court records are not available to the public. However, criminal history is available from the Ministry of Interior.

4. What other resources or types of information are regularly used by investigators in your country?

Employee files and criminal history are used by investigators in Egypt.

Legal and Regulatory Environment

6. What are the major data privacy laws in your country, and how do these affect most fraud investigations?

The Personal Status Law and the Criminal Code are the major data privacy laws in Egypt.

7. What type of legal system does your country have (e.g., civil law system, common law system, religious law system, hybrid)?

Egypt has a civil law system.

9. Is bribery a criminal offense in your country? If so, does it include payments to both government officials and private businesses?

The bribery of government officials is a crime in Egypt.

10. What are the primary financial and investment regulatory bodies in your country?

- Financial Supervisory Authority
- Administrative Control Authority

11. What are the most significant pieces of fraud-related legislation in your country?

- Penal Code
- Anti-Money Laundering Law

12. Does your country have laws in place to protect whistle-blowers? Please describe.

Egypt does not have laws protecting whistle-blowers.

Anti-Fraud Programs

13. What foundational frameworks for internal controls, risk management, corporate governance, and so on are commonly used by organizations in your country when designing or assessing their anti-fraud programs (e.g., COSO frameworks, specific ISO standards, OECD guidance)?

- COSO Internal Control Framework
- COSO Enterprise Risk Management Framework

14. What types of background checks, if any, are commonly run on prospective employees in your country (e.g., criminal, civil, credit, employment, educational)?

Criminal history background checks are commonly run on prospective employees in Egypt.

JORDAN

Contributors

Hazem Adel Shahin, CFE
Abdallah Alomari, CFE
Adel Ayyoub
Hossam El Shaffei, CFE
Fadi Daoud, MBA, CACM, CIPT
Sameh Abu Shamaleh, CFE
Qosai Obidat

Sources of Information

1. What types of information about individuals are available to the public?

No personal information is available to the public in Jordan.

2. What types of information about businesses are available to the public?

- Companies' registration data (e.g., names of owners, type and purpose of company, authorized personnel, ID number, changes in the company's legal status or signatories)
- Financial statements for listed companies

3. Are court records available to the public? If so, explain what types of civil and criminal records can be obtained by the public.

The only publicly available information is the status of the court case (i.e., session date and judge's name).

4. What other resources or types of information are regularly used by investigators in your country?

Investigators can obtain information about individuals by obtaining a letter of consent or seeking court permission.

5. What are some of the most useful Internet or online sources regularly used in fraud investigations?

Investigators can use the website for the Companies Control Department (www.ccd. gov.jo) for information about businesses.

Legal and Regulatory Environment

6. What are the major data privacy laws in your country, and how do these affect most fraud investigations?

No private information about individuals (e.g., bank records, real estate documents) can be obtained without court permission.

7. What type of legal system does your country have (e.g., civil law system, common law system, religious law system, hybrid)?

Jordan has a civil law system. Religious law governs family issues (e.g., marriages, legacies).

8. What laws governing the rights of individuals are of primary concern to investigators?

Civil laws governing the rights of individuals are of primary concern to investigators.

9. Is bribery a criminal offense in your country? If so, does it include payments to both government officials and private businesses?

Bribery is a crime in Jordan, and it includes payments to both government officials and private businesses.

10. What are the primary financial and investment regulatory bodies in your country?

- Ministry of Finance
- Ministry of Industry and Trade
- Jordan Securities Commission

11. What are the most significant pieces of fraud-related legislation in your country?

- Anti-Money Laundering and Counter Terrorist Financing Law
- Anti-Corruption Commission Law
- Penal Code

12. Does your country have laws in place to protect whistle-blowers? Please describe.

Jordan has no general laws protecting whistle-blowers. However, the Anti-Corruption Commission keeps information about whistle-blowers confidential.

Anti-Fraud Programs

13. What foundational frameworks for internal controls, risk management, corporate governance, and so on are commonly used by organizations in your country when designing or assessing their anti-fraud programs (e.g., COSO frameworks, specific ISO standards, OECD guidance)?

Corporate governance regulations issued by the Jordan Securities Commission are used by organizations for anti-fraud programs.

14. What types of background checks, if any, are commonly run on prospective employees in your country (e.g., criminal, civil, credit, employment, educational)?

Employees are asked to provide a noncriminal certificate issued by the Ministry of Justice.

Considerations in Fraud Investigations

15. Are there any special legal considerations that individuals from outside your country should be aware of when they are working on an investigation in your country? Examples might include licenses needed, special laws governing information gathering, or restrictions on transmitting personal data outside the country.

There is no license required to conduct investigations in Jordan. However, other local laws apply, such as the Electronic Transactions Law, the Information Systems and Cyber Crimes Law, the Companies Law, Central Bank regulations, arbitration law, and others.

OMAN

Contributor

Alison Benbow, CFE, CMIIA

Sources of Information

2. What types of information about businesses are available to the public?

- Commercial registration information (high-level only) is available from the Ministry of Commerce and Industry (www.business.gov.om/wps/portal).
- For listed companies, information availability is the same as elsewhere in the world.

3. Are court records available to the public? If so, explain what types of civil and criminal records can be obtained by the public.

Court records are not publicly available.

4. What other resources or types of information are regularly used by investigators in your country?

Public prosecutors and the Royal Oman Police have access to considerably more information than internal company investigators or consultants. In private investigations, any request for information must be sent to regulators or the courts.

5. What are some of the most useful Internet or online sources regularly used in fraud investigations?

- Google
- FBI's Internet Crime Complaint Center (www.ic3.gov)
- Association of Certified Fraud Examiners (www.acfe.com)
- Action Fraud UK (www.actionfraud.police.uk)
- Occasional circulars from regulators on common fraud schemes (e.g., Central Bank of Oman), but these tend to be after the event

Legal and Regulatory Environment

6. What are the major data privacy laws in your country, and how do these affect most fraud investigations?

Oman does not have a general data privacy law, but some individual laws contain privacy requirements (e.g., Banking Law, Article 70, Confidentiality of Banking Transactions). Commercial law also contains privacy rules to protect against unfair competition.

7. What type of legal system does your country have (e.g., civil law system, common law system, religious law system, hybrid)?

Oman has a civil law system.

9. Is bribery a criminal offense in your country? If so, does it include payments to both government officials and private businesses?

Bribery is a crime in Oman, and it includes payments to both government officials and private businesses.

10. What are the primary financial and investment regulatory bodies in your country?

- Central Bank of Oman
- Capital Market Authority

11. What are the most significant pieces of fraud-related legislation in your country?

- Criminal law: In Oman Penal Code 1974: Disgracing Crimes, Article 33, fraud is specifically mentioned.
- Law of Anti-Money Laundering and Combating the Financing of Terrorism (AM/CTF Law), Royal Decree No. 30/2016.

12. Does your country have laws in place to protect whistle-blowers? Please describe.

Oman does not have laws protecting whistle-blowers.

Anti-Fraud Programs

13. What foundational frameworks for internal controls, risk management, corporate governance, and so on are commonly used by organizations in your country when designing or assessing their anti-fraud programs (e.g., COSO frameworks, specific ISO standards, OECD guidance)?

In banking, anti-fraud programs have been developed in line with the Central Bank's guidance in its circulars BM 1078 and 1153.

14. What types of background checks, if any, are commonly run on prospective employees in your country (e.g., criminal, civil, credit, employment, educational)?

Criminal background checks with the local police are the most common.

UNITED ARAB EMIRATES

Contributors

Sagar Rajkumar, MBA, CFE, PJSC
Nagy Mohammed Ibrahim Yousef
Iyad Mourtada, CFE, CIA, CCSA, CRMA, CSX

Sources of Information

1. What types of information about individuals are available to the public?

- Al Etihad Credit Bureau (AECB) is a government-owned credit bureau that issues credit reports for a fee.
- Central Bank Rating Bureau (CBRB) issues credit ratings for businesses based on information given to the Central Bank by various other banks; can also be useful for individual ratings.
- Ministry of Labor (MOL) and Ministry of Human Resources (MOHRE) are useful for obtaining labor information, such as salaries, designations, and basic passport details, which come from labor contracts signed when joining organizations.
- SafeWatch and World-Check are used by organizations to conduct background checks on individuals.

2. What types of information about businesses are available to the public?

The CBRB has information regarding a company's liabilities and legal structure. Also, a Google search can reveal useful information about businesses.

3. Are court records available to the public? If so, explain what types of civil and criminal records can be obtained by the public.

Not all court records are available to the public. Lawyers and legal professionals must make an official request to the court for access to particular records. There is no central database for all cases in the United Arab Emirates. To determine whether there is current litigation against an individual, an investigator must proceed through a law firm or public prosecution. In some cases, local influence with the police or an immigration department can help. The collection/recovery departments of banks often have strong influence.

4. What other resources or types of information are regularly used by investigators in your country?

For internal investigations, fraud examiners rely on the organization's internal records, HR files, and financial documents, and they collect information from the government and banks as needed. Such examiners must contact the appropriate government authority and seek approval to obtain government records.

For external investigations by the government, examiners collect documents from policy records, court records, national security records, and other government records.

5. What are some of the most useful Internet or online sources regularly used in fraud investigations?

Depending on the nature of the investigation, commonly used resources may include online social media to trace whereabouts, as well as fraud forums that connect individuals from different fields and contain news and updates.

Legal and Regulatory Environment

6. What are the major data privacy laws in your country, and how do these affect most fraud investigations?

There is no general data protection law in the United Arab Emirates. However, Article 378 of the Penal Code (Federal Law 3 of 1987) prohibits the publication of any personal data that relates to an individual's private or family life. Disclosing secrets relating to someone's private life without that person's consent can result in liability. Similarly, disclosure of confidential information, such as information belonging to an employer, can result in liability. Federal Decree Law No. 5 of 2012 on Combating Cybercrimes (Cybercrime Law) prohibits the invasion of an individual's privacy by means of a computer network, electronic information system, or information technology without the individual's consent.

7. What type of legal system does your country have (e.g., civil law system, common law system, religious law system, hybrid)?

There is a civil law system in the United Arab Emirates.

8. What laws governing the rights of individuals are of primary concern to investigators?

- United Arab Emirates Federal Law No. 35 contains rules regarding arrests, searches, detentions, and imprisonment.
- Employment contracts contain the rights and duties of employers and employees.

9. Is bribery a criminal offense in your country? If so, does it include payments to both government officials and private businesses?

Anti-bribery legislation has been in place in the United Arab Emirates since the late 1980s in the form of the United Arab Emirates Federal Penal Code and the Federal Human Resources Law (Federal Law No. 11 of 2008) to prohibit public employees from accepting, offering, or requesting bribes, as well as several codes of conduct related to bribery that are published by various ministries and government departments. The United Arab Emirates is also a signatory to the United Nations Convention against Corruption, which prohibits the bribery of government officials.

The United Arab Emirates does not have a law prohibiting the bribery of private businesses.

10. What are the primary financial and investment regulatory bodies in your country?

- Dubai International Financial Centre (DIFC)
- Dubai Financial Services Authority (DFSA)
- Dubai courts
- DIFC Judicial Authority
- Central Bank of the United Arab Emirates
- Securities and Commodities Authority
- Insurance Authority (IA)

11. What are the most significant pieces of fraud-related legislation in your country?

- Federal Law No. 3 of 1987
- Federal Law No. 19 of 2016

In the United Arab Emirates, enforcement of the established anti-corruption laws received a boost with the Abu Dhabi Executive Council announcing the establishment of a new Anti-Corruption Unit in May 2015. The decision to establish a specialized department in the United Arab Emirates to combat corruption is considered one of the main cornerstones that will assist in the continuing development of the country, limiting the chances of corrupt individuals hindering such growth. The new anti-corruption unit is established within the Abu Dhabi Accountability Authority.

12. Does your country have laws in place to protect whistle-blowers? Please describe.

There is no general law in the United Arab Emirates protecting whistle-blowers. However, Dubai Law No. 4 of 2016 on Financial Crimes includes protections for those who report crimes to the newly established Dubai Centre for Economic Security. In addition, many organizations have adopted policies protecting whistle-blowers from retaliation. The Dubai Financial Services Authority has also taken certain initiatives to address the disclosure of information about market misconduct, financial crimes, and money laundering.

Anti-Fraud Programs

13. What foundational frameworks for internal controls, risk management, corporate governance, and so on are commonly used by organizations in your country when designing or assessing their anti-fraud programs (e.g., COSO frameworks, specific ISO standards, OECD guidance)?

The most commonly used framework is the COSO Internal Control – Integrated Framework. Many organizations have also implemented ISO 37001 – Anti-Bribery Management Systems and other internal fraud controls to prevent and detect fraud.

14. What types of background checks, if any, are commonly run on prospective employees in your country (e.g., criminal, civil, credit, employment, educational)?

Organizations usually verify the experience and education of potential employees by calling previous employers and educational institutions. Criminal background checks are also performed. Good Conduct Certificates (also called Police Clearance Certificates) can be obtained from the Dubai police for citizens and residents inside the United Arab Emirates. Organizations often hire corporate and commercial verifications firms to perform security background checks on foreign workers.

Considerations in Fraud Investigations

15. Are there any special legal considerations that individuals from outside your country should be aware of when they are working on an investigation in your country? Examples might include licenses needed, special laws governing information gathering, or restrictions on transmitting personal data outside the country.

In the United Arab Emirates, investigators must have government approval to perform private investigations, covert activities, or surveillance. Interview subjects must receive advance notice, information about the reason for the interview, and adequate time to prepare.

16. Are there any special cultural considerations that individuals from outside your country should be aware of when they are working on an investigation in your country? Examples might include who is present during an interview, how to address or greet individuals, inappropriate dress, and so on.

If the subject of the interview is a woman, at least two interviewers should be present in the room and one of them should be a woman.

CHAPTER 12

Southern Asia

REGIONAL FRAUD TRENDS

The 2018 *Report to the Nations on Occupational Fraud and Abuse* issued by the Association of Certified Fraud Examiners (ACFE) includes 96 cases from Southern Asia that were investigated between January 2016 and October 2017. These cases caused a median loss of US $100,000 per case.

As noted in Exhibit 12.1, corruption is the most common form of occupational fraud committed in Southern Asia; 62% of the cases analyzed involved some form of corruption, which is more than three times as frequent as any other type of fraud scheme. Theft of noncash assets is the second most common category of occupational fraud, occurring in 20% of the cases in the region. In addition, more than half of the fraud schemes in Southern Asia are detected by a tip, making this the most likely method of detection by far (see Exhibit 12.1).

The 2018 *Report to the Nations* also examines the anti-fraud controls that were present at victim organizations at the time the frauds being analyzed were committed. Exhibit 12.3 shows that external audits of the financial statements are the most commonly implemented anti-fraud control among victim organizations in Southern Asia, followed by an internal audit department. On the other end of the spectrum, only one-quarter of these organizations had a mandatory vacation or job rotation policy in place, and just 9% provided rewards to whistle-blowers.

Exhibit 12.1   Scheme Types – Southern Asia

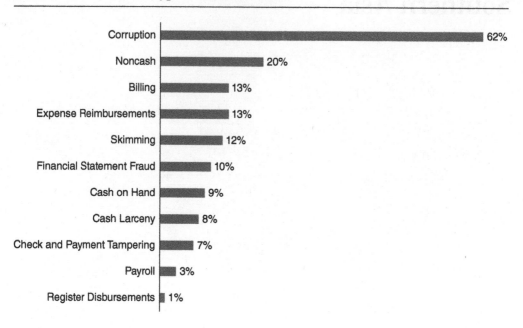

Exhibit 12.2   Initial Detection Method – Southern Asia

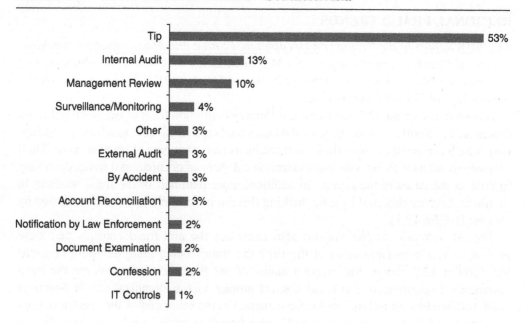

Exhibit 12.3   Frequency of Anti-Fraud Controls – Southern Asia

Control	% of Cases
External Audit of Financial Statements	90%
Internal Audit Department	88%
Code of Conduct	88%
Management Certification of Financial Statements	85%
External Audit of Internal Controls over Financial Reporting	77%
Independent Audit Committee	76%
Management Review	76%
Hotline	63%
Anti-Fraud Policy	58%
Fraud Training for Employees	56%
Surprise Audits	53%
Fraud Training for Managers/Executives	53%
Dedicated Fraud Department, Function, or Team	49%
Employee Support Programs	43%
Formal Fraud Risk Assessments	42%
Proactive Data Monitoring/Analysis	35%
Job Rotation/Mandatory Vacation	25%
Rewards for Whistle-Blowers	9%

The following discussions provide jurisdiction-specific information pertaining to the legal, investigatory, and general anti-fraud environment for several countries in Southern Asia.

INDIA

Contributors

India Chapter:

S.K. Bansal, CFE
Sumit Makhija, CFE
Sharad Kumar, CFE
Mukesh Arya, CFE

Mumbai Chapter:

Arpinder Singh, CFE, CA, Lawyer
Mukul Shrivastava, CFE, CA
Rajkumar Shriwastav, CFE, Lawyer
Aniket Kolge
Pooja Roy, CA

Sources of Information

1. What types of information about individuals are available to the public?

- Social networking websites provide individual and professional profiles.
- Electoral rolls contain information regarding age, address, and family.
- Property records are available in select states.
- Election Commission of India (eci.nic.in/eci/eci.html): If the individual was involved in a contested election, this free database provides information about sources of income, assets, liabilities, and criminal record.

Other information in the government's possession may be available through the Right to Information Act, including records regarding schools, taxes, property, public servants, and health care. However, banking secrecy laws prohibit banks from disclosing consumer information without a court order. Under the Lokpal Act, the financial information of public servants can be obtained from the government.

2. What types of information about businesses are available to the public?

Information about businesses is available for a fee at the office of the Registrar of Companies or at the website of the Ministry of Corporate Affairs (www.mca.gov.in). Such information may include the company's incorporation date, registration number, registered address, financial information, and the names of officers, directors, and shareholders.

The Securities and Exchange Board of India (www.sebi.gov.in) has information about companies that are listed on stock exchanges.

Commercial websites can provide additional information about companies, such as global and regional presence, number of employees, manufacturing units, business alliances, mergers and acquisitions, membership in associations, and political donations.

3. Are court records available to the public? If so, explain what types of civil and criminal records can be obtained by the public.

Information about pending and concluded lawsuits is available in databases of the Supreme Court, high courts, district courts, and consumer courts. Reported judgments are available from commercial databases. Certain information, such as affidavits and other evidence, is available only to interested parties.

4. What other resources or types of information are regularly used by investigators in your country?

In addition to the resources listed in the responses to Questions 1 and 2, investigators can refer to compliance and regulatory directives issued by the regulatory authorities. Investigators can use the Right to Information Act to obtain information in the government's possession. They can also petition the courts to gain access to information. Criminal records can be obtained from courts and police agencies.

5. What are some of the most useful Internet or online sources regularly used in fraud investigations?

- Ministry of Corporate Affairs (www.mca.gov.in)
- Commercial databases such as Lexis Diligence, Factiva, Emerging Markets Information System (EMIS), Bloomberg, Dow Jones, and World Compliance Online
- Social or professional networking sites
- Court databases
- Web sites providing information about loan defaults, insolvency, regulatory violations, and enforcement actions

Legal and Regulatory Environment

6. What are the major data privacy laws in your country, and how do these affect most fraud investigations?

- Right to Privacy as implicit in Articles 19 and 21 of the Constitution of India
- Information Technology Act
- Information Technology (Reasonable Security Practices and Procedures and Sensitive Personal Data or Information) Rules, 2011

7. What type of legal system does your country have (e.g., civil law system, common law system, religious law system, hybrid)?

India has a common law system.

Family law is mostly governed by religious laws, such as the Hindu Marriage Act, Transfer of Property Act, Muslim Personal Law, and Christian Marriage Act.

8. What laws governing the rights of individuals are of primary concern to investigators?

- Right to Privacy as implicit in Articles 19 and 21 of the Constitution of India
- Criminal Procedure Code
- Civil Procedure Code
- Information Technology Act
- Information Technology (Reasonable Security Practices and Procedures and Sensitive Personal Data or Information) Rules, 2011

9. Is bribery a criminal offense in your country? If so, does it include payments to both government officials and private businesses?

It is a crime to bribe a government official under the Indian Prevention of Corruption Act. The Act does not cover bribes to private businesses.

10. What are the primary financial and investment regulatory bodies in your country?

- Reserve Bank of India
- Securities and Exchange Board of India
- Insurance Regulatory and Development Authority
- Financial Intelligence Unit
- Pension Fund Regulatory and Development Authority
- Ministry of Corporate Affairs
- Forward Markets Commission

11. What are the most significant pieces of fraud-related legislation in your country?

- Banking Regulation Act
- Prevention of Money Laundering Act
- Criminal Procedure Code
- Penal Code
- Contract Act (Section 17 defines fraud)
- Companies Act (Section 447 defines fraud)
- Competition Act

12. Does your country have laws in place to protect whistle-blowers? Please describe.

India has laws protecting whistle-blowers, including the Whistle Blowers Protection Act.

Anti-Fraud Programs

13. What foundational frameworks for internal controls, risk management, corporate governance, and so on are commonly used by organizations in your country when designing or assessing their anti-fraud programs (e.g., COSO frameworks, specific ISO standards, OECD guidance)?

- COSO frameworks
- ISO 37001
- Internal Financial Controls compliance under the Companies Act

14. What types of background checks, if any, are commonly run on prospective employees in your country (e.g., criminal, civil, credit, employment, educational)?

The type and depth of background checks depend on the industry, company policies, and the seniority of the employee. For senior executives, organizations usually conduct a thorough background check, which includes educational and employment verification, reference checks, civil and criminal records, past regulatory enforcement actions, litigation history, and past conduct in relation to business associates, vendors, suppliers, and customers. For middle- and junior-level employees, pre-employment checks are usually basic and involve obtaining documentation for educational and professional qualifications, along with experience letters if applicable.

Considerations in Fraud Investigations

15. Are there any special legal considerations that individuals from outside your country should be aware of when they are working on an investigation in your country? Examples might include licenses needed, special laws governing information gathering, or restrictions on transmitting personal data outside the country.

There is no license requirement for private investigators. All investigations must comply with data privacy laws. Information should be obtained from the public domain, or with a court order or proper approvals from enforcement agencies.

16. Are there any special cultural considerations that individuals from outside your country should be aware of when they are working on an investigation in your country? Examples might include who is present during an interview, how to address or greet individuals, inappropriate dress, and so on.

Interviews should be conducted with one or two witnesses. Refrain from making comments on the person's background, cultural affinity, caste group, or religion. The interviewer should be serious and not casual in approach or attire. Proper respect, greetings, and introductions are expected. Never try to intimidate.

In India, there are number of festivals celebrated throughout the country and a few that have great regional significance. Assignments should be scheduled to account for these events so that required staff is available. During festivals, it is common practice to exchange gifts. Investigators must assess the value, reasonableness, and frequency of gifts along with adherence to relevant legislation and organization policies. This will help to identify any potential fraudulent activities or improper payments.

Hospitality in India tends to be more personal than in the West. Adequate caution and judgment must be exercised when accepting such hospitality.

PAKISTAN

Contributor

Syed Zubair Ahmed, MBA, CFE, MCom

Sources of Information

1. What types of information about individuals are available to the public?

Under the Freedom of Information Ordinance (FOIO), Pakistani citizens can request access to information held by the national government. The law allows access only to public records. It excludes documents such as notes and minutes of meetings, personal bank account data, classified information, and anything violating individual privacy. The FOIO application form is available online at foiapakistan.com/request.html. The application must be addressed to the appropriate person at the appropriate public body, it must contain the specific reasons the information is needed, and it must be accompanied by the requisite fee. If the requested information is not provided within 21 days, the applicant may file a complaint with the head of the public body.

The National Database and Registration Authority (NADRA) maintains the largest database registry of the people of Pakistan. NADRA issues a Computerized National Identity Card (CNIC) to every citizen of Pakistan over 18. Registration is technically voluntary, but a CNIC is required to open a bank account, obtain a gas or an electricity connection, pay utility bills, obtain a passport, or enter into any transaction with the state. NADRA will disclose personal information when it is legally obligated to do so. NADRA has a text messaging service for verifying family members. When a CNIC number is sent to 8008, the system will respond with the names of all registered persons in the family. If a person is incorrectly registered as a part of the family, this fact can be reported to NADRA.

The Federal Board of Revenue (FBR) is responsible for enforcing fiscal laws and collecting revenue for the government. The FBR's Taxpayer Online Verification System provides useful information regarding national tax numbers, CNIC numbers, passport numbers, and business registration numbers. In addition, the FBR prepares an annual Active Taxpayers List (ATL), which contains CNIC numbers, names of individuals, national tax numbers, and the names of companies associated with individual taxpayers. The ATL is available online at www.fbr.gov.pk/ActiveTaxpayersList.aspx.

Mobile phone users of any company (e.g., Telenor, Mobilink, Ufone, Warid, Zong) can send a blank text message to 667 to receive ownership information. When an investigator sends a blank text message (or anything if the phone does not allow blank messages) to 667, the system will respond with the owner's name and CNIC number.

There are many ways to obtain information about automobiles and other vehicles, including:

- Sending a text message to a particular telephone number, depending on where the vehicle is registered, to obtain title and ownership information
- Entering the vehicle's registration number on a public authority's Web site, depending on where the vehicle is registered, to obtain title and ownership information
- Visiting the offices of the appropriate public authority, depending on where the vehicle is registered, to obtain title and ownership information or check for any criminal activities associated with the vehicle

2. What types of information about businesses are available to the public?

Most of the resources listed in the response to Question 1 can also be used to obtain information about businesses. In addition, the Securities and Exchange Commission of Pakistan (SECP) is the primary national financial regulatory agency in Pakistan. Investigators can use the SECP's website (www.secp.gov.pk) to obtain or request information about companies.

3. Are court records available to the public? If so, explain what types of civil and criminal records can be obtained by the public.

Constitution

The Constitution of the Islamic Republic of Pakistan does not grant citizens the right to access judicial or other governmental information. The Constitution establishes an independent judicial branch composed of the Supreme Court, high courts, courts of district judges, courts of session judges, and courts of magistrates of varied subject matter jurisdictions.

Statutory Law

Under Pakistan's Right to Information Act, the public has the right to access the information of all public institutions, including courts. However, the public does not have the right to access information regarding criminal investigations or prosecutions if the disclosure of such information would endanger the investigation, the prosecution, or the defendant's rights.

Court Practice

Judicial case law in Pakistan is generally available on the Internet. The decisions of the Supreme Court and high courts are available in the Official Gazette, which is published periodically, and also on the Web sites of the Supreme Court (www.supremecourt.gov.pk/web) and the various high courts.

4. What other resources or types of information are regularly used by investigators in your country?

The Organisation for Economic Co-operation and Development (OECD) website for Pakistan (www.oecd.org/countries/pakistan) contains useful links to fraud-related government resources, legislation, and best practices.

5. What are some of the most useful Internet or online sources regularly used in fraud investigations?

The most effective way to search the Internet is to perform a keyword search with a search engine such as Google or Bing. Both have the ability to filter text, images, and video, and the investigator can filter the information by time, location, website, or related pages. While these search engines are good, they have their weaknesses. For example, they do not automatically search social media.

Social media, such as Twitter, Facebook, and LinkedIn, have embedded themselves in people's lives. Social media evidence (i.e., tweets, images, and videos) can be important in an investigation, often revealing key information about the subject. But such evidence must be gathered in a way that is legal so that it will be admissible in court.

Collecting evidence from social media sites can be challenging because of its evolving nature. Information on social media is easily updated and deleted. However, when an investigation is ongoing, the subject is generally required to preserve social media evidence just like any other type of evidence.

Legal and Regulatory Environment

6. What are the major data privacy laws in your country, and how do these affect most fraud investigations?

The Constitution of Pakistan states that the right to privacy is a fundamental right. Article 14(1) of the Constitution confirms that the "dignity of man and, subject to law, the privacy of home, shall be inviolable." However, the Constitution contains broad exceptions to fundamental rights, such as the ability of the armed forces or the police to discharge their duties.

Currently, Pakistan does not have data protection legislation. In the absence of such legislation, data protection is theoretically regulated through other pieces of legislation. For example, the Electronic Transactions Ordinance 2002 criminalizes unlawful or unauthorized access to information. The law provides for the establishment of a government body to draft information privacy regulations. However, no such body has been created, and no such regulations have been drafted.

As discussed in the response to Question 1, certain information is exempt from disclosure under the Freedom of Information Ordinance if its disclosure would involve the invasion of privacy of an identifiable individual other than the requester.

The Prevention of Electronic Crimes Act 2016 also contains a number of provisions related to data privacy. Under the law, it is a crime to gain unauthorized access to any data or information system. However, there are broad exceptions for law enforcement and other government entities.

Since 2004, network providers are required to comply with requests from law enforcement agencies for interception and access to network data as a standard condition of the Pakistan Telecommunication Authority's award of operating licenses to telephone companies.

7. What type of legal system does your country have (e.g., civil law system, common law system, religious law system, hybrid)?

Pakistan has a hybrid legal system. Pakistan's common law system, which emphasizes evolving precedent-based legal decisions, has origins in British practice. Civil and criminal procedural laws also come from the British colonial system, although they have been amended. Examples include the Criminal Procedure Code (1898) and the Civil Procedure Code (1908).

Over the course of its history, Pakistan has alternated between a parliamentary system and military rule. As a result, the country has a complex framework of laws that are often difficult to apply. Pakistan also has an Islamic system of law that is generally referred to as Shariah. Islamic law often applies to family relations, commercial transactions, crime and punishment, and inheritance. In Pakistan, the common law tradition, Islamic law, and customary practices have a complex relationship.

8. What laws governing the rights of individuals are of primary concern to investigators?

As discussed in the response to Question 6, the Constitution of Pakistan states that the right to privacy is a fundamental right. In addition, both the Electronic Transactions Ordinance 2002 and the Prevention of Electronic Crimes Act 2016 prohibit unlawful or unauthorized access to information.

9. Is bribery a criminal offense in your country? If so, does it include payments to both government officials and private businesses?

The bribery of government officials is a crime under the Pakistan Penal Code, the Prevention of Corruption Act 1947, the National Accountability Bureau Ordinance 1999, and provincial laws. Pakistani law does not specifically prohibit commercial bribery. However, commercial bribery can be prosecuted under Penal Code 1860, which covers crimes such as criminal breach of trust, cheating, mischief, making false documents, extortion, and theft.

Foreign companies operating in Pakistan must abide by Pakistan's anti-corruption laws. If a government official asks for a bribe or kickback, it must be reported to the appropriate government agencies as well as the company's embassy in Pakistan. It is difficult to claim coercion by a senior government official as a defense against improper practices in judicial proceedings.

10. What are the primary financial and investment regulatory bodies in your country?

- Securities and Exchange Commission of Pakistan (SECP) (www.secp.gov.pk) is Pakistan's primary national financial regulatory agency.
- National Accountability Bureau (NAB) (www.nab.gov.pk) investigates and prosecutes corruption and corrupt practices, misuse and abuse of powers, and assets held beyond known sources of income.
- Financial Monitoring Unit (FMU) (www.fmu.gov.pk) monitors suspicious transactions.
- Federal Investigation Agency (FIA) (www.fia.gov.pk) investigates corruption and economic crimes, such as counterfeit currencies, economic terrorism, and violations of intellectual property rights.
- State Bank of Pakistan (www.sbp.org.pk) conducts regulatory functions, such as issuing anti-money-laundering regulations.
- Federal Board of Revenue (FBR) (www.fbr.gov.pk) enforces fiscal laws and collects revenue for the government.

11. What are the most significant pieces of fraud-related legislation in your country?

- Contract Act, Sections 2(17) and (18), defining fraud and misrepresentation
- Penal Code
- Companies Act, 2017
- Anti-Money Laundering Ordinance, 2007
- Anti-Money Laundering Act, 2010
- Prevention of Corruption Act, 1947
- National Accountability Bureau Ordinance, 1999
- Anti-Terrorism Act, 1997
- Provincial laws

12. Does your country have laws in place to protect whistle-blowers? Please describe.

The Public Interest Disclosures Bill, 2017, is a national law providing protection to whistle-blowers in corruption cases.

In addition, the provincial government of Khyber Pakhtunkhwa approved the Khyber Pakhtunkhwa Whistleblower Protection and Vigilance Commission Bill, 2015, to protect whistle-blowers who make disclosures about irregular, illegal, or corrupt practices by individuals.

Anti-Fraud Programs

13. What foundational frameworks for internal controls, risk management, corporate governance, and so on are commonly used by organizations in your country when designing or assessing their anti-fraud programs (e.g., COSO frameworks, specific ISO standards, OECD guidance)?

The Securities and Exchange Commission of Pakistan (SECP) has issued mandatory corporate governance frameworks for both listed and nonlisted companies.

14. What types of background checks, if any, are commonly run on prospective employees in your country (e.g., criminal, civil, credit, employment, educational)?

Background checks are not a standard practice for employment and are not very common in Pakistan. Employers generally limit background checks to criminal, employment, and educational records, as well as Internet and social media searches.

In Pakistan, there is no specific law governing background checks. Therefore, background checks are generally permissible, especially with the consent of the applicant. However, the Constitution of Pakistan prohibits discrimination based on union affiliation or political views.

Employers should obtain consent before conducting background checks of existing employees, because background checks are less likely to be justifiable during employment. Before hiring foreign nationals, employers must confirm that they are legally authorized to work.

Considerations in Fraud Investigations

15. Are there any special legal considerations that individuals from outside your country should be aware of when they are working on an investigation in your country? Examples might include licenses needed, special laws governing information gathering, or restrictions on transmitting personal data outside the country.

Under the Constitution of Pakistan, the right to a fair trial is a fundamental right. The right to a fair trial is not limited to criminal matters; it is important in the context of caution warnings, custodial torture, confessions, identification parades, and nondisclosure of accusations and material evidence to the accused.

16. Are there any special cultural considerations that individuals from outside your country should be aware of when they are working on an investigation in your country? Examples might include who is present during an interview, how to address or greet individuals, inappropriate dress, and so on.

Investigators must be professional in their behavior and appearance. Decorum and politeness are important. Lawyers generally wear white shirts, black coats, ties, and trousers. Lawyers may wear a black *sherwani* (a long traditional Pakistani coat) over a white *shalwar* and *qamiz* (trousers and shirt).

CHAPTER 13

Sub-Saharan Africa

REGIONAL FRAUD TRENDS

The 2018 *Report to the Nations on Occupational Fraud and Abuse* issued by the Association of Certified Fraud Examiners (ACFE) includes 267 cases from sub-Saharan Africa that were investigated between January 2016 and October 2017. These cases caused a median loss of US $90,000 per case.

As noted in Exhibit 13.1, corruption is the most common form of occupational fraud committed in sub-Saharan Africa; 49% of the cases analyzed involved some form of corruption, which is more than twice as frequent as any other type of fraud scheme. Theft of cash on hand is the second most common category of occupational fraud, occurring in 21% of the cases in the region. In addition, fraud schemes in sub-Saharan Africa are more than twice as likely to be detected by a tip as by any other means (see Exhibit 13.2).

The 2018 *Report to the Nations* also examines the anti-fraud controls that were present at victim organizations at the time the frauds being analyzed were committed. Exhibit 13.3 shows that external audits of the financial statements are the most commonly implemented anti-fraud control among victim organizations in sub-Saharan Africa, followed by a formal code of conduct. On the other end of the spectrum, only one-quarter of these organizations had a mandatory vacation or job rotation policy in place, and just 20% provided rewards to whistle-blowers.

Exhibit 13.1   Scheme Types – Sub-Saharan Africa

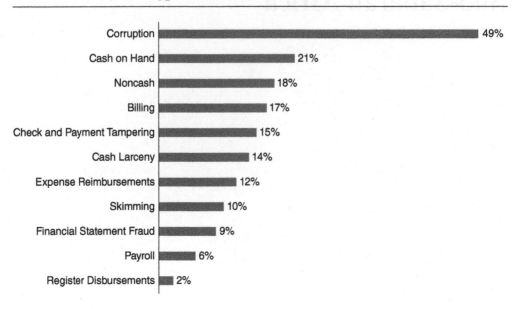

Exhibit 13.2   Initial Detection Method – Sub-Saharan Africa

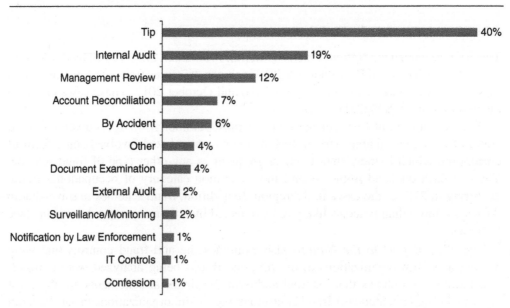

Exhibit 13.3   Frequency of Anti-Fraud Controls – Sub-Saharan Africa

Control	% of Cases
External Audit of Financial Statements	90%
Code of Conduct	89%
Internal Audit Department	87%
Management Certification of Financial Statements	81%
Independent Audit Committee	73%
External Audit of Internal Controls over Financial Reporting	72%
Hotline	70%
Management Review	69%
Anti-Fraud Policy	60%
Fraud Training for Employees	55%
Fraud Training for Managers/Executives	52%
Employee Support Programs	50%
Formal Fraud Risk Assessments	46%
Surprise Audits	46%
Dedicated Fraud Department, Function, or Team	43%
Proactive Data Monitoring/Analysis	40%
Job Rotation/Mandatory Vacation	25%
Rewards for Whistle-Blowers	20%

The following discussions provide jurisdiction-specific information pertaining to the legal, investigatory, and general anti-fraud environment for several countries in sub-Saharan Africa.

KENYA

Contributors

Bernard M. K. Muchere, CFE
Josephat K. Wainaina, CFE
Lukelesia Namarome, CFE
Shamsa Dagane, CFE

Sources of Information

1. What types of information about individuals are available to the public?

- Individual names under registration of persons
- Birth certificate showing date, place of birth, and parents
- Baptism certificate showing religion, names, date of birth, and location

2. What types of information about businesses are available to the public?

- Whether the company is blacklisted
- The location of the business
- Incorporation details
- Litigation information
- Property owned

3. Are court records available to the public? If so, explain what types of civil and criminal records can be obtained by the public.

Court records are available for a fee.

4. What other resources or types of information are regularly used by investigators in your country?

- Financial records
- Telephone records
- Computer data

5. What are some of the most useful Internet or online sources regularly used in fraud investigations?

- Commercial databases
- Social networking websites
- Internet search engines

Legal and Regulatory Environment

6. What are the major data privacy laws in your country, and how do these affect most fraud investigations?

- Constitution of Kenya
- Official Secrets Act
- Evidence Act

A court order is often required to access personal information, which can delay the gathering of evidence.

7. What type of legal system does your country have (e.g., civil law system, common law system, religious law system, hybrid)?

The Kenyan legal system is a hybrid of common law, civil law, and religious law (Kadhis court).

8. What laws governing the rights of individuals are of primary concern to investigators?

Human rights under the Kenyan Constitution are of primary concern to investigators.

9. Is bribery a criminal offense in your country? If so, does it include payments to both government officials and private businesses?

Bribery is a crime in Kenya, and it includes payments to both government officials and private businesses.

10. What are the primary financial and investment regulatory bodies in your country?

- Capital Markets Authority
- Insurance Regulatory Authority
- SACOO Societies Regulatory Authority
- Central Bank of Kenya

11. What are the most significant pieces of fraud-related legislation in your country?

- Prevention of Fraud (Investments) Act
- Anti-Corruption and Economic Crimes Act
- Bribery Act
- Anti-Counterfeit Act
- Extradition (Contiguous and Foreign Countries) Act
- Banking Act

12. Does your country have laws in place to protect whistle-blowers? Please describe.

Kenya has laws protecting whistle-blowers, including the Anti-Corruption and Economic Crimes Act and the Witness Protection Act.

Anti-Fraud Programs

13. What foundational frameworks for internal controls, risk management, corporate governance, and so on are commonly used by organizations in your country when designing or assessing their anti-fraud programs (e.g., COSO frameworks, specific ISO standards, OECD guidance)?

- Fraud Risk Management Framework (COSO Model)
- OECD Principles of Corporate Governance
- ISO standards compliance

14. **What types of background checks, if any, are commonly run on prospective employees in your country (e.g., criminal, civil, credit, employment, educational)?**

- Employment references
- Character references
- Gaps in employment history
- Identity and address verification
- Credit history
- Whether the applicant holds a directorship in another company
- Medical records
- Bankruptcies
- Academic and professional records
- Criminal records

Considerations in Fraud Investigations

15. **Are there any special legal considerations that individuals from outside your country should be aware of when they are working on an investigation in your country? Examples might include licenses needed, special laws governing information gathering, or restrictions on transmitting personal data outside the country.**

- Constitution of Kenya
- Regional and International Convention
- Evidence Act
- Official Secrets Act
- National Intelligence Service Act

16. **Are there any special cultural considerations that individuals from outside your country should be aware of when they are working on an investigation in your country? Examples might include who is present during an interview, how to address or greet individuals, inappropriate dress, and so on.**

Investigators should be aware of religious and cultural practices in Kenya.

MAURITIUS

Contributors

Deoraj Juggoo
Bandish Bundhoo, CFE

Sources of Information

1. **What types of information about individuals are available to the public?**

- Land Registry contains information regarding real property owned and sold, mortgages, and property rights.

- Registry of Associations contains information regarding membership in associations and trade unions.
- Media and social media have general information about individuals.

Other information about individuals, such as motor vehicle registrations, overseas travel, and bank statements, is available only to government authorities (see response to Question 4).

2. What types of information about businesses are available to the public?

The sources listed in the response to Question 1 can also be used to obtain information about businesses. In addition, the Corporate and Business Registration Department (companies.govmu.org) collects information about businesses, such as business registration number, type of business, names of officers and directors, data about shareholders, and financial statements.

3. Are court records available to the public? If so, explain what types of civil and criminal records can be obtained by the public.

Court judgments are available online.

4. What other resources or types of information are regularly used by investigators in your country?

See the responses to Questions 1 and 2 for public information available to private investigators. Government investigators may also have access to the following resources:

- National Transport Authority – information regarding motor vehicles owned and sold
- Passport and Immigration Office – information about overseas travel
- Civil Status Division – births, deaths, and marriages
- Banking institutions – bank statements
- Telecommunications companies – telephone records
- Local governments – permits

5. What are some of the most useful Internet or online sources regularly used in fraud investigations?

- Social media (Facebook, Instagram, Twitter)
- Internet search engines (Google, Yahoo)
- Company websites

Legal and Regulatory Environment

6. What are the major data privacy laws in your country, and how do these affect most fraud investigations?

- Constitution of Mauritius
- Data Protection Act
- Information and Communications Technologies Act

7. What type of legal system does your country have (e.g., civil law system, common law system, religious law system, hybrid)?

Mauritius has a hybrid legal system.

8. What laws governing the rights of individuals are of primary concern to investigators?

- Constitution of Mauritius
- Protection of Human Rights Act
- Data Protection Act
- Information and Communications Technologies Act

9. Is bribery a criminal offense in your country? If so, does it include payments to both government officials and private businesses?

Bribery is a crime in Mauritius. Most laws concern the bribery of government officials (e.g., the Prevention of Corruption Act). However, payments to private businesses might also be subject to prosecution.

10. What are the primary financial and investment regulatory bodies in your country?

- Financial Services Commission
- Bank of Mauritius
- Board of Investment

11. What are the most significant pieces of fraud-related legislation in your country?

- Prevention of Corruption Act
- Financial Intelligence and Anti-Money Laundering Act
- Mauritius Revenue Authority Act

12. Does your country have laws in place to protect whistle-blowers? Please describe.

Mauritius does not have laws protecting whistle-blowers, although such laws are under discussion.

Anti-Fraud Programs

13. What foundational frameworks for internal controls, risk management, corporate governance, and so on are commonly used by organizations in your country when designing or assessing their anti-fraud programs (e.g., COSO frameworks, specific ISO standards, OECD guidance)?

All of the major international frameworks, ISO standards, and OECD guidance are used for anti-fraud programs.

14. What types of background checks, if any, are commonly run on prospective employees in your country (e.g., criminal, civil, credit, employment, educational)?

Employers generally verify the employment and educational backgrounds of applicants. To be employed in the public sector, applicants generally must submit to a background check performed by the police department. In addition, a certificate of morality is required for some jobs.

SOUTH AFRICA

Contributors

Jaco de Jager, CFE
Adv. Jan Henning, SQ
Adv. Chris van Vuuren, CFE

Sources of Information

1. What types of information about individuals are available to the public?

- Any information published on a social media site (e.g., name, race, gender, place of work, contact details, etc.)
- Birth and death records
- ID confirmation
- Company registration and directorships
- Address confirmation
- Default judgments
- Notary bond information
- Employment
- Vehicle ownership
- Education
- Life insurance policy details
- Golf membership
- Confirmation of property ownership (deeds)
- Accounts opened at retailers
- Third-party inquiries on credit profiles

2. What types of information about businesses are available to the public?

- Any and all information that the company makes available on the company website
- Company registration date
- Company address
- Financial statements
- Directors' information (e.g., names, addresses, and, in some instances, shareholding percentages)

- Inquiries received from other companies and their details
- Details of company accountant

3. Are court records available to the public? If so, explain what types of civil and criminal records can be obtained by the public.

Generally, the records of court cases heard in open court are available to the public. Such courts may include the magistrates' courts, equality courts, small claims courts, high courts, appeals courts, and labour courts, as well as the Constitutional Court. Cases that involve children are generally not available to the public because the law protects information about persons under the age of 18. In addition, some cases involving rape are not available to the public.

Information about cases can be obtained via JUTA Law Reports and LexisNexis Law Reports. Another useful tool is the website for the Southern African Legal Information Institute (www.saflii.org).

4. What other resources or types of information are regularly used by investigators in your country?

Investigators can register for access to information through the ACFE South Africa, or in some instances directly with the information provider, to obtain access to:

- Criminal records
- Cross-border movement
- Passport verification
- Bank verification
- Cell phone and other telephone numbers – confirmation of ownership
- Confirmation of short-term insurance coverage
- Life insurance coverage
- Consumer profile on accounts indicates number of payments, duration of payments made from date of invoice, account risk indicator, and so on.
- Identity confirmation
- Vehicle ownership confirmation
- Fingerprint confirmation

5. What are some of the most useful Internet or online sources regularly used in fraud investigations?

- Search engines, such as Google
- Social media, such as Facebook, Twitter, Instagram, and LinkedIn
- Deeds – property searches (www.windeed.co.za)
- TransUnion ITC (www.transunion.co.za)
- XDS (www.xds.co.za)
- Experian (www.experian.co.za)
- Consumer Profile Bureau (www.consumerprofilebureau.com)
- Companies and Intellectual Property Commission (www.cipc.co.za)
- News websites such as News24 (www.news24.com), Media24 (www.media24.com), and Times Live (www.timeslive.co.za/news/south-africa)

Legal and Regulatory Environment

6. What are the major data privacy laws in your country, and how do these affect most fraud investigations?

South Africa's Protection of Personal Information Act (POPI) restricts the use and processing of personal information. The major principles of POPI are:

- Personal information must be obtained in a fair and lawful manner.
- Personal information can be used only for the specified purpose for which it was originally obtained. Processing for other purposes is prohibited.
- The person who processes the personal information must take reasonable steps to ensure that the information is complete, up to date, accurate, and not misleading.
- The person who processes the personal information should have a degree of openness. The data subject and the Information Regulator must be notified that the information is being processed.
- The person who processes the personal information must implement security measures to safeguard against loss, damage, destruction, and unauthorized or unlawful access, or processing of the information.
- The data subject must be able to access and correct the personal information.
- The person who processes the personal information is responsible for complying with these principles and providing proof of compliance.

Under the Promotion of Access to Information Act, persons can request information held by the state and certain information held by private bodies.

The Constitution of South Africa states that people have a right of confidentiality. Personal information must be treated confidentially, and no other person has a right to access the information except through the proper channels or legal action.

The South African Revenue Services Act prohibits companies from providing any information regarding a person's income or taxes to any other company or person. This law restricts the ability of investigators to obtain financial information.

Last, the Electronic Communications and Transactions Act, No. 25 of 2002, and the Interception Act, No. 70 of 2002, regulate the interception of communications.

7. What type of legal system does your country have (e.g., civil law system, common law system, religious law system, hybrid)?

South Africa has a hybrid legal system based in part on common law, which is based on Roman-Dutch law, with important influences by English law. Statutory law is also an important source of law.

8. What laws governing the rights of individuals are of primary concern to investigators?

South African citizens have a right to privacy and confidentiality; therefore, investigators generally do not have access to financial records such as bank statements. South African legislation governs when and how such information can be obtained.

The South African Revenue Services Act prohibits companies from providing any information regarding a person's income or taxes to any other company or person. This law restricts the ability of investigators to obtain financial information.

9. Is bribery a criminal offense in your country? If so, does it include payments to both government officials and private businesses?

Bribery, which includes payments to both government officials and private businesses, is a criminal offense under South Africa's Prevention of Corruption Act, Prevention and Combating of Corrupt Activities Act, and Prevention of Organised Crime Act. Failing to report bribery is also a crime. The maximum sentence for such corrupt activities is 15 years in prison.

10. What are the primary financial and investment regulatory bodies in your country?

The Financial Services Board is the overseeing regulator.

11. What are the most significant pieces of fraud-related legislation in your country?

- The Auditing Profession Act, No. 26 of 2005
- The Civil Proceedings Act, No. 25 of 1965
- The Close Corporations Act, No. 69 of 1984
- The Companies Act, No. 71 of 2008
- The Constitution of the Republic of South Africa Act, No. 108 of 1996
- The Copyright Act, No. 98 of 1978
- The Counterfeit Goods Act, No. 37 of 1997
- The Criminal Law Amendment Act, No. 105 of 1997
- The Criminal Procedure Act, No. 51 of 1977 (CPA)
- The Electronic Communications and Transactions Act, No. 25 of 2002
- The Financial Intelligence Centre Act, No. 38 of 2001 (FICA)
- The General Law Amendment Act, No. 62 of 1955
- The General Law Amendment Act, No. 50 of 1956
- The General Law Amendment Act, No. 139 of 1992
- The General Law Third Amendment Act, No. 129 of 1993
- The Income Tax Act, No. 58 of 1962
- The Insolvency Act, No. 24 of 1936
- The Inspection of Financial Institutions Act, No. 80 of 1998
- The Labour Relations Act, No. 66 of 1995
- The Law of Evidence Amendment Act, No. 45 of 1988
- The Magistrates' Courts Act, No. 32 of 1944
- The National Prosecuting Authority Act, No. 32 of 1998
- The National Road Traffic Act, No. 93 of 1996
- The Prevention and Combating of Corrupt Activities Act, No. 12 of 2004
- The Prevention of Corruption Act, No. 12 of 2004
- The Prevention of Counterfeiting of Currency Act, No. 16 of 1965
- The Prevention of Organised Crime Act, No. 121 of 1998
- The Protected Disclosures Act, No. 26 of 2000

- The Regulation of Interception of Communications and Provision of Communication-Related Information Act, No. 70 of 2002
- The Right of Appearance Act, No. 62 of 1995
- The Securities Services Act, No. 36 of 2004
- The Small Claims Courts Act, No. 61 of 1984, as amended
- The South African Police Service Act, No. 68 of 1995
- The South African Reserve Bank Act, No. 117 of 1998
- The Special Investigating Units and Special Tribunal Act, No. 74 of 1996
- The Superior Courts Act, No. 10 of 2013
- The Trust Property Control Act, No. 57 of 1988
- The Witness Protection Act, No. 112 of 1998

12. Does your country have laws in place to protect whistle-blowers? Please describe.

The South African Protected Disclosures Act, No. 26 of 2000, protects employees who report unlawful or irregular conduct by their employers or fellow employees.

Anti-Fraud Programs

13. What foundational frameworks for internal controls, risk management, corporate governance, and so on are commonly used by organizations in your country when designing or assessing their anti-fraud programs (e.g., COSO frameworks, specific ISO standards, OECD guidance)?

ISO standards, COSO frameworks, OECD guidance, and frameworks instituted by the African Organisation of Supreme Audit Institutions (AFROSAI) and International Organisation of Supreme Audit Institutions (INTOSAI) are used for anti-fraud programs.

14. What types of background checks, if any, are commonly run on prospective employees in your country (e.g., criminal, civil, credit, employment, educational)?

Criminal, civil, credit, employment, and educational background checks are commonly run on prospective employees.

In some instances, applicants provide false salary slips to potential employers to increase the offer amount. The only way to verify salaries is to look at bank statements or contact the HR department of the applicant's current or previous employer.

Considerations in Fraud Investigations

15. Are there any special legal considerations that individuals from outside your country should be aware of when they are working on an investigation in your country? Examples might include licenses needed, special laws governing information gathering, or restrictions on transmitting personal data outside the country.

If an investigation involves security-related issues, the investigator must register with the Private Security Industry Regulatory Authority (PSIRA), which regulates the security industry. Foreign investigators should involve local investigative and/or law enforcement agencies such as the South African Police Service and the National Prosecuting Authority where applicable. It is also important to comply with the International Co-operation in Criminal Matters Act, No. 75/1996.

16. Are there any special cultural considerations that individuals from outside your country should be aware of when they are working on an investigation in your country? Examples might include who is present during an interview, how to address or greet individuals, inappropriate dress, and so on.

There are various cultures in South Africa and 11 different official languages. It is best to involve a local who understands the cultures and languages. If the interview subject is a woman, it is best to have another woman present during the interview to protect against allegations such as sexual harassment.

CHAPTER 14

United States

REGIONAL FRAUD TRENDS

The 2018 *Report to the Nations on Occupational Fraud and Abuse* issued by the Association of Certified Fraud Examiners (ACFE) includes 1,000 cases from the US that were investigated between January 2016 and October 2017. These cases caused a median loss of US $108,000 per case.

As noted in Exhibit 14.1, corruption is the most common form of occupational fraud committed in the US; 30% of the cases analyzed involved some form of corruption. Billing schemes are the second most common category of occupational fraud, occurring in just over one-quarter of the cases. In addition, fraud schemes in the US are more than twice as likely to be detected by a tip as by any other means (see Exhibit 14.2).

The 2018 *Report to the Nations* also examines the anti-fraud controls that were present at victim organizations at the time the frauds being analyzed were committed. Exhibit 14.3 shows that a formal code of conduct is the most commonly implemented anti-fraud control among victim organizations in the US, followed by external audits of financial statements. On the other end of the spectrum, only 15% of these organizations had a mandatory vacation or job rotation policy in place, and just 12% provided rewards to whistle-blowers.

Exhibit 14.1   Scheme Types – United States

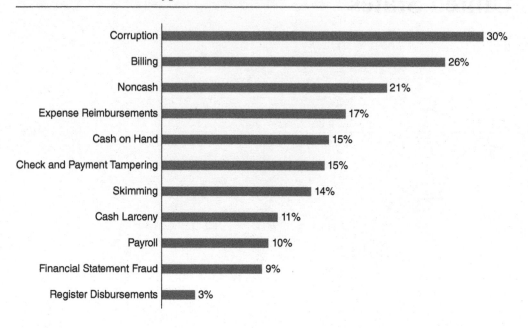

Exhibit 14.2   Initial Detection Method – United States

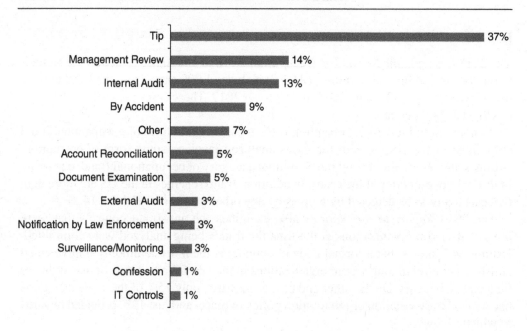

Exhibit 14.3   Frequency of Anti-Fraud Controls – United States

Control	% of Cases
Code of Conduct	73%
External Audit of Financial Statements	69%
Employee Support Programs	62%
Management Certification of Financial Statements	61%
Internal Audit Department	60%
External Audit of Internal Controls over Financial Reporting	60%
Management Review	59%
Hotline	56%
Fraud Training for Employees	50%
Fraud Training for Managers/Executives	49%
Independent Audit Committee	49%
Anti-Fraud Policy	47%
Formal Fraud Risk Assessments	37%
Proactive Data Monitoring/Analysis	36%
Dedicated Fraud Department, Function, or Team	35%
Surprise Audits	31%
Job Rotation/Mandatory Vacation	15%
Rewards for Whistle-Blowers	12%

The following discussion provides country-specific information pertaining to the legal, investigatory, and general anti-fraud environment for the US.

UNITED STATES

Contributors

ACFE Research Department

Sources of Information

1. What types of information about individuals are available to the public?

The best sources of information about individuals are Internet search engines (e.g., Google) and publicly available social media websites (e.g., Facebook, LinkedIn, Twitter). Such sources can reveal important information, including an individual's full name, marital status, occupation, current and former employers, current and former addresses, hobbies, social status, and more.

331

In the US, each state is composed of multiple counties. For example, California has 58 counties and Texas has 254. Each county maintains records regarding real property ownership. Investigators can search a county's land and property tax records to determine whether an individual owns real property in that county.

When a consumer uses personal property as collateral for a loan, the lender generally files a financing statement with the state government to notify other parties of its interest in the property. These documents are sometimes called "UCC filings" (referring to the Uniform Commercial Code), and they are generally publicly available. Searching UCC filings can reveal useful information about individuals, including property they have financed, the names of lenders, home and business addresses, and tax liens. Some states charge fees for searches of UCC filings. In other states, they are free.

In addition, investigators can search certain public records for free at the Search Systems website (publicrecords.searchsystems.net).

2. What types of information about businesses are available to the public?

In the US, business records are maintained by a government agency in the state where the business is registered. Depending on the state, the agency may be called the Secretary of State, Department of State, Division of Corporations, or something similar. Investigators can search the agency's business records via an online database or at the agency's office. Generally, such records include the following:

- Business name
- Names of owners, directors, officers, and registered agent
- Address of principal office
- Legal form of the business (e.g., corporation, partnership, limited liability company)
- Business purpose (e.g., grocery store, accounting firm)
- Articles of incorporation, partnership agreement, or other formation documents
- Any other required business filings

Publicly traded companies are required to file certain documents with the US Securities and Exchange Commission. These documents are publicly available via an online database called EDGAR, which stands for Electronic Data Gathering, Analysis, and Retrieval (www.sec.gov/edgar/searchedgar/companysearch.html).

In addition, there are a number of paid commercial services that provide information about businesses, including:

- Dun & Bradstreet (www.dnb.com)
- Kompass (us.kompass.com)
- SkyMinder (www.skyminder.com)
- LexisNexis (www.lexisnexis.com)
- Bureau Van Dijk (www.bvdinfo.com/en-us/home)

3. Are court records available to the public? If so, explain what types of civil and criminal records can be obtained by the public.

In the US, civil and criminal court records are generally considered public information, but such records are not always easy to find. Generally, any public information filed with a court can be accessed by visiting the court or searching the court's website. However, the investigator must know the name of the state or federal court in which the proceeding occurred. There is no free central database that covers all court proceedings.

For a fee, investigators can access the Public Access to Court Electronic Records (PACER) (www.pacer.gov), a paid online database of federal court records, including bankruptcies. In addition, the National Center for State Courts (www.ncsc.org) is a useful free resource for information about state courts in the US.

Attorneys use commercial services, such as LexisNexis (www.lexisnexis.com) and Westlaw (https://westlaw.com), to perform legal research. These databases generally contain the decisions of appellate and high courts; they usually do not contain lower court decisions from state courts.

See the response to Question 14 for a discussion of background checks.

4. What other resources or types of information are regularly used by investigators in your country?

A search of media outlets and press releases might be a helpful source of information about a business or, in some cases, an individual. Most search engines allow users to target news publications with searches, and the PR Newswire website (prnewswire. com) hosts a wide range of archived press releases.

5. What are some of the most useful Internet or online sources regularly used in fraud investigations?

See the responses to Questions 1, 2, 3, and 4.

Legal and Regulatory Environment

6. What are the major data privacy laws in your country, and how do these affect most fraud investigations?

Unlike most countries, the US does not have a comprehensive federal data privacy law. However, there are state and federal laws that impose conditions on the collection, use, and transfer of certain types of personal information. For example, a federal law called the Health Insurance Portability and Accountability Act of 1996 (HIPAA) protects the privacy of medical records. Another federal law, the Gramm-Leach-Bliley Act, restricts the disclosure of personal information by financial institutions.

7. What type of legal system does your country have (e.g., civil law system, common law system, religious law system, hybrid)?

The US has a common law system.

8. What laws governing the rights of individuals are of primary concern to investigators?

The laws most important to fraud investigators are state laws regarding:

- Invasion of privacy
- False imprisonment

- Defamation
- Attorney-client privilege
- Rules of evidence, such as maintaining a chain of custody and the admission and exclusion of evidence

In addition, if the investigator works for the government, various constitutional rights are important, such as the Fourth Amendment prohibition against unreasonable searches and seizures.

9. Is bribery a criminal offense in your country? If so, does it include payments to both government officials and private businesses?

It is a crime under federal and state laws to bribe public officials working for federal or state government. The bribery of foreign public officials is also a crime under the US Foreign Corrupt Practices Act.

There is no federal law that criminalizes commercial bribery. However, commercial bribery is a crime under the laws of many states.

10. What are the primary financial and investment regulatory bodies in your country?

- Federal Reserve System (Fed) is the central bank of the US and has responsible for the overall stability of the financial system.
- Securities and Exchange Commission (SEC) regulates the securities industry and enforces federal securities laws.
- Commodity Futures Trading Commission (CFTC) regulates commodity futures and options markets.
- Financial Industry Regulatory Authority (FINRA) is a self-regulatory organization that regulates the broker-dealer industry.
- Financial Crimes Enforcement Network (FinCEN) collects and analyzes financial intelligence to prevent money laundering and promote national security.
- Federal Deposit Insurance Corporation (FDIC) provides deposit insurance to bank customers.
- State financial regulators: States have their own regulatory bodies that oversee financial matters.

11. What are the most significant pieces of fraud-related legislation in your country?

- Foreign Corrupt Practices Act requires accounting transparency and prohibits the bribery of foreign public officials.
- Sarbanes-Oxley Act contains accounting, reporting, and auditing requirements for public companies and enhanced penalties for corporate fraud.
- Computer Fraud and Abuse Act prohibits computer-related fraud.
- False Claims Act prohibits false claims to the government.
- 18 U.S.C. §§ 1341 and 1343 are federal mail and wire fraud statutes.
- 18 U.S.C. § 1344 is the federal bank fraud statute.
- 18 U.S.C. § 1001 prohibits false statements to federal officials.

- State laws prohibit fraudulent misrepresentation, extortion, larceny, embezzlement, conflicts of interest, and more.

12. Does your country have laws in place to protect whistle-blowers? Please describe.

There are numerous federal laws protecting whistle-blowers, including:

- Sarbanes-Oxley Act (SOX) protects employees of public companies who report violations of SOX.
- Dodd-Frank Act protects whistle-blowers who report misconduct by public companies.
- Whistleblower Protection Act protects government employees who report misconduct by government agencies.
- Patient Protection and Affordable Care Act (ACA) protects employees from retaliation for obtaining health care under the ACA or reporting violations of the ACA by their employer.

In addition, every state has laws protecting whistle-blowers who report certain offenses.

Anti-Fraud Programs

13. What foundational frameworks for internal controls, risk management, corporate governance, and so on are commonly used by organizations in your country when designing or assessing their anti-fraud programs (e.g., COSO frameworks, specific ISO standards, OECD guidance)?

The following publications are commonly used by organizations in the US in creating and evaluating their anti-fraud and anti-corruption programs:

- COSO, Internal Control – Integrated Framework
- COSO, Enterprise Risk Management Framework
- *The Fraud Risk Management Guide*, jointly published by COSO and the ACFE
- Federal Sentencing Guidelines for Organizations and related guidance put forth by the US Department of Justice
- ISO 31000:2009, Risk Management – Principles and Guidelines
- OECD, Good Practice Guidance on Internal Controls, Ethics, and Compliance
- US Department of Justice publication *A Resource Guide to the US Foreign Corrupt Practices Act*
- ISO 37001:2016, Anti-Bribery Management Systems

14. What types of background checks, if any, are commonly run on prospective employees in your country (e.g., criminal, civil, credit, employment, educational)?

Employers commonly run criminal, employment, and educational background checks. Civil and credit checks are less common.

Generally, employers must obtain written consent before checking an applicant's criminal or credit history, or hiring a company to provide an investigative report about the applicant. The employer also must provide certain notices to the applicant.

Some state and local laws prohibit employers from inquiring about an applicant's criminal record on an employment application or early in the screening process. Under other laws, employers cannot inquire about an applicant's criminal record until after a conditional job offer is made. There are exceptions for certain occupations (e.g., child care) and where criminal background checks are required by law.

Considerations in Fraud Investigations

15. Are there any special legal considerations that individuals from outside your country should be aware of when they are working on an investigation in your country? Examples might include licenses needed, special laws governing information gathering, or restrictions on transmitting personal data outside the country.

Most states have license requirements for private investigators.

16. Are there any special cultural considerations that individuals from outside your country should be aware of when they are working on an investigation in your country? Examples might include who is present during an interview, how to address or greet individuals, inappropriate dress, and so on.

In the US, there is no uniform dress code for the workplace. Some workplaces require conservative business attire, while others encourage their employees to dress casually. Generally, an interviewer should not be dressed less formally than the interviewee. If the dress code is unknown, a dark suit (with or without a tie) is generally a safe option for a male interviewer. A suit or a dress with a jacket is generally a good option for a female interviewer.

Americans tend to require more personal space than other cultures. They may feel discomfort or anxiety when someone stands too close to them, especially a stranger. In a business environment, it is best to keep at least an arm's length, or two to three feet, between oneself and other people.

Punctuality is generally expected for business meetings. The usual greeting is a firm handshake, brief eye contact, and an introduction and greeting such as, "I'm John Smith. Nice to meet you."

CHAPTER 15

Western Europe

REGIONAL FRAUD TRENDS

The 2018 *Report to the Nations on Occupational Fraud and Abuse* issued by the Association of Certified Fraud Examiners (ACFE) includes 130 cases from Western Europe that were investigated between January 2016 and October 2017. These cases caused a median loss of US $200,000 per case.

As noted in Exhibit 15.1, corruption is the most common form of occupational fraud committed in Western Europe; 36% of the cases analyzed involved some form of corruption. Billing schemes are the second most common category of occupational fraud, occurring in 28% of the cases in the region. In addition, fraud schemes in Western Europe are more than four times more likely to be detected by a tip than by any other means (see Exhibit 15.2).

The 2018 *Report to the Nations* also examines the anti-fraud controls that were present at victim organizations at the time the frauds being analyzed were committed. Exhibit 15.3 shows that a formal code of conduct is the most commonly implemented anti-fraud control among victim organizations in Western Europe, followed by management certification of the financial statements and external audits of the financial statements. On the other end of the spectrum, only 22% of these organizations had a mandatory vacation or job rotation policy in place, and just 10% provided rewards to whistle-blowers.

Exhibit 15.1 Scheme Types – Western Europe

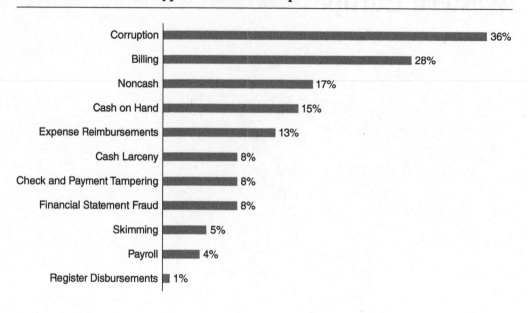

Exhibit 15.2 Initial Detection Method – Western Europe

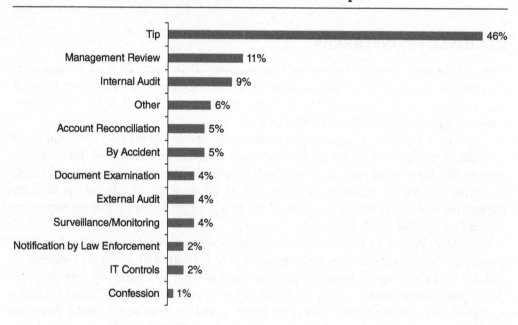

Exhibit 15.3   Frequency of Anti-Fraud Controls – Western Europe

Control	% of Cases
Code of Conduct	93%
Management Certification of Financial Statements	88%
External Audit of Financial Statements	88%
External Audit of Internal Controls over Financial Reporting	85%
Management Review	83%
Internal Audit Department	80%
Independent Audit Committee	78%
Hotline	76%
Anti-Fraud Policy	65%
Fraud Training for Managers/Executives	63%
Fraud Training for Employees	59%
Formal Fraud Risk Assessments	53%
Dedicated Fraud Department, Function, or Team	49%
Employee Support Programs	48%
Surprise Audits	41%
Proactive Data Monitoring/Analysis	38%
Job Rotation/Mandatory Vacation	22%
Rewards for Whistle-Blowers	10%

The following discussions provide jurisdiction-specific information pertaining to the legal, investigatory, and general anti-fraud environment for several countries in Western Europe.

DENMARK

Contributors

Carsten Allerslev Olsen, CFE
Thomas Bøgballe, CFE
Nicoleta Mehlsen, MBA, CFE

Sources of Information

1. What types of information about individuals are available to the public?

The home addresses and telephone numbers of individuals are available on the Internet if the individuals allow them to be public. In addition, the following websites might contain relevant information:

- www.boliga.dk – public records regarding real property
- www.ois.dk – additional information about real property, such as historical sales prices, public valuation, and so on
- www.tinglysning.dk – information about loans, debtors, and financed property
- www.nummerplade.net – information about vehicle financing
- www.tingbogen.dk – information about mortgages and the ownership of property and vehicles

2. What types of information about businesses are available to the public?

The Central Business Register (www.cvr.dk) is Denmark's master register of information about businesses. Searching for a business on the website can reveal its government registration number, industry code, type of business, number of employees, business address, the names of its directors and legal auditors, published financial reports (if any), and more.

3. Are court records available to the public? If so, explain what types of civil and criminal records can be obtained by the public.

Under the Administration of Justice Act, individuals can ask a court for a copy of any judgment or conviction.

5. What are some of the most useful Internet or online sources regularly used in fraud investigations?

See responses to Questions 1 and 2.

Legal and Regulatory Environment

6. What are the major data privacy laws in your country, and how do these affect most fraud investigations?

The major data privacy laws include the Danish Act on Processing of Personal Data (Act No. 429 of May 31, 2000), the EU's General Data Protection Regulation (effective May 25, 2018), and EU Regulation 2016/679 of the European Parliament and of the Council of April 27, 2016. These laws are embedded into everyday life and business; there are systems built around them to support the need for personal data. Fraud investigations must be supported by a legal framework, and no personal data can be obtained without support from the Danish police or the Court of Justice.

7. What type of legal system does your country have (e.g., civil law system, common law system, religious law system, hybrid)?

Scandinavian civil law is the system applicable in Denmark. The district courts, the high courts, and the Supreme Court represent the three basic levels of the Danish legal system.

8. What laws governing the rights of individuals are of primary concern to investigators?

The Administration of Justice Act, the Criminal Code, and the Act on Processing of Personal Data are the most important laws for investigators.

9. Is bribery a criminal offense in your country? If so, does it include payments to both government officials and private businesses?

It is a criminal offense to bribe a public official. In private business, bribery is a criminal offense if a present or an advantage is given or received contrary to one's duty in connection with business negotiations.

10. What are the primary financial and investment regulatory bodies in your country?

In Denmark, there is a dual system. The Danish Financial Supervisory Authority (*Finanstilsynet*) regulates companies working in the financial industry (banks, insurance companies, etc.). All other companies are regulated by the Danish Business Authority (*Erhversstyrelsen*), which also regulates certified auditors.

11. What are the most significant pieces of fraud-related legislation in your country?

The Criminal Code is the most significant piece of fraud-related legislation in Denmark.

12. Does your country have laws in place to protect whistle-blowers? Please describe.

There is no law protecting whistle-blowers in Denmark. This is mainly due to two factors: (1) the duty of loyalty and (2) the limited rights of employees who are dismissed without cause (e.g., small amount of damages, scarce chance of reinstatement).

Anti-Fraud Programs

13. What foundational frameworks for internal controls, risk management, corporate governance, and so on are commonly used by organizations in your country when designing or assessing their anti-fraud programs (e.g., COSO frameworks, specific ISO standards, OECD guidance)?

Enterprise risk management is the foundation for the establishment of controls to mitigate risks; the COSO Enterprise Risk Management Framework is the most common framework used. Also important is paragraph 107 of the Danish Financial Statement Act, which governs internal controls over financial reporting.

14. What types of background checks, if any, are commonly run on prospective employees in your country (e.g., criminal, civil, credit, employment, educational)?

Background checks often include an applicant's criminal record and employment history. They do not usually include an applicant's educational background or financial situation.

Considerations in Fraud Investigations

15. Are there any special legal considerations that individuals from outside your country should be aware of when they are working on an investigation in your country? Examples might include licenses needed, special laws governing information gathering, or restrictions on transmitting personal data outside the country.

See response to Question 8.

16. Are there any special cultural considerations that individuals from outside your country should be aware of when they are working on an investigation in your country? Examples might include who is present during an interview, how to address or greet individuals, inappropriate dress, and so on.

If an employee is a member of a union, in some cases a union representative must be present during an interview.

FRANCE

Contributors

Francis Hounnongandji, CFE, CFA
Eric Lasry
Sara Koski
Hervé Zany, CFE

Sources of Information

1. What types of information about individuals are available to the public?

France has strict data privacy laws. Generally, government records regarding individuals are not available to the public, unless the records are more than 75 years old.

An individual's residential address is deemed private. Unless the individual's address is voluntarily listed in the telephone directory or another directory, this information is not publicly accessible. There are no databases compiling the residential address histories of individuals.

If an individual holds a directorship in a business or has a declared commercial activity, the individual's basic identifiers (full name, date and place of birth, and self-declared residential address) are publicly available through government registries and private services (see response to Question 2). Searching for directorships can unveil the existence of private companies, such as personal real estate holding companies. There is no public database for shareholdings. However, an individual's shareholdings can be identified by searching the corporate filings of companies in which the individual is believed to have an interest.

Members of the public can use the website of the *Service de la Publicité Foncière* (www2.impots.gouv.fr/contacts/spf/index.htm), or visit one of the agency's more than 400 offices, to search for real estate records by address. The search can reveal financial and ownership information if there is only one property at the address. To search for property in the name of a particular individual, a request must be made at the correct regional office where the property is located.

The High Authority for Transparency in Public Life maintains a public website (www.hatvp.fr) that contains declarations of interests made by about 15,000 elected officials.

2. What types of information about businesses are available to the public?

Information about businesses is available through government registries and private services. Local business and companies' registers, such as the Registry of Commerce and Companies (*Registre du Commerce et des Sociétés*), are kept by registrars of the commercial courts and of the civil courts with commercial jurisdiction. Such registrars issue *Kbis* extracts, which are official documents confirming the legal existence of a company; they are the true "identity cards" of companies in France. The extract contains information about the company's business activities, management, administrative or supervisory bodies, registered agents, and whether collective proceedings have been brought against the company.

Other information available from business and companies registers can include:

- Articles of association
- Minutes of corporate meetings
- Management reports
- Insolvency proceedings against the company

Most commercial companies (whether listed or not) are required to file annual financial statements (including balance sheet, income statement, and notes) and a management report in the month following the general assembly that approved them (i.e., within seven months maximum after closing the fiscal year in question). Under some conditions, small companies can voluntarily declare their annual accounts to be confidential and the register will not make them available to the public.

The commercial website Infogreffe (www.infogreffe.com) provides centralized access to information contained in the business and companies registers. The service is offered in French and English. There are many other proprietary commercial databases that offer information on businesses.

The website of the National Institute for Industrial Property (www.inpi.fr/fr) contains information regarding intellectual property rights held by companies and individuals.

3. Are court records available to the public? If so, explain what types of civil and criminal records can be obtained by the public.

Criminal records are not publicly available. For each individual, the French government maintains a criminal record (*casier judiciaire*), which includes a list of the individual's convictions for serious offenses. Convictions are removed from the individual's record after a specified time period (three to 40 years, depending on the seriousness of the offense). Only a judge or a law enforcement officer may access an individual's full *casier judiciaire*. However, individuals may request an extract of their own *casier judiciaire*. Such extracts include convictions for serious offenses that have not been removed.

Although most civil and criminal judgments are publicly available in France, accessing a judgment requires precise indexing information that cannot be obtained through a searchable database because most judgments are not available in digitalized form. Only a fraction of civil and criminal litigation records are publicly available through databases that can be searched by keyword (although not specifically by party name). French litigation databases are exhaustive for only the highest court (*Cour de cassation*) and include only a small selection of lower court cases. In addition, cases involving individuals are usually reported anonymously to meet privacy law requirements. Information regarding current litigation is not a matter of public record.

French high court decisions are published in the following reports:

- *Bulletins de la Cour de Cassation* cover civil and criminal cases in the *Cour de cassation*.
- *Recueil Lebon (Recueil des décisions du Conseil d'État)* covers administrative law.
- *Recueil des décisions du Conseil Constitutionnel* covers decisions of the Constitutional Council.

Other useful resources include the following:

- Jurisprudence database in *Légifrance* is a free resource that covers constitutional case law, administrative decisions, and private case law.
- *Bulletin des arrêts de la Cour de cassation rendus en matière civile* is a free resource for civil cases in the *Cour de cassation*.
- *ArianeWeb* is a free resource for administrative decisions by the *Conseil d'Etat*.

Other sources of French court decisions include legal reviews, such as *La Semaine Juridique* or *La Gazette du Palais*. If a specific case is not available online, individuals can request information from the registry (*greffe*) of the relevant court.

4. What other resources or types of information are regularly used by investigators in your country?

Investigators perform Web and deep Web research, covering online documents, cached pages, groups, images, news pages, and the main social networks through focused, combined keyword searches. Investigators also rely upon proprietary screening solutions or risk compliance databases that provide coverage of known money launderers, financial criminals, terrorists, and other individuals and businesses from other categories, including politically exposed persons (PEPs). These databases correlate with leading sanctions regimes from around the world (EU, UN, US Office of Foreign Assets Control, UK, Switzerland's State Secretariat for Economic Affairs, Australia's Department of Foreign Affairs and Trade, etc.), global PEP databases, and watch lists.

Licensed private investigators (*agents de recherches privées*) are allowed to conduct reputational and business information interviews with third parties without revealing the purpose of their mission. They often assist fraud examiners in their investigations.

5. What are some of the most useful Internet or online sources regularly used in fraud investigations?

Investigators often use Internet search tools, such as Google, Yahoo, and Bing. Furthermore, investigators can consult the website of the subject entity or individual. Social media (such as LinkedIn, Facebook, Twitter, blogs, etc.) and search engine records (Infogreffe, Societe.com) also provide investigators with public information. Some proprietary tools search the Web and deep Web sources for adverse media information filtered by a wide range of financial and nonfinancial crimes, including corporate scandals, corruption, and terrorism.

Other sources used in fraud investigations include:

- Kompass France (fr.kompass.com) – information about companies, such as trade names, executives, products and services offered, and more
- Skyminder (www.skyminder.com) – company profiles, as well as credit and financial information, on 50 million public and private entities worldwide
- Bureau van Dijk France (www.bvdinfo.com) – information on businesses, mergers and acquisitions, and other business-related data
- Trace route sites such as YouGetSignal.com (https://yougetsignal.com) – used to determine where a website's server is located
- Infogreffe (www.infogreffe.com) – information contained in business and companies registers
- Societe.com – legal and financial information about companies
- Zoominfo.com – information about companies and individuals
- France's patent and trademark sites, such as *Institut national de la propriété industrielle*
- France's stock exchange sites (e.g., Euronext)

Legal and Regulatory Environment

6. What are the major data privacy laws in your country, and how do these affect most fraud investigations?

Data collected in the context of fraud investigations is subject to the French Data Protection Act (FDPA), which governs the collection, storage, and use of personal data. The FDPA incorporates and enhances many of the principles of the EU Data Protection Directive. The French Data Protection Authority (*Commission Nationale de L'Informatique et des Libertés* or CNIL) enforces the FDPA and informs data subjects and controllers of their rights and duties.

7. What type of legal system does your country have (e.g., civil law system, common law system, religious law system, hybrid)?

France has a civil law system. The doctrine of *stare decisis* does not apply in France in the same way it does in common law jurisdictions. Indeed, each case is decided on its own merits according to how it relates to the various codified laws and how the judge decides to interpret their contents.

Furthermore, the French legal system can be described as dual, as it is divided into two branches:

- Administrative law (*Droit administratif*), which covers public law matters involving the state and state-owned entities
- Private law (*Droit privé*), which relates to individuals and private entities

French courts also reflect this duality, and they are divided into two orders:

- Judicial courts, which enforce criminal, commercial, civil, and labor laws
- Administrative courts, which enforce public law

The judicial court of last resort is the *Cour de cassation*. The *Conseil d'Etat* is the highest administrative court.

8. What laws governing the rights of individuals are of primary concern to investigators?

- The right to privacy, as defined in Article 9 of the French Civil Code
- The French Data Protection Act, regarding the processing of personal data
- Labor law provisions (*Code du travail*) governing employee investigations, which require justification, proportionality, and prior warning for certain surveillance activities

9. Is bribery a criminal offense in your country? If so, does it include payments to both government officials and private businesses?

French law prohibits the bribery of government officials and private businesses. The prohibition includes active bribery (offering or paying a bribe) and passive bribery (soliciting or receiving a bribe).

10. What are the primary financial and investment regulatory bodies in your country?

The Financial Markets Authority (*Autorité des Marchés Financiers* or AMF) is an independent public body responsible for regulating the participants and products of French financial markets. The AMF monitors transactions, conducts investigations, and issues sanctions. It also ensures that investors receive relevant material information, and it provides mediation services for investor disputes. The AMF has the power to require regulated entities to produce all documents and information necessary for its investigations.

The Supervisory Control and Resolution Authority (*Autorité de Contrôle Prudentiel et de résolution* or ACPR) is an independent public authority attached to the French Central Bank (*Banque de France*). The ACPR governs the insurance and banking sectors in France. It has supervisory and disciplinary powers and may impose sanctions.

The Competition Authority (*Autorité de la concurrence*) is the national competition regulator. It is an independent administrative body, and its purpose is fighting anti-competitive practices and overseeing how markets function. The Competition Authority is not considered a court, but it makes decisions, issues injunctions, and, if necessary, imposes penalties that are subject to appeal to the Court of Appeal of Paris and the *Cour de cassation*.

The National Financial Prosecutor's Office (*Parquet National Financier* or PNF) is an administrative body created in 2013 to fight corruption and financial fraud. The PNF is designed to address highly complex cases, often involving tax or securities fraud. Unlike other prosecution offices, the PNF's jurisdiction is nationwide. The PNF has been particularly active in its enforcement activity, prosecuting several major financial entities for money laundering and tax fraud.

11. What are the most significant pieces of fraud-related legislation in your country?

Fraud is not a separately defined crime under French law. Rather, fraudulent conduct is defined by various pieces of legislation, many of them in the Criminal Code and the Criminal Procedure Code. Some of the most significant fraud-related legislation include:

- The Law on Transparency, the Fight Against Corruption, and Modernization of Economic Life (also known as Sapin II) (Law No. 2016-1691) contains whistle-blower protections and requires companies to take steps to prevent corruption, such as adopting a code of conduct, creating training and whistle-blowing programs, performing risk mapping analysis, and conducting due diligence to verify third parties. The law also created an anti-corruption agency with extraterritorial jurisdiction for offenses committed outside of France.
- The Law on Transparency in Public Affairs (Law No. 2013-906) contains reporting requirements for certain high-ranking public officials (ministers, members of Parliament, and any other elected public representative, as well as nonelected high-ranking officials). The law created a new independent entity, the High Authority for Transparency in Public Affairs, which reviews and discloses submissions and statements of interest by officials.
- Law No. 2013-1117 and Law No. 2013-1115 increased penalties for tax fraud and other serious financial crimes. Moreover, the laws include provisions protecting whistle-blowers, permitting organizations to join criminal proceedings as civil claimants, and permitting new investigation techniques (e.g., use of undercover investigators).
- The Law on Moralization of Public Affairs was adopted in 2017 and includes the following provisions:
  - Members of Parliament, ministers, and local government members are prohibited from employing close family members.
  - The so-called *parliamentary reserve*, which allows members of Parliament to provide subsidies to not-for-profit organizations, is no longer permitted.
  - The monthly indemnity paid to members of Parliament to cover expenses incurred in the performance of their duties is replaced by a reimbursement of their expenses via supporting vouchers.

○ New conflict of interest provisions are adopted, including the creation of a register.

○ Members of Parliament cannot engage in a newly created consulting business during their term of office.

12. Does your country have laws in place to protect whistle-blowers? Please describe.

The 2016 Sapin II law created a single regime protecting whistle-blowers in all legal areas. Whistle-blowers cannot be barred from recruitment, discriminated against, sanctioned, terminated, or subjected to any direct or indirect retaliation. In addition, whistle-blowers are protected by strict confidentiality throughout the reporting procedure and afterward. Under Sapin II, an attempt to hinder a whistle-blower from reporting is a criminal offense punishable by one year imprisonment and a fine of €15,000.

Whistle-blower reporting procedures must be readily accessible (e.g., posted on the Internet), and such procedures cannot be so complex that they hinder effective reporting. Disclosure of matters involving national defense, confidential medical issues, or legal privilege are excluded from protection and cannot be disclosed.

Anti-Fraud Programs

13. What foundational frameworks for internal controls, risk management, corporate governance, and so on are commonly used by organizations in your country when designing or assessing their anti-fraud programs (e.g., COSO frameworks, specific ISO standards, OECD guidance)?

- COSO framework
- Risk management and internal control systems (reference framework, AMF)
- AFEP-MEDEF Code, published by the French business groups *Association Française des Entreprises Privées* (AFEP) and *Mouvement des Entreprises de France* (MEDEF)
- ISO 37001:2016 and available guidance documentation relating to the US Foreign Corrupt Practices Act (e.g., US Sentencing Guidelines) and the UK Bribery Act

Also note that the new French anti-bribery authority will issue detailed recommendations to the companies required to adopt compliance programs under the Sapin II law.

14. What types of background checks, if any, are commonly run on prospective employees in your country (e.g., criminal, civil, credit, employment, educational)?

In general, there are few educational and professional background checks carried out by employers. Such background checks must be proportionate to the purpose sought, and the employee should be made aware of such verification. As a matter of principle, criminal or personal credit checks and drug testing are not permissible except in very limited cases where such checks are justified by the specifics of the position.

Considerations in Fraud Investigations

15. Are there any special legal considerations that individuals from outside your country should be aware of when they are working on an investigation in your country? Examples might include licenses needed, special laws governing information gathering, or restrictions on transmitting personal data outside the country.

EU regulations and French data protection laws restrict the transfer of French personal data to other countries. The CNIL generally must authorize transfers of personal data from France to the US, subject to limited exceptions.

16. Are there any special cultural considerations that individuals from outside your country should be aware of when they are working on an investigation in your country? Examples might include who is present during an interview, how to address or greet individuals, inappropriate dress, and so on.

Approximately two-thirds of the persons living in France are fluent in French only. Only one-fifth of the persons residing in France are fluent in English.

History (namely, the German occupation of France) still shapes attitudes toward whistle-blowing and data privacy. Memories of abusive denunciations cause many observers to associate whistle-blowing with pernicious behavior, exposing potentially innocent persons to intrusive authorities. This especially applies to anonymous whistle-blowing.

Business professionals, rather than judges, preside over French Labor Courts (*Conseils des Prudhommes*); their rulings can be appealed to a higher jurisdiction (the Social Chamber of the Court of Appeal) presided over by magistrates, but the resulting legal procedures are lengthy.

GERMANY

Contributors

Ralf Neese, CIA
Robert Kilian, CFE

Sources of Information

1. What types of information about individuals are available to the public?

Generally, the law restricts access to personal information without the individual's knowledge and explicit approval. Information posted on social media by an individual can be accessed as long as public access is not restricted in the settings.

2. What types of information about businesses are available to the public?

Information about businesses is available in the public register. Such information can include the names of directors and shareholders, the legal form and status of the business, and its registered business address. Financial statements are available for public companies that are required to publish such information. Private companies are not required to publish their financial statements.

3. Are court records available to the public? If so, explain what types of civil and criminal records can be obtained by the public.

Civil and criminal court records are generally not available to the public unless the person seeking the records can demonstrate a legal interest in them. Generally, crime victims are granted access to criminal records upon application.

4. What other resources or types of information are regularly used by investigators in your country?

Upon proof of a justified interest, an investigator might be able to obtain a report from a private credit rating company.

5. What are some of the most useful Internet or online sources regularly used in fraud investigations?

- Business registration information: www.handelsregister.de
- Insolvencies by companies and individuals: www.insolvenzbekanntmachungen.de
- Social media websites

Legal and Regulatory Environment

6. What are the major data privacy laws in your country, and how do these affect most fraud investigations?

- Federal Data Protection Act (*Bundesdatenschutzgesetz* or BDSG)
- Federal Telecommunications Act (*Telekommunikationsgeset* or TKG)
- German Banking Act (*Kreditwesengesetz* or KWG)
- The EU's General Data Protection Regulation (effective May 25, 2018)

7. What type of legal system does your country have (e.g., civil law system, common law system, religious law system, hybrid)?

Germany has a civil law system.

8. What laws governing the rights of individuals are of primary concern to investigators?

The German Constitution (*Grundgesetz*) grants individuals certain basic rights, including individual freedom and data privacy. These rights must be observed during an investigation. With judicial approval, official authorities may restrict these rights in criminal cases.

Investigators also must comply with German and EU data protection laws.

9. Is bribery a criminal offense in your country? If so, does it include payments to both government officials and private businesses?

Bribery is a criminal offense and includes payments to both government officials and private businesses.

10. What are the primary financial and investment regulatory bodies in your country?

The primary financial and investment regulatory authority in Germany is the Federal Financial Supervisory Authority (*Bundesanstalt für Finanzdienstleistungsaufsicht* or BaFin). However, the European Central Bank is increasingly involved in financial regulation in Germany.

11. What are the most significant pieces of fraud-related legislation in your country?

Fraud-related legislation is located in the German Criminal Code (*Strafgesetzbuch* or StGB).

12. Does your country have laws in place to protect whistle-blowers? Please describe.

There are no German laws protecting whistle-blowers. However, there are leniency programs that apply in certain court cases.

Anti-Fraud Programs

13. What foundational frameworks for internal controls, risk management, corporate governance, and so on are commonly used by organizations in your country when designing or assessing their anti-fraud programs (e.g., COSO frameworks, specific ISO standards, OECD guidance)?

- COSO framework for big companies
- ISO certification for medium-sized companies
- MaRisk (minimum requirements) for financial institutions

14. What types of background checks, if any, are commonly run on prospective employees in your country (e.g., criminal, civil, credit, employment, educational)?

Due to very restrictive legislation, only 10% of big companies perform background checks on prospective employees. However, employers commonly ask applicants to provide a police clearance certificate. Furthermore, employers often verify any documents provided by applicants. All of these activities require the applicant's consent.

Considerations in Fraud Investigations

15. Are there any special legal considerations that individuals from outside your country should be aware of when they are working on an investigation in your country? Examples might include licenses needed, special laws governing information gathering, or restrictions on transmitting personal data outside the country.

Data protection laws generally prohibit the collection and processing of personal data without the individual's consent. Investigators have no special rights in this area, and violations of these laws may result in criminal penalties. Illegally gathered information generally cannot be used in court. All investigation activities should be coordinated with an investigator who is familiar with German and European legislation.

GREECE

Contributors

Dr. Anna Damaskou, CFE, PhD, LLM
Evangelia Dimitroulia, CFE, CIA

Sources of Information

1. What types of information about individuals are available to the public?

Greece follows EU standards with regard to the protection of sensitive personal data, meaning that such data enjoys full protection. Moreover, personal data is generally unavailable to the public, even if it is not sensitive.

2. What types of information about businesses are available to the public?

Information about businesses is generally available to the public.

Under a 2010 transparency initiative called Diavgeia, all government institutions must upload their acts and decisions to the Internet. Uploaded documents are assigned a unique Internet Uploading Number (IUN). Such documents can be viewed for free by the public.

3. Are court records available to the public? If so, explain what types of civil and criminal records can be obtained by the public.

Generally, civil and criminal court records are not available to the public.

Legal and Regulatory Environment

6. What are the major data privacy laws in your country, and how do these affect most fraud investigations?

- Greek Law 2472/1997 on the Protection of Individuals with Regard to the Processing of Personal Data
- Greek Law 3471/2006 on the Protection of Personal Data and Privacy in the Electronic Telecommunications Sector
- The EU's General Data Protection Regulation (effective May 25, 2018)

7. What type of legal system does your country have (e.g., civil law system, common law system, religious law system, hybrid)?

Greece has a civil law system.

9. Is bribery a criminal offense in your country? If so, does it include payments to both government officials and private businesses?

In Greece, active and passive bribery in both the public sector and the private sector is a criminal offense.

10. What are the primary financial and investment regulatory bodies in your country?

- Bank of Greece
- Hellenic Capital Market Commission

11. What are the most significant pieces of fraud-related legislation in your country?

The Greek Criminal Code is the most significant piece of fraud-related legislation.

12. Does your country have laws in place to protect whistle-blowers? Please describe.

The Greek Criminal Procedure Code and the Greek Civil Servants Code contain provisions for the protection of whistle-blowers regarding a number of financial crimes. Greek Law 4254/2014 added Article 45B on "public interest witnesses" to the Code of Criminal Procedure, and it extended protection to individuals reporting corruption and related wrongdoing. The law also amended the Civil Service Code to ensure that no disciplinary or other internal procedure may be taken against a public official who is a public interest witness.

Anti-Fraud Programs

13. What foundational frameworks for internal controls, risk management, corporate governance, and so on are commonly used by organizations in your country when designing or assessing their anti-fraud programs (e.g., COSO frameworks, specific ISO standards, OECD guidance)?

Many companies use the COSO frameworks and ISO standards. Recently, there was an OECD initiative for anti-corruption in Greece for the public and private sectors. As a result, OECD guidance might become more popular among Greek companies.

14. What types of background checks, if any, are commonly run on prospective employees in your country (e.g., criminal, civil, credit, employment, educational)?

Criminal, employment, and educational background checks are commonly conducted on prospective employees.

Considerations in Fraud Investigations

15. Are there any special legal considerations that individuals from outside your country should be aware of when they are working on an investigation in your country? Examples might include licenses needed, special laws governing information gathering, or restrictions on transmitting personal data outside the country.

When personal data is transferred outside of the EU, data protection laws require the company transferring the data to verify that the country receiving the data maintains a level of protection equivalent to the protection required in EU countries.

Under Article 371 of the Greek Criminal Code, it is a crime for certain professionals to reveal private secrets that were entrusted to them. Article 371 applies to clergymen, lawyers and other legal professionals, notaries, doctors, midwives, nurses, pharmacists, and others to whom private secrets are routinely entrusted because of their profession. Violations of Article 371 can result in a fine or imprisonment for up to one year.

NETHERLANDS

Contributors

Gertjan Groen
Sabrina Tatli-Van der Valk
Loes Wenink, CFE
Sandra Hauwert, CFE

Sources of Information

1. What types of information about individuals are available to the public?

- Ownership of real estate, including mortgages (available from paid service)
- Directorships and sole shareholderships (available from paid service)
- Ownership of ships (available from paid service)
- Bankruptcy (available from free service)
- Court decisions (available from both free and paid services)

In the Netherlands, other information about individuals is rarely available from government or semi-governmental sources. More information is available from commercial sources.

2. What types of information about businesses are available to the public?

The Dutch Chamber of Commerce offers a paid service that contains information on directors, sole shareholders, annual accounts, dates of incorporation, addresses, statutory names, trading names, statutes, and so on. There are also commercial services that offer this information (e.g., Company.info and LexisNexis).

3. Are court records available to the public? If so, explain what types of civil and criminal records can be obtained by the public.

The following types of (partly anonymous) judicial decisions are available to the public:

- Debt restructurings (private persons)
- Receiverships
- Bankruptcies
- Civil court cases
- Penal court cases
- Administrative court cases
- International public law cases

4. What other resources or types of information are regularly used by investigators in your country?

- Internet and online resources (see response to Question 5)
- Information provided by clients

5. What are some of the most useful Internet or online sources regularly used in fraud investigations?

- Social media (e.g., Facebook, LinkedIn, Twitter, Strava)
- Internet search engines
- News websites (e.g., with regard to bad press)
- Wayback Machine
- Whois IP lookup
- Website with tax value of houses (Netherlands)
- Open and semi-open sources, including:
  - National and International Chambers of Commerce
  - National and International Land Register
  - LexisNexis
  - Company.info
  - Dun & Bradstreet
  - Experian Autotrace
  - OpenCorporates
  - World-Check

Legal and Regulatory Environment

6. What are the major data privacy laws in your country, and how do these affect most fraud investigations?

- Dutch Personal Data Protection Act (*Wet bescherming persoonsgegevens*)
- The EU's General Data Protection Regulation (effective May 25, 2018)

7. What type of legal system does your country have (e.g., civil law system, common law system, religious law system, hybrid)?

The Netherlands is a civil law country. The laws are commonly divided into the legal areas described in the response to Question 11.

8. What laws governing the rights of individuals are of primary concern to investigators?

- Civil law
- Dutch Personal Data Protection Act
- The European Convention on Human Rights (specifically Article 6)
- Anti-Money Laundering and Anti-Terrorist Financing Act, which describes what kind of information gatekeepers (such as banks, real estate agents, insurance companies, etc.) need to collect about their customers to comply with due diligence requirements

9. Is bribery a criminal offense in your country? If so, does it include payments to both government officials and private businesses?

Bribery is a criminal offense and includes payments to both government officials and private businesses.

10. What are the primary financial and investment regulatory bodies in your country?

- Dutch Central Bank (*De Nederlandsche Bank* or DNB)
- Authority for Financial Markets (*Autoriteit Financiële Markten* or AFM)
- Financial Supervision Office (*Bureau Financieel Toezicht* or BFT)

11. What are the most significant pieces of fraud-related legislation in your country?

The fraudulent act must be in violation of a valid law. Since there is no specific law on fraud in the Netherlands, relevant laws might include:

- Civil law
- Criminal law
- Tax law
- Sector-specific regulations

Usually, fraud is linked to criminal acts, such as scams, money laundering, forgery, and deceit. Other relevant areas of law might include administrative law, European law, and international law.

12. Does your country have laws in place to protect whistle-blowers? Please describe.

The rights of whistle-blowers are protected by the Civil Code, which states that an employer cannot disadvantage an employee who reports a suspected abuse in good faith. In addition, a 2016 law created a new government agency to advise whistle-blowers and investigate their claims.

Anti-Fraud Programs

13. What foundational frameworks for internal controls, risk management, corporate governance, and so on are commonly used by organizations in your country when designing or assessing their anti-fraud programs (e.g., COSO frameworks, specific ISO standards, OECD guidance)?

- COSO frameworks
- ISO 37001
- ISO 31000

14. What types of background checks, if any, are commonly run on prospective employees in your country (e.g., criminal, civil, credit, employment, educational)?

Most organizations require that an employee provide an employer with a certificate of conduct (*Verklaring Omtrent het Gedrag* or VOG) prior to the start of the employment. Provided by the Dutch State Secretary for Security and Justice, a VOG declares that the applicant has not committed any relevant criminal offenses. For example, a VOG would probably not be issued to a taxi driver with several drunken driving convictions or an accountant with a fraud conviction. Furthermore, most organizations require applicants to provide references.

Considerations in Fraud Investigations

15. Are there any special legal considerations that individuals from outside your country should be aware of when they are working on an investigation in your country? Examples might include licenses needed, special laws governing information gathering, or restrictions on transmitting personal data outside the country.

Hearing Both Sides of the Argument

Dutch law requires fraud examiners to give the involved parties an opportunity to comment on the findings of the investigation. This principle is called hearing both sides of the argument (*hoor en wederhoor*).

Strict Guidelines with Regard to Investigations into Individuals

For chartered accountants, there are strict guidelines regarding investigations of both persons and legal entities. Guideline 1112, Investigations into Persons, of the Royal Netherlands Institute of Chartered Accountants, includes the principles of informing the subject of the investigation, hearing both sides of the argument, and factual reporting.

Anti-Money Laundering and Anti-Terrorist Financing Act

Under the Anti-Money Laundering and Anti-Terrorist Financing Act, external auditors, accountants, and persons and consultants comparable to auditors or accountants must report unusual transactions to the Dutch Financial Intelligence Unit when such transactions are identified during an investigation.

Other

It is not common practice to record interviews, especially without the permission of the interviewee.

NORWAY

Contributors

Vibeke Bisschop-Mørland, CFE
Katie Huchler, CFE

Sources of Information

1. What types of information about individuals are available to the public?

Shareholdings

The shareholder register contains information about the shareholdings of all Norwegian companies, as well as any foreign companies that are registered on the Oslo Stock Exchange. The register displays the shareholder's birth year, home address, and the number of shares owned in each company. The register contains information submitted to the Norwegian Tax Administration by all public and private limited companies, as well as savings banks with equity certificates.

Directorships

The Register of Business Enterprises includes the names of individuals who constitute the boards of directors of Norwegian companies (see also response to Question 2). Investigators can search the register by company name but not by an individual's name. To search for directorships by an individual's name, investigators must use private services (e.g., Bisnode or Proff).

Land Ownership

The Norwegian Mapping Authority's Cadastre and Land Registry is the public register for property rights registration in real property and flats in cooperative housing. Anyone can use the register to search for information about a particular property. However, to determine whether an individual owns property in Norway, investigators must use a private service (e.g., Infotorg).

2. What types of information about businesses are available to the public?

Information about businesses is available from the Brønnøysund Register Centre (BRC). The BRC is a government agency responsible for the regulation and registration of businesses and industries. The BRC maintains multiple state electronic registers, including the Register of Business Enterprises. The types of information available for registered companies include date of incorporation, legal form, address, officers and members of the board of directors, and the statutory auditor.

3. Are court records available to the public? If so, explain what types of civil and criminal records can be obtained by the public.

Most records of the Supreme Court are available through the online legal resources Lovdata (https://lovdata.no) and Rettsdata (www.rettsdata.no). These records are usually made to be anonymous. Some key judgments from district courts and courts of appeal are also available through the same portal, but users must pay for access. Full anonymous judgments can be obtained directly from the court if the case number is known.

4. What other resources or types of information are regularly used by investigators in your country?

The Norwegian Bar Association has issued general guidelines for private investigations. Online legal resources include the public website of Lovdata and the commercial website of Rettsdata. See also the responses to Questions 1 and 2.

5. What are some of the most useful Internet or online sources regularly used in fraud investigations?

- Norwegian Register of Business Enterprises (www.brreg.no)
- Shareholder Register (www.aksjeeiere.no)
- Legal information (https://lovdata.no)
- www.Rettsdata.no
- www.Bisnode.no
- www.Forvalt.no
- Norwegian Bar Association's guidelines for private investigations (www.advokat-foreningen.no/PageFiles/1092/Retningslinjer_for_private_granskninger.PDF)
- Land Registry and Cadastre (www.kartverket.no/en/Land-Registry-and-Cadestre)

Legal and Regulatory Environment

6. What are the major data privacy laws in your country, and how do these affect most fraud investigations?

Fraud investigations must comply with the Norwegian Personal Data Act and EU data protection laws. The EU's General Data Protection Regulation takes effect on May 25, 2018.

7. What type of legal system does your country have (e.g., civil law system, common law system, religious law system, hybrid)?

Norway has a civil law system.

8. What laws governing the rights of individuals are of primary concern to investigators?

Private investigations are subject to the Personal Data Act and the Personal Data Regulations. Police investigations are governed by the Criminal Procedure Act.

The Norwegian Bar Association has published guidelines for private investigations. The guidelines are not binding, but in practice they serve as a guide for conducting investigations. The guidelines attempt to safeguard legal principles such as the right to privacy, the right to a fair trial, protection against self-incrimination, and so on.

9. Is bribery a criminal offense in your country? If so, does it include payments to both government officials and private businesses?

Bribery is a criminal offense in Norway. The basic provisions on bribery and corruption are found in the Norwegian Penal Code, Chapter 30, Sections 387, 388, and 389. These provisions apply to both foreign and domestic bribery within the public and the private sectors. Offering or providing bribes (active bribery) as well as requesting or receiving bribes (passive bribery) are offenses under Section 387. The influencing of conduct of any position, office, or assignment by offering or requesting an improper advantage is an offense according to Section 389 (trading in influence). The penalty for corruption is a fine or imprisonment for up to three years. Gross corruption is punishable by imprisonment for up to 10 years. A company that is found guilty of bribery can be barred from conducting business in Norway.

10. What are the primary financial and investment regulatory bodies in your country?

Cases of corruption are prosecuted by the Norwegian Public Prosecution Authority and investigated by the Norwegian police. There is one national police and prosecution authority in Norway, the National Authority for Investigation and Prosecution of Economic and Environmental Crime in Norway (ØKOKRIM), which consists of highly specialized and trained investigators and prosecutors. ØKOKRIM is both a police specialist agency and a public prosecutor's office with national authority. Within the ordinary police force, there are specific law enforcement teams consisting of financial and white-collar crime experts.

The Financial Supervisory Authority of Norway (*Finanstilsynet*) monitors businesses in the financial sector and ensures compliance with relevant laws and regulations related to banking, insurance, and securities. *Finanstilsynet* has no investigative authority, but may in some cases impose administrative fines.

11. What are the most significant pieces of fraud-related legislation in your country?

The basic provisions on bribery and corruption are found in the Norwegian Penal Code, Chapter 30, Sections 387–389. The Norwegian Penal Code also includes provisions regarding embezzlement (Chapter 27, Sections 324–326), asset misappropriation (Chapter 30, Sections 390–391), handling of stolen goods (Chapter 27, Sections 332–336), money laundering (Chapter 27, Sections 337–341), fraud (Chapter 30, Sections 371–377), extortion (Chapter 27, Sections 330–331), accounting violations (Chapter 30, Sections 392–394), and criminal acts relating to bankruptcy (Chapter 31).

12. Does your country have laws in place to protect whistle-blowers? Please describe.

Norway has laws that protect whistle-blowers. Whistle-blowing is regulated by the Norwegian Working Environment Act, which stipulates that whistle-blowers are protected from any retaliation as a result of reporting suspected wrongdoing. Any retribution against whistle-blowers who report in good faith is prohibited. Under the Act, employers have a duty to implement procedures that allow for the reporting of concerns.

Anti-Fraud Programs

13. What foundational frameworks for internal controls, risk management, corporate governance, and so on are commonly used by organizations in your country when designing or assessing their anti-fraud programs (e.g., COSO frameworks, specific ISO standards, OECD guidance)?

Some Norwegian companies use COSO in relation to frameworks for internal controls and the Three Lines of Defense model as a framework for corporate governance. In the context of fraud risk management, companies use a variety of best practice standards, which include guidance from the UK Ministry of Justice, the US Department of Justice and Securities and Exchange Commission (SEC), the British Standard, the OECD, and Transparency International. Norwegian companies might also use guidance issued by the Norwegian National Authority for Investigation and Prosecution of Economic and

Environmental Crime (ØKOKRIM), particularly in relation to anti-bribery and corruption risk management, as well as the 2016 ISO 37001 standards for Anti-Bribery Management Systems.

14. What types of background checks, if any, are commonly run on prospective employees in your country (e.g., criminal, civil, credit, employment, educational)?

Routine background checks are typically performed to verify work history, education, current certifications, and so on. In Norway, only the police have access to an individual's criminal record, which is contained in a document called a police attestation (*politiattest*). Employers cannot request a police attestation from an applicant unless explicitly authorized by law. In accordance with the Norwegian Data Protection Agency (*Datatilsynet*), credit checks can be performed only on applicants for a senior position or a position with a financial function.

Considerations in Fraud Investigations

15. Are there any special legal considerations that individuals from outside your country should be aware of when they are working on an investigation in your country? Examples might include licenses needed, special laws governing information gathering, or restrictions on transmitting personal data outside the country.

EU data protection laws govern the transfer of personal data to countries outside the EU.

16. Are there any special cultural considerations that individuals from outside your country should be aware of when they are working on an investigation in your country? Examples might include who is present during an interview, how to address or greet individuals, inappropriate dress, and so on.

Norwegian culture is egalitarian in its nature, and cultural norms in Norway dictate equal status between women and men. The organizational structure in Norway is characteristically flat. Office attire is often less formal than abroad, and Norwegians are often direct in their communication. Interview styles are typically nonconfrontational. Interviewees are given the opportunity to have another individual present during the interview, if desired. This individual may be a colleague, legal representative, family member, friend, or other.

SPAIN

Contributors

Gertrudis Alarcon, CFE
Jose Damian Garcia Medina, CFE
Miguel Angel Osma, CFE
Dr. Jose A. Brandin, MBA, CFE, CIA, CISA

Sources of Information

1. What types of information about individuals are available to the public?

Spanish law restricts the availability of certain information about individuals. The most reliable data is provided by public administrations and some private databases. Publicly available data generally includes information about real estate ownership, corporate directorships, interactions with government agencies, bankruptcies, and civil and social proceedings.

In some cases, information about individuals cannot be accessed without a legal reason (contractual relationship, solvency investigation, etc.). Generally, personal information is made anonymous before it is made public. Personal information obtained via the Internet (e.g., social networks) can be used only for personal purposes or in the context of an investigation conducted by authorized professionals.

In 2016, most public administrations began the process of making the transition to electronic data. Most of these systems have limited search functions, and some information is available online for only a limited period of time.

2. What types of information about businesses are available to the public?

- Data about the foundation of the company
- Certain changes to the company (e.g., change of address or name, new appointments, mergers, etc.)
- The names of officers, directors, and sometimes shareholders
- Accounts and auditors' reports
- Records of real property associated with the company (e.g., loans and liens on property)
- Credit reports
- Litigation records
- Bankruptcy records
- Regulatory checks
- Licenses or authorizations to conduct regulated activities

As mentioned, the most reliable information is provided by public administrations and some private databases. Many companies fail to report to the Companies Register, so sometimes the information is limited and outdated.

3. Are court records available to the public? If so, explain what types of civil and criminal records can be obtained by the public.

Civil litigation records are publicly available in Spain. However, the information can be incomplete due to slow data entry in some jurisdictions. In addition, most court records are not computerized.

Bankruptcy filings are publicly available in the Official Gazettes. General liens and judgments are not publicly available, unless they are released by the Constitutional Court and published in the Official Gazettes. Dispute communications from government agencies are publicly available.

The criminal records of individuals are not publicly available. Such information is contained in the Central Register of Convicted Persons (*Registro Central de Penados*), which is used by public administrations (e.g., the national police, border agents, passport agency). Employers generally cannot request an applicant's criminal record unless the applicant authorizes the request and criminal background checks are legally permitted for the job (e.g., cashier, security guard, teacher).

4. What other resources or types of information are regularly used by investigators in your country?

Source inquiries, the Internet, and surveillance are used by investigators.

5. What are some of the most useful Internet or online sources regularly used in fraud investigations?

- Social and professional networks
- Professionals associations
- Public administration contractors
- Companies Register
- Real estate register
- Regulatory bodies

Legal and Regulatory Environment

6. What are the major data privacy laws in your country, and how do these affect most fraud investigations?

The Spanish Data Protection Act (Law 15/1999) as well as Law 62/2003 restrict access to personal data. Due to these laws, public registers and administrations might deny access to documents that contain personal information or might redact the personal information.

7. What type of legal system does your country have (e.g., civil law system, common law system, religious law system, hybrid)?

Spain has a civil law system.

8. What laws governing the rights of individuals are of primary concern to investigators?

- The Spanish Workers' Statute
- Data Protection Act (Law 15/1999)

9. Is bribery a criminal offense in your country? If so, does it include payments to both government officials and private businesses?

In Spain, bribery is a criminal offense and includes payments to both government officials and private businesses.

10. What are the primary financial and investment regulatory bodies in your country?

- National Securities Market Commission (*Comisión Nacional del Mercado de Valores*)
- Bank of Spain (*Banco de España*)

11. What are the most significant pieces of fraud-related legislation in your country?

The Spanish Anti-Tax-Fraud Law (Law 7/2012) is the most significant piece of fraud-related legislation.

12. Does your country have laws in place to protect whistle-blowers? Please describe.

Spain has no laws protecting whistle-blowers.

Anti-Fraud Programs

13. What foundational frameworks for internal controls, risk management, corporate governance, and so on are commonly used by organizations in your country when designing or assessing their anti-fraud programs (e.g., COSO frameworks, specific ISO standards, OECD guidance)?

- COSO frameworks
- ISO standards
- UNE standards issued by the Spanish Association for Standardization and Certification (AENOR)

14. What types of background checks, if any, are commonly run on prospective employees in your country (e.g., criminal, civil, credit, employment, educational)?

The most common types of background checks include:

- Civil
- Credit
- Employment
- Education
- Negative media

Employers generally cannot perform a criminal background check unless the applicant authorizes it and criminal background checks are legally permitted for the job (e.g., cashier, security guard, teacher).

Considerations in Fraud Investigations

15. Are there any special legal considerations that individuals from outside your country should be aware of when they are working on an investigation in your country? Examples might include licenses needed, special laws governing

information gathering, or restrictions on transmitting personal data outside the country.

Special legal considerations in Spain include the following:

- Investigations are regulated by Private Security Law 23/92.
- Information must be obtained legally.
- Generally, personal data can be transmitted only to countries with similar or more demanding data protection legislation.
- Workers' rights are protected by the Spanish Workers' Statute.

SWITZERLAND

Contributors

Peter Juestel, CFE, CAMS
John Ederer, CFE, FCA

Sources of Information

1. What types of information about individuals are available to the public?

Swiss law is relatively restrictive regarding public access to information about individuals. Sources of information about individuals include:

- Commercial Register on state/cantonal level (*Handelsregister*)
- Commercial Register on federal/national level (*Zefix*)
- Official Gazette of Commerce (*Schweizerisches Handelsamtsblatt* or SHAB)
- Bankruptcy/collection records (*Betreibungsregister*)

2. What types of information about businesses are available to the public?

In addition to the sources listed in the response to Question 1, the following sources contain information about businesses:

- Swiss Financial Market Supervisory Authority (FINMA) for financial intermediaries, banks, insurances, fund managers, and traders
- Temporary staff agencies, which must be registered
- Trade associations, which voluntarily publish information

3. Are court records available to the public? If so, explain what types of civil and criminal records can be obtained by the public.

Generally, court records are not published unless a case sets a legal precedent, but then the personal details are made anonymous. However, all bankruptcy cases are published in the Official Gazette of Commerce (SHAB).

4. What other resources or types of information are regularly used by investigators in your country?

Open sources, newspapers, and journalist commentaries are used by investigators.

5. What are some of the most useful Internet or online sources regularly used in fraud investigations?

- www.zefix.ch (commercial register)
- www.SHAB.ch (Official Gazette of Commerce)
- www.finma.ch (Swiss Financial Market Supervisory Authority)

Legal and Regulatory Environment

6. What are the major data privacy laws in your country, and how do these affect most fraud investigations?

- Federal Act on Data Protection (*Datenschutzgesetz* or DSG).
- Swiss Code of Obligations (*Obligationenrecht* or OR), especially employment and labor law and contractual confidentiality rules.
- Swiss Penal Code (*Strafgesetzbuch* or STGB) contains legal privilege and confidentiality (*Anwaltsgeheimnis*).
- Swiss banking law (*Bankengesetz* or BankG) contains bank secrecy (*Bankkundengeheimnis*).

7. What type of legal system does your country have (e.g., civil law system, common law system, religious law system, hybrid)?

Switzerland has a civil law system.

8. What laws governing the rights of individuals are of primary concern to investigators?

- United Nations Universal Declaration of Human Rights
- European Union Charter of Fundamental Rights
- Swiss Federal Constitution

9. Is bribery a criminal offense in your country? If so, does it include payments to both government officials and private businesses?

In Switzerland, bribery is a criminal offense and includes payments to both government officials and private businesses.

10. What are the primary financial and investment regulatory bodies in your country?

- Swiss Financial Market Supervisory Authority (FINMA)
- Swiss Stock Exchange

11. What are the most significant pieces of fraud-related legislation in your country?

- Swiss Penal Code (STGB)
- Swiss Code of Obligations (OR)
- Swiss Federal Unfair Competition Act (UWG)
- Swiss Pharmaceutical Act (TRA)
- Swiss Anti-Money Laundering Act (GwG)

12. Does your country have laws in place to protect whistle-blowers? Please describe.

Switzerland does not have laws protecting whistle-blowers.

Anti-Fraud Programs

13. What foundational frameworks for internal controls, risk management, corporate governance, and so on are commonly used by organizations in your country when designing or assessing their anti-fraud programs (e.g., COSO frameworks, specific ISO standards, OECD guidance)?

- COSO frameworks
- OECD guidance
- US Sentencing Guidelines
- Federal Corrupt Practices Act (Q&A guidelines)
- UK Bribery Act

14. What types of background checks, if any, are commonly run on prospective employees in your country (e.g., criminal, civil, credit, employment, educational)?

Many employers conduct national criminal background checks with the specific permission of the prospective employee. Employers often require testimonial letters from all previous employers and references, which are often verified by the hiring employer.

Considerations in Fraud Investigations

15. Are there any special legal considerations that individuals from outside your country should be aware of when they are working on an investigation in your country? Examples might include licenses needed, special laws governing information gathering, or restrictions on transmitting personal data outside the country.

It is a crime to cooperate directly or indirectly with non-Swiss governmental agencies unless specific approval is obtained from the Swiss courts or the Swiss government. Violations of this law may result in fines and imprisonment.

In addition, there are strict limitations on cross-border data transfers, subject to pre-approved safe harbor destinations.

16. Are there any special cultural considerations that individuals from outside your country should be aware of when they are working on an investigation in your country? Examples might include who is present during an interview, how to address or greet individuals, inappropriate dress, and so on.

Linguistic issues often arise in Swiss society. Though many managers speak English (perhaps 60 to 70%), this is not always the case. In serious circumstances, individuals may prefer to communicate in a national language. In Switzerland, the national languages are German, French, Italian, and Romansh. Otherwise, it is important to remain polite, nonaggressive, and factual. Normal business dress is standard.

UNITED KINGDOM

Contributor

Tim Harvey, CFE, JP

Sources of Information

1. What types of information about individuals are available to the public?

The following resources contain information about individuals:

- Records of births, deaths, and marriages: www.gov.uk/browse/births-deaths-marriages
- An electoral roll that displays the addresses of voters (however, individuals can opt out): www.gov.uk/electoral-register/overview

Criminal records are not publicly available. Individuals can access their own criminal records by filing an application and paying a fee.

2. What types of information about businesses are available to the public?

The public website for Companies House (www.gov.uk/government/organisations/companies-house) permits individuals to search for company information, such as the names of officers, directors, and shareholders. Information about disqualified directors and bankruptcies is also publicly available. In addition, there are many commercial services that offer information about businesses.

3. Are court records available to the public? If so, explain what types of civil and criminal records can be obtained by the public.

Criminal records are not publicly available. However, criminal court proceedings are generally open to the public. There are some exceptions, including certain juvenile cases and cases involving national security.

Civil proceedings are not public, and only those who are parties to the proceedings can attend.

4. What other resources or types of information are regularly used by investigators in your country?

Many investigators use the commercial service at www.192.com to search for information about individuals and businesses. There are many other commercial resources available in the UK (see response to Question 5).

5. What are some of the most useful Internet or online sources regularly used in fraud investigations?

Legal Resources:

- Access to Law (www.accesstolaw.com)
- Centre for Commercial Studies, Queen Mary University of London (www.ccls.qmul.ac.uk)
- InfoLaw Gateway (www.infolaw.co.uk)
- LawLink (www.lawlink.co.uk)
- Her Majesty's Courts and Tribunals Service (www.gov.uk/government/organisations/hm-courts-and-tribunals-service)
- The Law Commission (www.lawcom.gov.uk)
- The Law Society (www.lawsociety.org.uk)

Government and Law Enforcement:

- Government Information Center (www.gov.uk)
- Information Commissioner's Office (ico.org.uk)
- Serious Fraud Office (www.sfo.gov.uk)
- Financial Conduct Authority (www.fca.org.uk)
- Prudential Regulation Authority (www.bankofengland.co.uk/pra/Pages/default.aspx)
- Foreign and Commonwealth Office (www.gov.uk/government/organisations/foreign-commonwealth-office)
- Her Majesty's Treasury (www.gov.uk/government/organisations/hm-treasury)
- UK Police Forces (www.police.uk)
- International Centre for Criminal Law Reform and Criminal Justice Policy (icclr.law.ubc.ca)
- National Crime Agency (www.nationalcrimeagency.gov.uk)
- Intellectual Property Office (www.gov.uk/government/organisations/intellectual-property-office)
- Insolvency Service (www.gov.uk/government/organisations/insolvency-service)
- National Archives (www.nationalarchives.gov.uk)
- European Commission (ec.europa.eu/commission/index_en)
- Home Office (www.gov.uk/government/organisations/home-office)
- Parliament (www.parliament.uk)

Legal and Regulatory Environment

6. What are the major data privacy laws in your country, and how do these affect most fraud investigations?

- UK Freedom of Information Act
- UK Data Protection Act
- EU's General Data Protection Regulation (effective May 25, 2018)

7. What type of legal system does your country have (e.g., civil law system, common law system, religious law system, hybrid)?

The UK has a common law system.

8. What laws governing the rights of individuals are of primary concern to investigators?

Data protection laws and laws against false imprisonment, libel, and slander are of primary concern to investigators.

9. Is bribery a criminal offense in your country? If so, does it include payments to both government officials and private businesses?

Under the UK Bribery Act, bribery is a criminal offense and includes payments to both government officials and private businesses. A company can also violate the Act by failing to prevent bribery.

10. What are the primary financial and investment regulatory bodies in your country?

The Financial Conduct Authority is the primary financial and investment regulatory body in the UK.

11. What are the most significant pieces of fraud-related legislation in your country?

In the UK, the most significant piece of fraud-related legislation is the Fraud Act 2006. Under the Act, fraud can be committed by false representation, failing to disclose information, or abuse of position. The Act also makes it a criminal offense to possess any article for use in the course of, or in connection with, any fraud. This is extremely useful for fraud examiners because *any article* means exactly that, and it includes any data held in electronic format (e.g., an email or false invoice). The act creates an offense of carrying on fraudulent business as a sole trader (i.e., activity not subject to the Companies Act).

Another significant fraud-related law is the Proceeds of Crime Act 2002, which is the primary anti-money-laundering legislation in the UK.

12. Does your country have laws in place to protect whistle-blowers? Please describe.

Yes, the UK has laws protecting whistle-blowers.

Anti-Fraud Programs

13. What foundational frameworks for internal controls, risk management, corporate governance, and so on are commonly used by organizations in your country when designing or assessing their anti-fraud programs (e.g., COSO frameworks, specific ISO standards, OECD guidance)?

- COSO frameworks
- ISO 9001
- *At the Juncture of Corporate Governance and Cybersecurity*, issued by the Federation of European Risk Management Associations (FERMA) and the European Confederation of Institutes of Internal Auditing (ECIIA)

14. What types of background checks, if any, are commonly run on prospective employees in your country (e.g., criminal, civil, credit, employment, educational)?

Employers must perform criminal background checks for certain occupations, including anyone working with children, nurses in a position of trust, first responders, magistrates, and others. For other positions, employers are generally prohibited from performing criminal background checks. However, they can ask applicants to provide a basic disclosure certificate, which is a government-issued document showing criminal convictions.

Considerations in Fraud Investigations

15. Are there any special legal considerations that individuals from outside your country should be aware of when they are working on an investigation in your country? Examples might include licenses needed, special laws governing information gathering, or restrictions on transmitting personal data outside the country.

UK and EU data protection rules restrict the collection and transfer of personal information.

Qichacha (website), 218
Question(s):
answering with, as sign of deception, 202
presenting alternative, in interviews, 199–200
repetition of the, as sign of deception, 201
sensitive, in interviews, 205
types of, in interviews, 188–194

Ranking, of fraud risk, 93
Ransomware, 39–40
Rationalizations:
as component of Fraud Triangle, 6
establishing, 198
reinforcing, 200
Real evidence, 45
Realistic goals, 148
Reasonableness, of searches, 64
Receivables skimming, 11–12
Receiving reports, falsified, 23–24
Recommendations, in fraud risk assessment, 98
Reconciliations, 130
Recording, of interviews, 184–185
Reference checks, 123–124
Refunds, false, 18
Register, theft of cash from, 12
Registry Court (Poland), 259
Registry of Commerce and Companies (France), 343
Regulations, compliance with, 79
Regulatory issues, in international whistle-blowing, 119
Regulatory misconduct, risk of, 87–88
Reimbursements, duplicate/multiple, 19–20
Related-party transactions, 34
Relevant evidence, 46–47, 58
Relevant parties, notification of, 149–150
Religious legal systems, 43
Remediation, following fraud, 137–138
Remote interviews, 183–184
Reporting:
of cases, 166–171
confidentiality in, 107
in good faith, 107
requirements outlined in anti-fraud policy, 105
results of fraud risk assessment, 97–98
Reporting mechanisms:
accessibility of, 120
in whistle-blowing policies, 117–118

Report to the Nations on Occupational Fraud and Abuse, 7, 10, 13, 116, 117, 126, 130, 211, 217, 251, 265, 287, 303, 315, 329, 337
Reputation risk, 88, 108
Requisitions, fraudulent, 23
Reserve Bank of Australia, 216
Residual fraud risks, 76, 93–97
Response:
to fraud, as component of anti-fraud program, 136–138
to fraud risk, 93
Responsibility:
for anti-fraud programs, 111–116
for fraud prevention and detection, 104
for fraud risk assessment, 79–82
for fraud risk management, 99
for investigations, 105
of investigation team members, 147
Revenues, overstated, 30–32
Reviews, 130
Rewards, for whistle-blowers, 120–121
Rights:
of employees, 56–61
of individuals, 56–57, 61–63
Risk:
categories of, 108
identifying contributors to, 78
Risk and control personnel, 115
Risk management, 108–109
Roman law, 44
Rotation, of job duties, 128
Rutificador, 270

Safety concerns, in cross-border investigations, 177
Sales skimming, 11
Sanctions, as ineffective deterrent, 6–7
Sarbanes-Oxley Act of 2002 (SOX), 240, 334, 335
Scheme-specific control activities, 131–136
Scheme types:
in Asia-Pacific region, 211, 212e
in Canada, 245, 246e
in Eastern Europe and Western/Central Asia, 251, 252e
in Latin America and the Caribbean, 265, 266e
in Middle East and North Africa, 287, 288e